EARTHLIGHT

VOL. I

**WRITTEN BY
STUART MOORE**

**ILLUSTRATED BY
CHRISTOPHER SCHONS**

HAMBURG // LONDON // LOS ANGELES // TOKYO

Earthlight Vol. 1
Written by Stuart Moore
Illustrated by Christopher Schons

Development Editor - Aaron Suhr
Copy Editor - Ao Ringo
Lettering and Production Artist - Lucas Rivera
Cover Design - Christian Lownds

Editor - Bryce P. Coleman
Digital Imaging Manager - Chris Buford
Pre-Production Supervisor - Erika Terriquez
Art Director - Anne Marie Horne
Managing Editor - Vy Nguyen
Production Manager - Elisabeth Brizzi
VP of Production - Ron Klamert
Editor-in-Chief - Rob Tokar
Publisher - Mike Kiley
President and C.O.O. - John Parker
C.E.O. and Chief Creative Officer - Stuart Levy

A  Manga

TOKYOPOP Inc.
5900 Wilshire Blvd. Suite 2000
Los Angeles, CA 90036

E-mail: info@TOKYOPOP.com
Come visit us online at www.TOKYOPOP.com

ISBN: 1-59816-705-7

First TOKYOPOP printing: October 2006
10 9 8 7 6 5 4 3 2 1
Printed in the USA

TABLE OF CONTENTS

EARTHLIGHT

VOL. 1

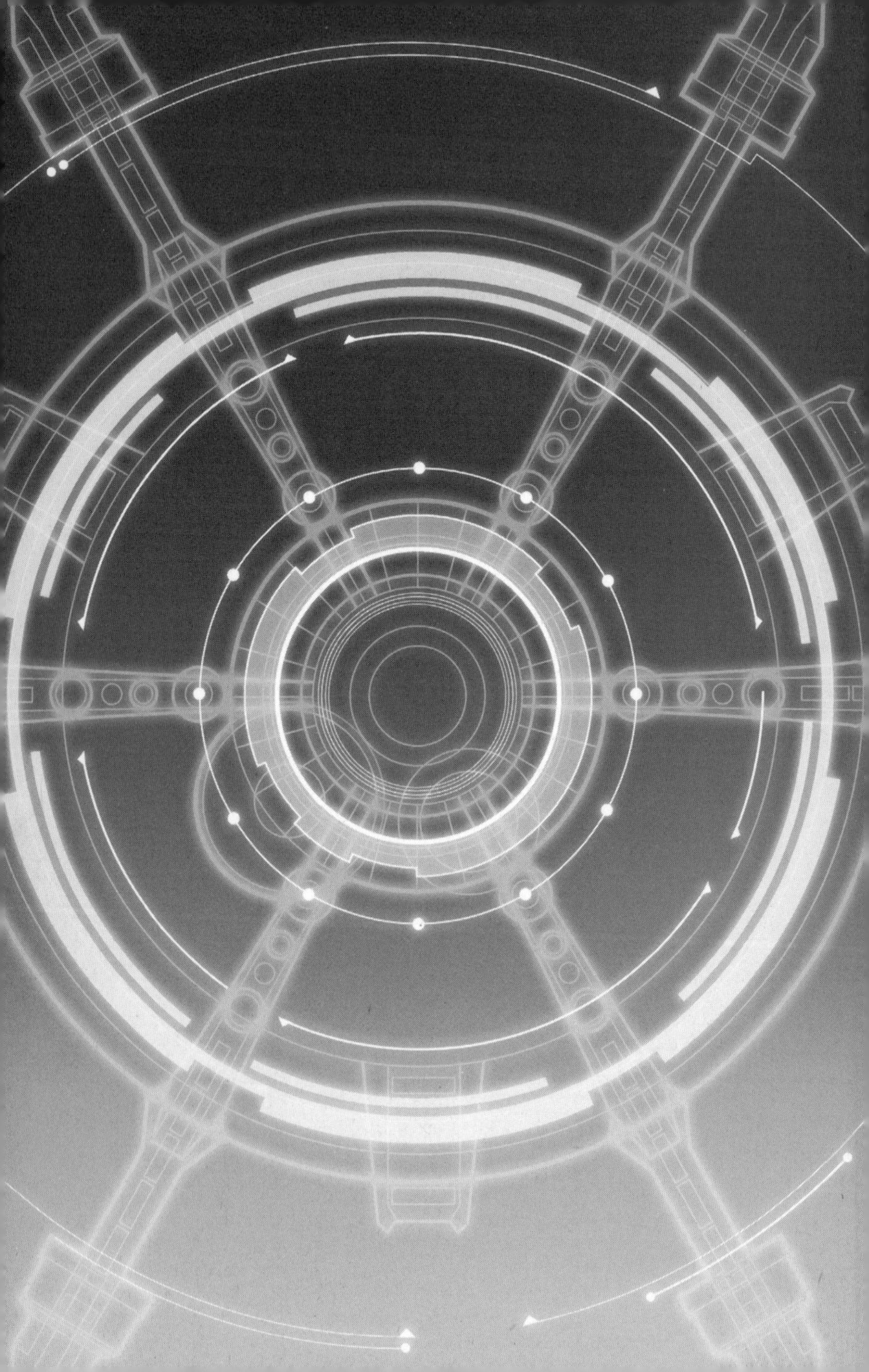

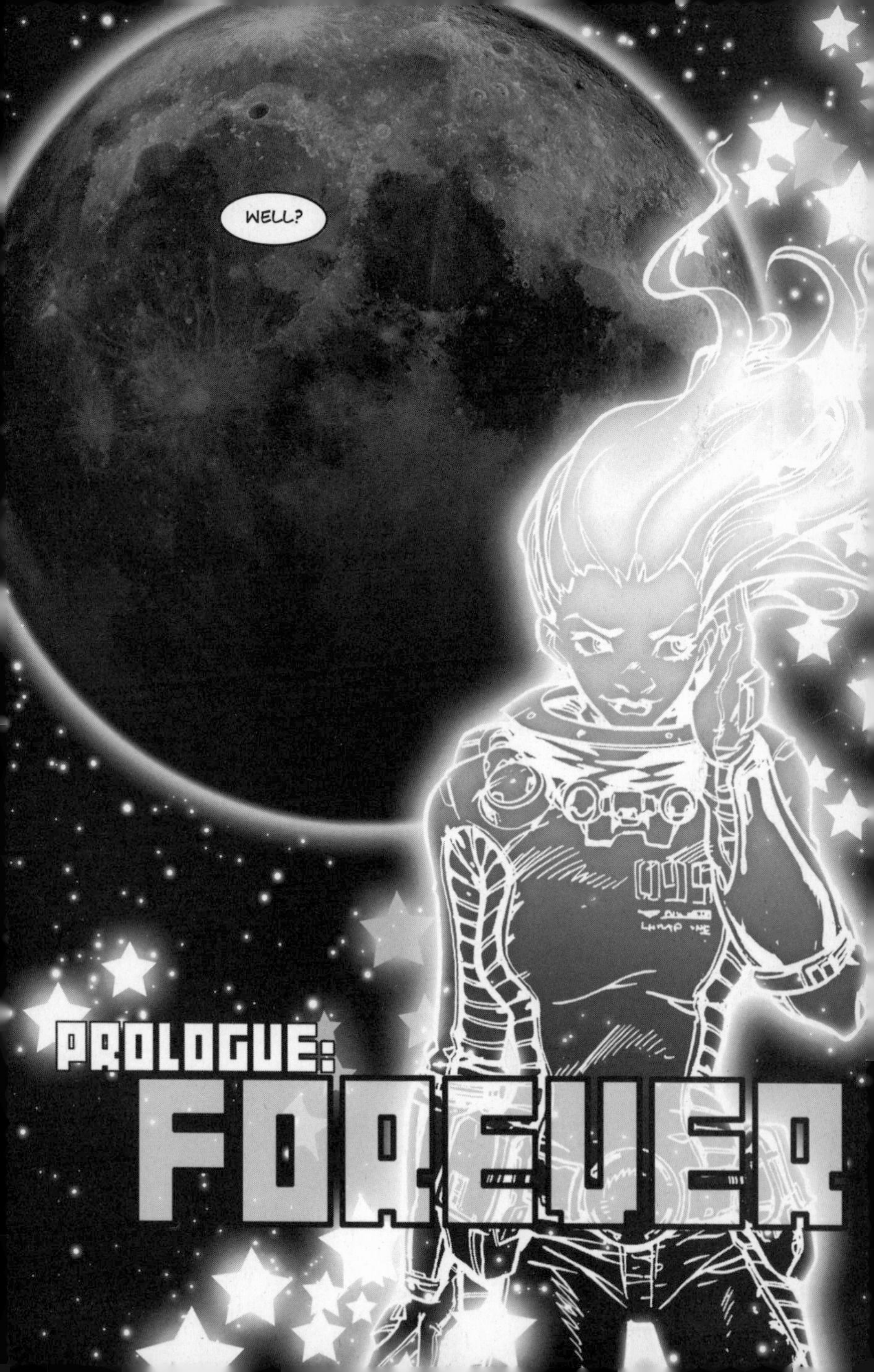
WELL?
PROLOGUE:
FOREVER

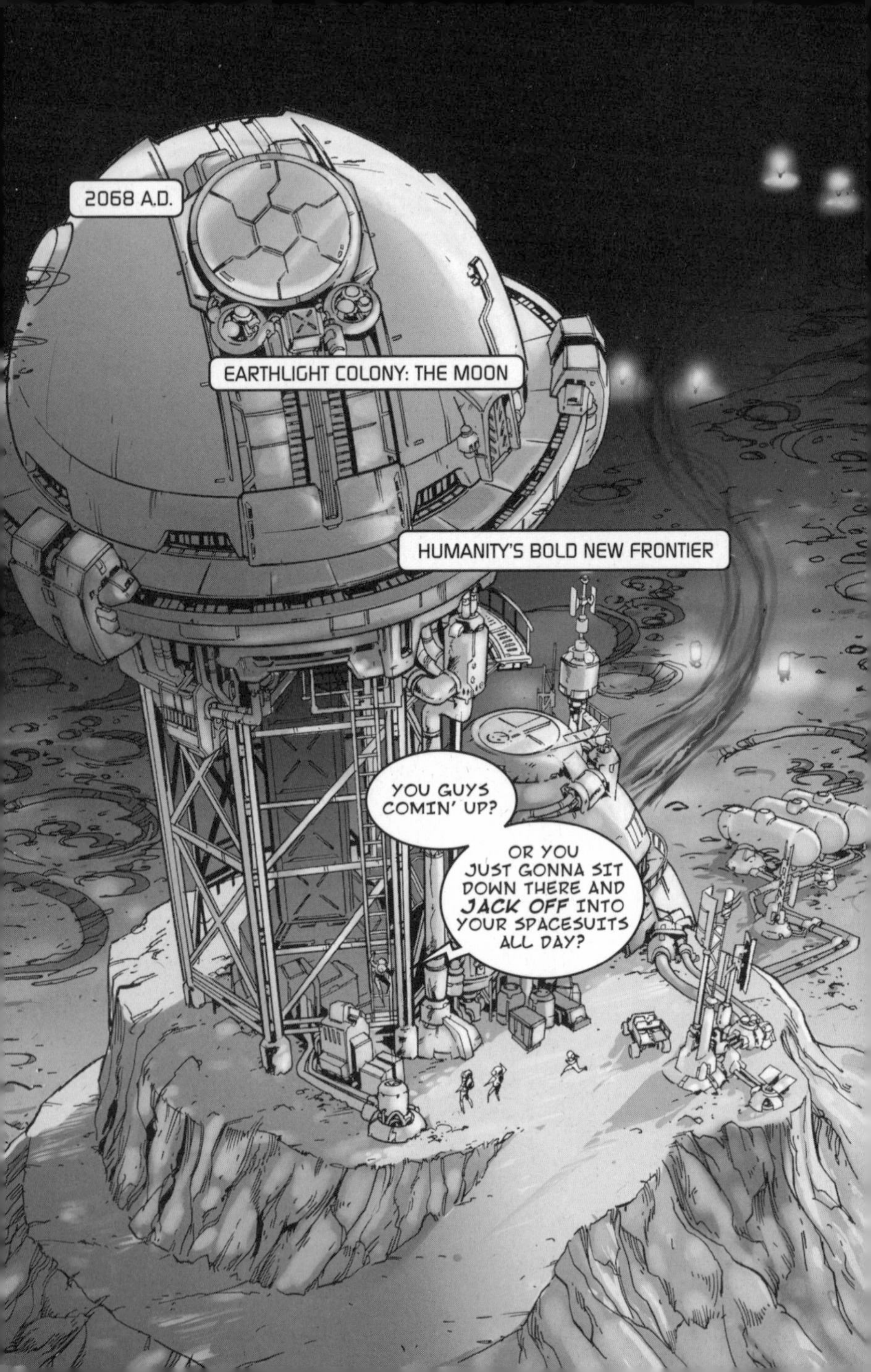
2068 A.D.
EARTHLIGHT COLONY: THE MOON
HUMANITY'S BOLD NEW FRONTIER
YOU GUYS COMIN' UP?
OR YOU JUST GONNA SIT DOWN THERE AND JACK OFF INTO YOUR SPACESUITS ALL DAY?

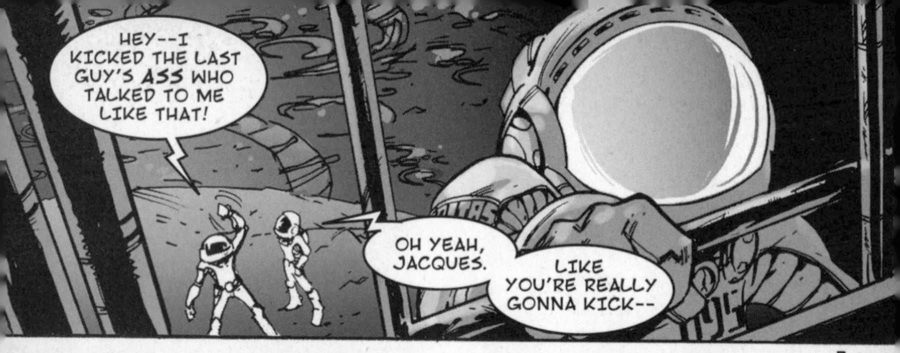
HEY--I KICKED THE LAST GUY'S **ASS** WHO TALKED TO ME LIKE THAT!
OH YEAH, JACQUES.
LIKE YOU'RE REALLY GONNA KICK--

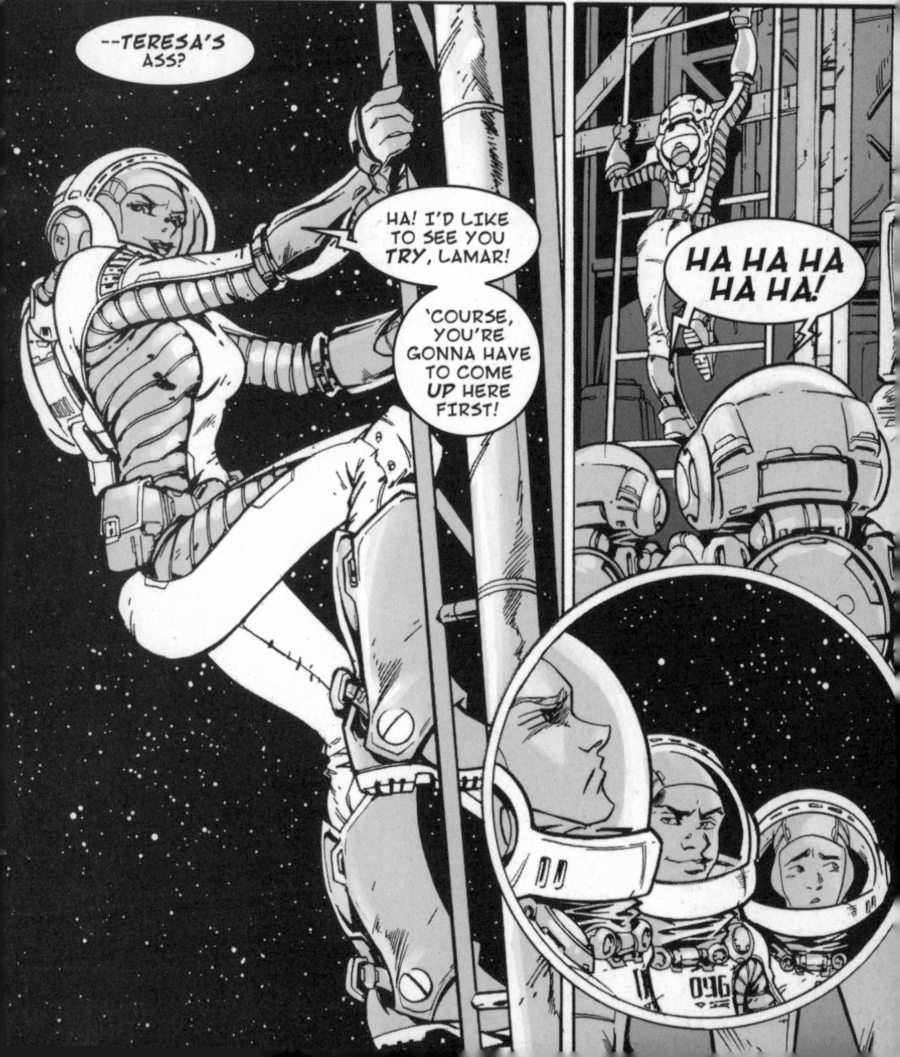
--*TERESA'S* ASS?
HA! I'D LIKE TO SEE YOU *TRY*, LAMAR!
'COURSE, YOU'RE GONNA HAVE TO COME **UP** HERE FIRST!
HA HA HA HA HA!

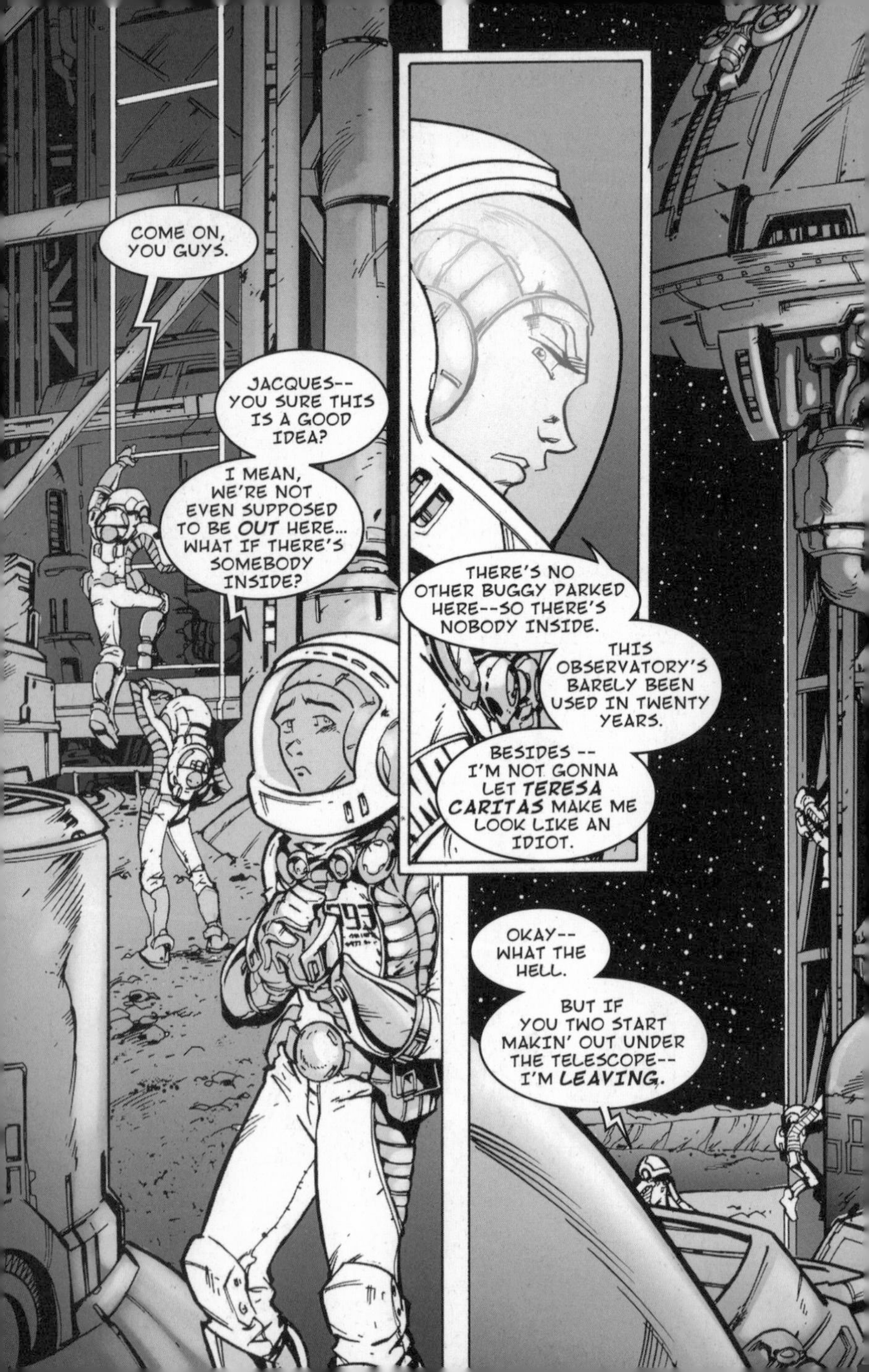
COME ON, YOU GUYS.
JACQUES-- YOU SURE THIS IS A GOOD IDEA?
I MEAN, WE'RE NOT EVEN SUPPOSED TO BE OUT HERE... WHAT IF THERE'S SOMEBODY INSIDE?
THERE'S NO OTHER BUGGY PARKED HERE--SO THERE'S NOBODY INSIDE.
THIS OBSERVATORY'S BARELY BEEN USED IN TWENTY YEARS.
BESIDES -- I'M NOT GONNA LET TERESA CARITAS MAKE ME LOOK LIKE AN IDIOT.
OKAY-- WHAT THE HELL.
BUT IF YOU TWO START MAKIN' OUT UNDER THE TELESCOPE-- I'M LEAVING.

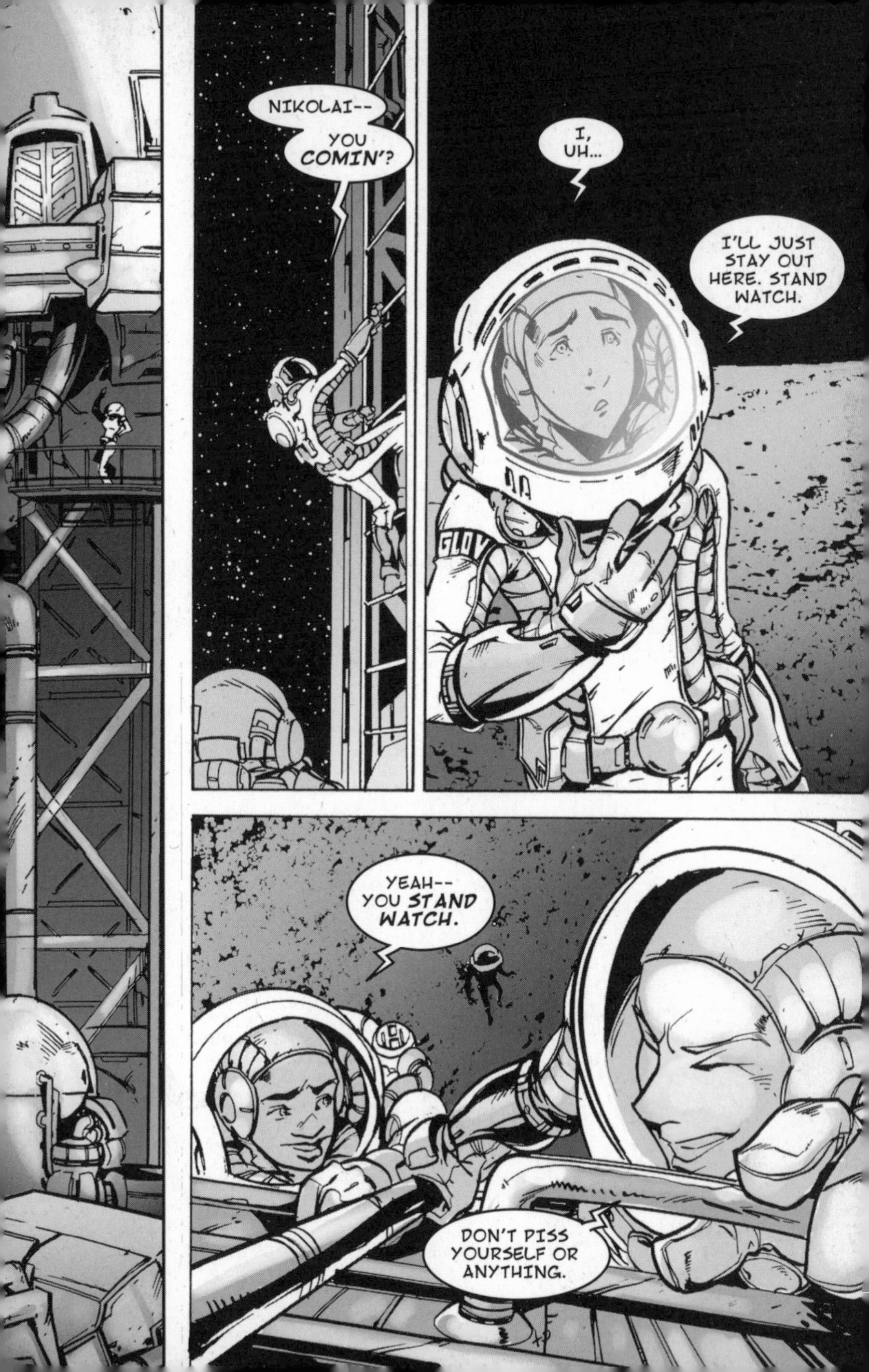
NIKOLAI--
YOU COMIN'?
I, UH...
I'LL JUST STAY OUT HERE. STAND WATCH.
YEAH-- YOU STAND WATCH.
DON'T PISS YOURSELF OR ANYTHING.

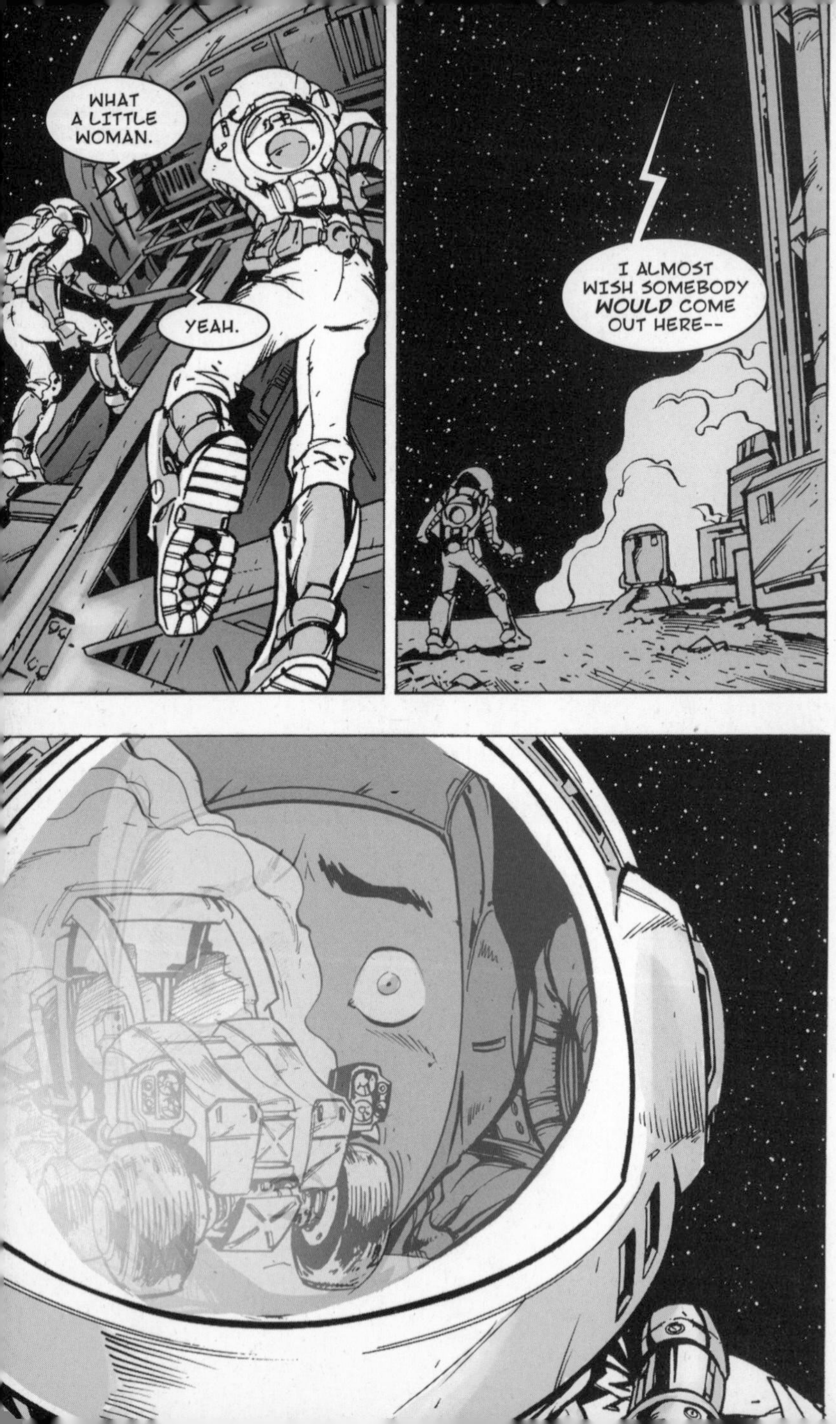
WHAT A LITTLE WOMAN.
YEAH.
I ALMOST WISH SOMEBODY WOULD COME OUT HERE--

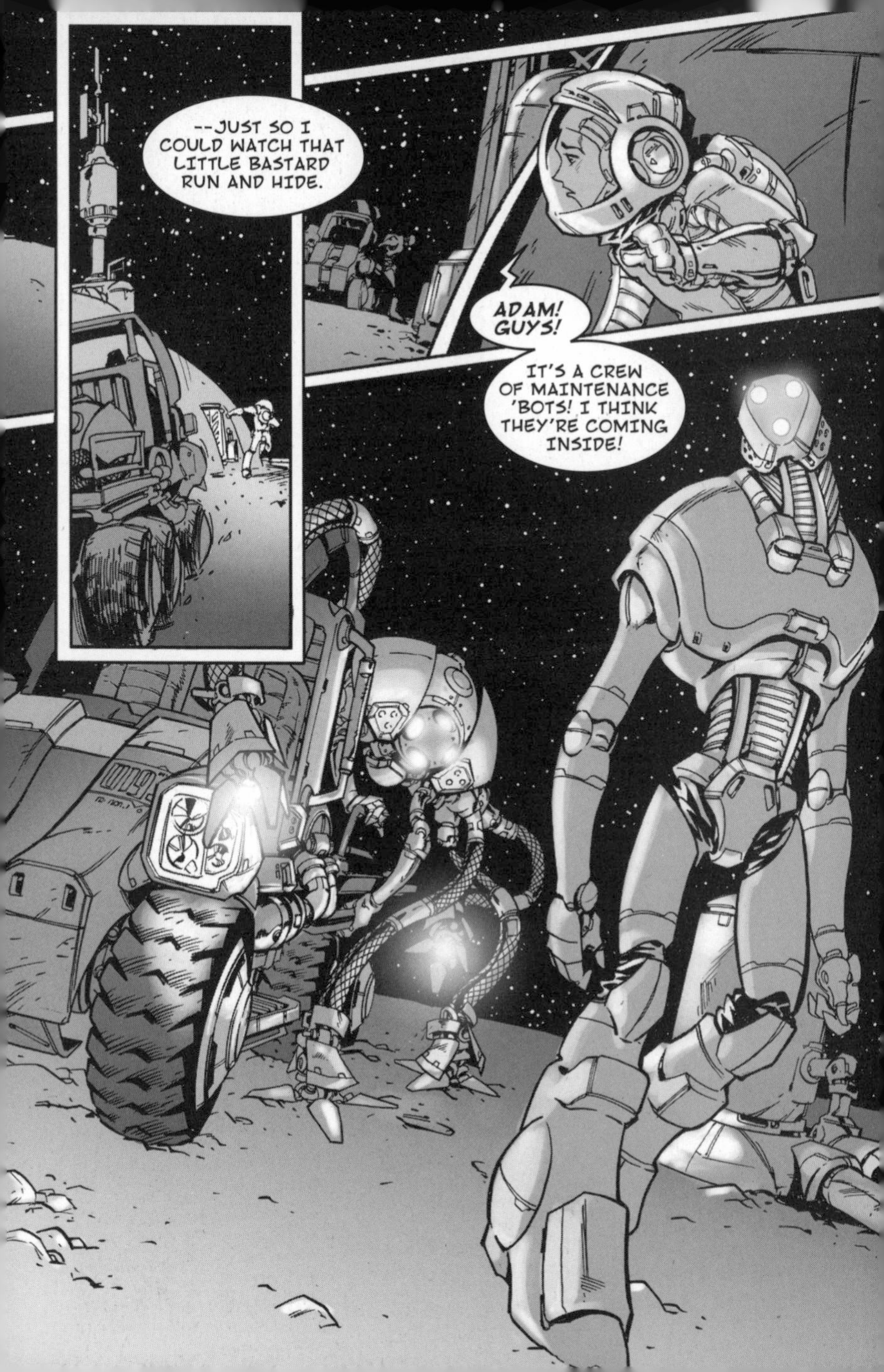
--JUST SO I COULD WATCH THAT LITTLE BASTARD RUN AND HIDE.
ADAM! GUYS!
IT'S A CREW OF MAINTENANCE 'BOTS! I THINK THEY'RE COMING INSIDE!

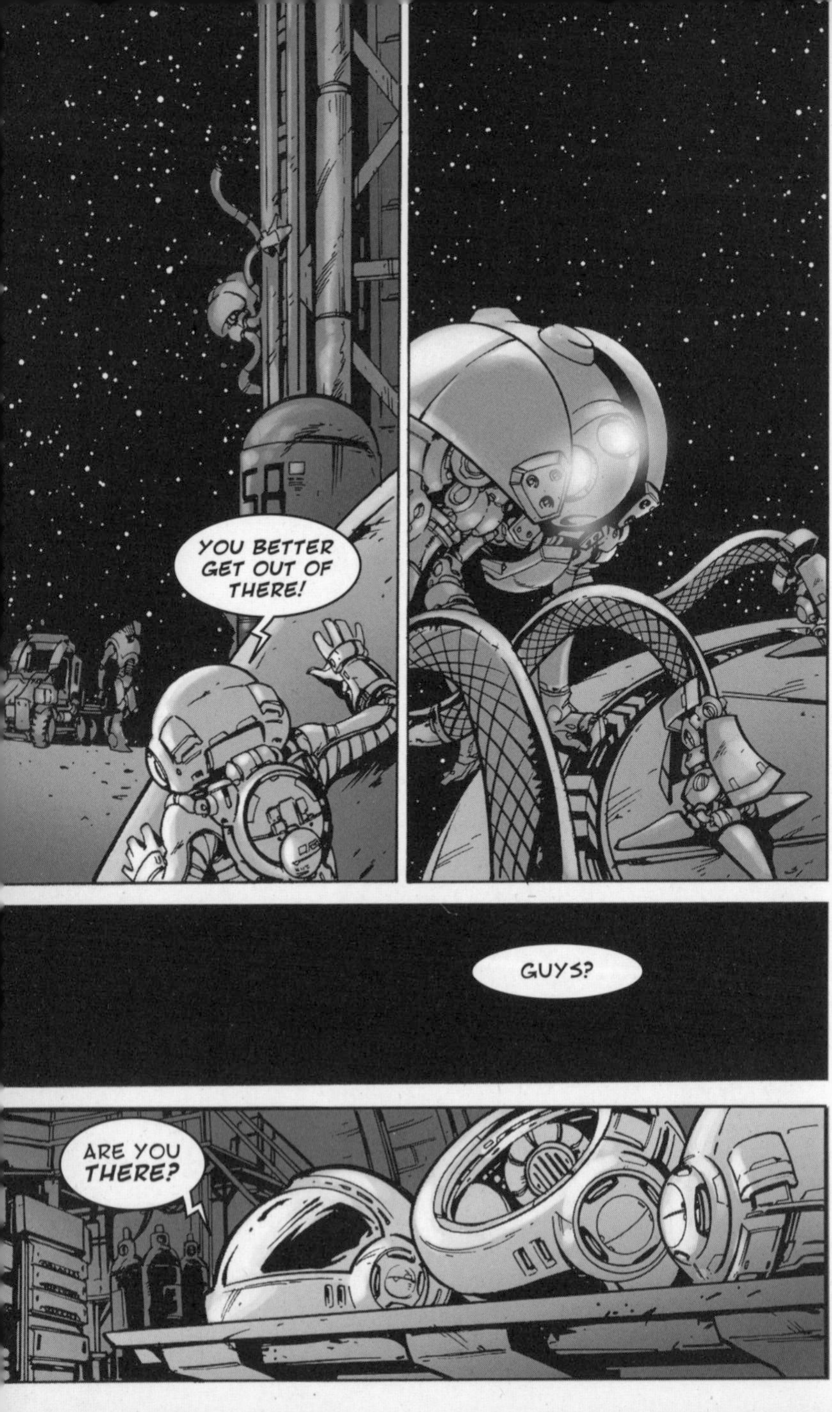
YOU BETTER GET OUT OF THERE!
GUYS?
ARE YOU THERE?

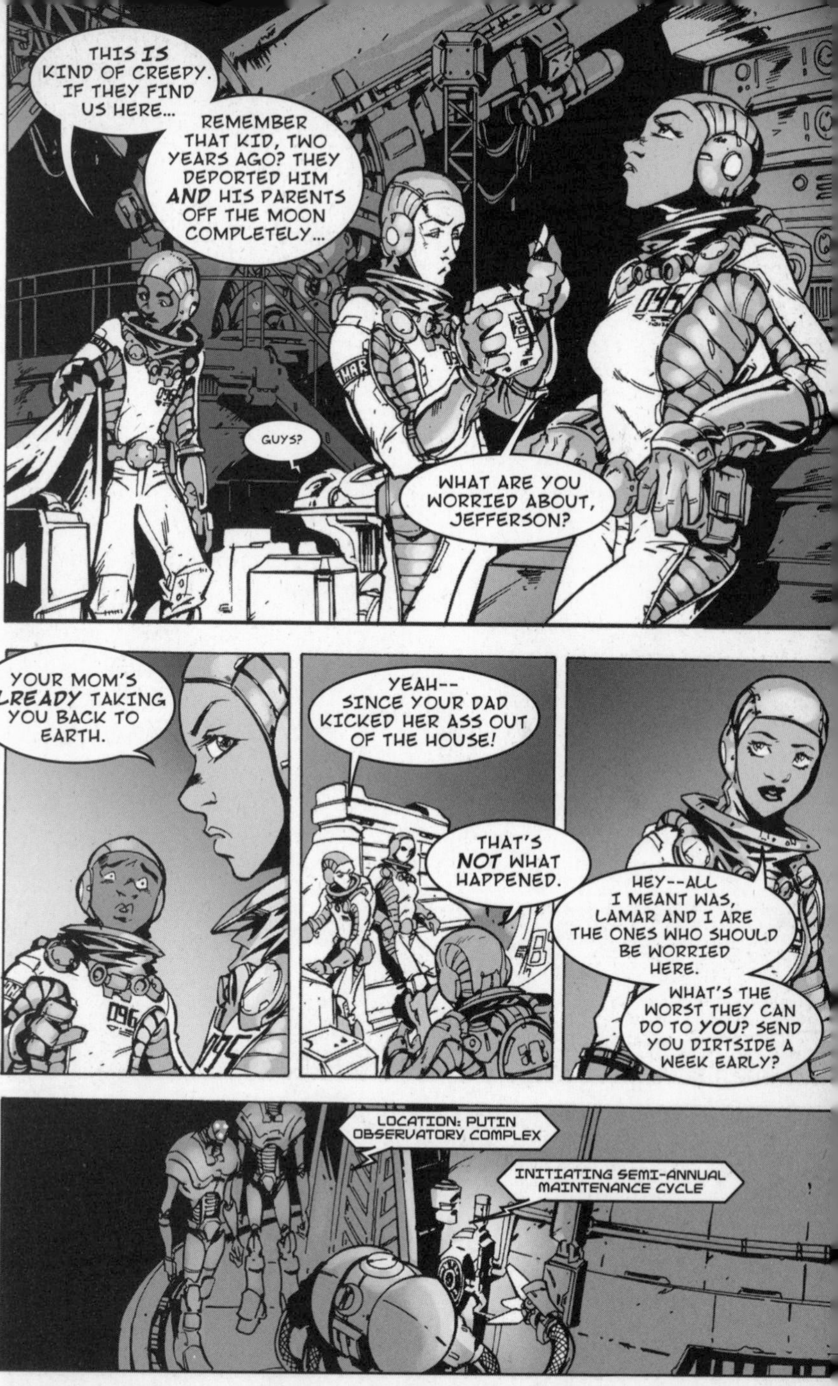
THIS *IS* KIND OF CREEPY. IF THEY FIND US HERE...
REMEMBER THAT KID, TWO YEARS AGO? THEY DEPORTED HIM *AND* HIS PARENTS OFF THE MOON COMPLETELY...
GUYS?
WHAT ARE YOU WORRIED ABOUT, JEFFERSON?
YOUR MOM'S *ALREADY* TAKING YOU BACK TO EARTH.
YEAH-- SINCE YOUR DAD KICKED HER ASS OUT OF THE HOUSE!
THAT'S *NOT* WHAT HAPPENED.
HEY--ALL I MEANT WAS, LAMAR AND I ARE THE ONES WHO SHOULD BE WORRIED HERE.
WHAT'S THE WORST THEY CAN DO TO *YOU*? SEND YOU DIRTSIDE A WEEK EARLY?
LOCATION: PUTIN OBSERVATORY COMPLEX
INITIATING SEMI-ANNUAL MAINTENANCE CYCLE

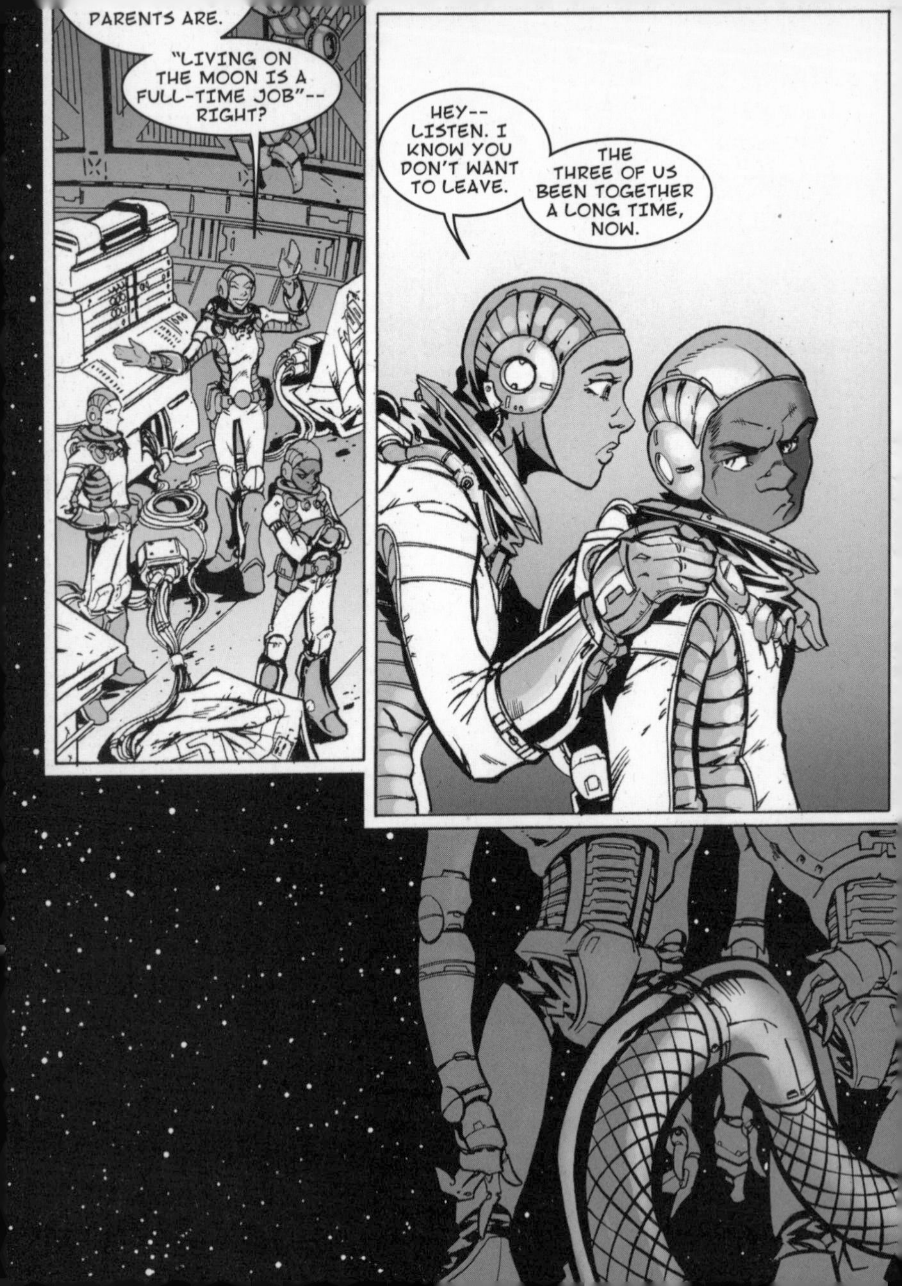
PARENTS ARE.
"LIVING ON THE MOON IS A FULL-TIME JOB"-- RIGHT?
HEY-- LISTEN. I KNOW YOU DON'T WANT TO LEAVE.
THE THREE OF US BEEN TOGETHER A LONG TIME, NOW.

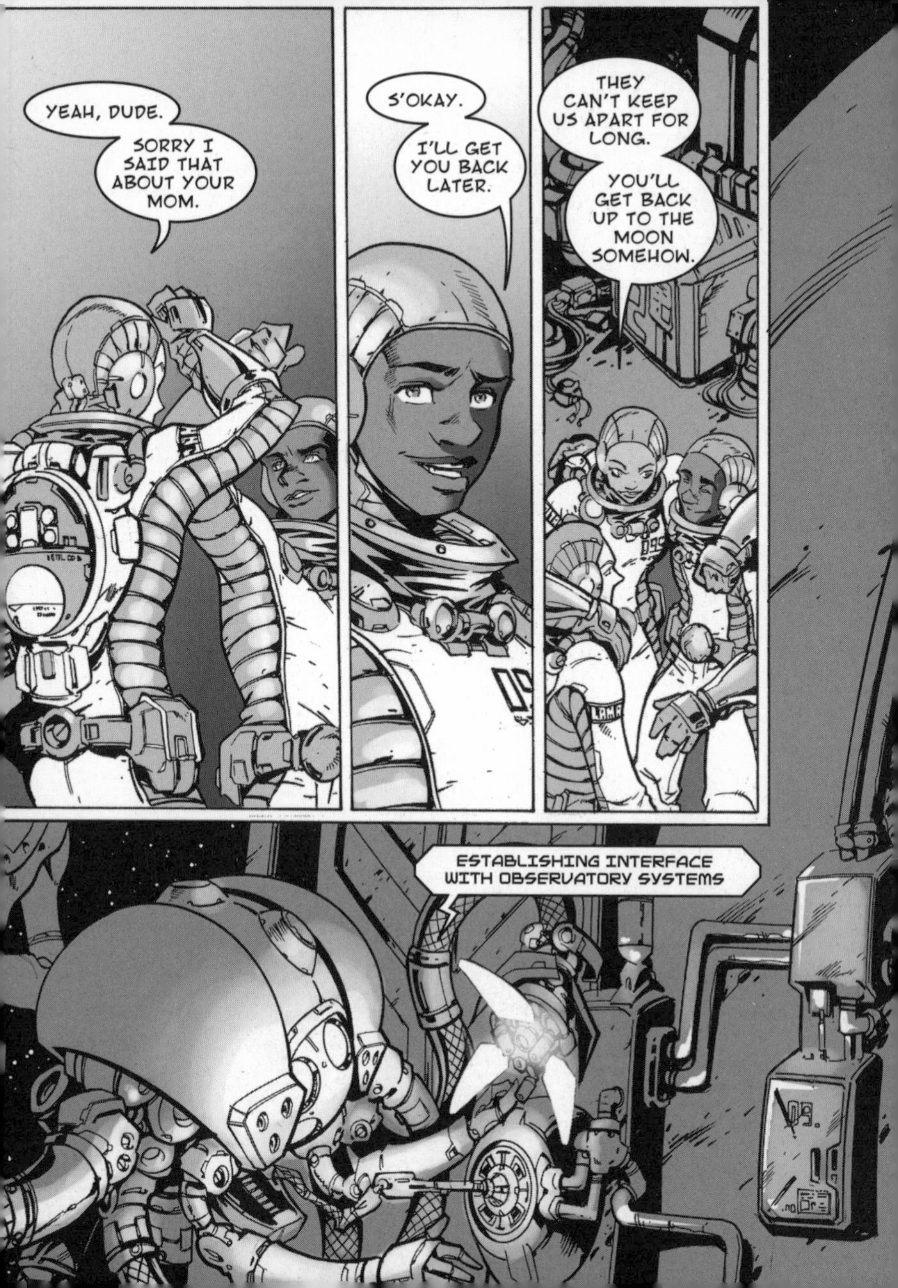
YEAH, DUDE.
SORRY I SAID THAT ABOUT YOUR MOM.
S'OKAY.
I'LL GET YOU BACK LATER.
THEY CAN'T KEEP US APART FOR LONG.
YOU'LL GET BACK UP TO THE MOON SOMEHOW.
ESTABLISHING INTERFACE WITH OBSERVATORY SYSTEMS

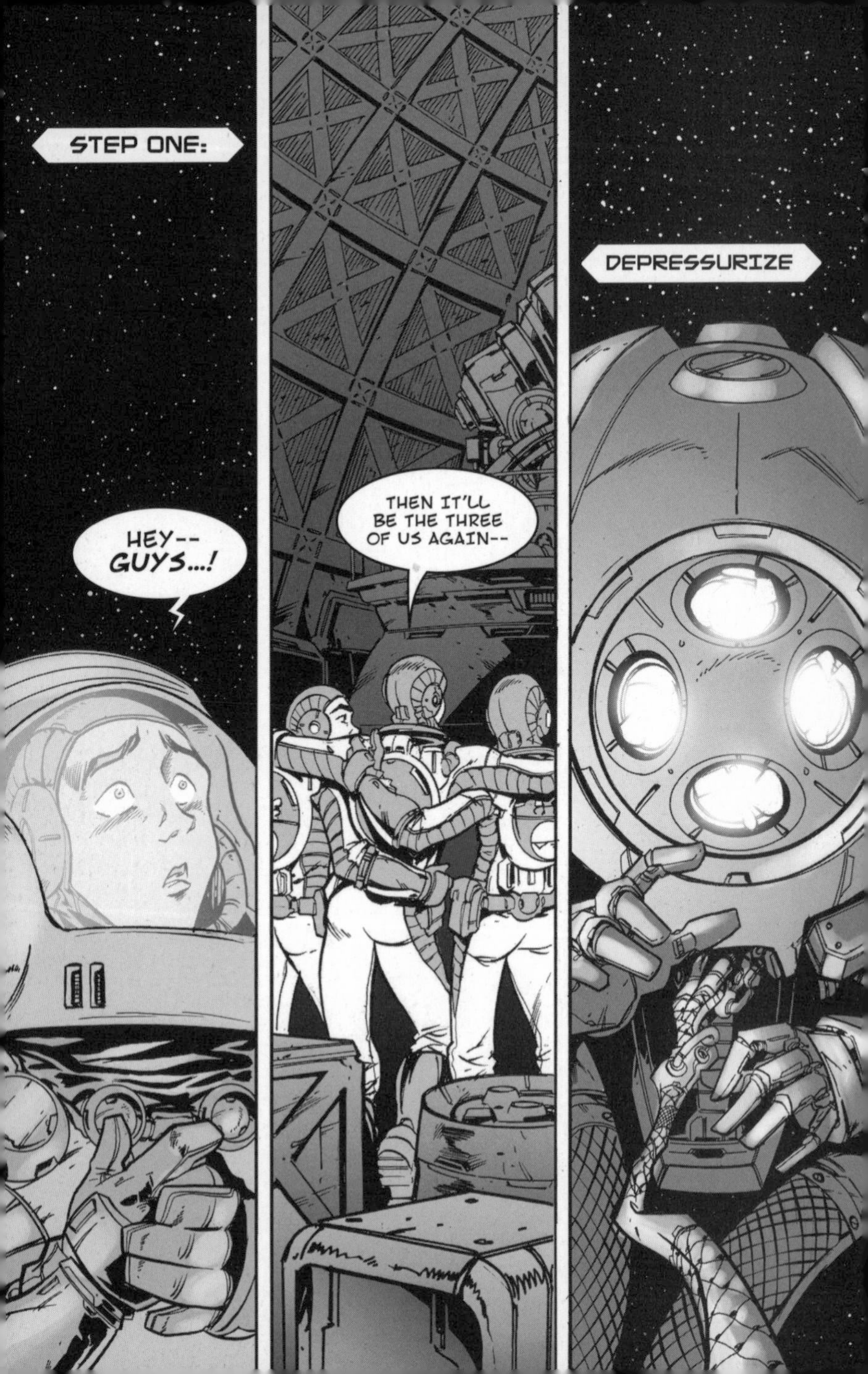
STEP ONE:
HEY-- GUYS...!
THEN IT'LL BE THE THREE OF US AGAIN--
DEPRESSURIZE

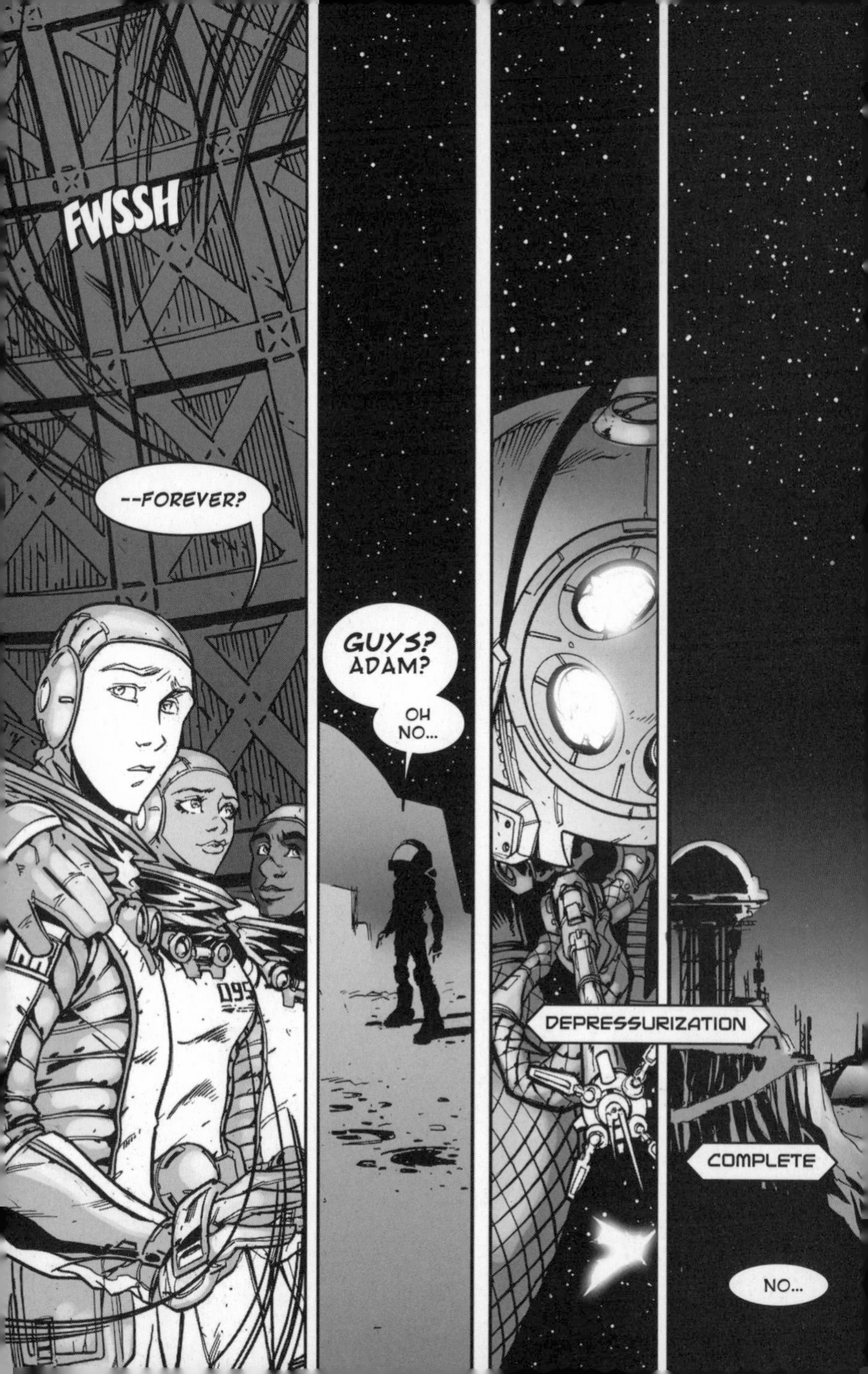
FWSSH
--FOREVER?
GUYS? ADAM?
OH NO...
DEPRESSURIZATION
COMPLETE
NO...

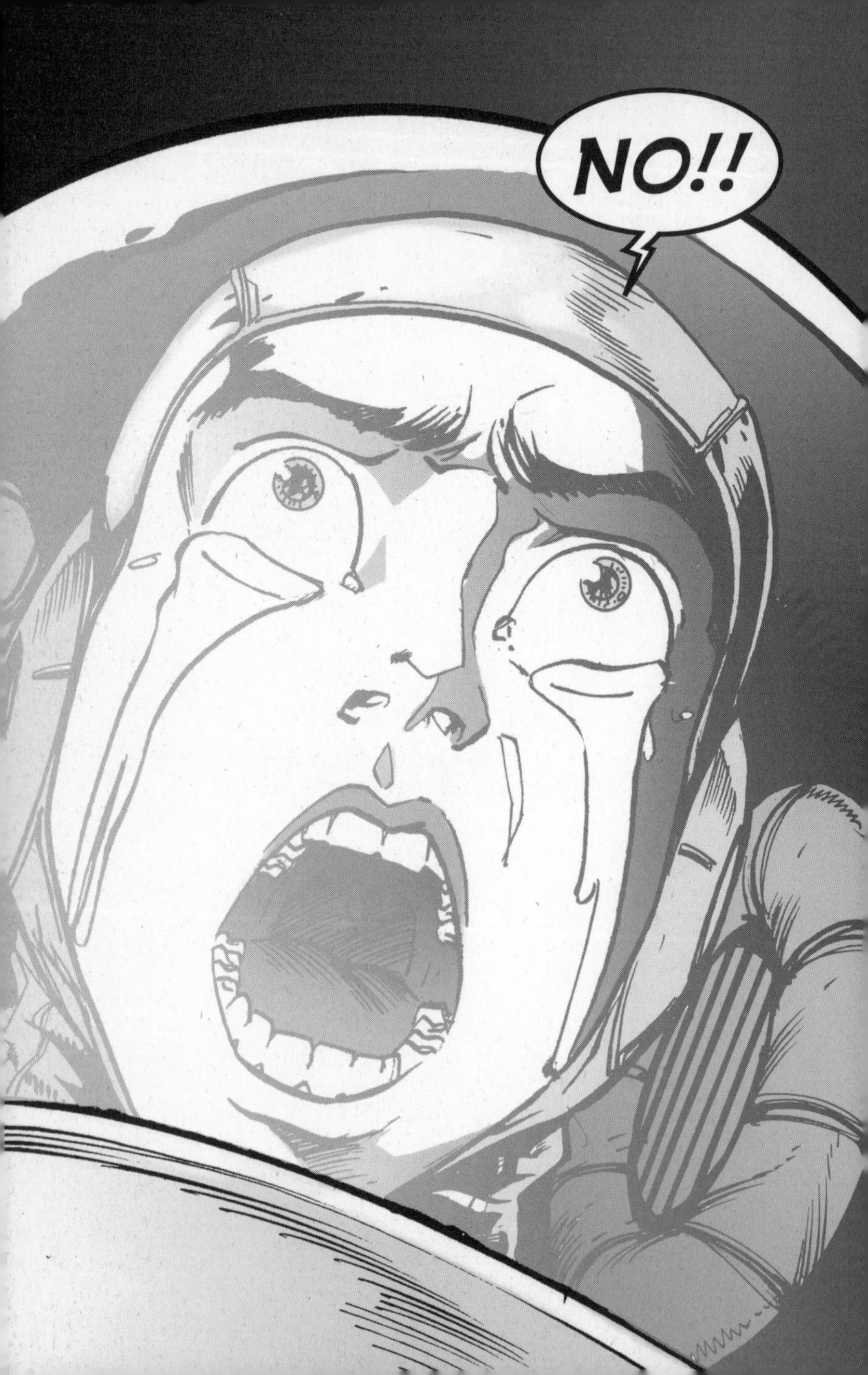
NO!!

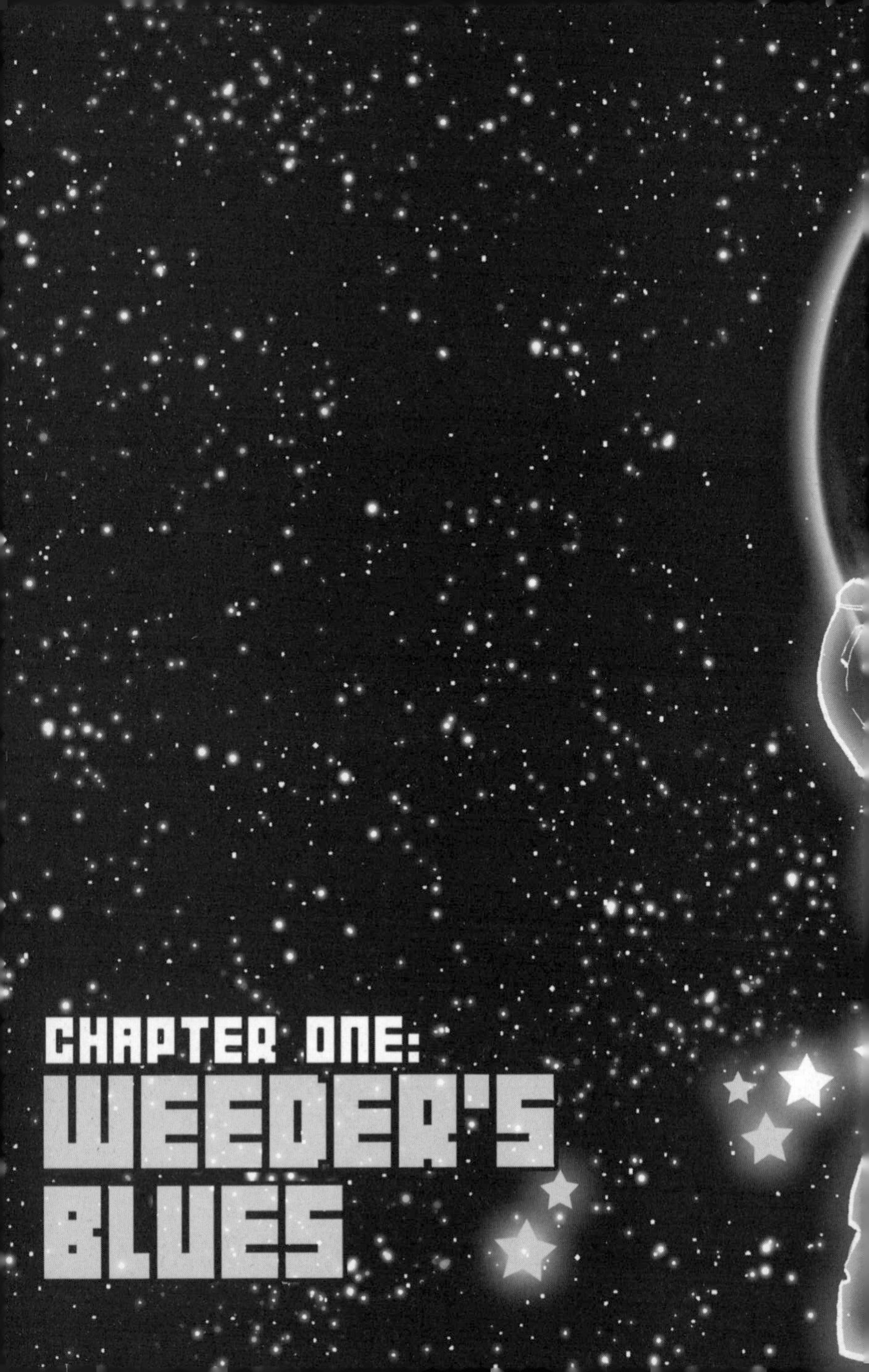

CHAPTER ONE:
WEEDER'S BLUES

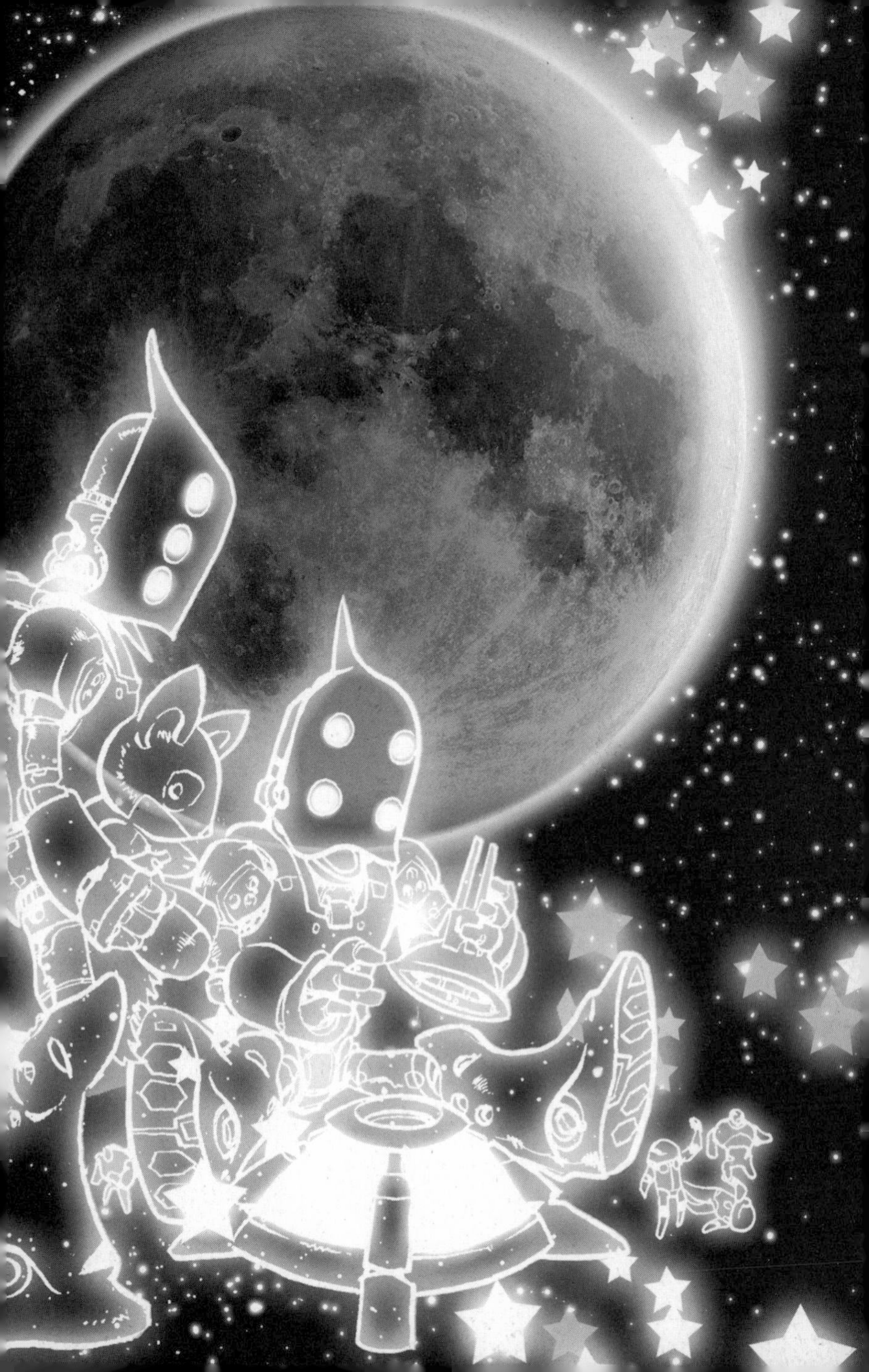

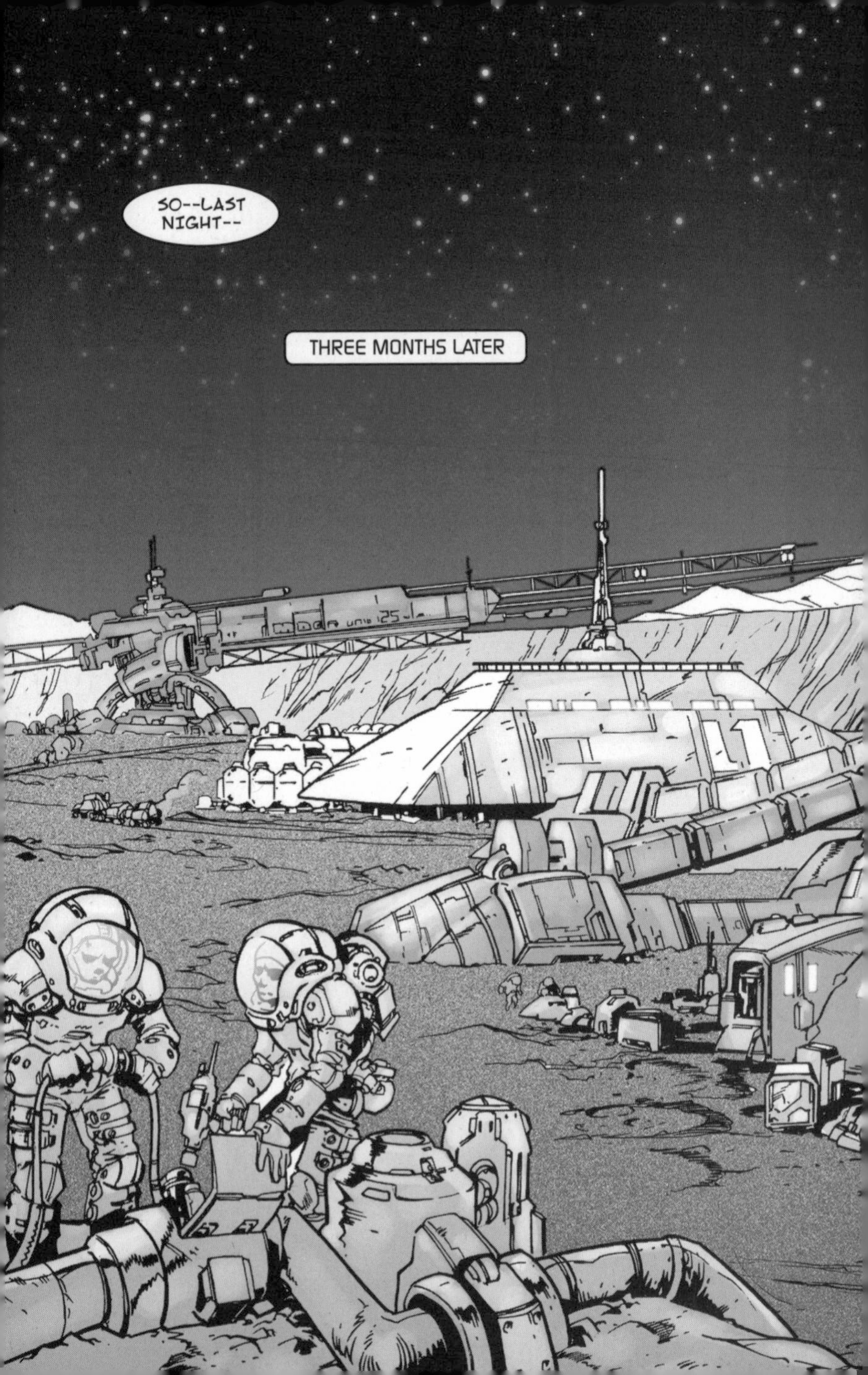
SO--LAST NIGHT--
THREE MONTHS LATER

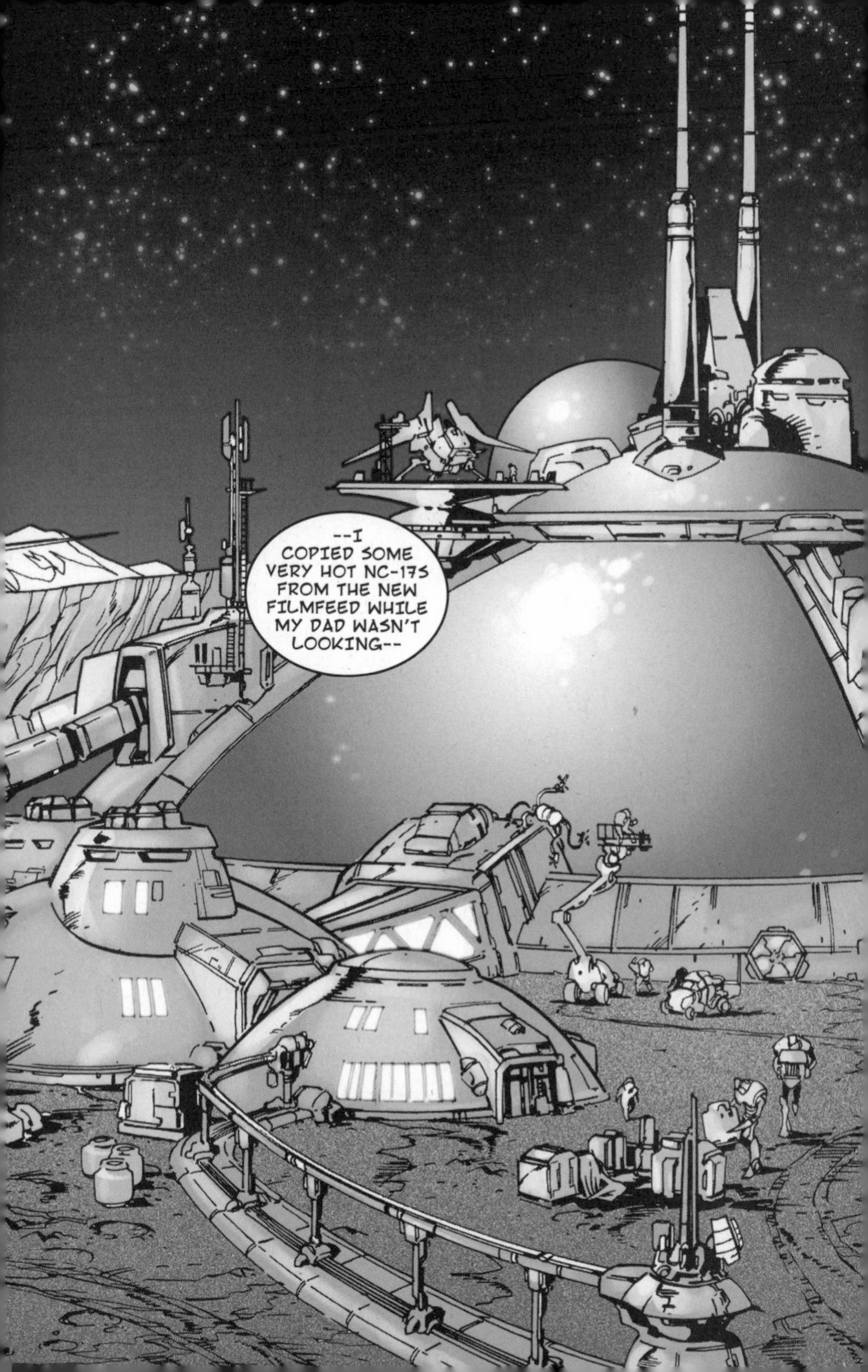
--I COPIED SOME VERY HOT NC-17S FROM THE NEW FILMFEED WHILE MY DAD WASN'T LOOKING--

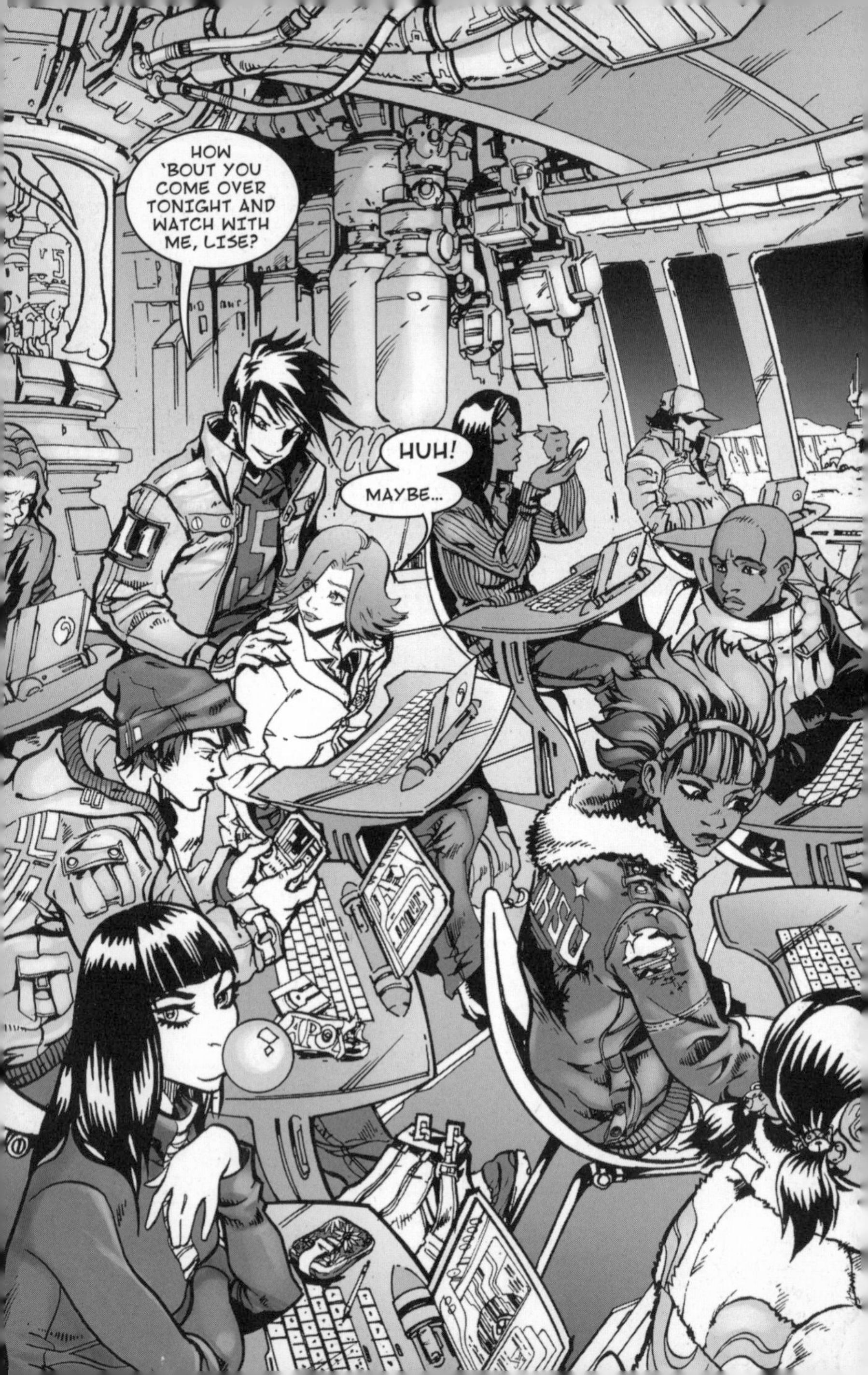
HOW 'BOUT YOU COME OVER TONIGHT AND WATCH WITH ME, LISE?
HUH!
MAYBE...

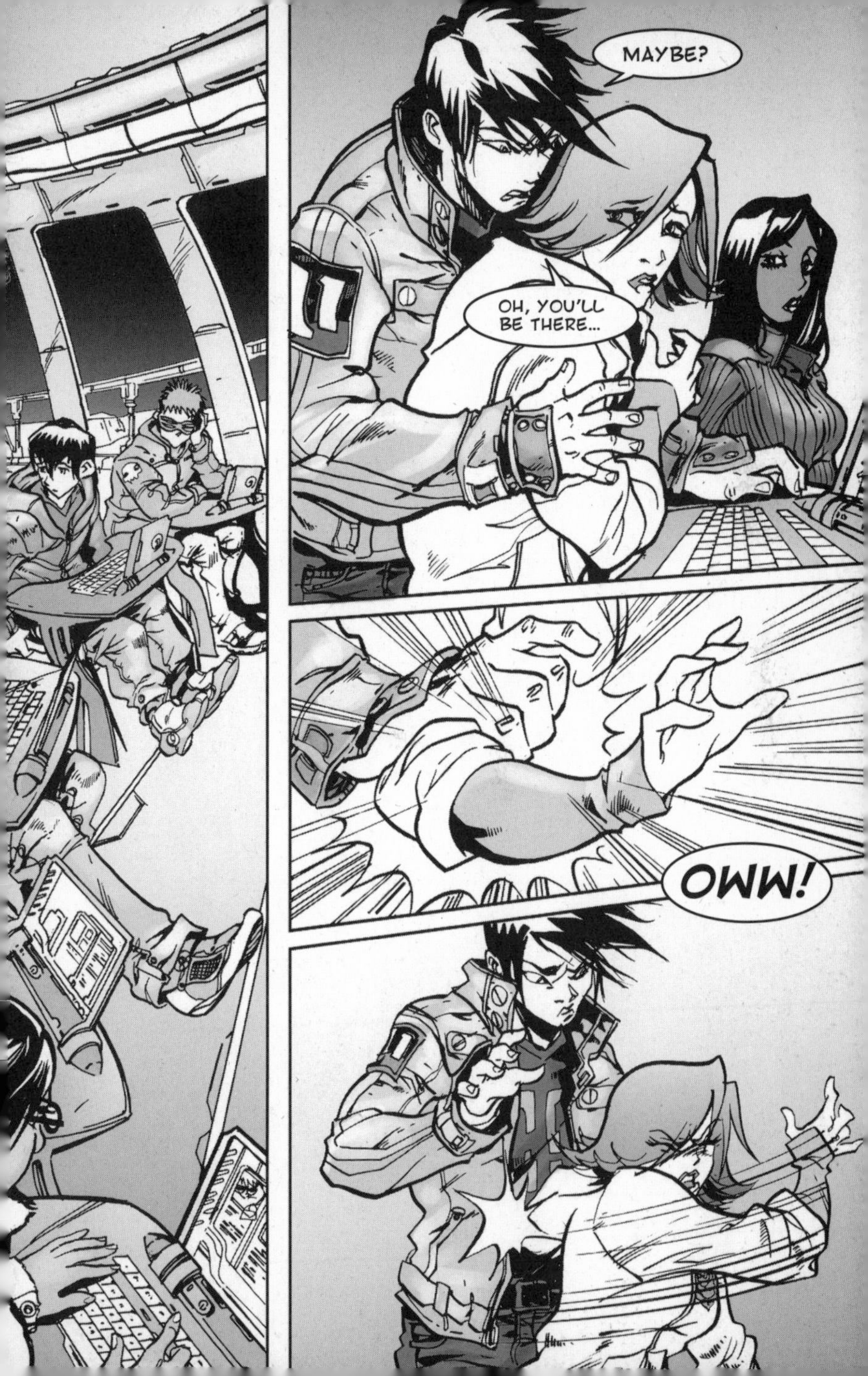
MAYBE?
OH, YOU'LL BE THERE...
OWW!

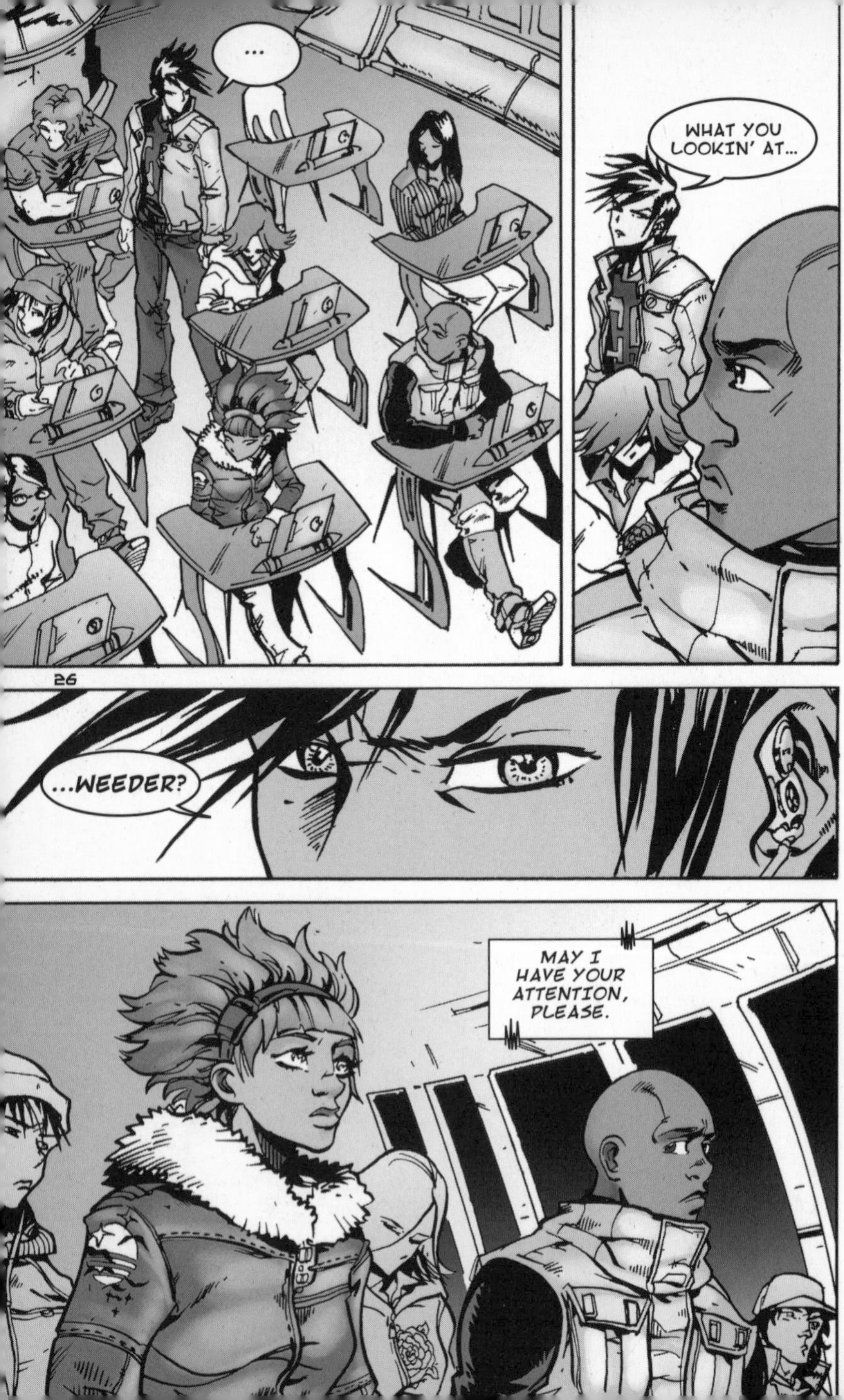
...
WHAT YOU LOOKIN' AT...
...WEEDER?
MAY I HAVE YOUR ATTENTION, PLEASE.

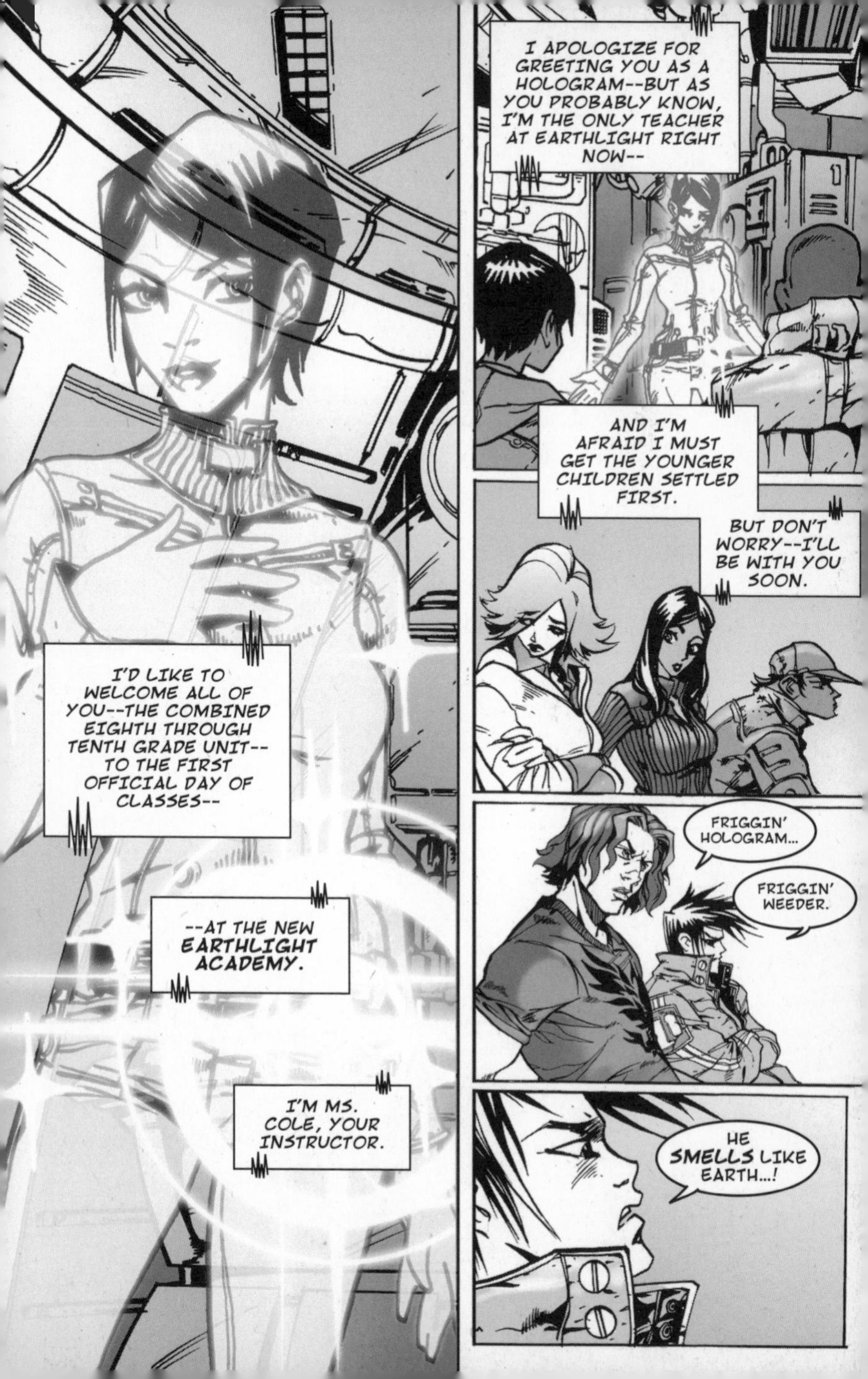
I'D LIKE TO WELCOME ALL OF YOU--THE COMBINED EIGHTH THROUGH TENTH GRADE UNIT--TO THE FIRST OFFICIAL DAY OF CLASSES--
--AT THE NEW EARTHLIGHT ACADEMY.
I'M MS. COLE, YOUR INSTRUCTOR.
I APOLOGIZE FOR GREETING YOU AS A HOLOGRAM--BUT AS YOU PROBABLY KNOW, I'M THE ONLY TEACHER AT EARTHLIGHT RIGHT NOW--
AND I'M AFRAID I MUST GET THE YOUNGER CHILDREN SETTLED FIRST.
BUT DON'T WORRY--I'LL BE WITH YOU SOON.
FRIGGIN' HOLOGRAM...
FRIGGIN' WEEDER.
HE SMELLS LIKE EARTH...!

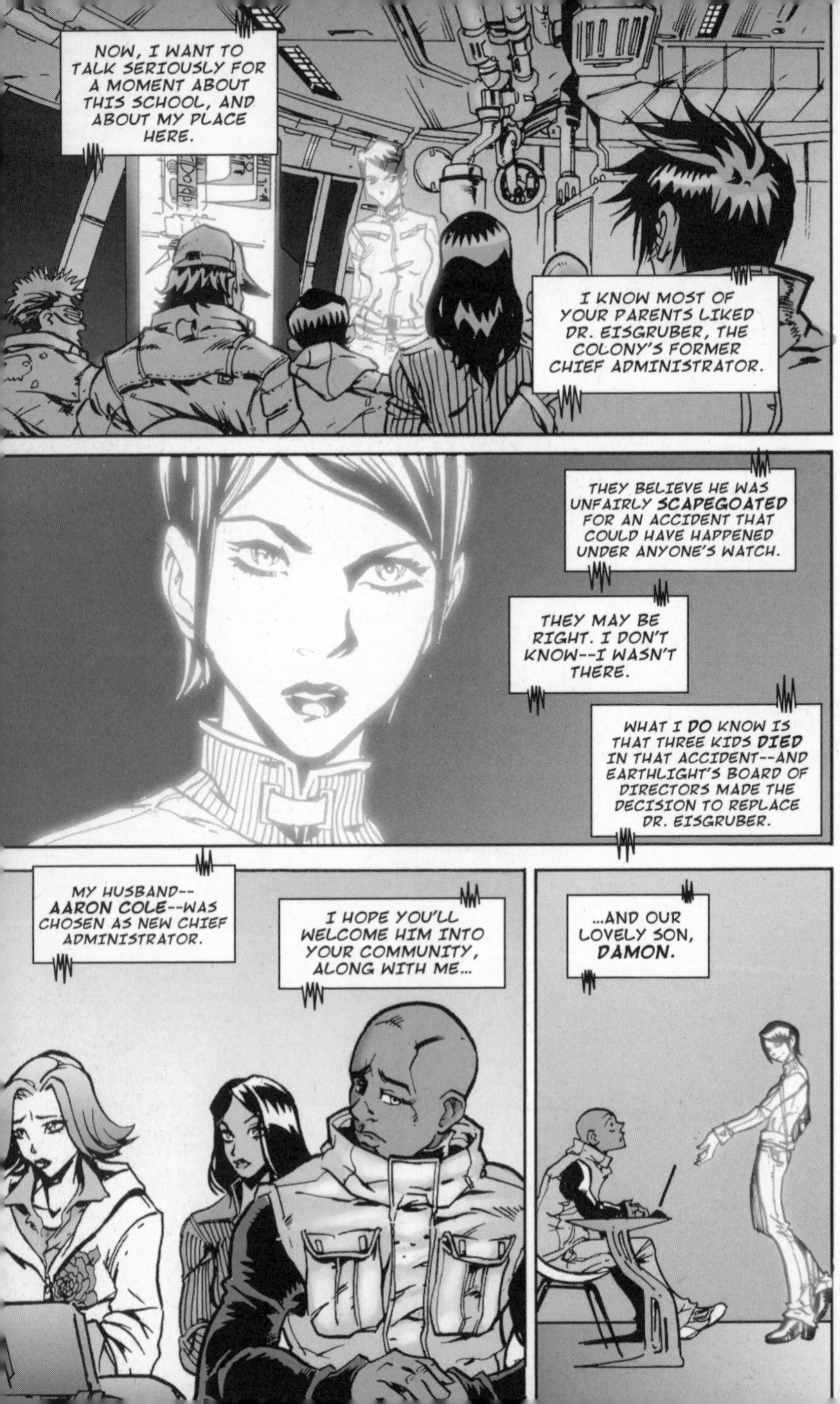
NOW, I WANT TO TALK SERIOUSLY FOR A MOMENT ABOUT THIS SCHOOL, AND ABOUT MY PLACE HERE.
I KNOW MOST OF YOUR PARENTS LIKED DR. EISGRUBER, THE COLONY'S FORMER CHIEF ADMINISTRATOR.
THEY BELIEVE HE WAS UNFAIRLY **SCAPEGOATED** FOR AN ACCIDENT THAT COULD HAVE HAPPENED UNDER ANYONE'S WATCH.
THEY MAY BE RIGHT. I DON'T KNOW--I WASN'T THERE.
WHAT I **DO** KNOW IS THAT THREE KIDS **DIED** IN THAT ACCIDENT--AND EARTHLIGHT'S BOARD OF DIRECTORS MADE THE DECISION TO REPLACE DR. EISGRUBER.
MY HUSBAND--**AARON COLE**--WAS CHOSEN AS NEW CHIEF ADMINISTRATOR.
I HOPE YOU'LL WELCOME HIM INTO YOUR COMMUNITY, ALONG WITH ME...
...AND OUR LOVELY SON, **DAMON.**

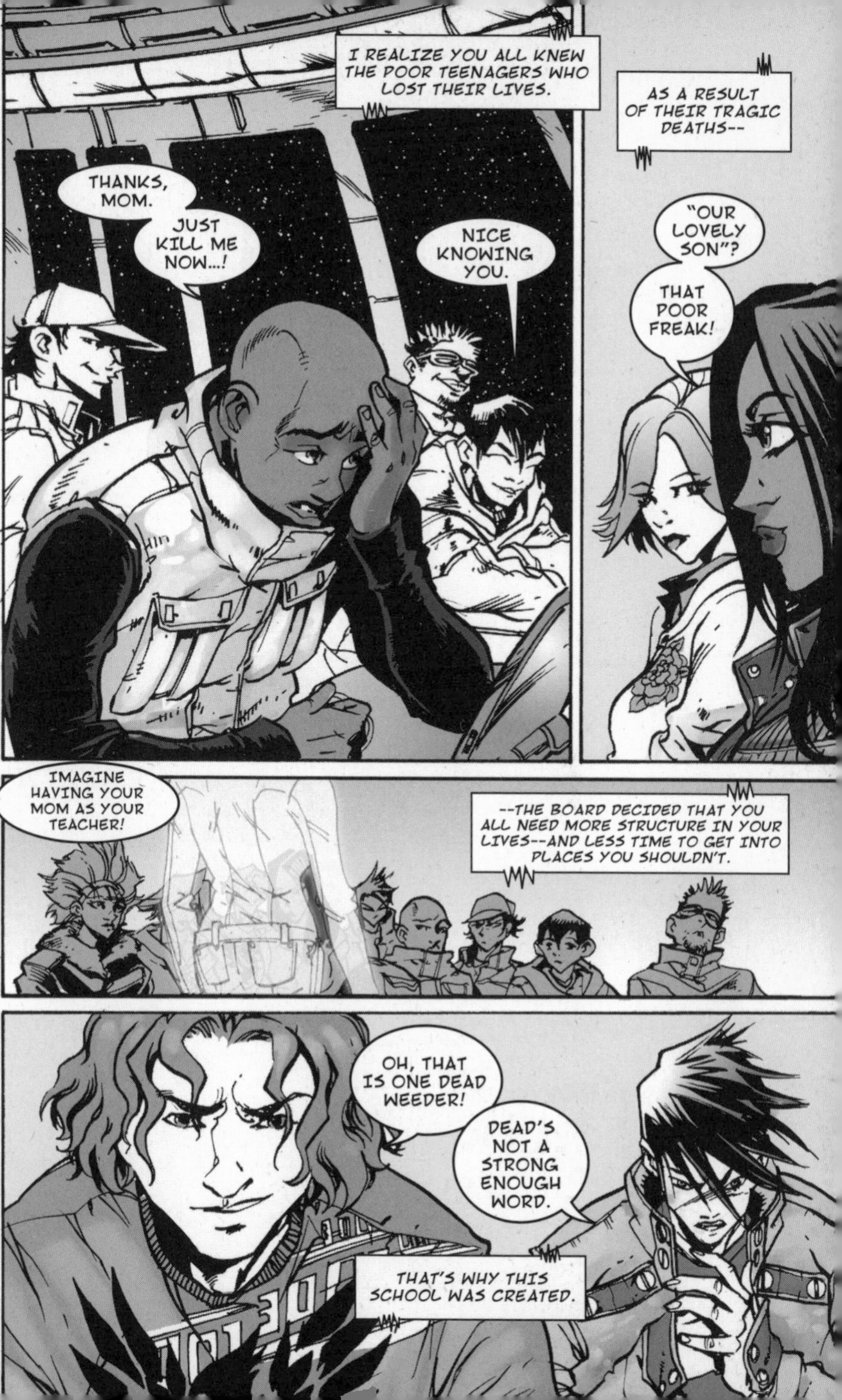
I REALIZE YOU ALL KNEW THE POOR TEENAGERS WHO LOST THEIR LIVES.
THANKS, MOM.
JUST KILL ME NOW...!
NICE KNOWING YOU.
AS A RESULT OF THEIR TRAGIC DEATHS--
"OUR LOVELY SON"?
THAT POOR FREAK!
IMAGINE HAVING YOUR MOM AS YOUR TEACHER!
--THE BOARD DECIDED THAT YOU ALL NEED MORE STRUCTURE IN YOUR LIVES--AND LESS TIME TO GET INTO PLACES YOU SHOULDN'T.
OH, THAT IS ONE DEAD WEEDER!
DEAD'S NOT A STRONG ENOUGH WORD.
THAT'S WHY THIS SCHOOL WAS CREATED.

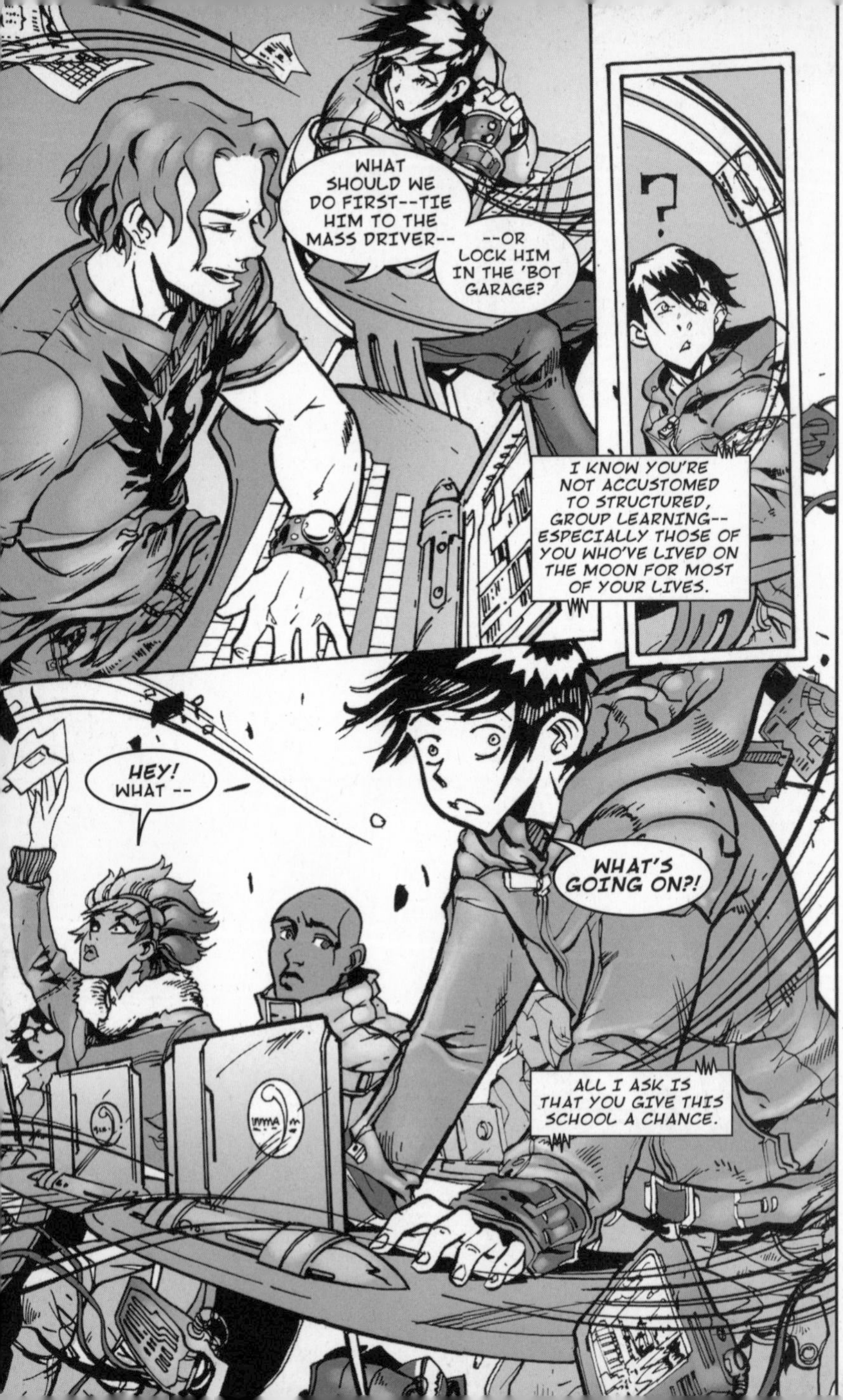

WHAT SHOULD WE DO FIRST--TIE HIM TO THE MASS DRIVER--
--OR LOCK HIM IN THE 'BOT GARAGE?
?
I KNOW YOU'RE NOT ACCUSTOMED TO STRUCTURED, GROUP LEARNING--ESPECIALLY THOSE OF YOU WHO'VE LIVED ON THE MOON FOR MOST OF YOUR LIVES.
HEY! WHAT --
WHAT'S GOING ON?!
ALL I ASK IS THAT YOU GIVE THIS SCHOOL A CHANCE.

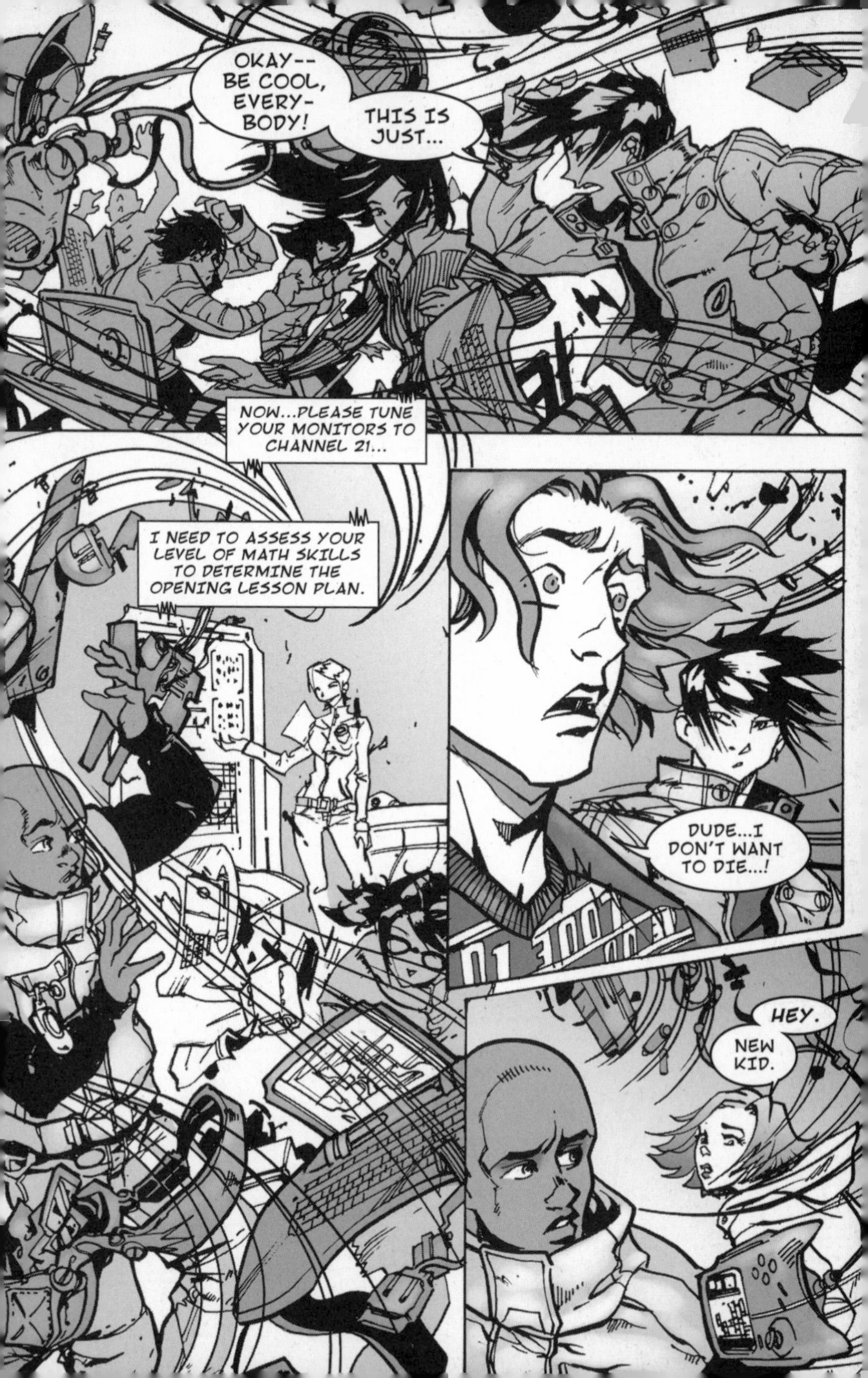
OKAY--BE COOL, EVERY-BODY!
THIS IS JUST...
NOW...PLEASE TUNE YOUR MONITORS TO CHANNEL 21...
I NEED TO ASSESS YOUR LEVEL OF MATH SKILLS TO DETERMINE THE OPENING LESSON PLAN.
DUDE...I DON'T WANT TO DIE...!
HEY.
NEW KID.

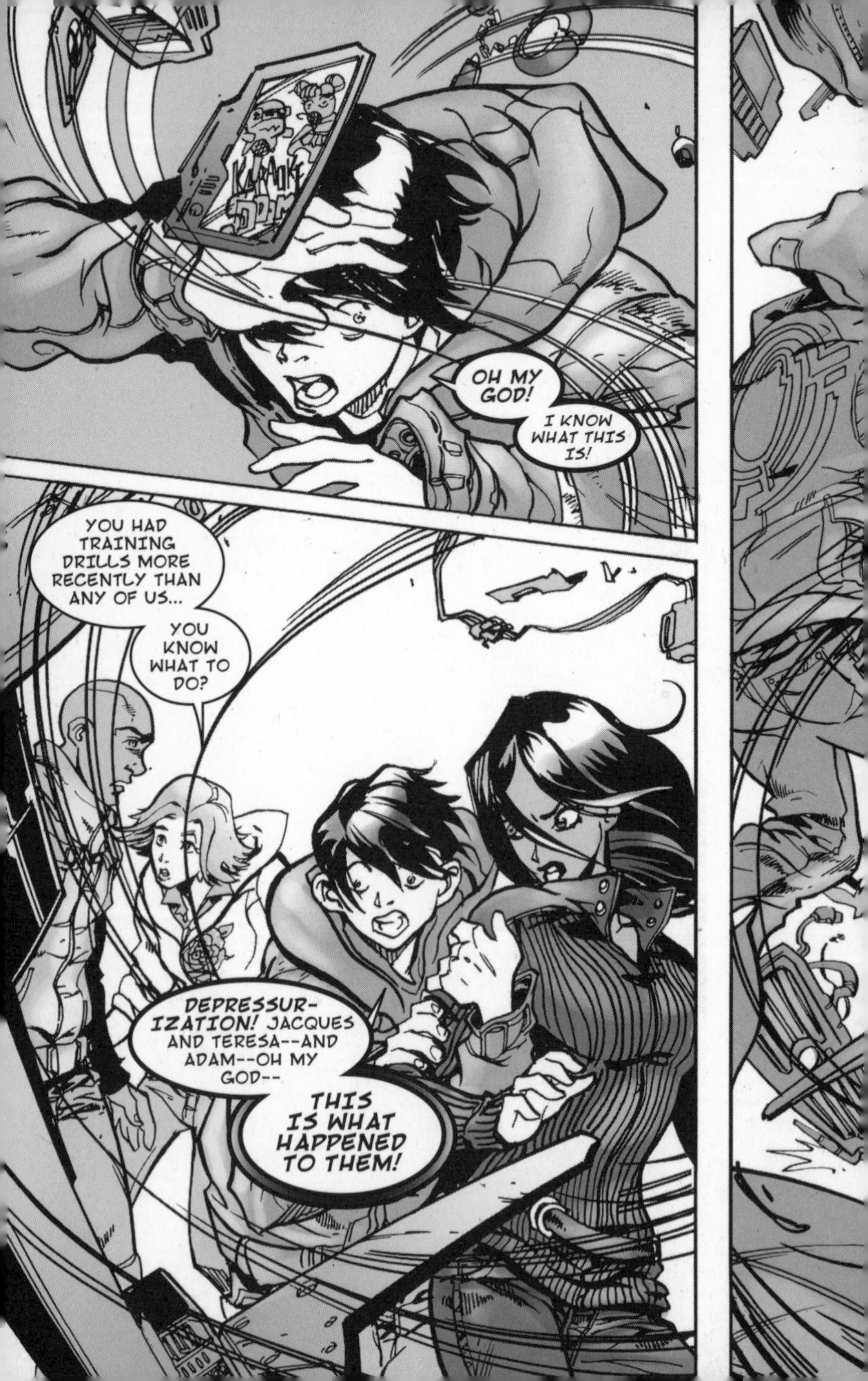
KARAOKE DOOM
OH MY GOD!
I KNOW WHAT THIS IS!
YOU HAD TRAINING DRILLS MORE RECENTLY THAN ANY OF US...
YOU KNOW WHAT TO DO?
DEPRESSUR-IZATION! JACQUES AND TERESA--AND ADAM--OH MY GOD--
THIS IS WHAT HAPPENED TO THEM!

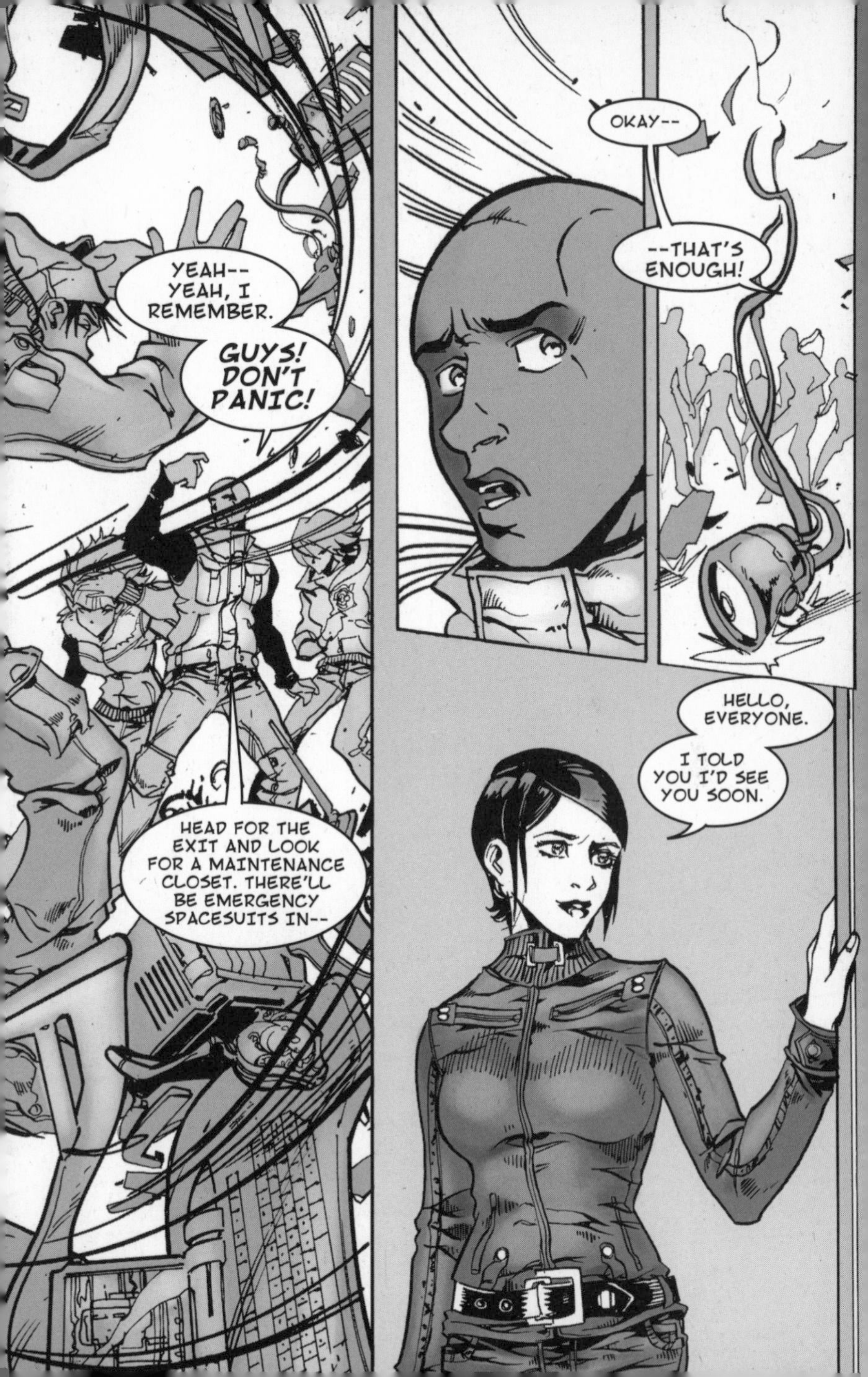
YEAH-- YEAH, I REMEMBER.
GUYS! DON'T PANIC!
HEAD FOR THE EXIT AND LOOK FOR A MAINTENANCE CLOSET. THERE'LL BE EMERGENCY SPACESUITS IN--
OKAY--
--THAT'S ENOUGH!
HELLO, EVERYONE.
I TOLD YOU I'D SEE YOU SOON.

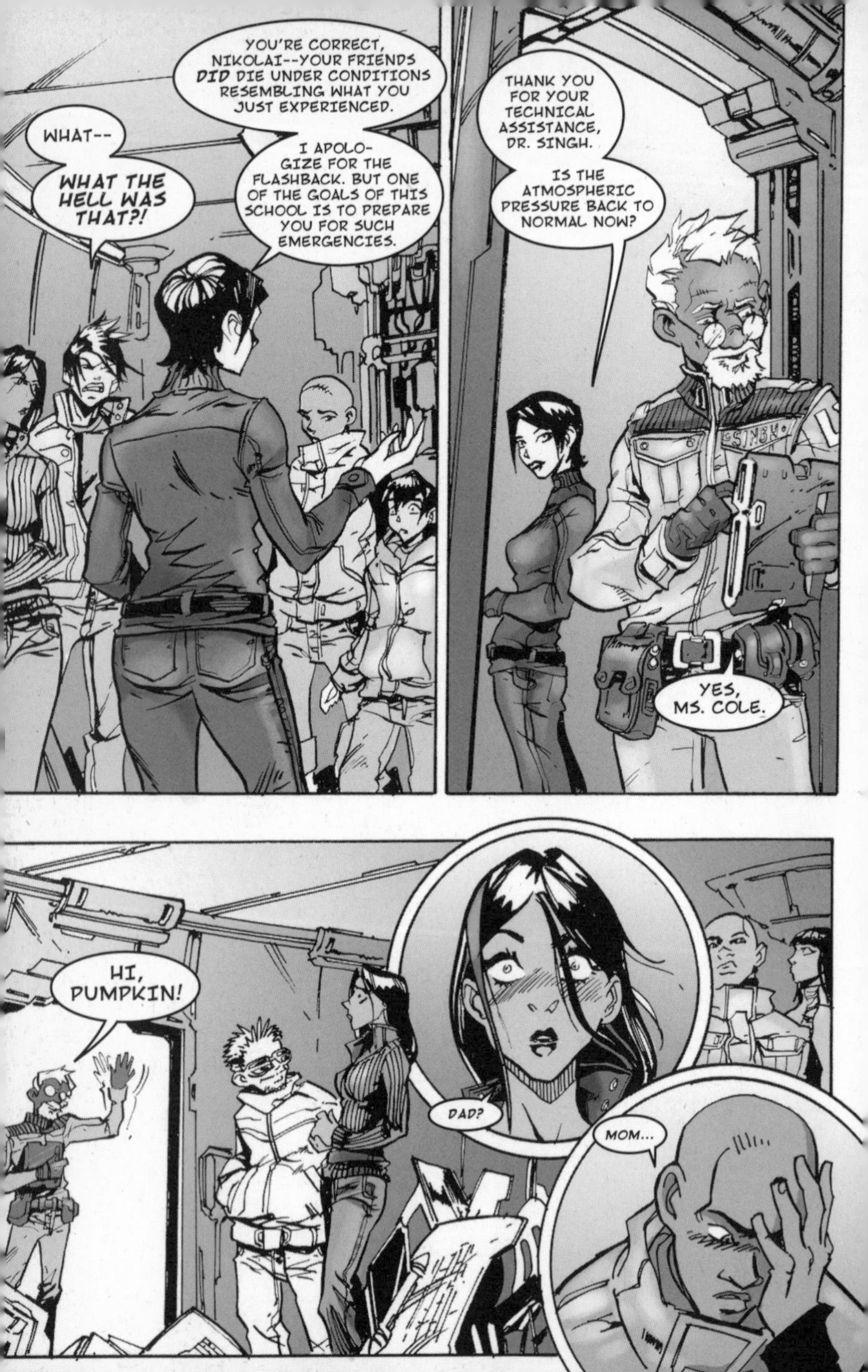
WHAT--
WHAT THE HELL WAS THAT?!
YOU'RE CORRECT, NIKOLAI--YOUR FRIENDS DID DIE UNDER CONDITIONS RESEMBLING WHAT YOU JUST EXPERIENCED.
I APOLOGIZE FOR THE FLASHBACK. BUT ONE OF THE GOALS OF THIS SCHOOL IS TO PREPARE YOU FOR SUCH EMERGENCIES.
THANK YOU FOR YOUR TECHNICAL ASSISTANCE, DR. SINGH.
IS THE ATMOSPHERIC PRESSURE BACK TO NORMAL NOW?
SINGH
YES, MS. COLE.
HI, PUMPKIN!
DAD?
MOM...

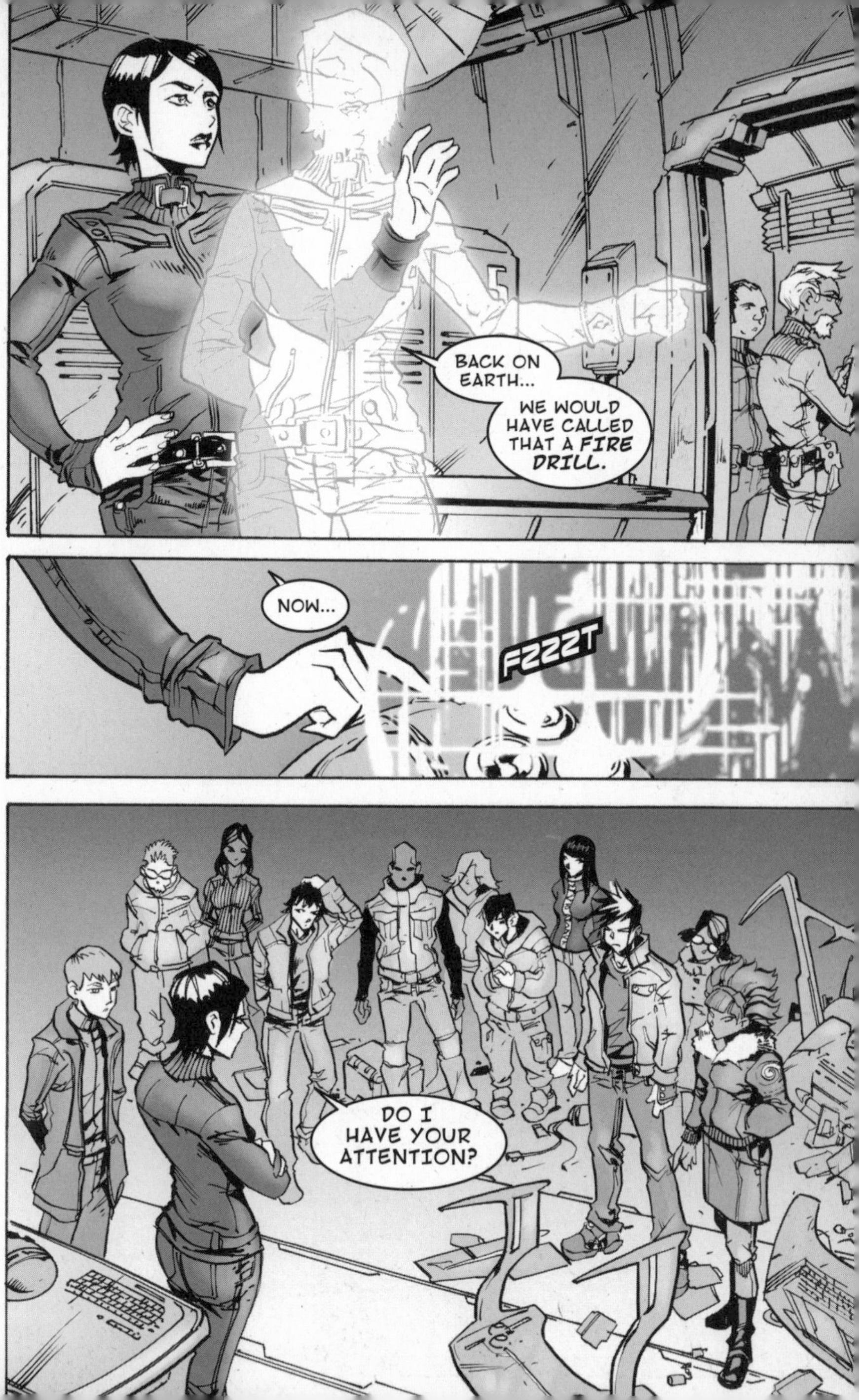
BACK ON EARTH...
WE WOULD HAVE CALLED THAT A FIRE DRILL.
NOW...
FZZZT
DO I HAVE YOUR ATTENTION?

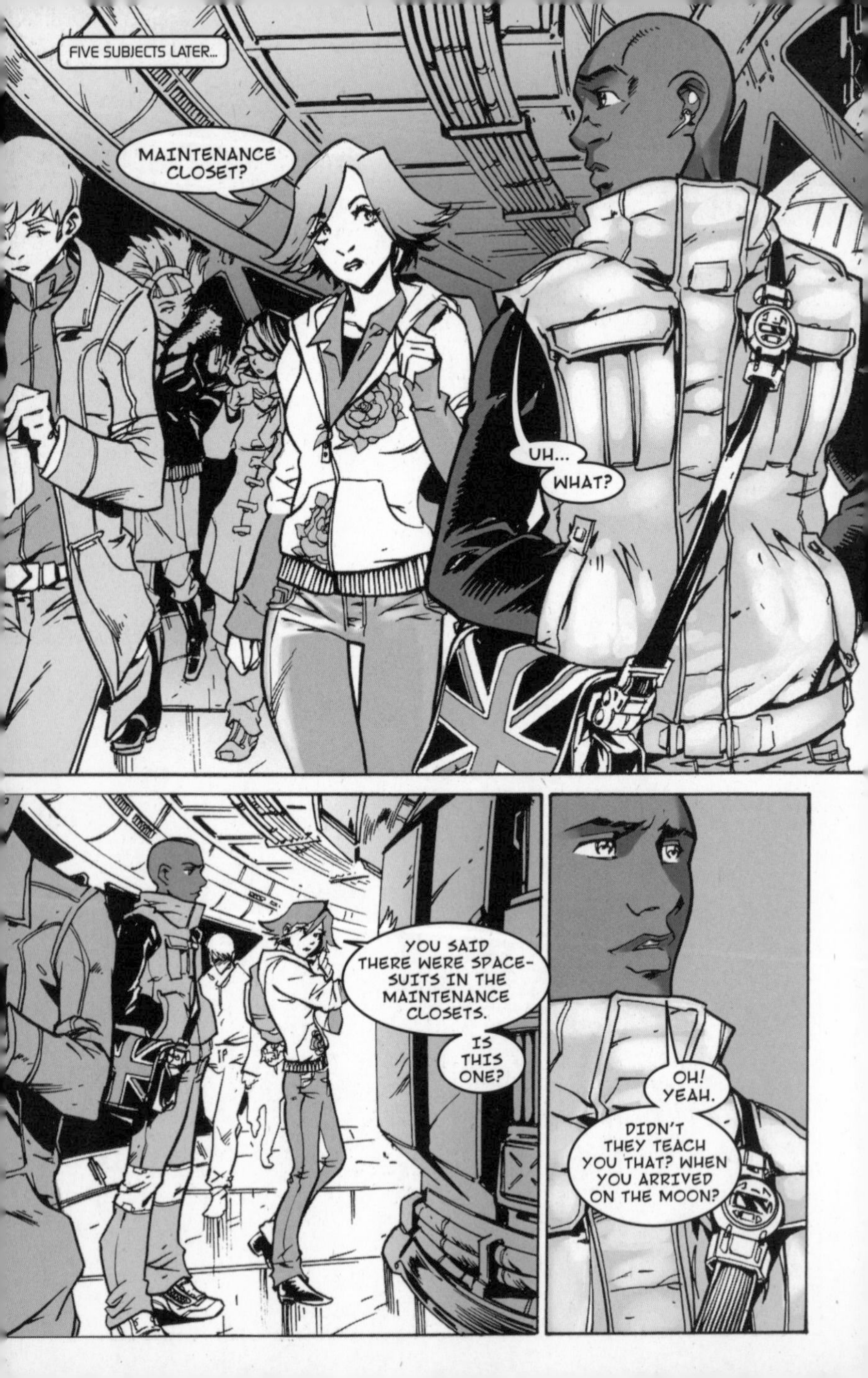
FIVE SUBJECTS LATER...
MAINTENANCE CLOSET?
UH... WHAT?
YOU SAID THERE WERE SPACE-SUITS IN THE MAINTENANCE CLOSETS.
IS THIS ONE?
OH! YEAH.
DIDN'T THEY TEACH YOU THAT? WHEN YOU ARRIVED ON THE MOON?

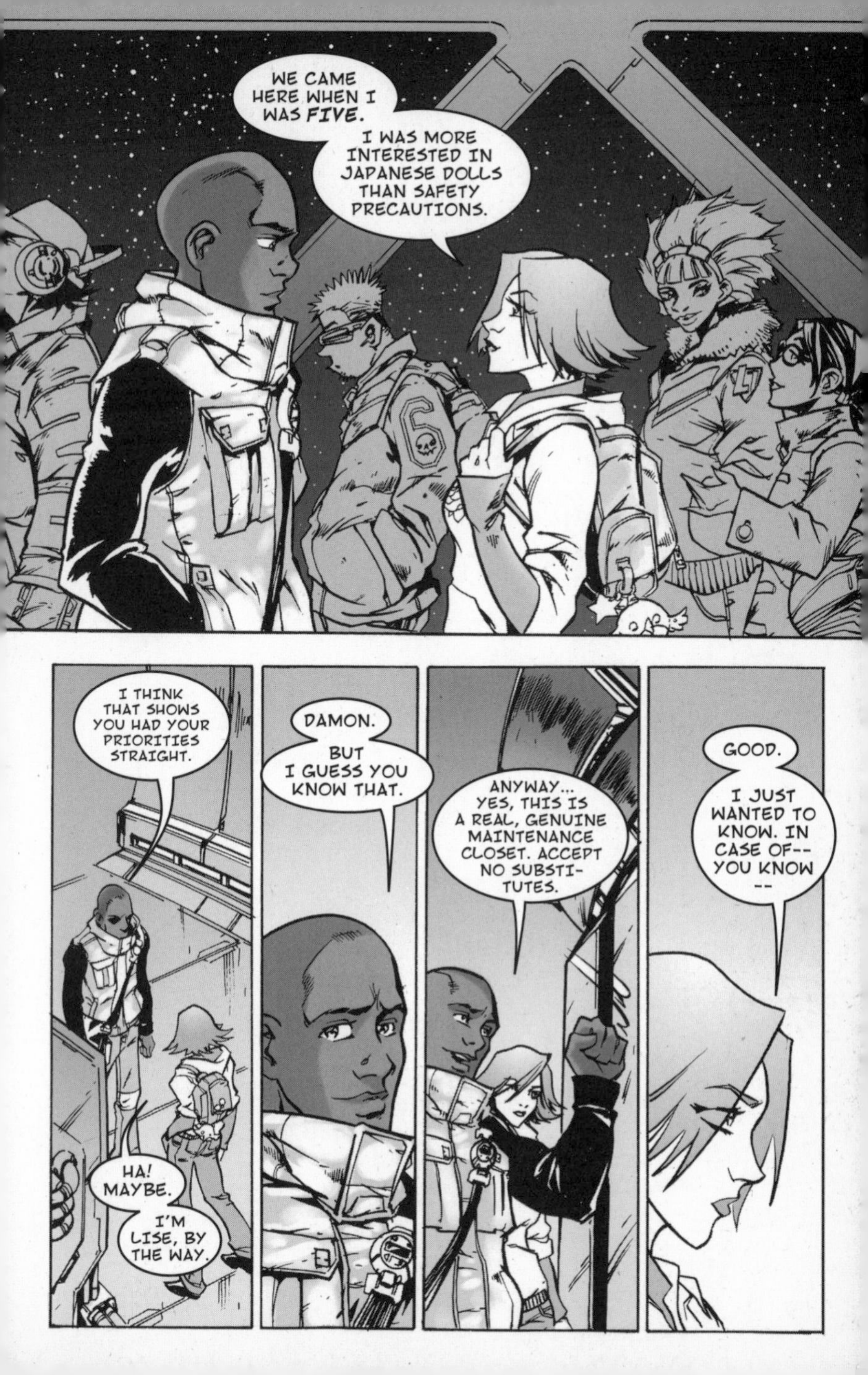
WE CAME HERE WHEN I WAS FIVE.
I WAS MORE INTERESTED IN JAPANESE DOLLS THAN SAFETY PRECAUTIONS.
I THINK THAT SHOWS YOU HAD YOUR PRIORITIES STRAIGHT.
HA! MAYBE.
I'M LISE, BY THE WAY.
DAMON.
BUT I GUESS YOU KNOW THAT.
ANYWAY... YES, THIS IS A REAL, GENUINE MAINTENANCE CLOSET. ACCEPT NO SUBSTI-TUTES.
GOOD.
I JUST WANTED TO KNOW. IN CASE OF-- YOU KNOW --

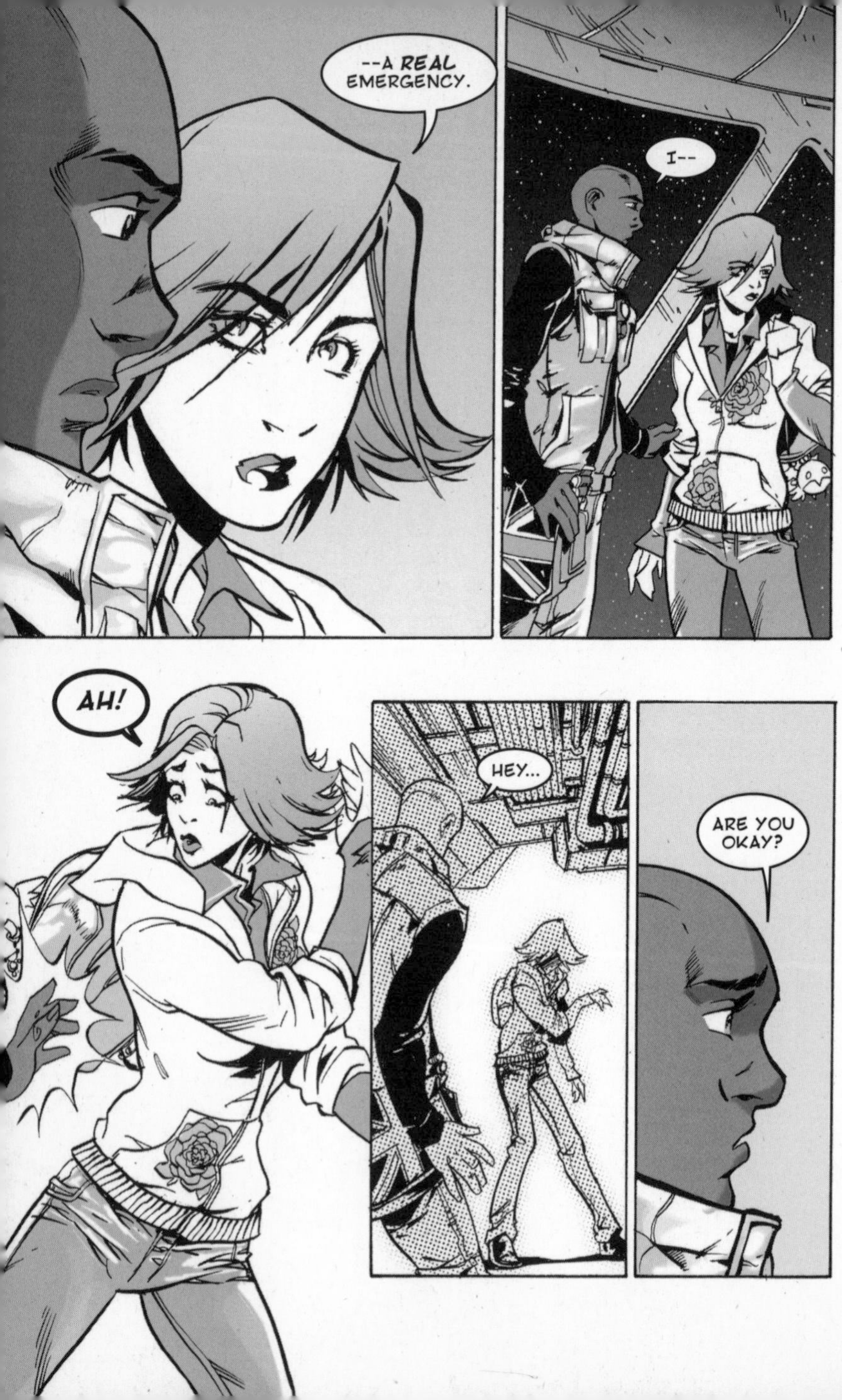
--A **REAL** EMERGENCY.
I--
AH!
HEY...
ARE YOU OKAY?

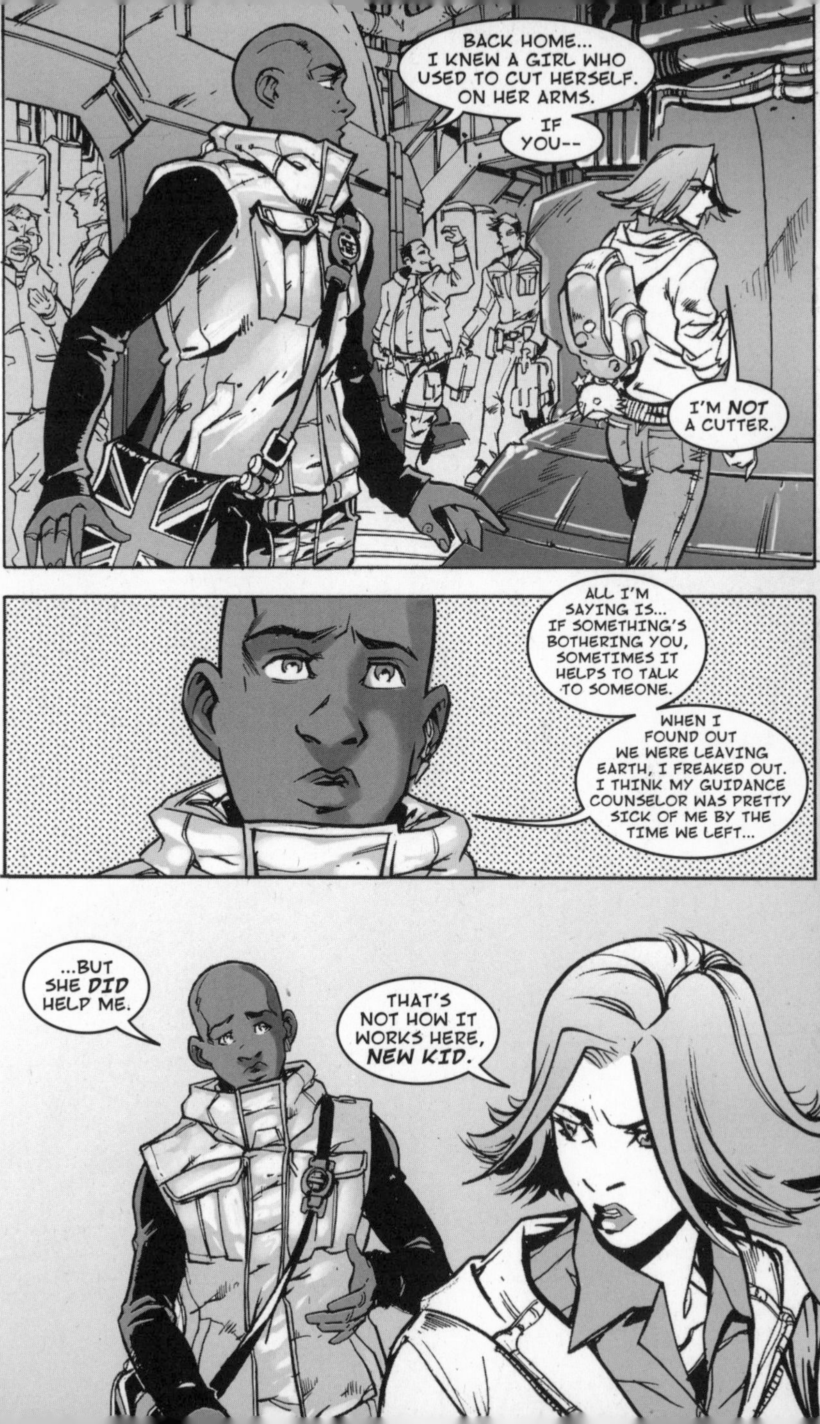

BACK HOME... I KNEW A GIRL WHO USED TO CUT HERSELF. ON HER ARMS.
IF YOU--
I'M **NOT** A CUTTER.
ALL I'M SAYING IS... IF SOMETHING'S BOTHERING YOU, SOMETIMES IT HELPS TO TALK TO SOMEONE.
WHEN I FOUND OUT WE WERE LEAVING EARTH, I FREAKED OUT. I THINK MY GUIDANCE COUNSELOR WAS PRETTY SICK OF ME BY THE TIME WE LEFT...
...BUT SHE **DID** HELP ME.
THAT'S NOT HOW IT WORKS HERE, **NEW KID**.

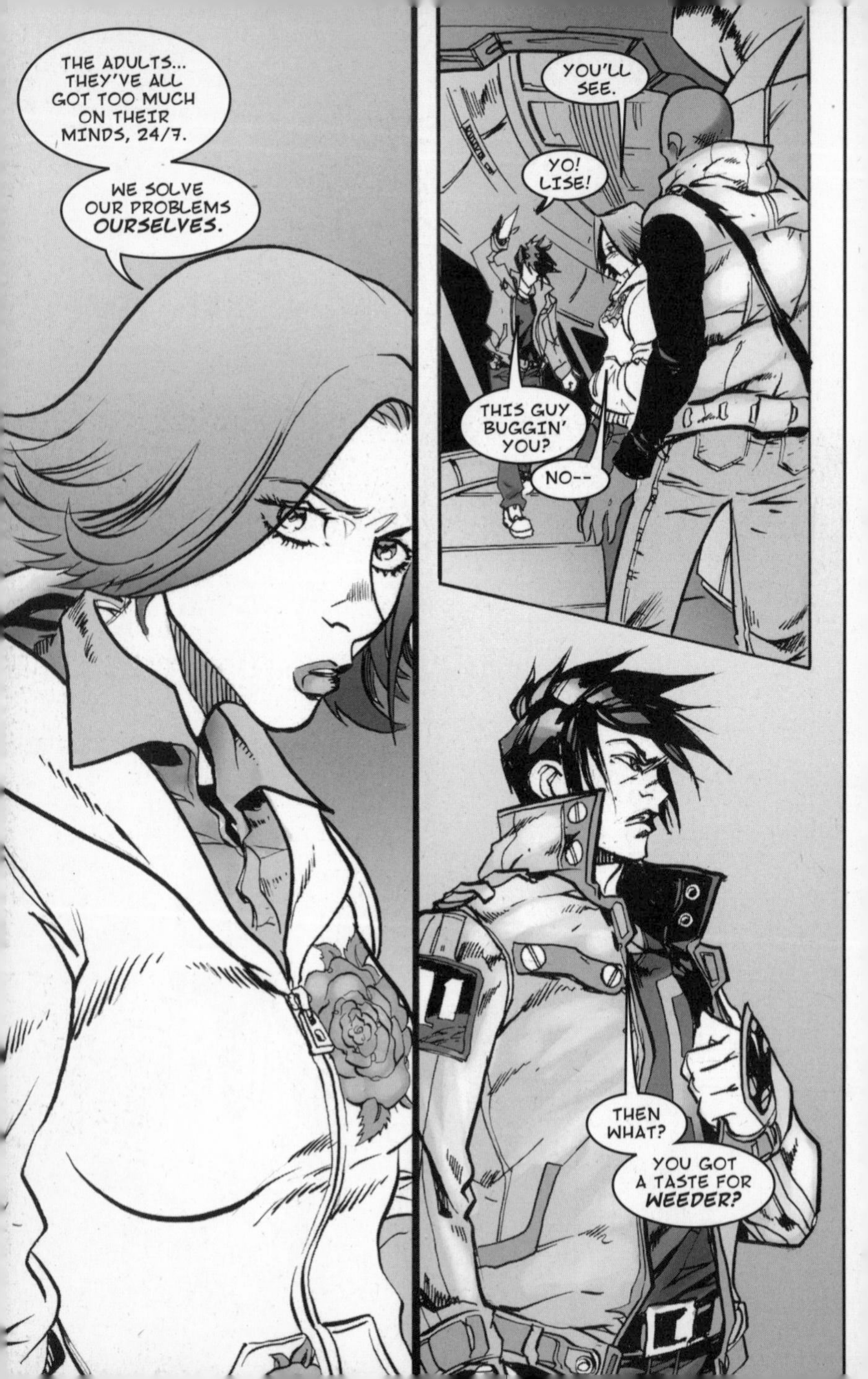
THE ADULTS... THEY'VE ALL GOT TOO MUCH ON THEIR MINDS, 24/7.
WE SOLVE OUR PROBLEMS **OURSELVES.**
YOU'LL SEE.
YO! LISE!
THIS GUY BUGGIN' YOU?
NO--
THEN WHAT?
YOU GOT A TASTE FOR **WEEDER?**

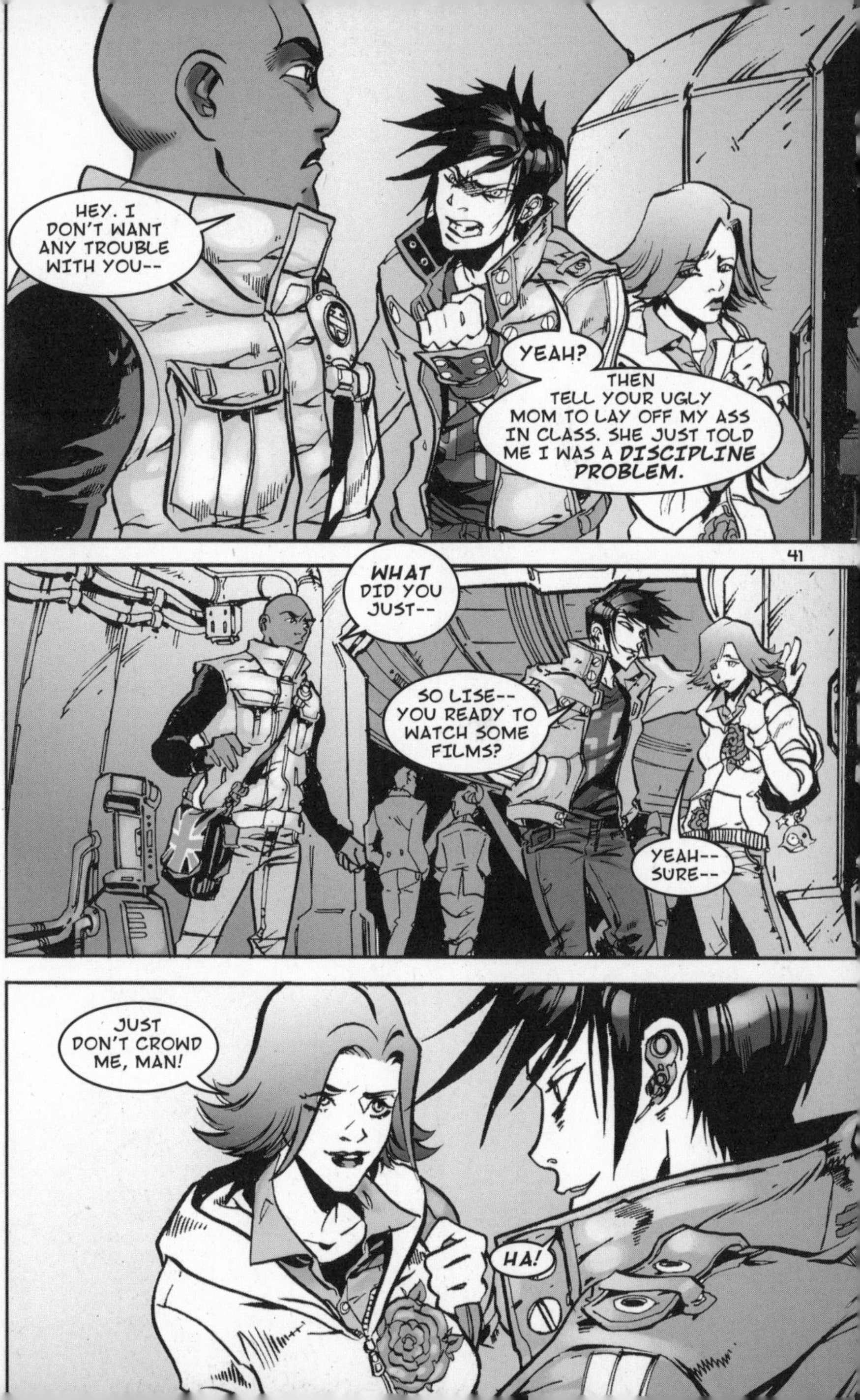
HEY. I DON'T WANT ANY TROUBLE WITH YOU--
YEAH?
THEN TELL YOUR UGLY MOM TO LAY OFF MY ASS IN CLASS. SHE JUST TOLD ME I WAS A DISCIPLINE PROBLEM.
WHAT DID YOU JUST--
SO LISE-- YOU READY TO WATCH SOME FILMS?
YEAH-- SURE--
JUST DON'T CROWD ME, MAN!
HA!

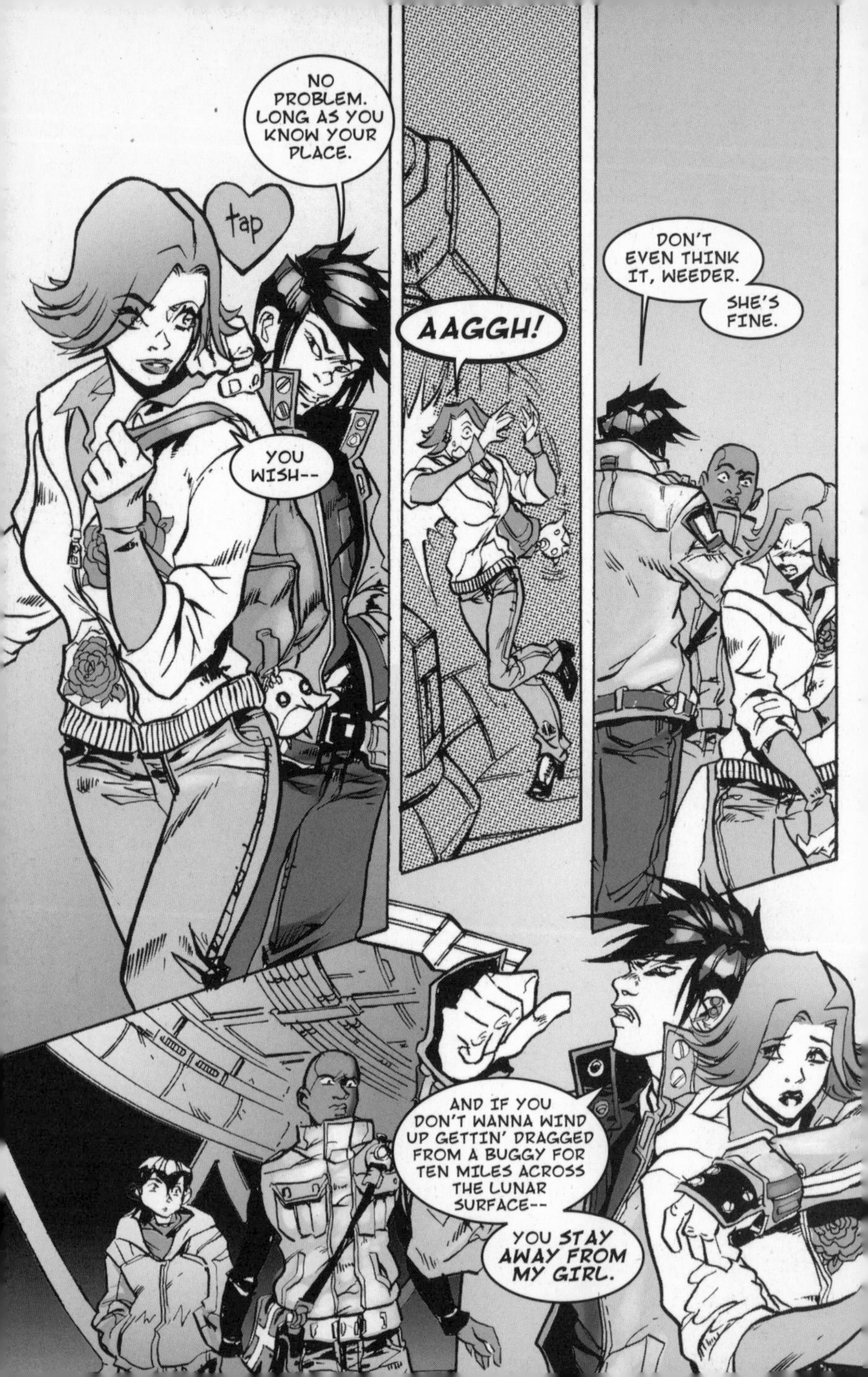

NO PROBLEM. LONG AS YOU KNOW YOUR PLACE.
tap
YOU WISH--
AAGGH!
DON'T EVEN THINK IT, WEEDER.
SHE'S FINE.
AND IF YOU DON'T WANNA WIND UP GETTIN' DRAGGED FROM A BUGGY FOR TEN MILES ACROSS THE LUNAR SURFACE--
YOU STAY AWAY FROM MY GIRL.

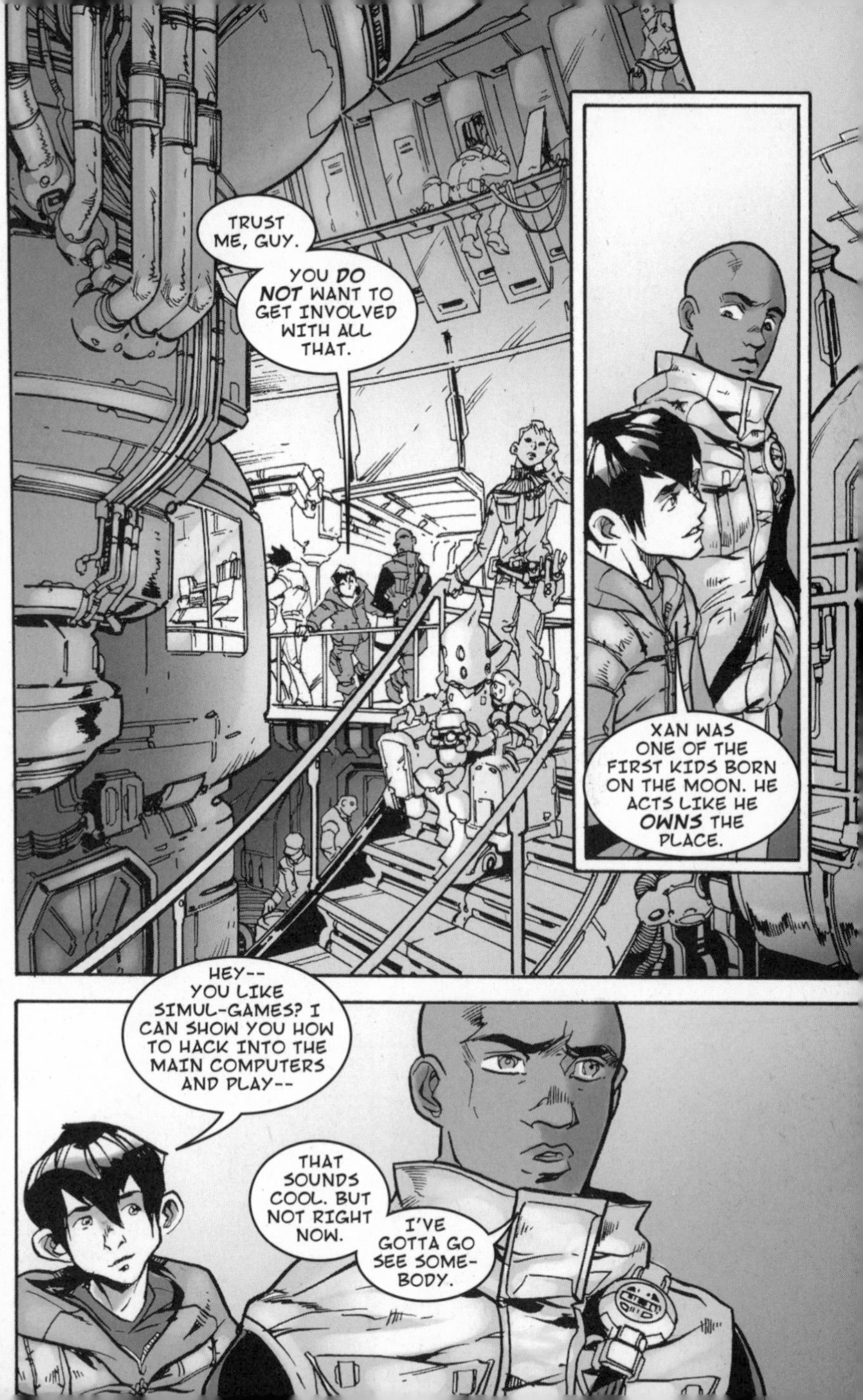
TRUST ME, GUY.
YOU DO NOT WANT TO GET INVOLVED WITH ALL THAT.
XAN WAS ONE OF THE FIRST KIDS BORN ON THE MOON. HE ACTS LIKE HE OWNS THE PLACE.
HEY-- YOU LIKE SIMUL-GAMES? I CAN SHOW YOU HOW TO HACK INTO THE MAIN COMPUTERS AND PLAY--
THAT SOUNDS COOL. BUT NOT RIGHT NOW.
I'VE GOTTA GO SEE SOME-BODY.

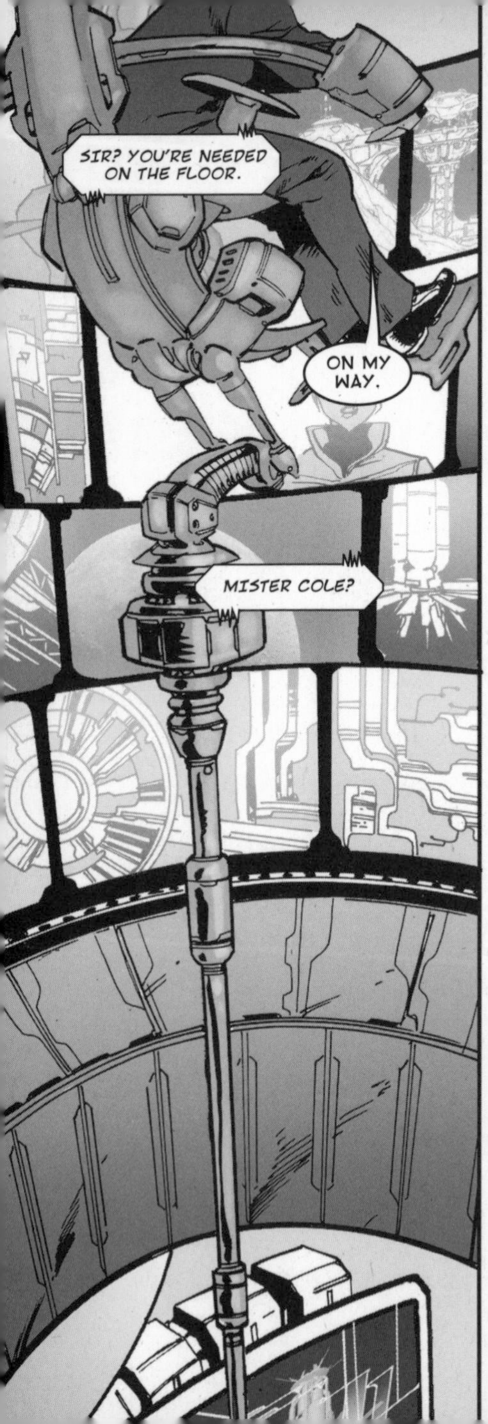
SIR? YOU'RE NEEDED ON THE FLOOR.
ON MY WAY.
MISTER COLE?

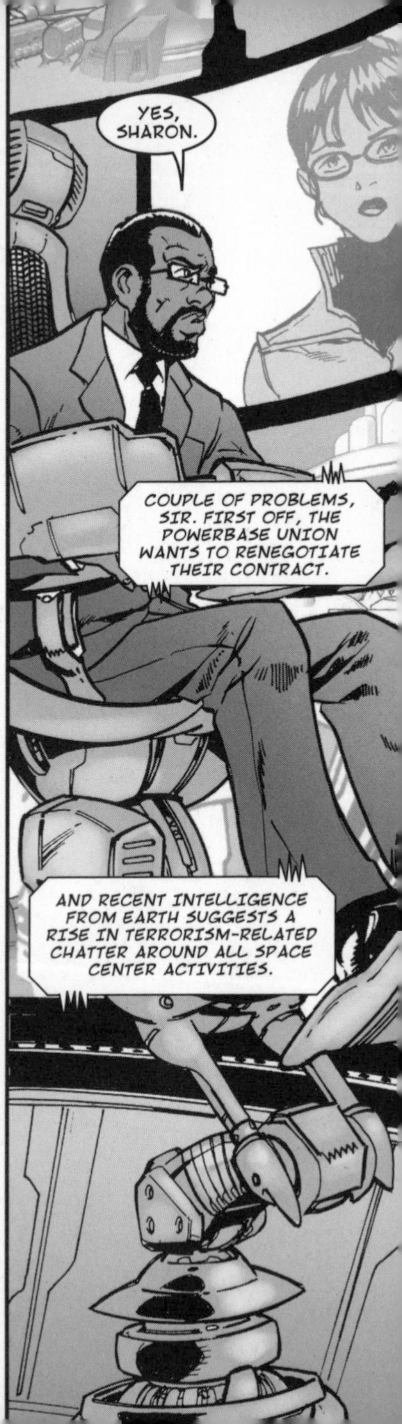
YES, SHARON.
COUPLE OF PROBLEMS, SIR. FIRST OFF, THE POWERBASE UNION WANTS TO RENEGOTIATE THEIR CONTRACT.
AND RECENT INTELLIGENCE FROM EARTH SUGGESTS A RISE IN TERRORISM-RELATED CHATTER AROUND ALL SPACE CENTER ACTIVITIES.

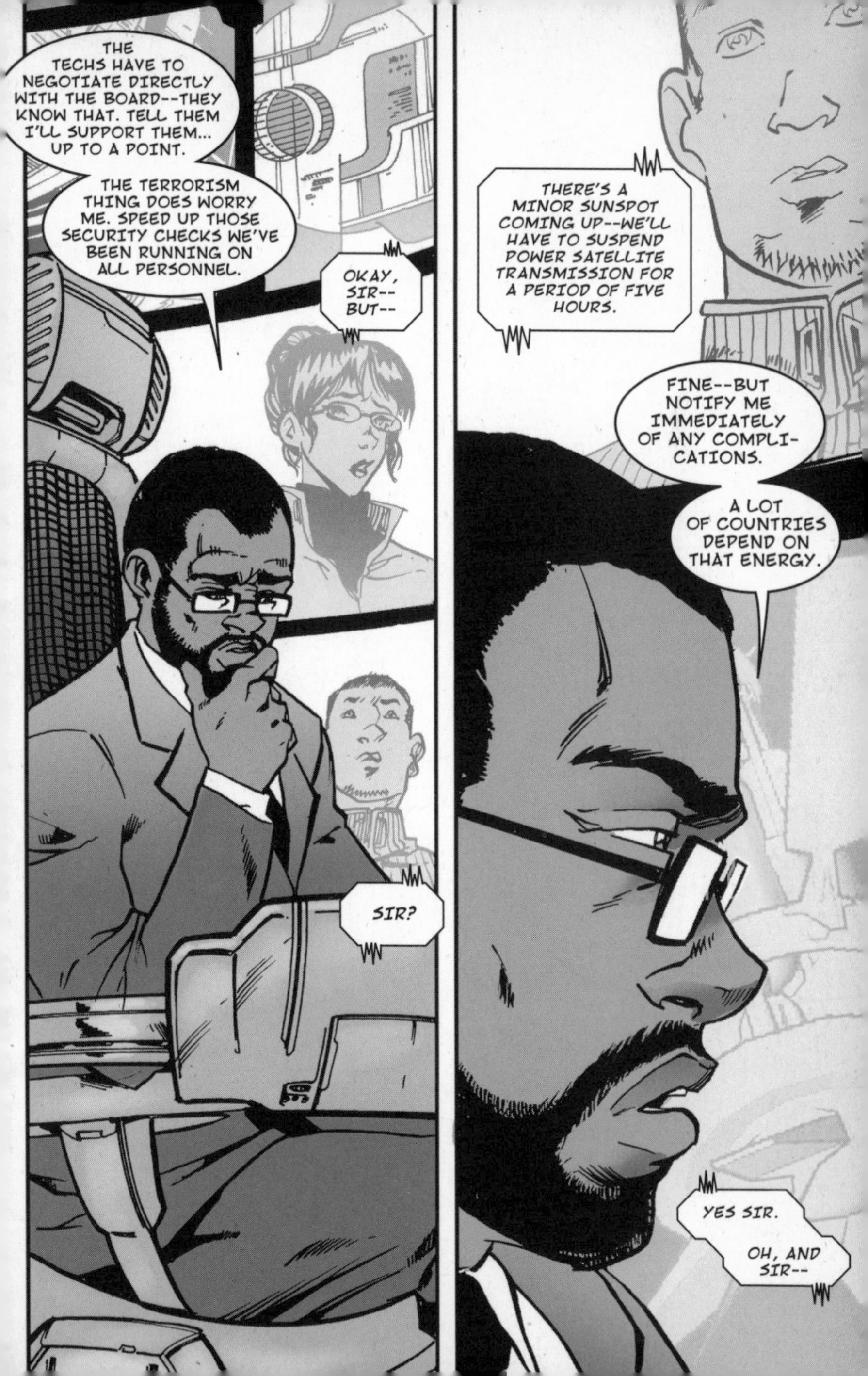
THE TECHS HAVE TO NEGOTIATE DIRECTLY WITH THE BOARD--THEY KNOW THAT. TELL THEM I'LL SUPPORT THEM... UP TO A POINT.
THE TERRORISM THING DOES WORRY ME. SPEED UP THOSE SECURITY CHECKS WE'VE BEEN RUNNING ON ALL PERSONNEL.
OKAY, SIR-- BUT--
SIR?
THERE'S A MINOR SUNSPOT COMING UP--WE'LL HAVE TO SUSPEND POWER SATELLITE TRANSMISSION FOR A PERIOD OF FIVE HOURS.
FINE--BUT NOTIFY ME IMMEDIATELY OF ANY COMPLI- CATIONS.
A LOT OF COUNTRIES DEPEND ON THAT ENERGY.
YES SIR.
OH, AND SIR--

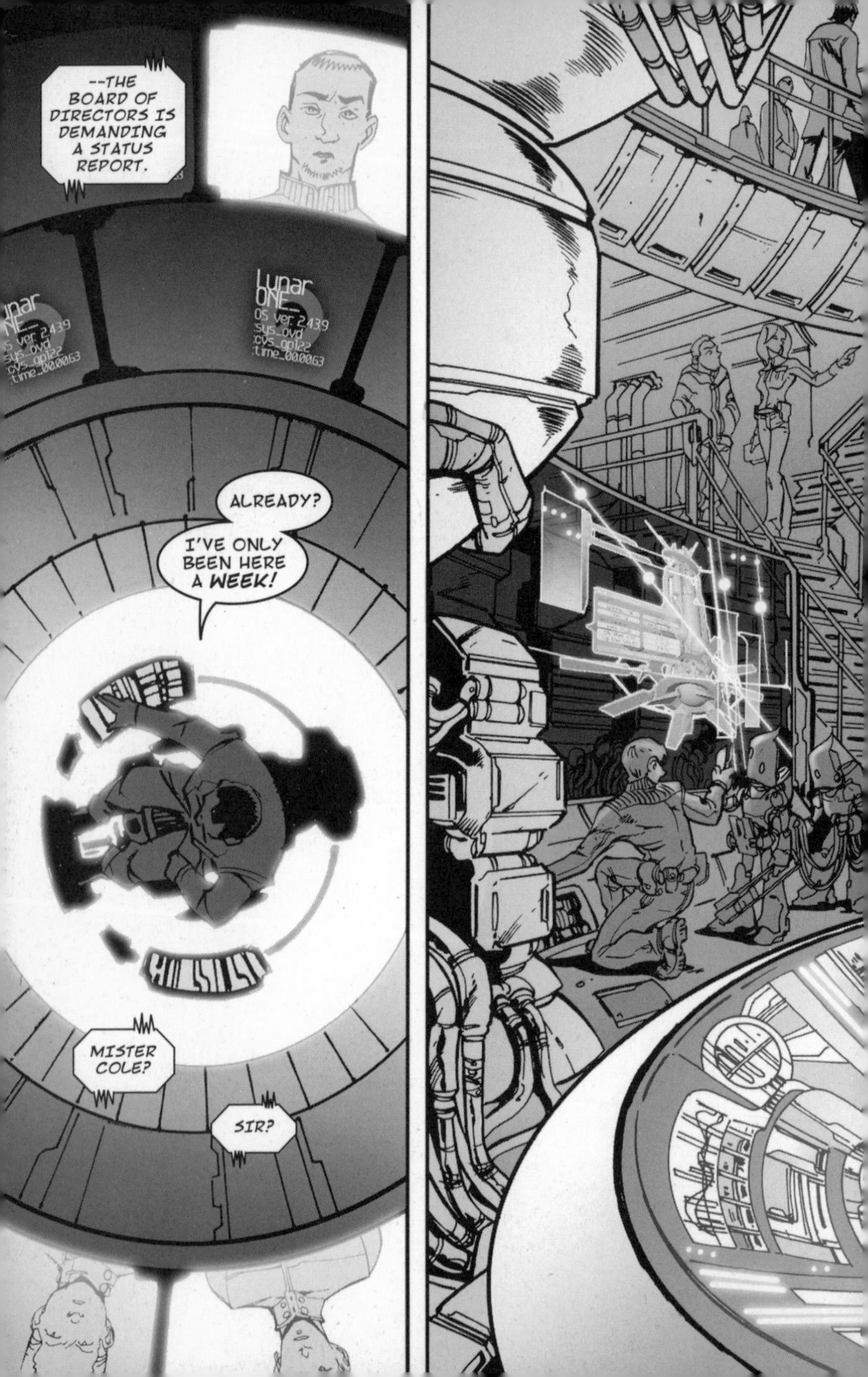
--THE BOARD OF DIRECTORS IS DEMANDING A STATUS REPORT.
Lunar ONE_
OS ver 2.439
sys_ovd
cys_gp122
time_00.0063
ALREADY?
I'VE ONLY BEEN HERE A **WEEK!**
MISTER COLE?
SIR?

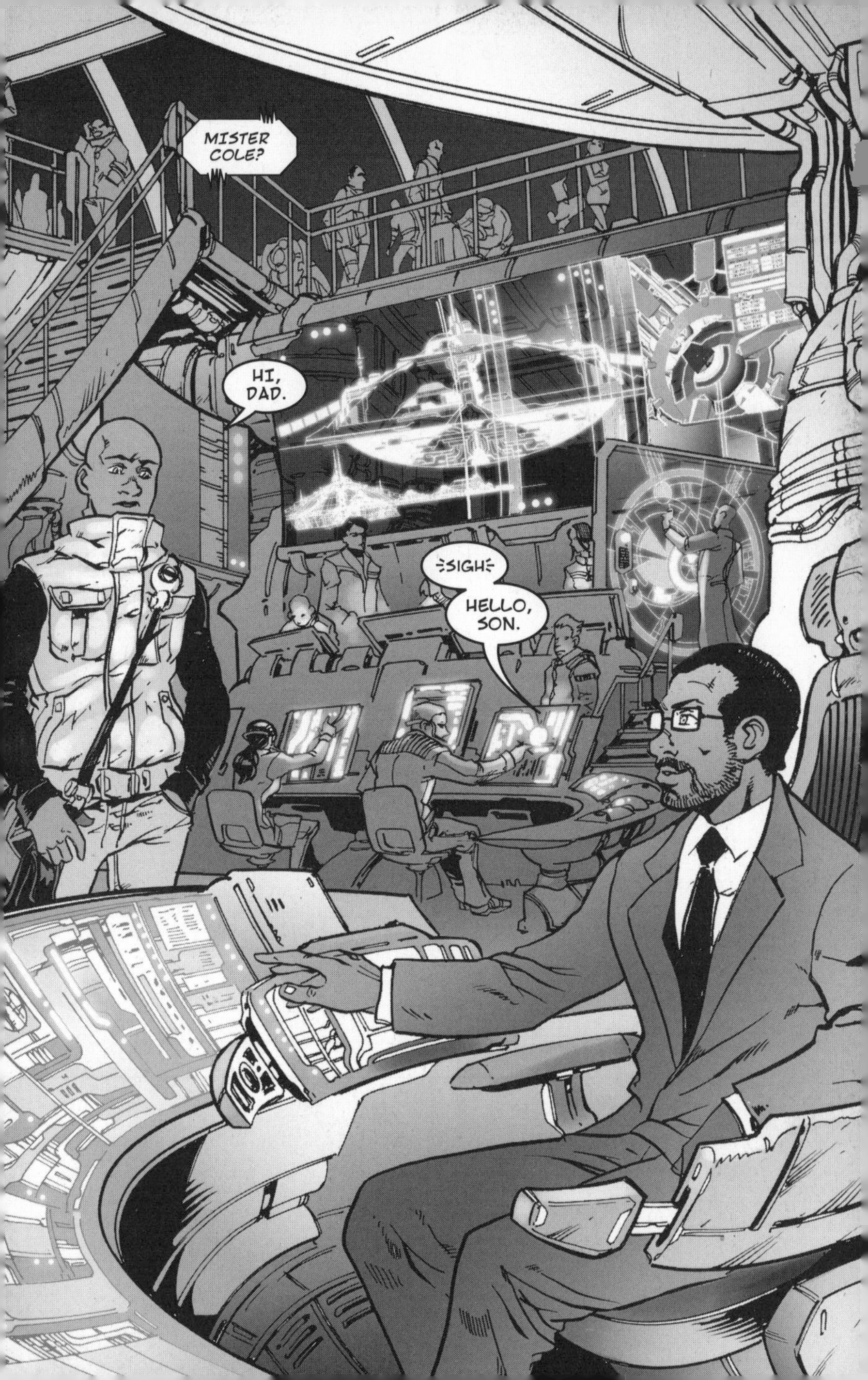
MISTER COLE?
HI, DAD.
SIGH
HELLO, SON.

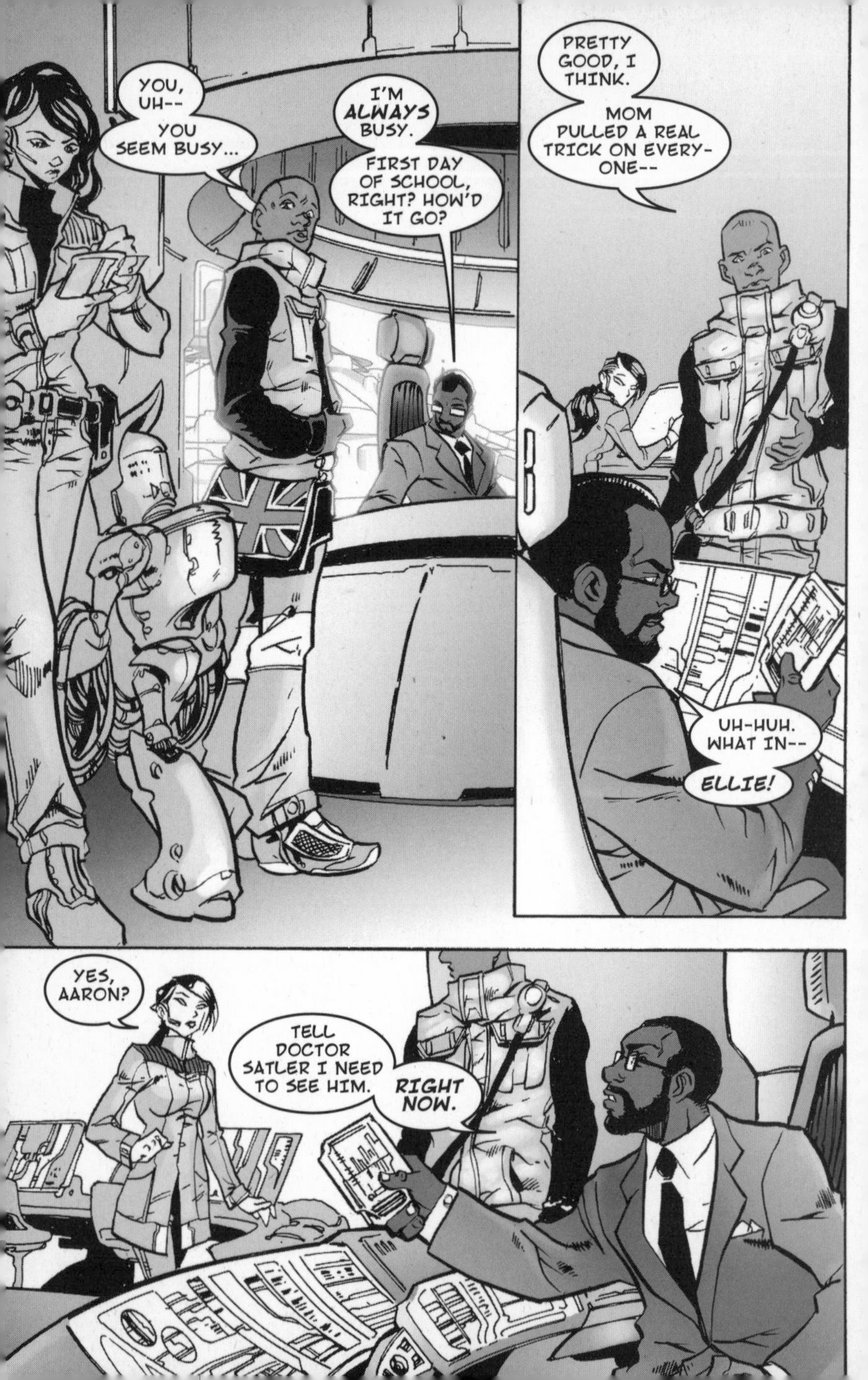
YOU, UH--
YOU SEEM BUSY...
I'M ALWAYS BUSY.
FIRST DAY OF SCHOOL, RIGHT? HOW'D IT GO?
PRETTY GOOD, I THINK.
MOM PULLED A REAL TRICK ON EVERY-ONE--
UH-HUH. WHAT IN--
ELLIE!
YES, AARON?
TELL DOCTOR SATLER I NEED TO SEE HIM.
RIGHT NOW.

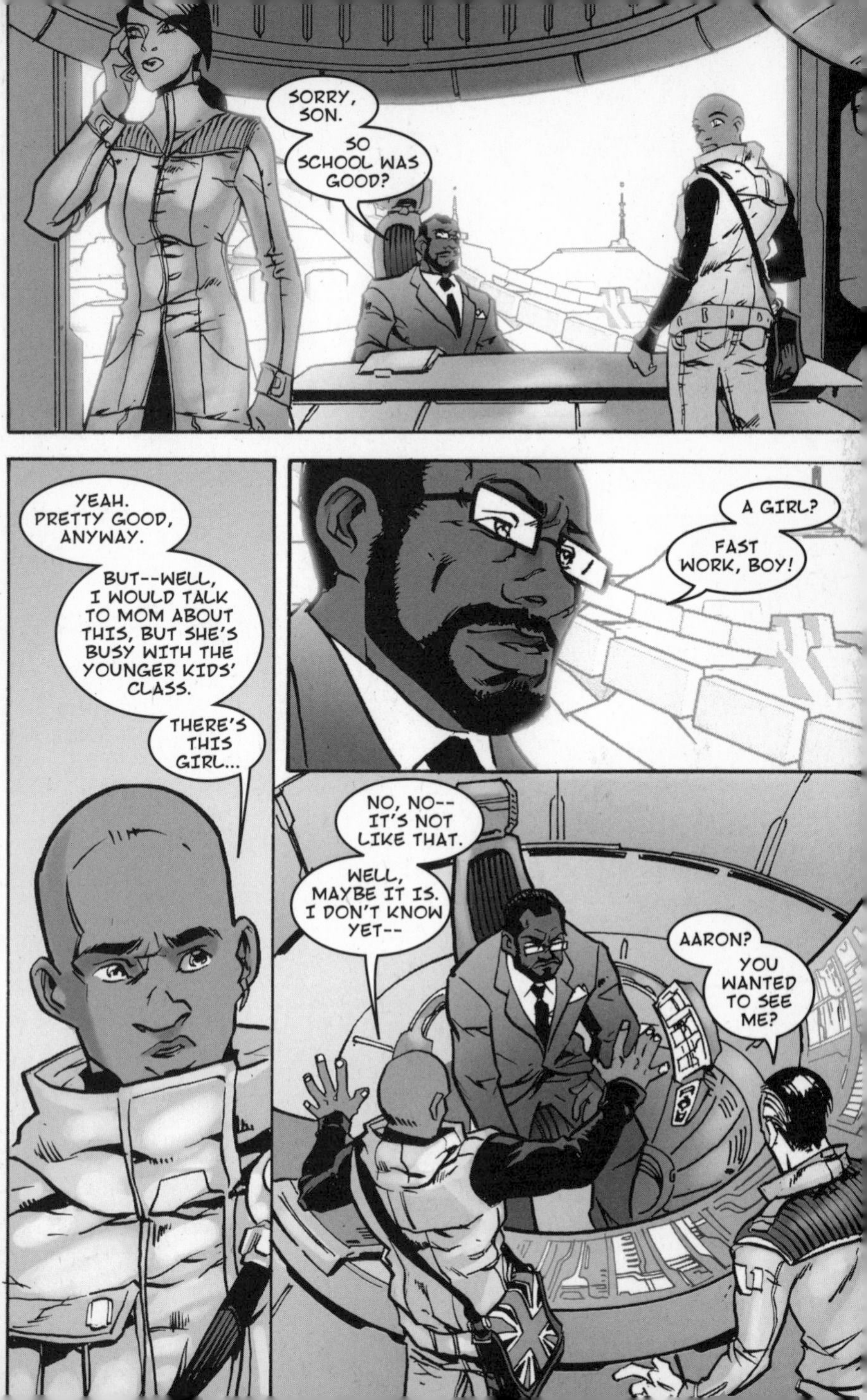
SORRY, SON.
SO SCHOOL WAS GOOD?
YEAH. PRETTY GOOD, ANYWAY.
BUT--WELL, I WOULD TALK TO MOM ABOUT THIS, BUT SHE'S BUSY WITH THE YOUNGER KIDS' CLASS.
THERE'S THIS GIRL...
A GIRL?
FAST WORK, BOY!
NO, NO-- IT'S NOT LIKE THAT.
WELL, MAYBE IT IS. I DON'T KNOW YET--
AARON?
YOU WANTED TO SEE ME?

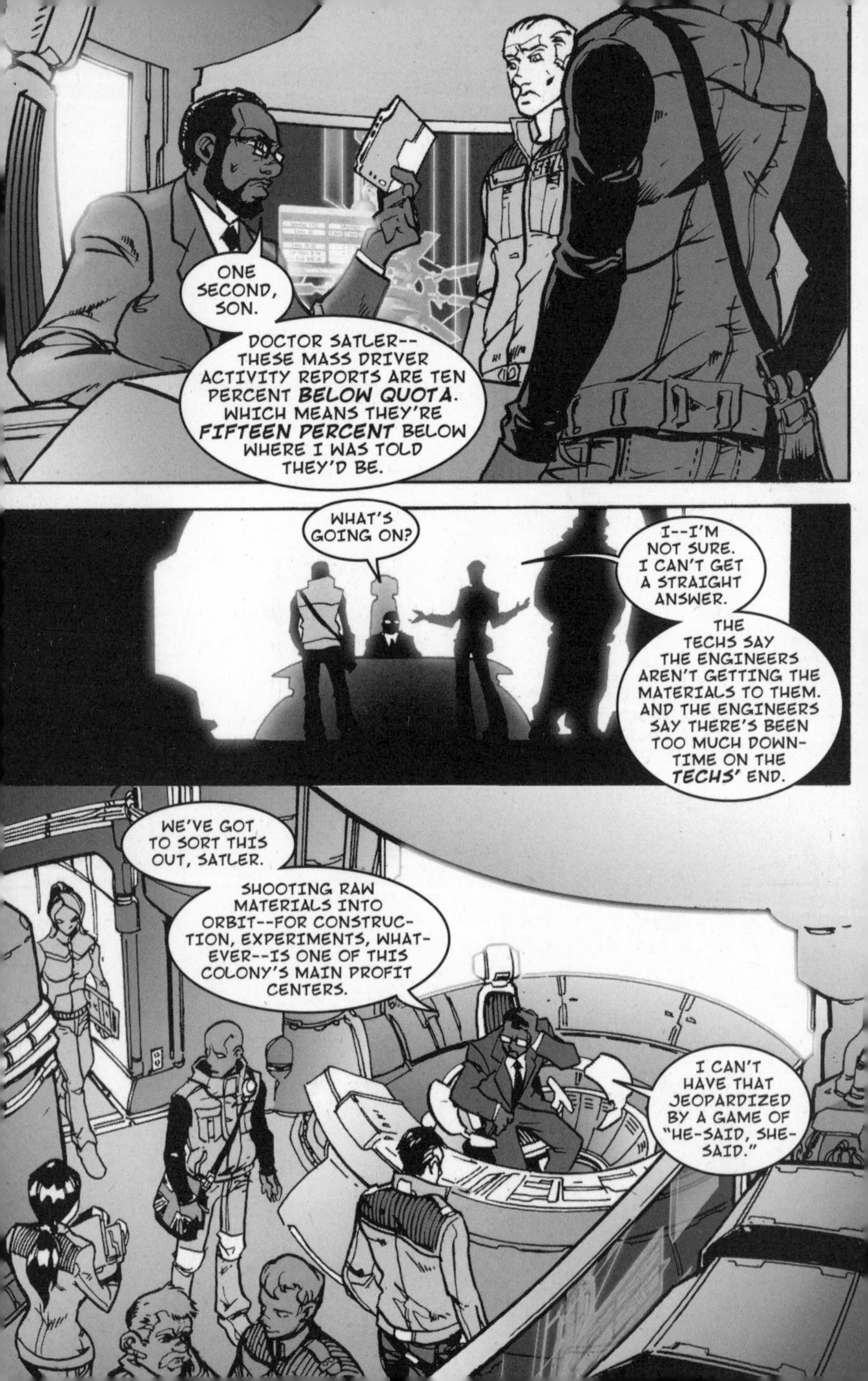
ONE SECOND, SON.
DOCTOR SATLER-- THESE MASS DRIVER ACTIVITY REPORTS ARE TEN PERCENT **BELOW QUOTA**. WHICH MEANS THEY'RE ***FIFTEEN PERCENT*** BELOW WHERE I WAS TOLD THEY'D BE.
WHAT'S GOING ON?
I--I'M NOT SURE. I CAN'T GET A STRAIGHT ANSWER.
THE TECHS SAY THE ENGINEERS AREN'T GETTING THE MATERIALS TO THEM. AND THE ENGINEERS SAY THERE'S BEEN TOO MUCH DOWN-TIME ON THE ***TECHS'*** END.
WE'VE GOT TO SORT THIS OUT, SATLER.
SHOOTING RAW MATERIALS INTO ORBIT--FOR CONSTRUC-TION, EXPERIMENTS, WHAT-EVER--IS ONE OF THIS COLONY'S MAIN PROFIT CENTERS.
I CAN'T HAVE THAT JEOPARDIZED BY A GAME OF "HE-SAID, SHE-SAID."

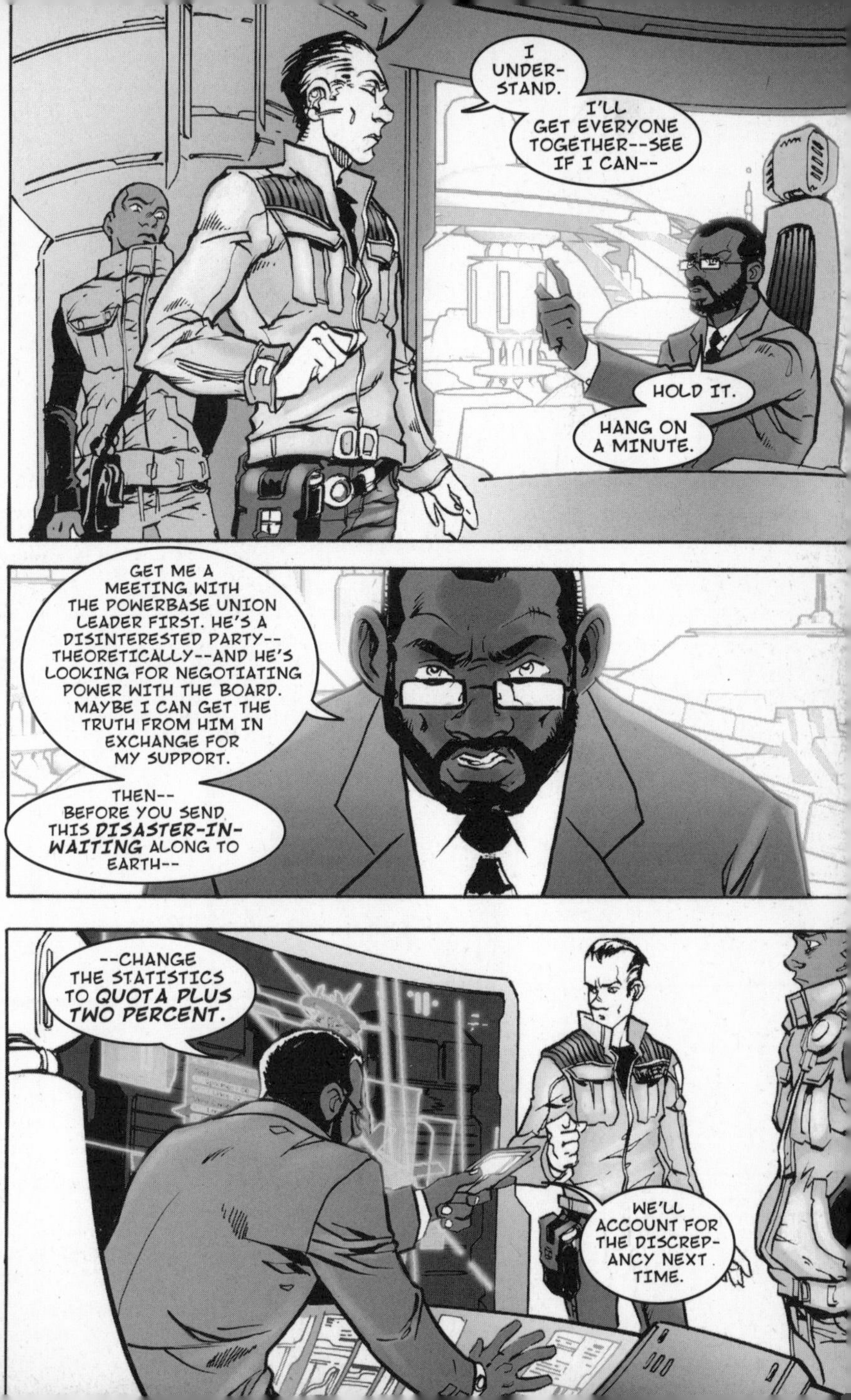
I UNDER-STAND.
I'LL GET EVERYONE TOGETHER--SEE IF I CAN--
HOLD IT.
HANG ON A MINUTE.
GET ME A MEETING WITH THE POWERBASE UNION LEADER FIRST. HE'S A DISINTERESTED PARTY--THEORETICALLY--AND HE'S LOOKING FOR NEGOTIATING POWER WITH THE BOARD. MAYBE I CAN GET THE TRUTH FROM HIM IN EXCHANGE FOR MY SUPPORT.
THEN--BEFORE YOU SEND THIS ***DISASTER-IN-WAITING*** ALONG TO EARTH--
--CHANGE THE STATISTICS TO ***QUOTA PLUS TWO PERCENT.***
WE'LL ACCOUNT FOR THE DISCREP-ANCY NEXT TIME.

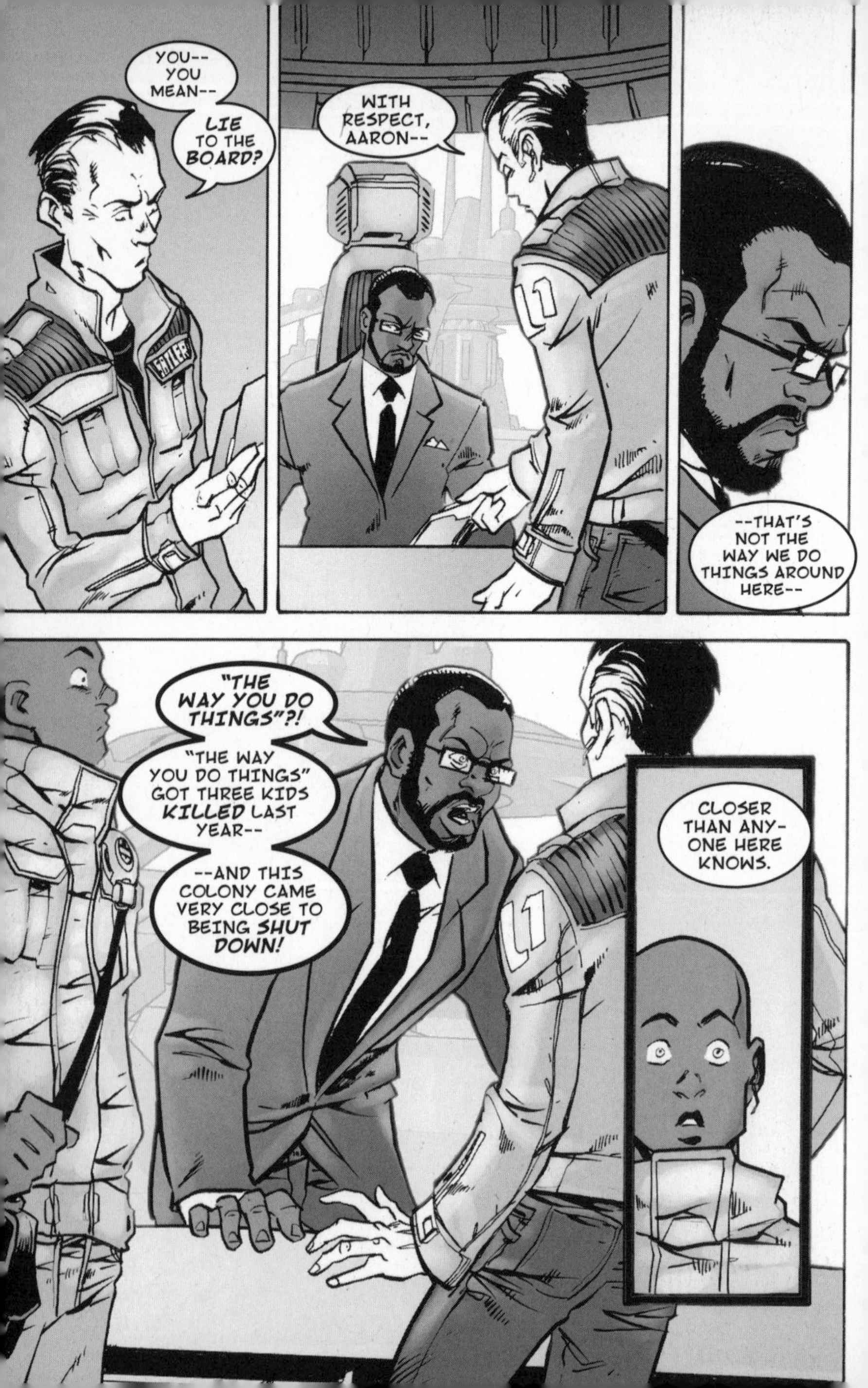
YOU-- YOU MEAN--
LIE TO THE BOARD?
WITH RESPECT, AARON--
--THAT'S NOT THE WAY WE DO THINGS AROUND HERE--
"THE WAY YOU DO THINGS"?!
"THE WAY YOU DO THINGS" GOT THREE KIDS KILLED LAST YEAR--
--AND THIS COLONY CAME VERY CLOSE TO BEING SHUT DOWN!
CLOSER THAN ANY-ONE HERE KNOWS.

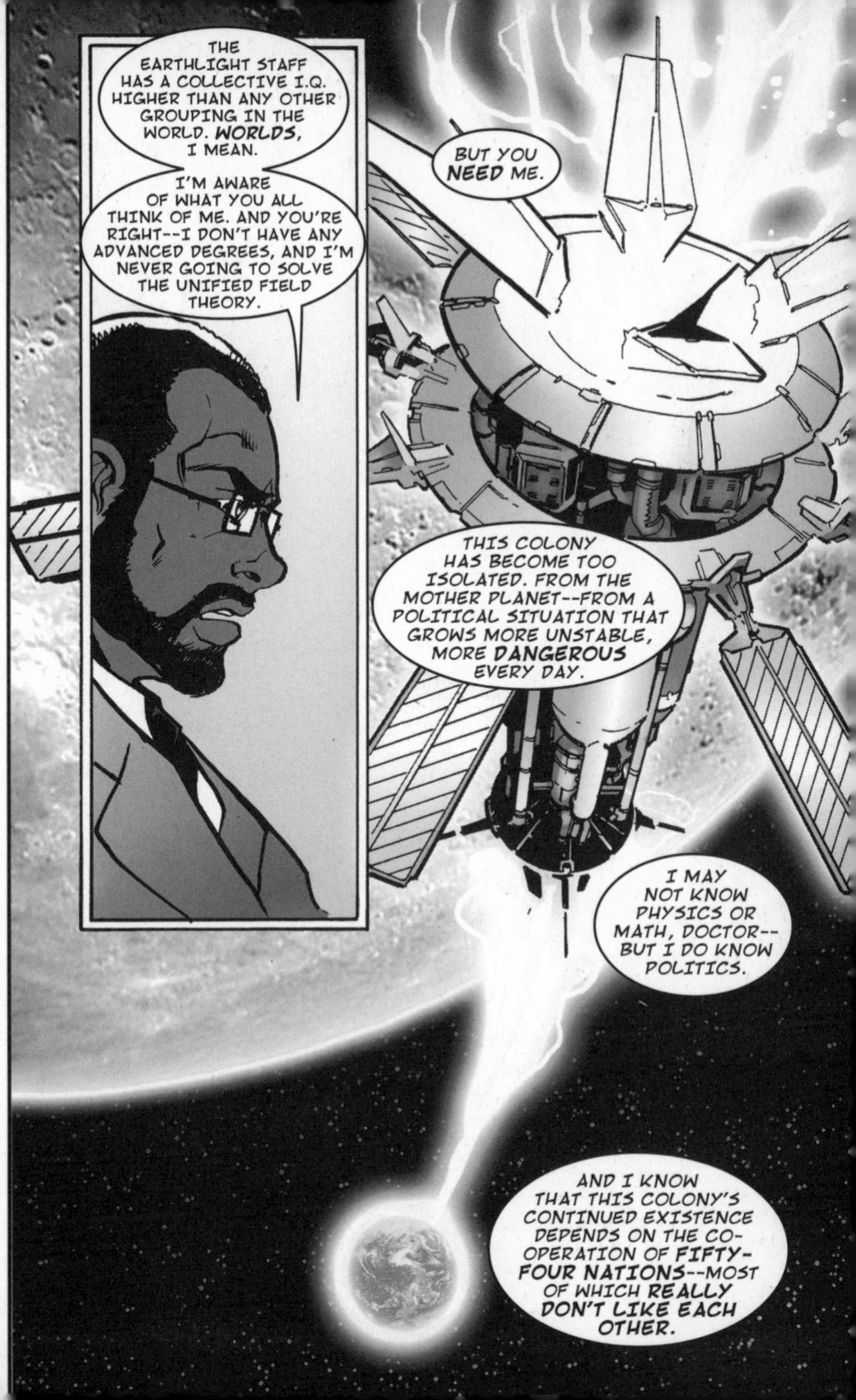
THE EARTHLIGHT STAFF HAS A COLLECTIVE I.Q. HIGHER THAN ANY OTHER GROUPING IN THE WORLD. **WORLDS,** I MEAN.
I'M AWARE OF WHAT YOU ALL THINK OF ME. AND YOU'RE RIGHT--I DON'T HAVE ANY ADVANCED DEGREES, AND I'M NEVER GOING TO SOLVE THE UNIFIED FIELD THEORY.
BUT YOU **NEED** ME.
THIS COLONY HAS BECOME TOO ISOLATED. FROM THE MOTHER PLANET--FROM A POLITICAL SITUATION THAT GROWS MORE UNSTABLE, MORE **DANGEROUS** EVERY DAY.
I MAY NOT KNOW PHYSICS OR MATH, DOCTOR--BUT I DO KNOW POLITICS.
AND I KNOW THAT THIS COLONY'S CONTINUED EXISTENCE DEPENDS ON THE CO-OPERATION OF **FIFTY-FOUR NATIONS**--MOST OF WHICH **REALLY DON'T LIKE EACH OTHER.**

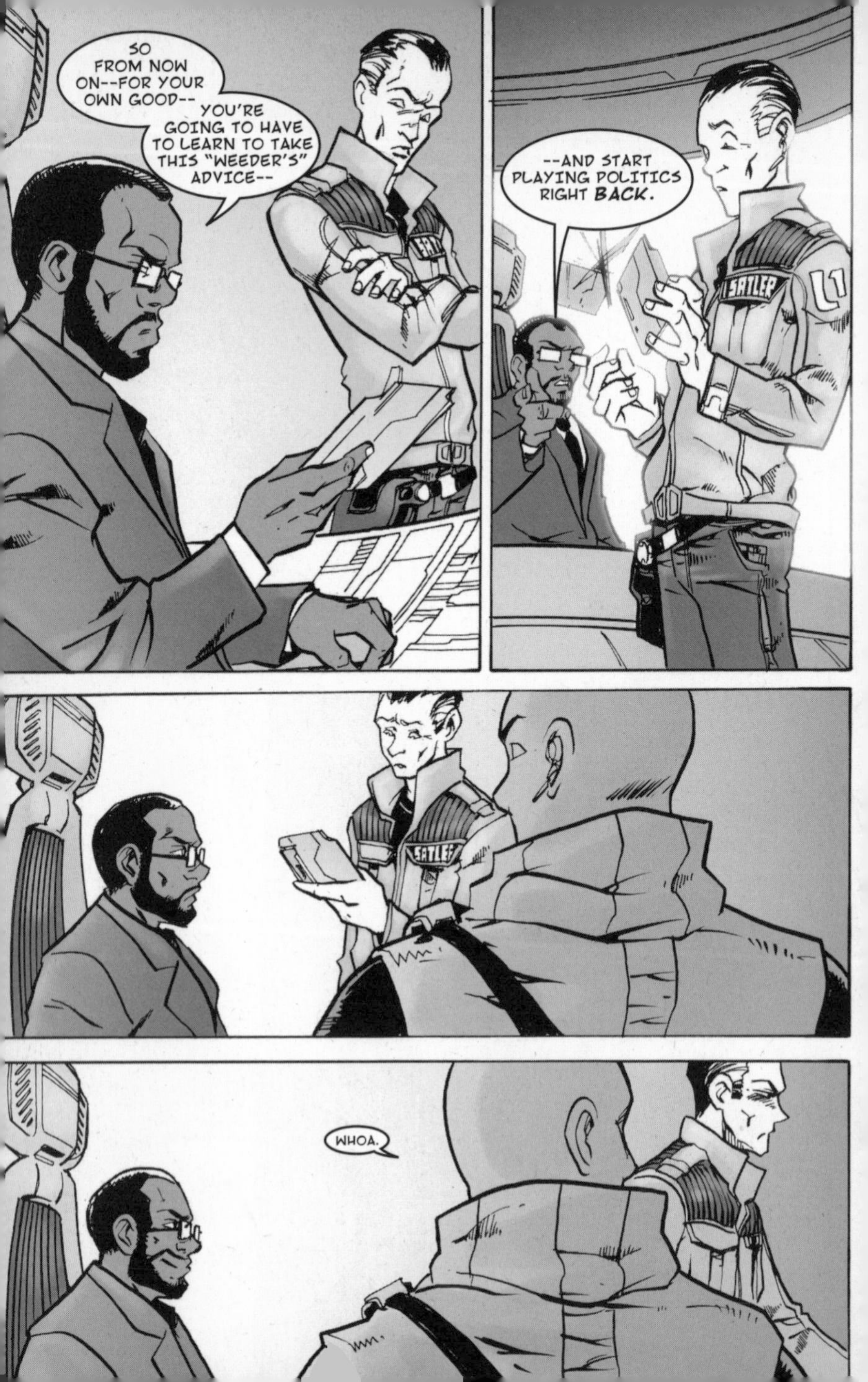
SO FROM NOW ON--FOR YOUR OWN GOOD--
YOU'RE GOING TO HAVE TO LEARN TO TAKE THIS "WEEDER'S" ADVICE--
--AND START PLAYING POLITICS RIGHT **BACK**.
SATLER
L1
SATLER
WHOA.

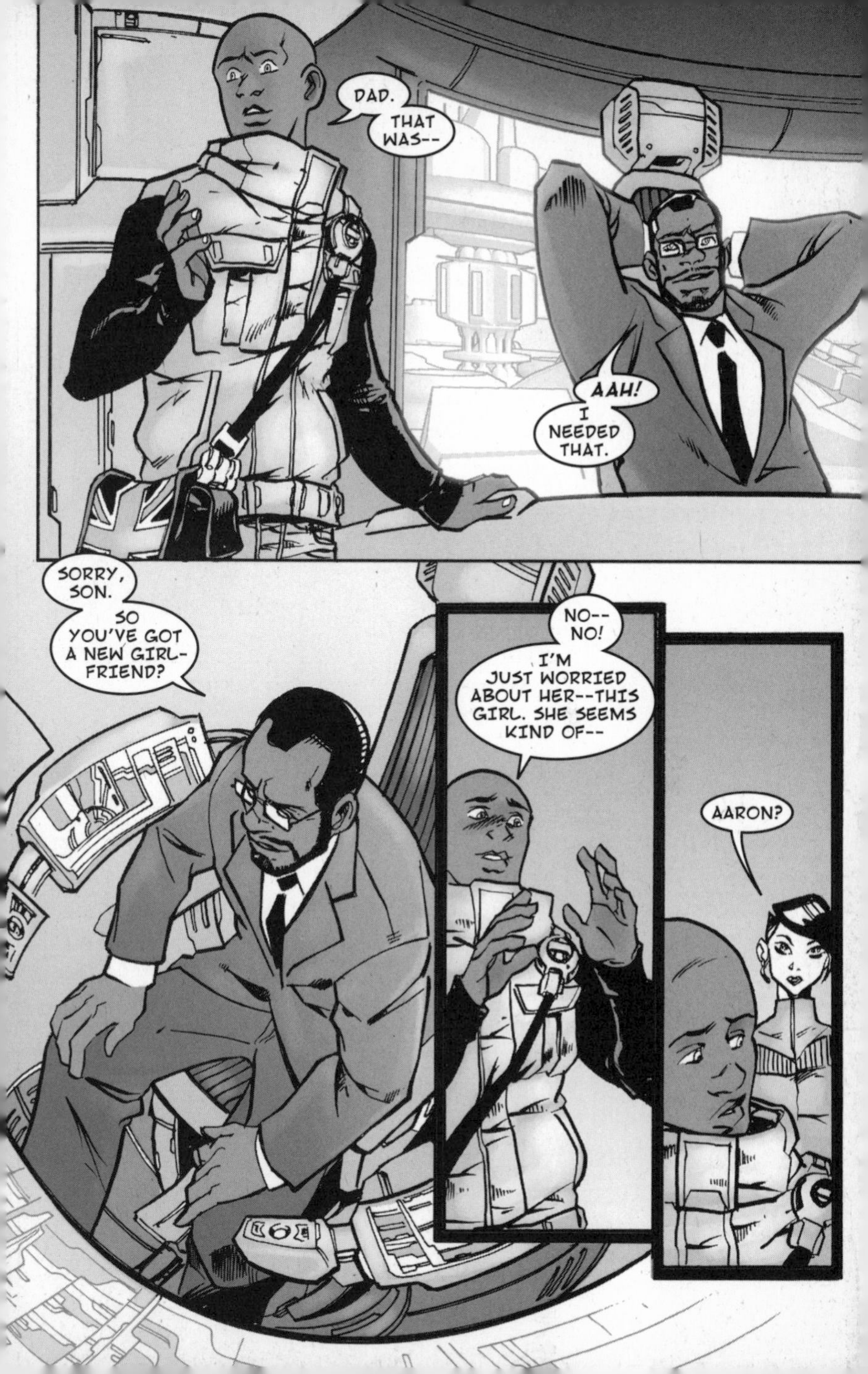
DAD.
THAT WAS--
AAH! I NEEDED THAT.
SORRY, SON.
SO YOU'VE GOT A NEW GIRL-FRIEND?
NO-- NO!
I'M JUST WORRIED ABOUT HER--THIS GIRL. SHE SEEMS KIND OF--
AARON?

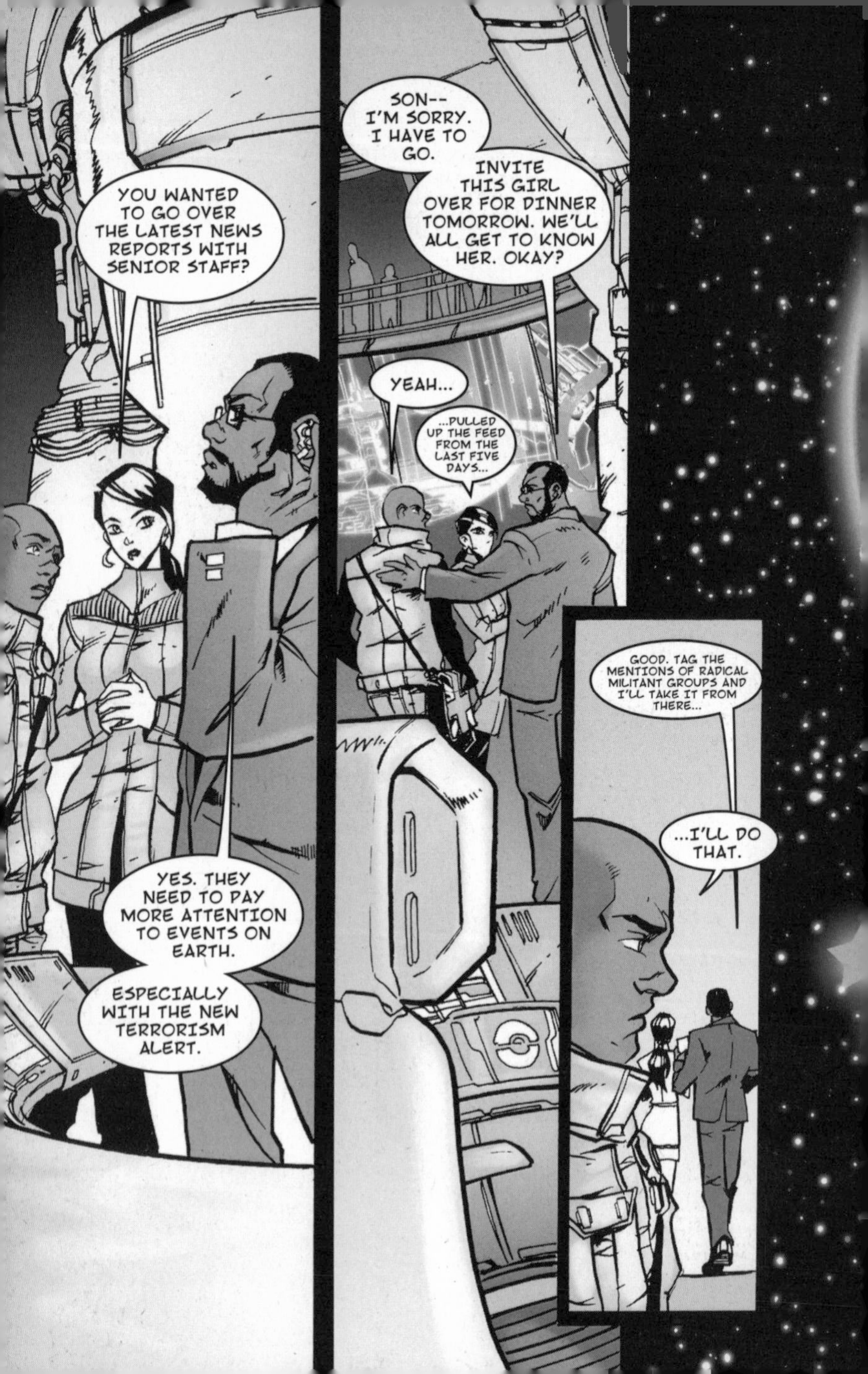
YOU WANTED TO GO OVER THE LATEST NEWS REPORTS WITH SENIOR STAFF?
YES. THEY NEED TO PAY MORE ATTENTION TO EVENTS ON EARTH.
ESPECIALLY WITH THE NEW TERRORISM ALERT.
SON-- I'M SORRY. I HAVE TO GO.
INVITE THIS GIRL OVER FOR DINNER TOMORROW. WE'LL ALL GET TO KNOW HER. OKAY?
YEAH...
...PULLED UP THE FEED FROM THE LAST FIVE DAYS...
GOOD. TAG THE MENTIONS OF RADICAL MILITANT GROUPS AND I'LL TAKE IT FROM THERE...
...I'LL DO THAT.

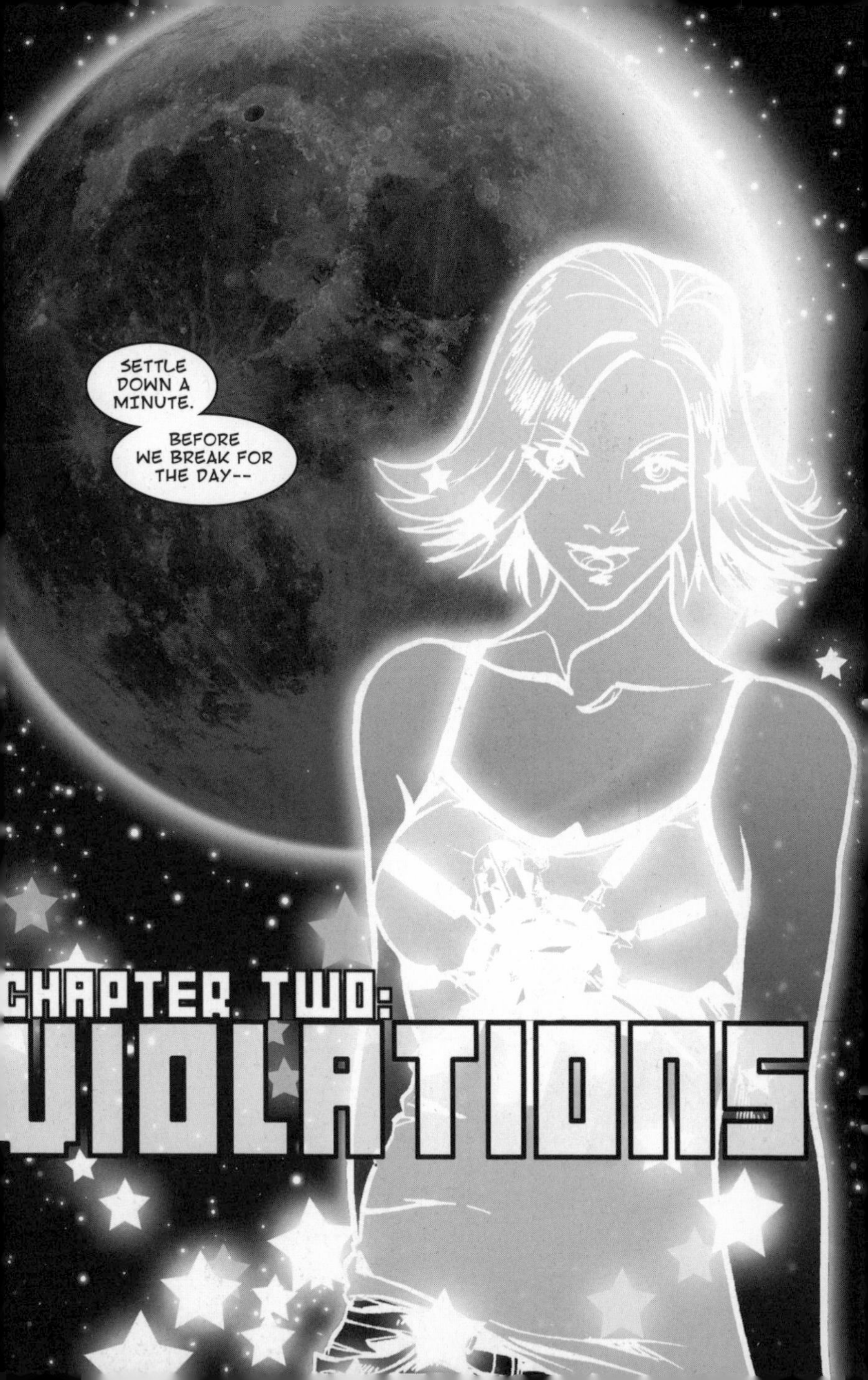
SETTLE DOWN A MINUTE.
BEFORE WE BREAK FOR THE DAY--
CHAPTER TWO:
VIOLATIONS

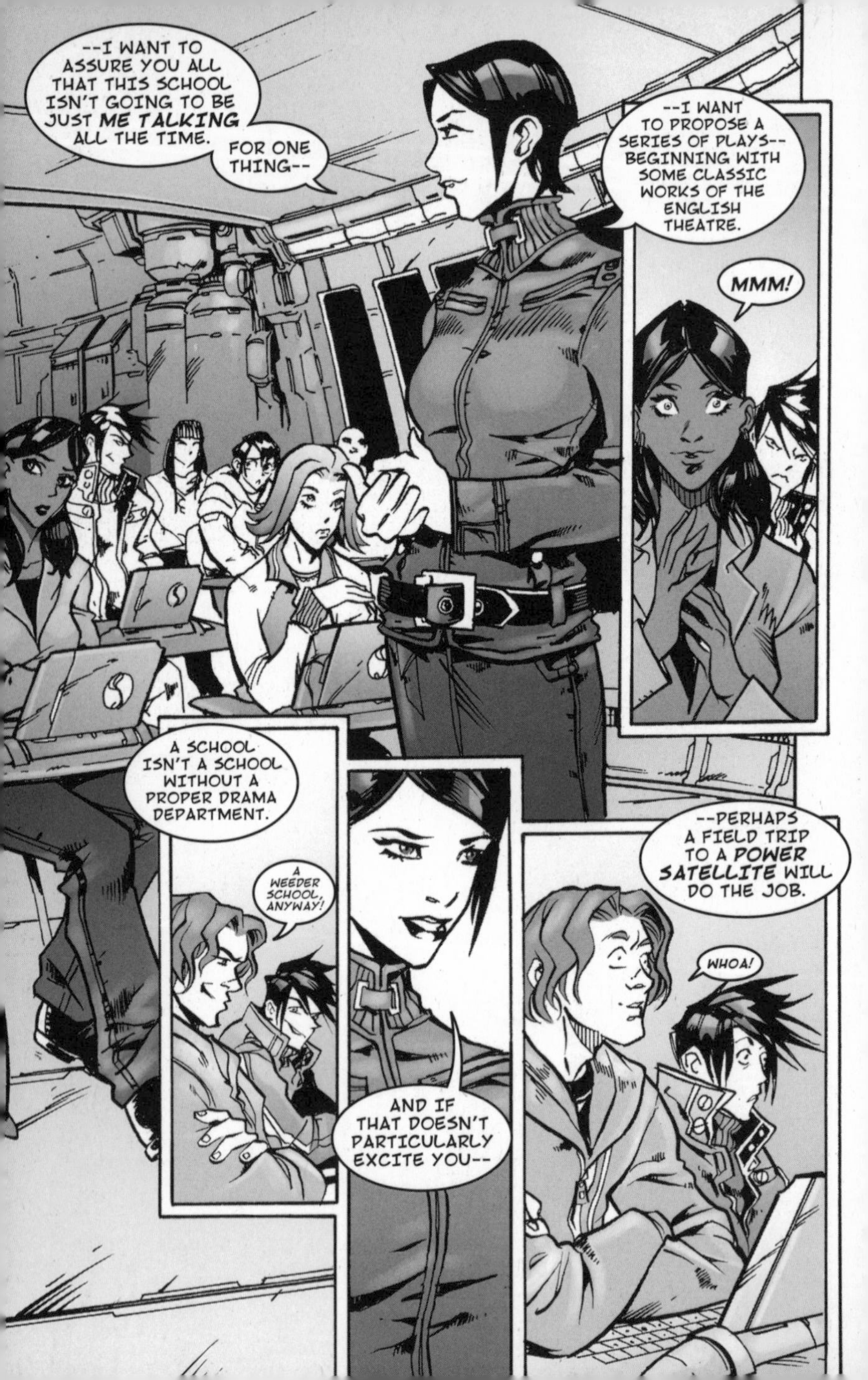
--I WANT TO ASSURE YOU ALL THAT THIS SCHOOL ISN'T GOING TO BE JUST ME TALKING ALL THE TIME.
FOR ONE THING--
--I WANT TO PROPOSE A SERIES OF PLAYS--BEGINNING WITH SOME CLASSIC WORKS OF THE ENGLISH THEATRE.
MMM!
A SCHOOL ISN'T A SCHOOL WITHOUT A PROPER DRAMA DEPARTMENT.
A WEEDER SCHOOL, ANYWAY!
AND IF THAT DOESN'T PARTICULARLY EXCITE YOU--
--PERHAPS A FIELD TRIP TO A POWER SATELLITE WILL DO THE JOB.
WHOA!

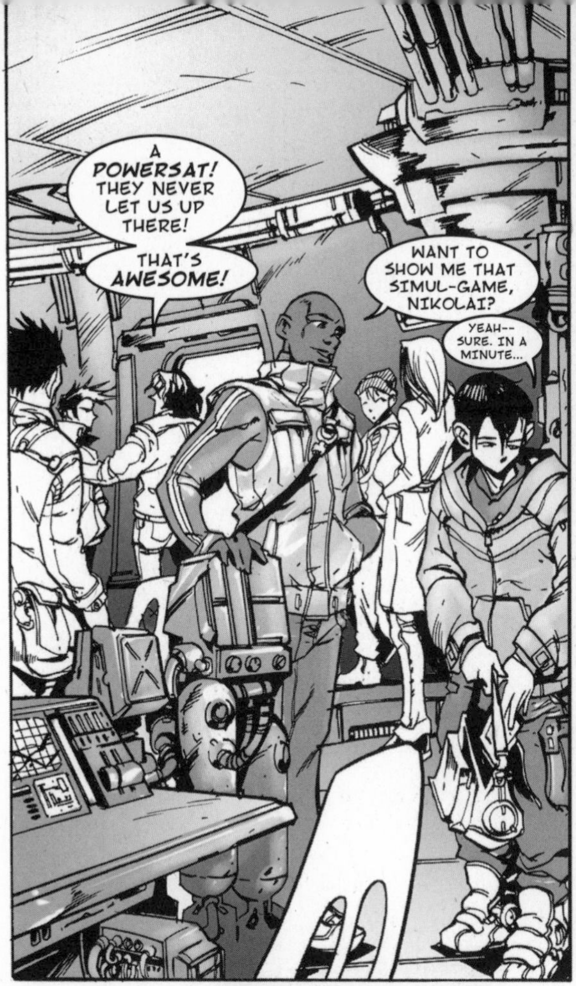
A POWERSAT! THEY NEVER LET US UP THERE!
THAT'S AWESOME!
WANT TO SHOW ME THAT SIMUL-GAME, NIKOLAI?
YEAH-- SURE. IN A MINUTE...

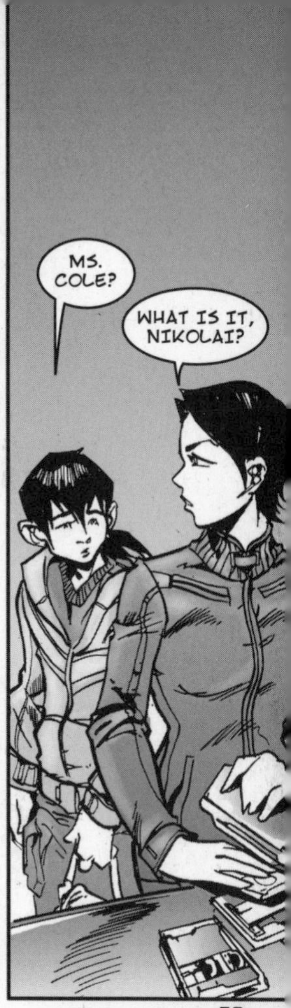
MS. COLE?
WHAT IS IT, NIKOLAI?

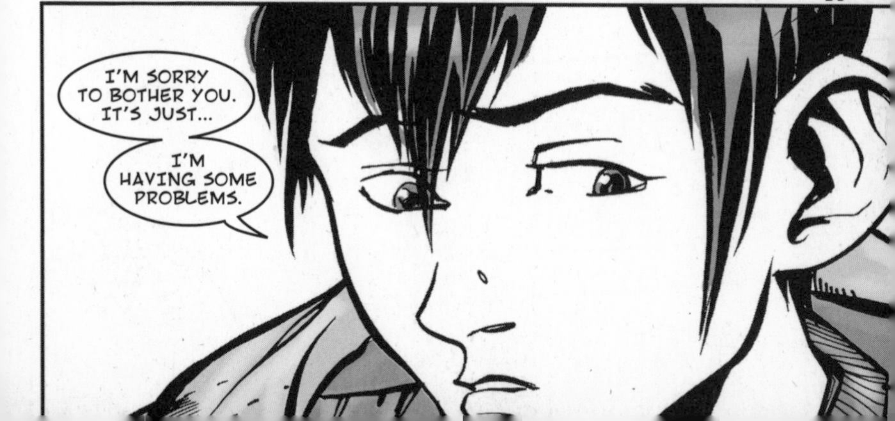
I'M SORRY TO BOTHER YOU. IT'S JUST...
I'M HAVING SOME PROBLEMS.

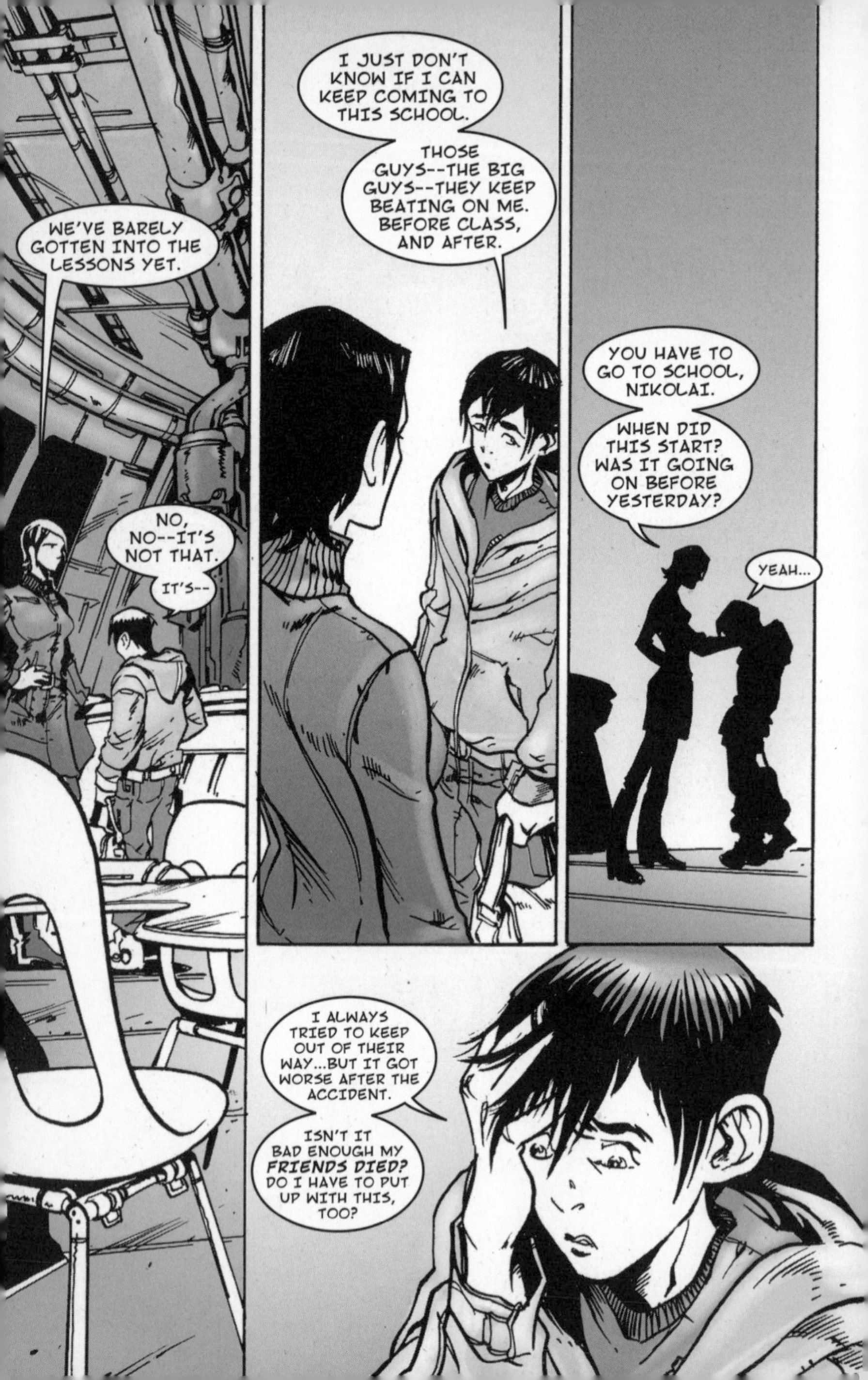
WE'VE BARELY GOTTEN INTO THE LESSONS YET.
NO, NO--IT'S NOT THAT.
IT'S--
I JUST DON'T KNOW IF I CAN KEEP COMING TO THIS SCHOOL.
THOSE GUYS--THE BIG GUYS--THEY KEEP BEATING ON ME. BEFORE CLASS, AND AFTER.
YOU HAVE TO GO TO SCHOOL, NIKOLAI.
WHEN DID THIS START? WAS IT GOING ON BEFORE YESTERDAY?
YEAH...
I ALWAYS TRIED TO KEEP OUT OF THEIR WAY...BUT IT GOT WORSE AFTER THE ACCIDENT.
ISN'T IT BAD ENOUGH MY *FRIENDS DIED?* DO I HAVE TO PUT UP WITH THIS, TOO?

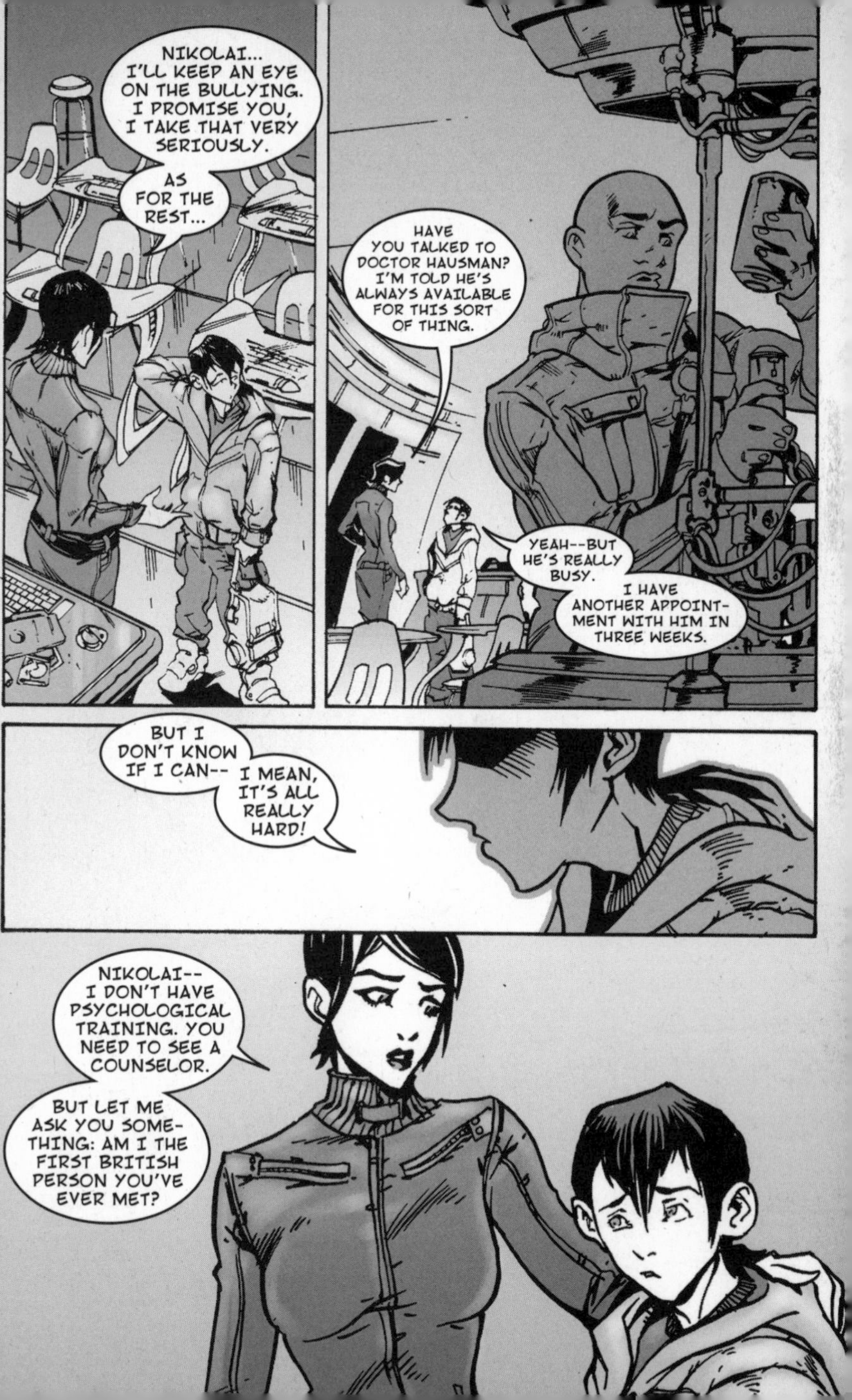
NIKOLAI... I'LL KEEP AN EYE ON THE BULLYING. I PROMISE YOU, I TAKE THAT VERY SERIOUSLY.
AS FOR THE REST...
HAVE YOU TALKED TO DOCTOR HAUSMAN? I'M TOLD HE'S ALWAYS AVAILABLE FOR THIS SORT OF THING.
YEAH--BUT HE'S REALLY BUSY.
I HAVE ANOTHER APPOINT-MENT WITH HIM IN THREE WEEKS.
BUT I DON'T KNOW IF I CAN--
I MEAN, IT'S ALL REALLY HARD!
NIKOLAI-- I DON'T HAVE PSYCHOLOGICAL TRAINING. YOU NEED TO SEE A COUNSELOR.
BUT LET ME ASK YOU SOME-THING: AM I THE FIRST BRITISH PERSON YOU'VE EVER MET?

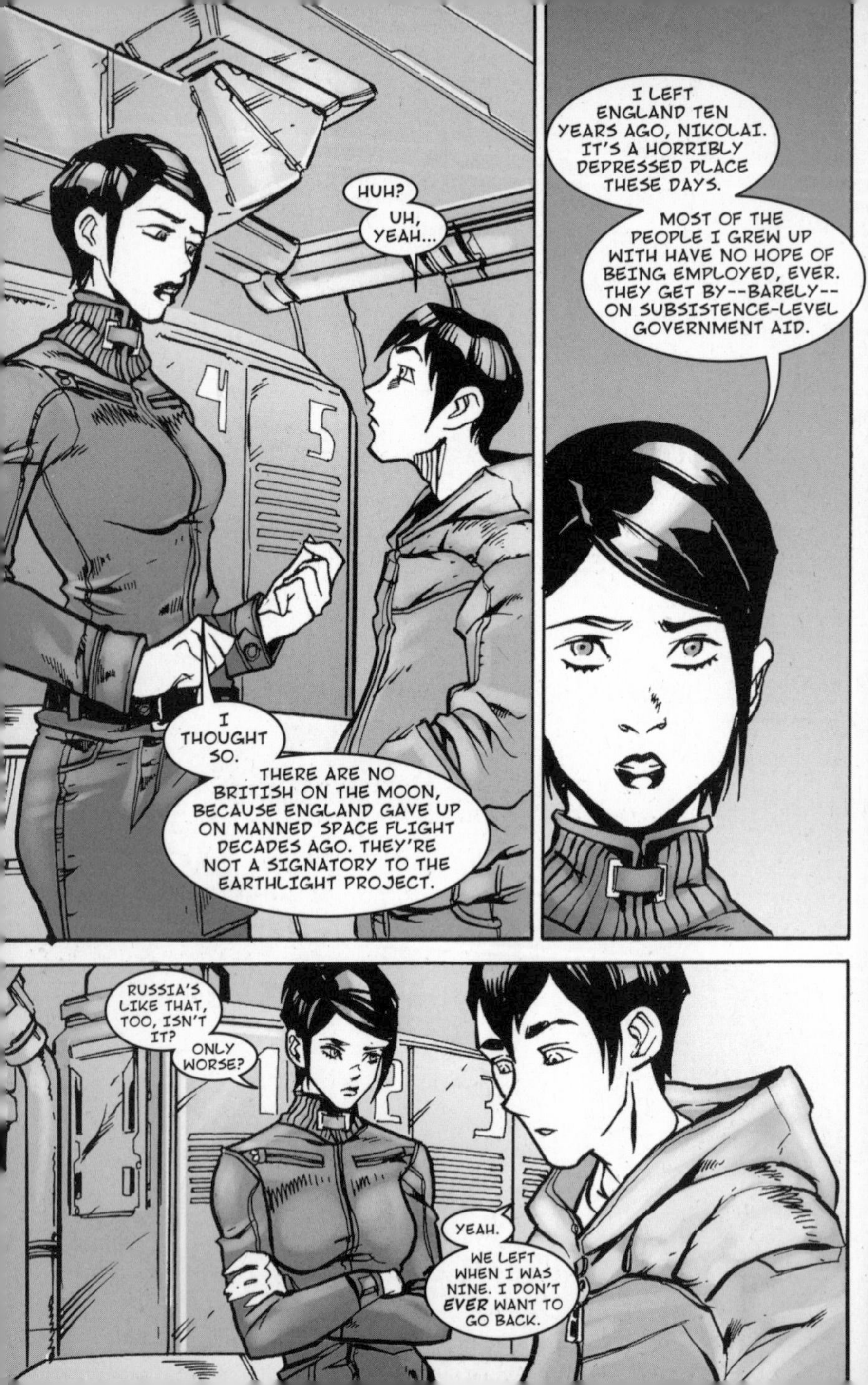
HUH?
UH, YEAH...
I THOUGHT SO.
THERE ARE NO BRITISH ON THE MOON, BECAUSE ENGLAND GAVE UP ON MANNED SPACE FLIGHT DECADES AGO. THEY'RE NOT A SIGNATORY TO THE EARTHLIGHT PROJECT.
I LEFT ENGLAND TEN YEARS AGO, NIKOLAI. IT'S A HORRIBLY DEPRESSED PLACE THESE DAYS.
MOST OF THE PEOPLE I GREW UP WITH HAVE NO HOPE OF BEING EMPLOYED, EVER. THEY GET BY--BARELY--ON SUBSISTENCE-LEVEL GOVERNMENT AID.
RUSSIA'S LIKE THAT, TOO, ISN'T IT?
ONLY WORSE?
YEAH.
WE LEFT WHEN I WAS NINE. I DON'T **EVER** WANT TO GO BACK.

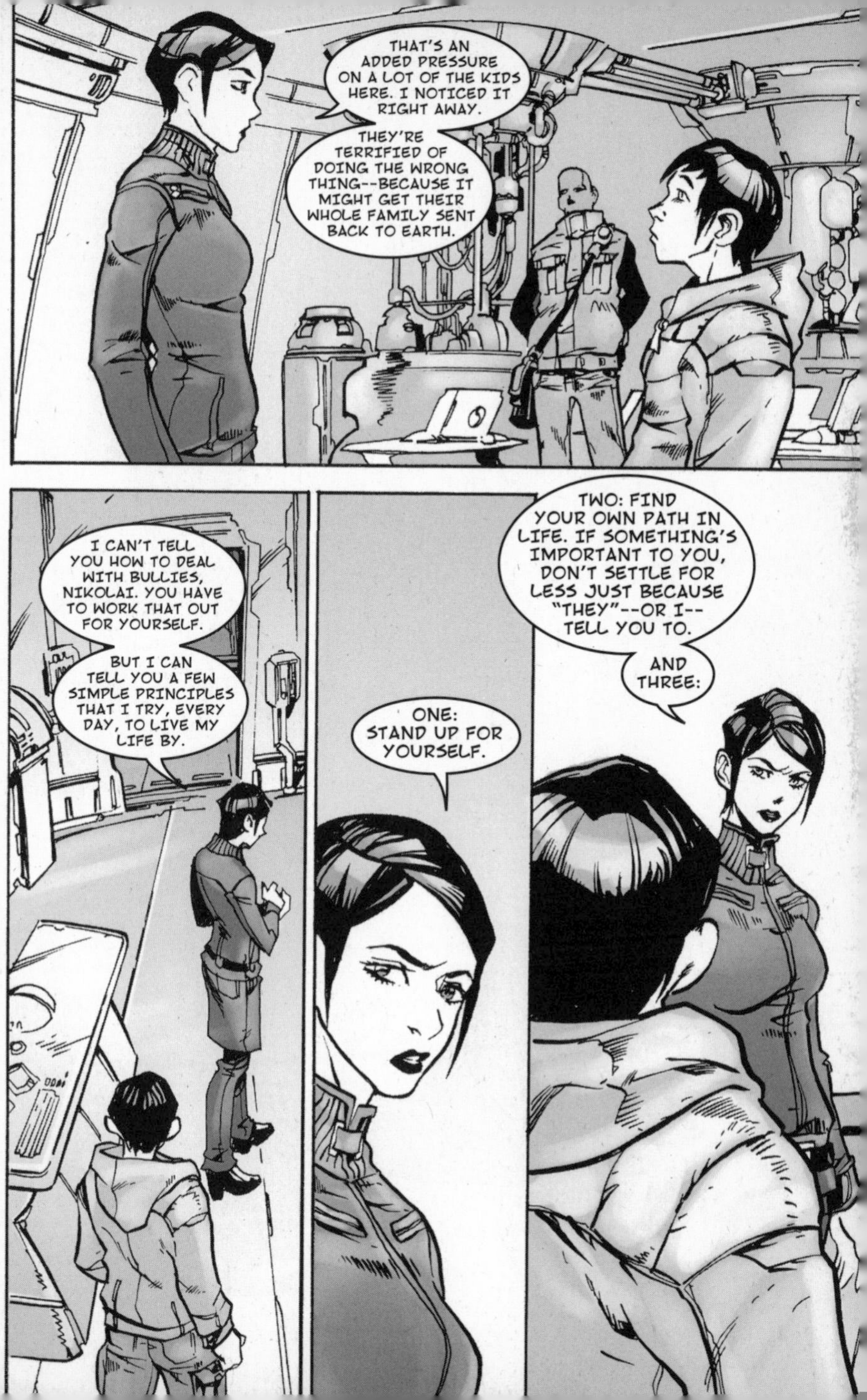
THAT'S AN ADDED PRESSURE ON A LOT OF THE KIDS HERE. I NOTICED IT RIGHT AWAY.
THEY'RE TERRIFIED OF DOING THE WRONG THING--BECAUSE IT MIGHT GET THEIR WHOLE FAMILY SENT BACK TO EARTH.
I CAN'T TELL YOU HOW TO DEAL WITH BULLIES, NIKOLAI. YOU HAVE TO WORK THAT OUT FOR YOURSELF.
BUT I CAN TELL YOU A FEW SIMPLE PRINCIPLES THAT I TRY, EVERY DAY, TO LIVE MY LIFE BY.
ONE: STAND UP FOR YOURSELF.
TWO: FIND YOUR OWN PATH IN LIFE. IF SOMETHING'S IMPORTANT TO YOU, DON'T SETTLE FOR LESS JUST BECAUSE "THEY"--OR I--TELL YOU TO.
AND THREE:

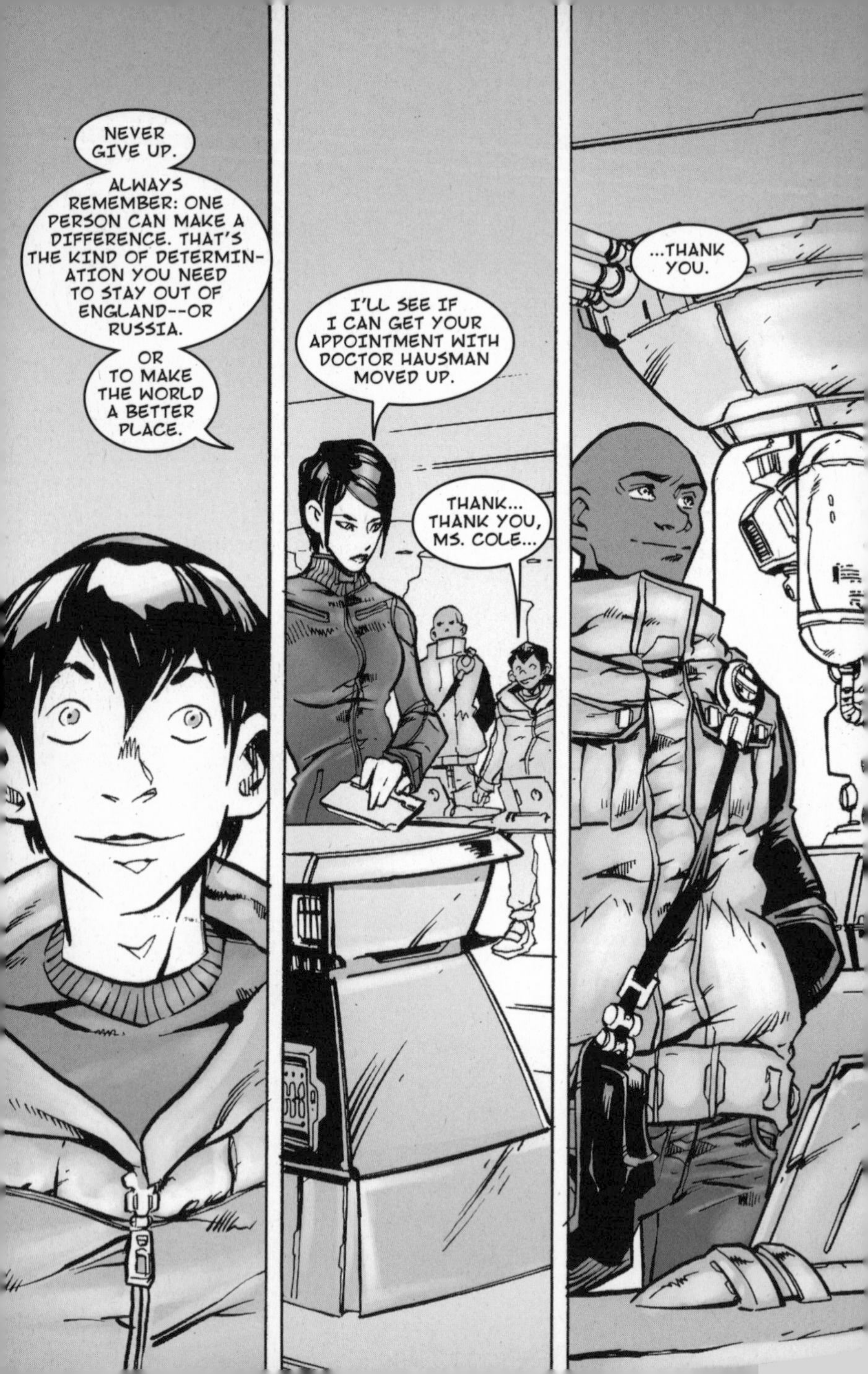
NEVER GIVE UP.
ALWAYS REMEMBER: ONE PERSON CAN MAKE A DIFFERENCE. THAT'S THE KIND OF DETERMIN-ATION YOU NEED TO STAY OUT OF ENGLAND--OR RUSSIA.
OR TO MAKE THE WORLD A BETTER PLACE.
I'LL SEE IF I CAN GET YOUR APPOINTMENT WITH DOCTOR HAUSMAN MOVED UP.
THANK... THANK YOU, MS. COLE...
...THANK YOU.

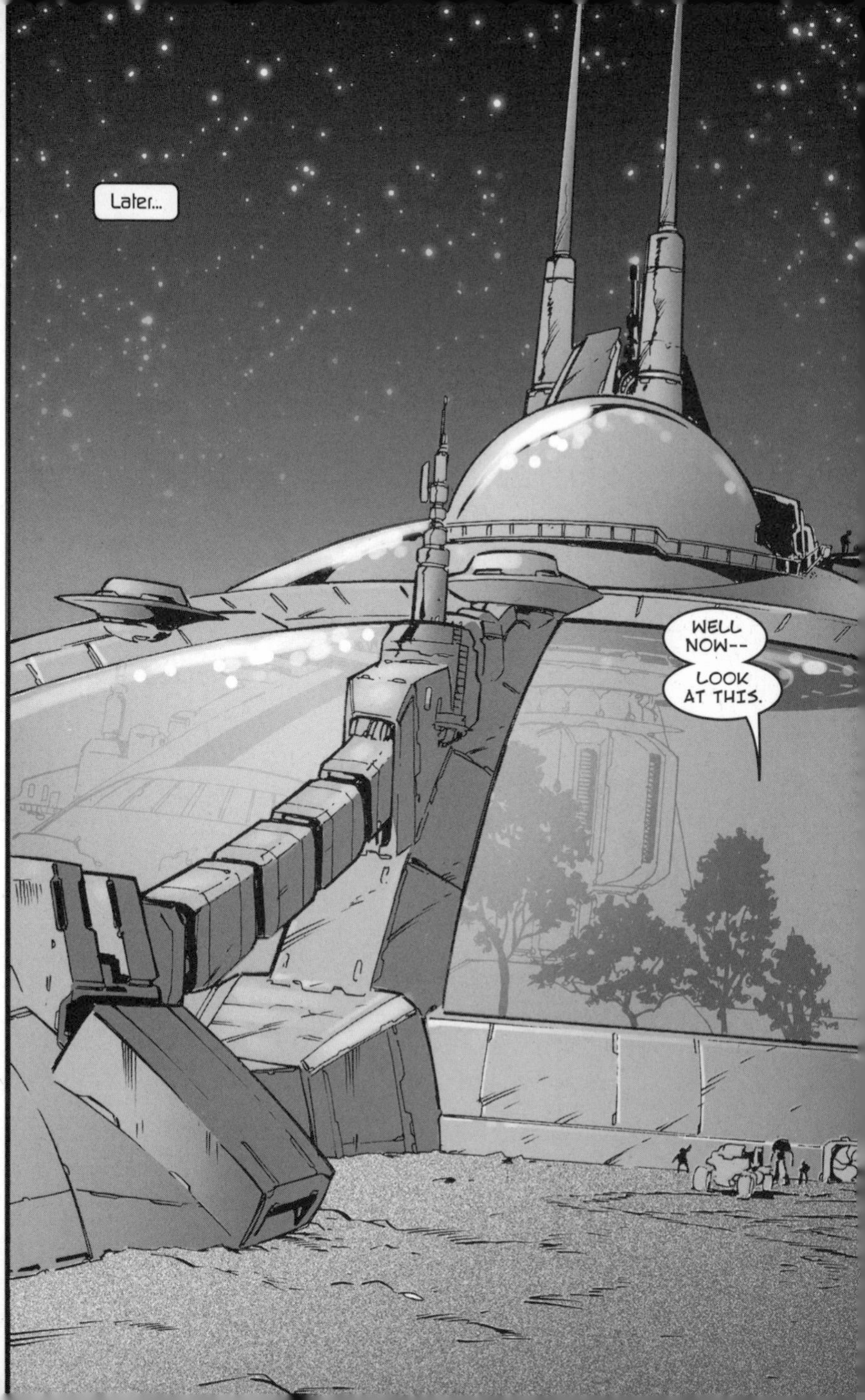
Later...
WELL NOW--
LOOK AT THIS.

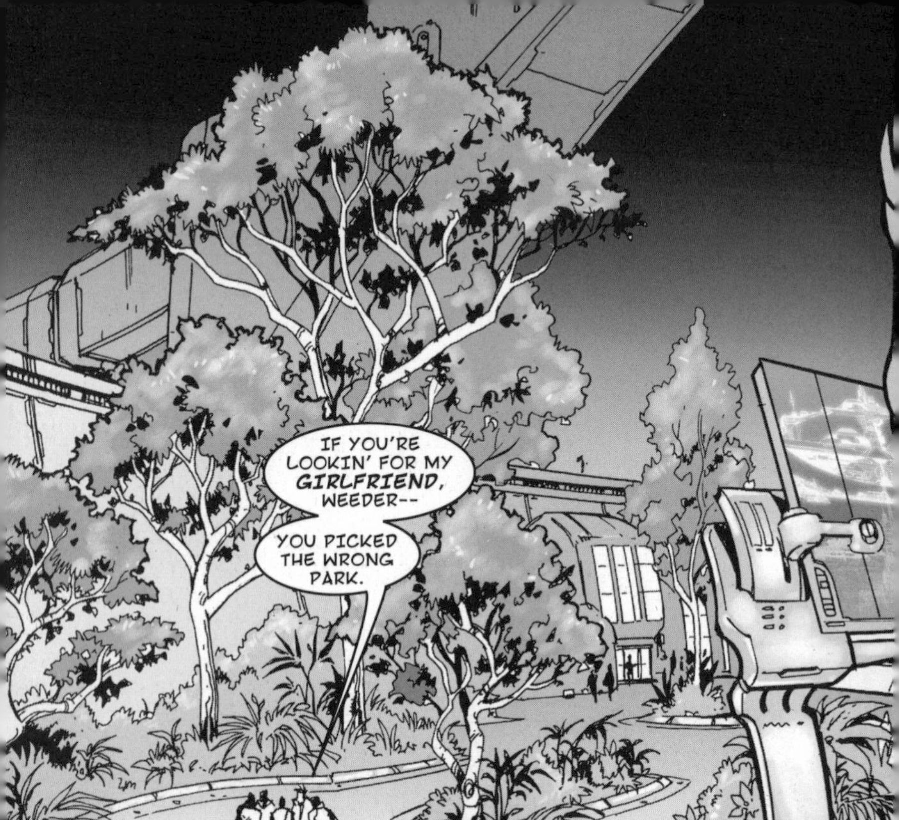
IF YOU'RE LOOKIN' FOR MY **GIRLFRIEND**, WEEDER--
YOU PICKED THE WRONG PARK.

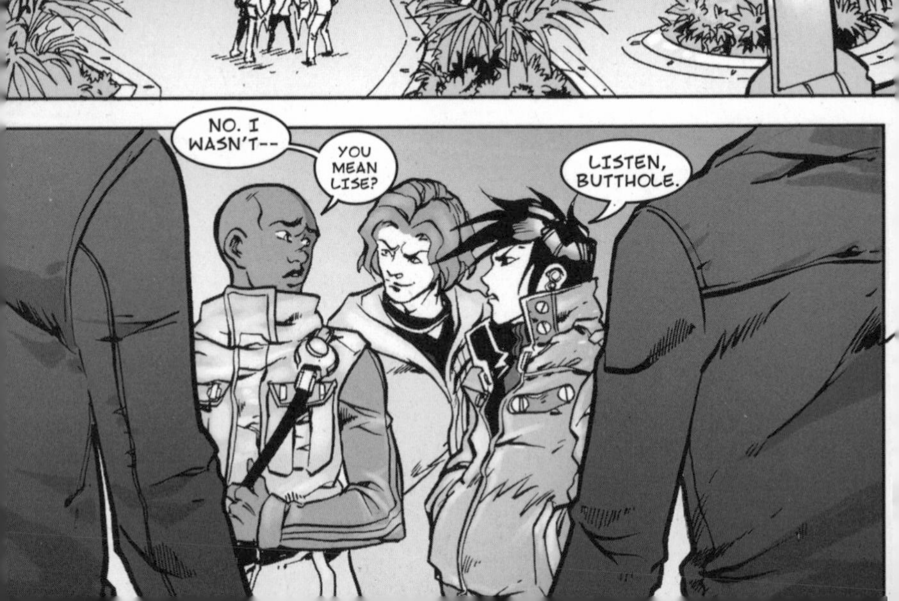
NO. I WASN'T--
YOU MEAN LISE?
LISTEN, BUTTHOLE.

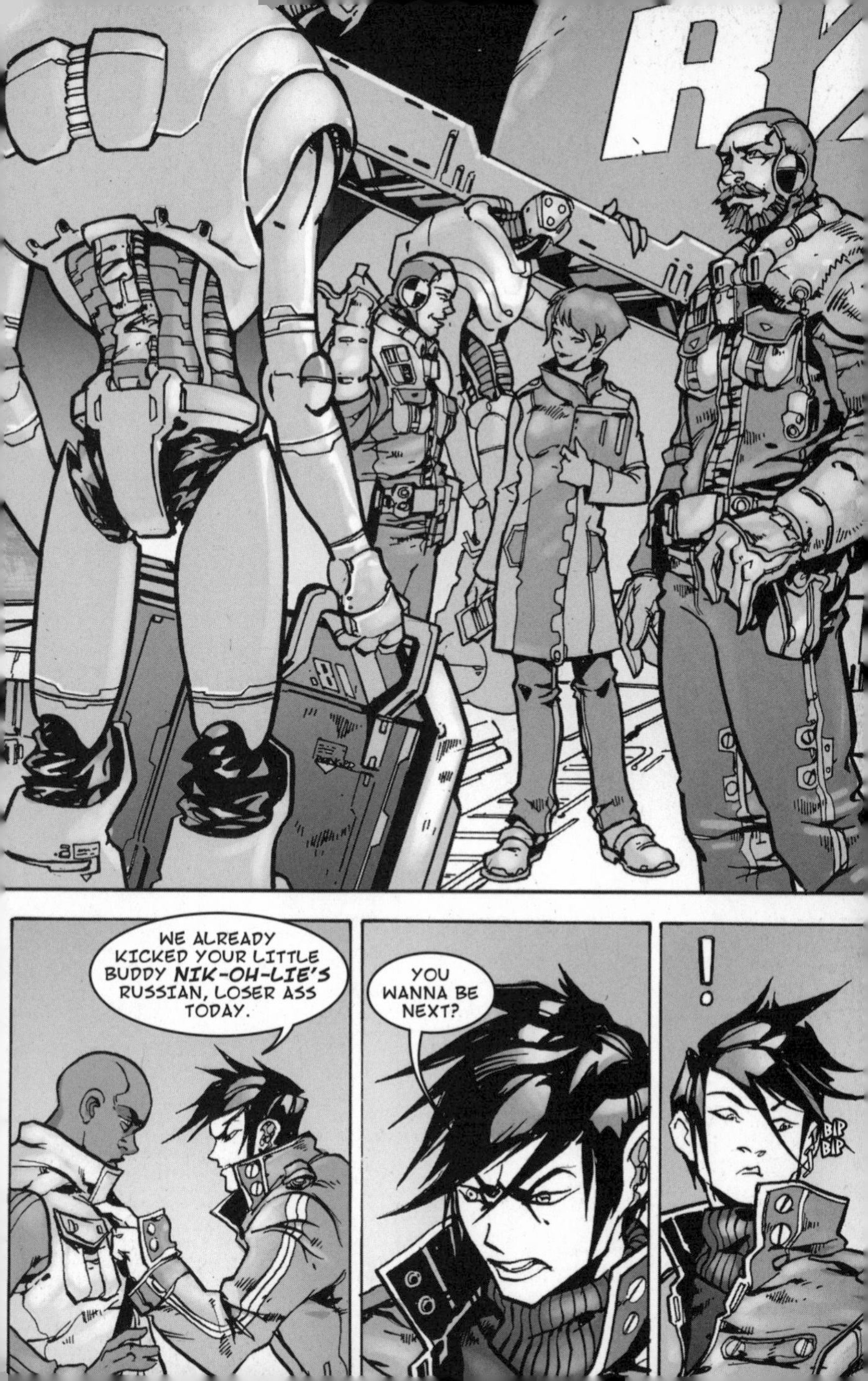
RY
WE ALREADY KICKED YOUR LITTLE BUDDY NIK-OH-LIE'S RUSSIAN, LOSER ASS TODAY.
YOU WANNA BE NEXT?
!
BIP BIP

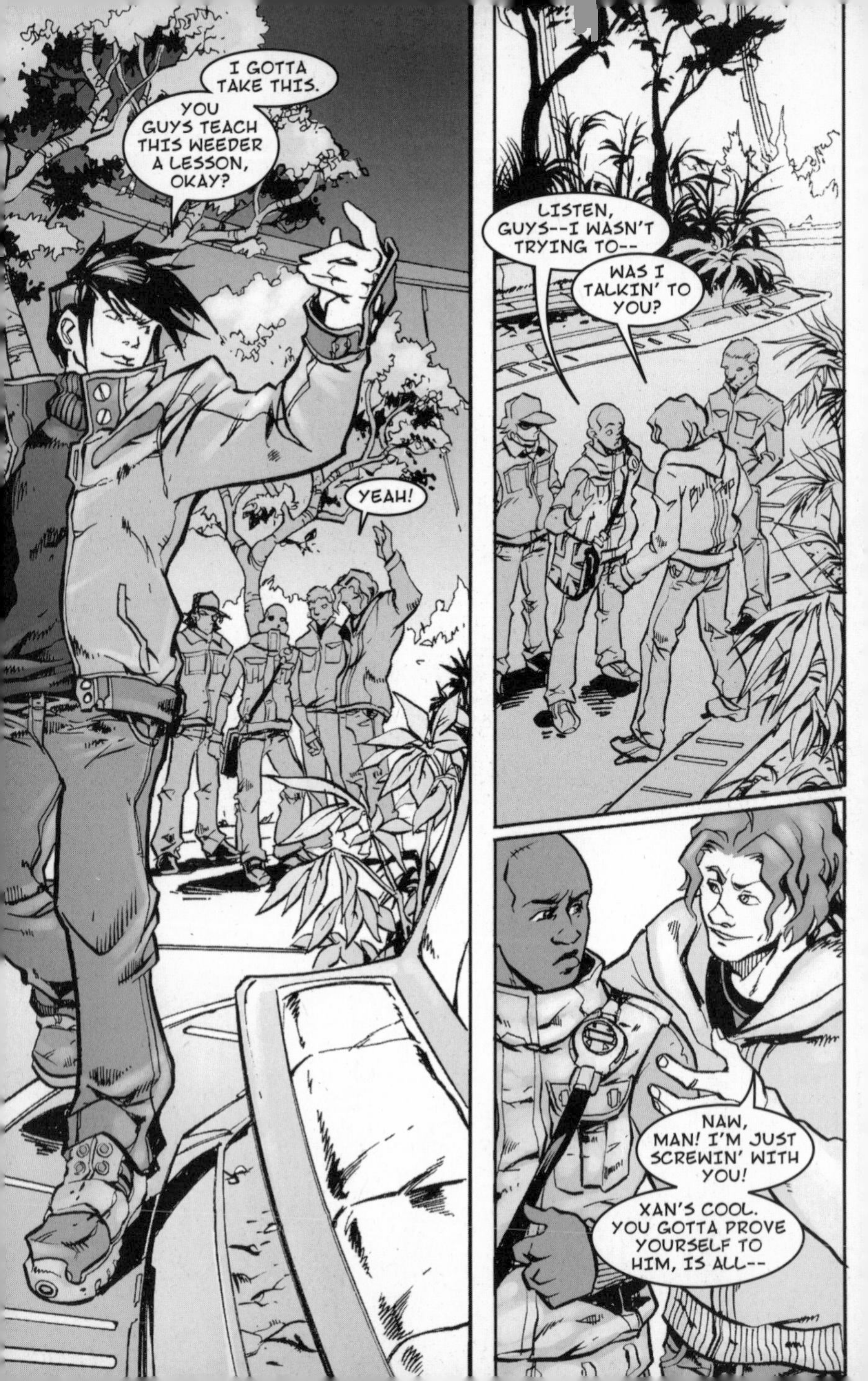
I GOTTA TAKE THIS.
YOU GUYS TEACH THIS WEEDER A LESSON, OKAY?
YEAH!
LISTEN, GUYS--I WASN'T TRYING TO--
WAS I TALKIN' TO YOU?
NAW, MAN! I'M JUST SCREWIN' WITH YOU!
XAN'S COOL. YOU GOTTA PROVE YOURSELF TO HIM, IS ALL--

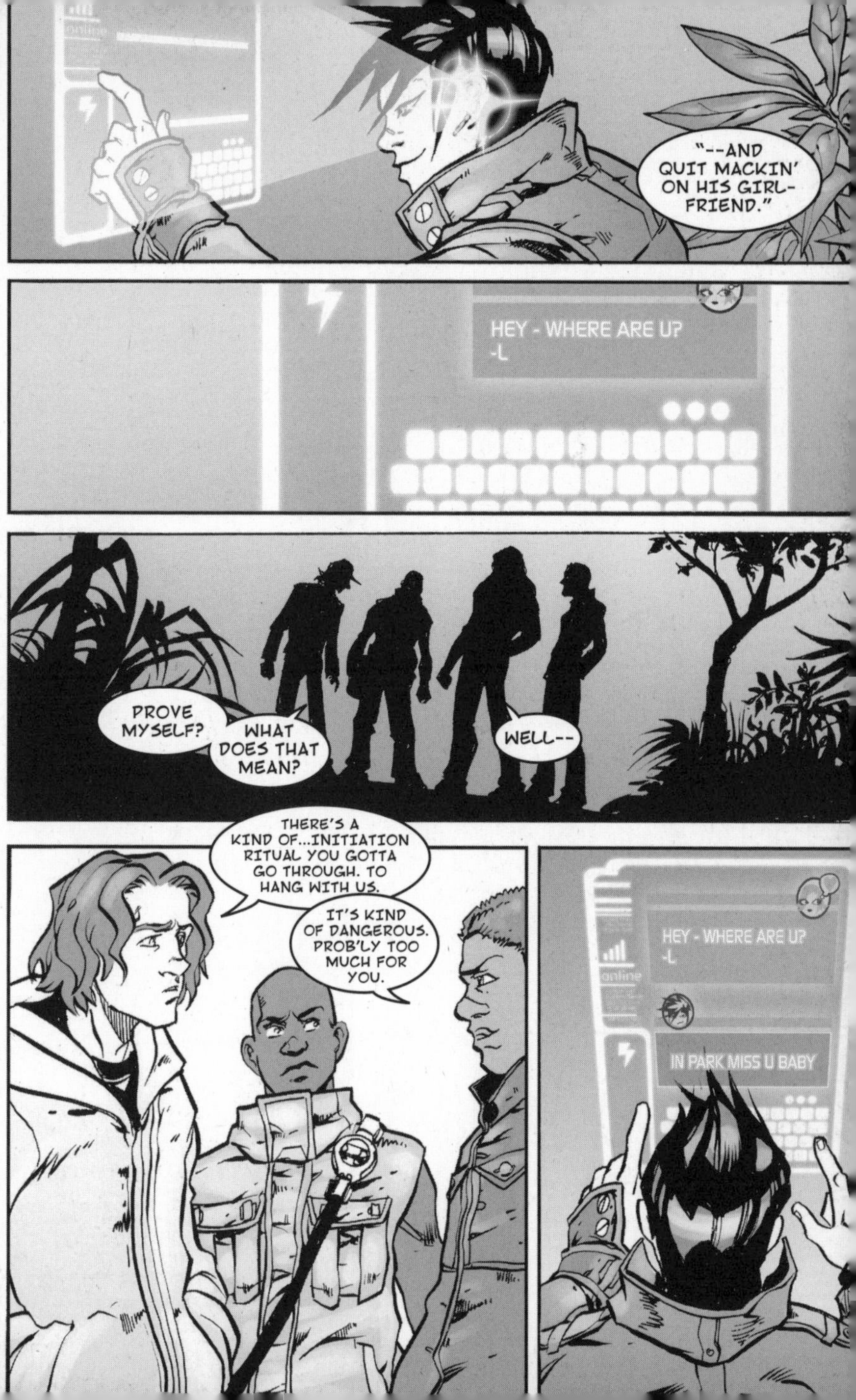
"--AND QUIT MACKIN' ON HIS GIRL-FRIEND."
HEY - WHERE ARE U? -L
PROVE MYSELF?
WHAT DOES THAT MEAN?
WELL--
THERE'S A KIND OF...INITIATION RITUAL YOU GOTTA GO THROUGH. TO HANG WITH US.
IT'S KIND OF DANGEROUS. PROB'LY TOO MUCH FOR YOU.
HEY - WHERE ARE U? -L
IN PARK MISS U BABY

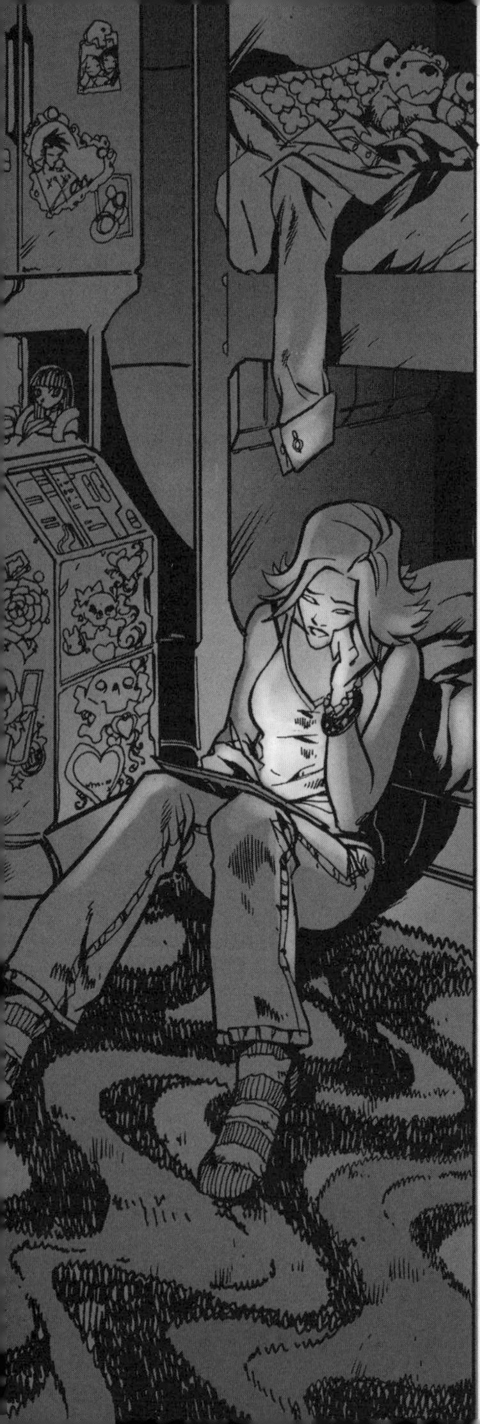

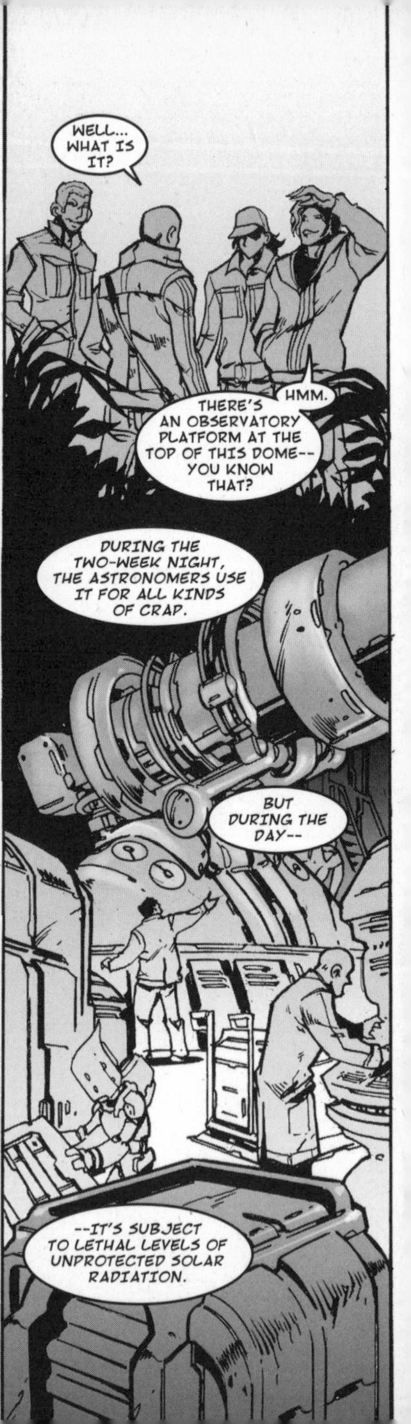
WELL... WHAT IS IT?
HMM.
THERE'S AN OBSERVATORY PLATFORM AT THE TOP OF THIS DOME-- YOU KNOW THAT?
DURING THE TWO-WEEK NIGHT, THE ASTRONOMERS USE IT FOR ALL KINDS OF CRAP.
BUT DURING THE DAY--
--IT'S SUBJECT TO LETHAL LEVELS OF UNPROTECTED SOLAR RADIATION.

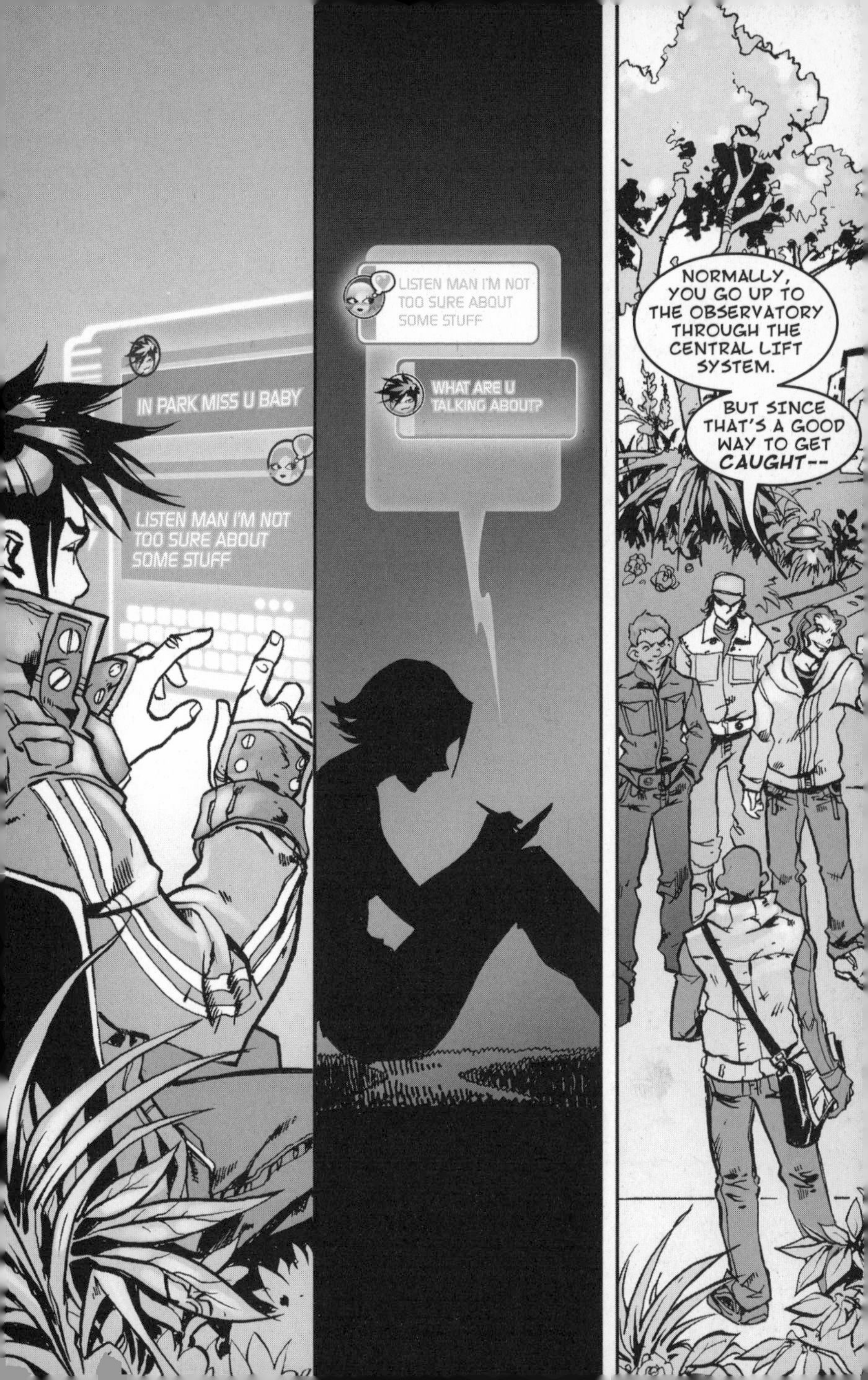
IN PARK MISS U BABY
LISTEN MAN I'M NOT TOO SURE ABOUT SOME STUFF
LISTEN MAN I'M NOT TOO SURE ABOUT SOME STUFF
WHAT ARE U TALKING ABOUT?
NORMALLY, YOU GO UP TO THE OBSERVATORY THROUGH THE CENTRAL LIFT SYSTEM.
BUT SINCE THAT'S A GOOD WAY TO GET CAUGHT--

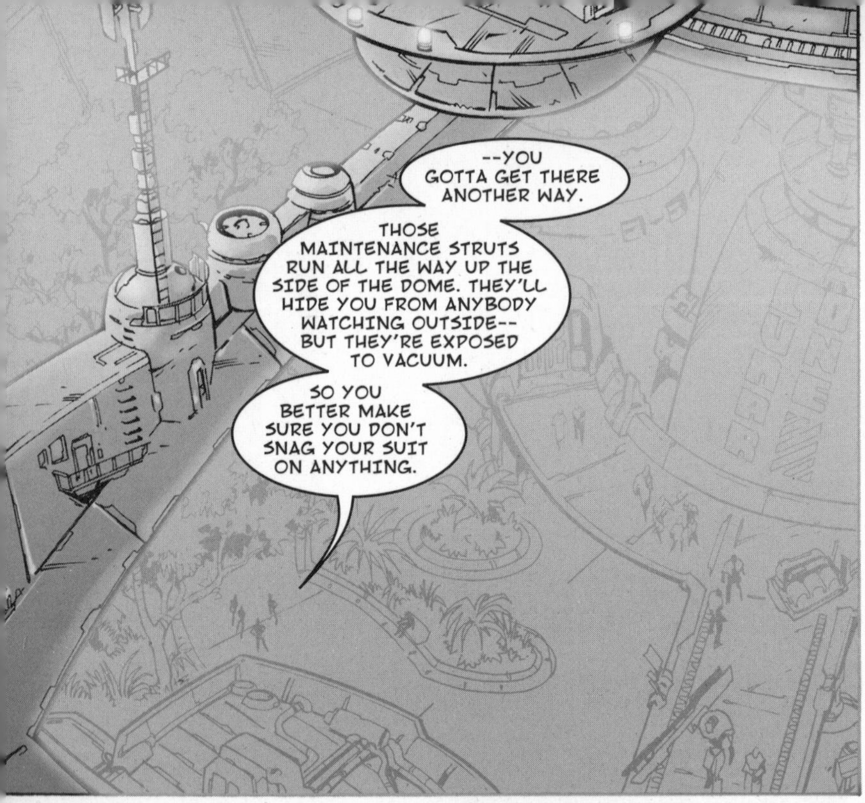
--YOU GOTTA GET THERE ANOTHER WAY.
THOSE MAINTENANCE STRUTS RUN ALL THE WAY UP THE SIDE OF THE DOME. THEY'LL HIDE YOU FROM ANYBODY WATCHING OUTSIDE-- BUT THEY'RE EXPOSED TO VACUUM.
SO YOU BETTER MAKE SURE YOU DON'T SNAG YOUR SUIT ON ANYTHING.
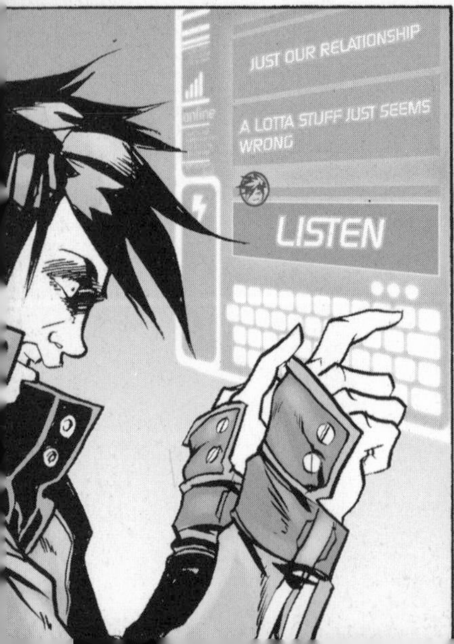
JUST OUR RELATIONSHIP
A LOTTA STUFF JUST SEEMS WRONG
LISTEN
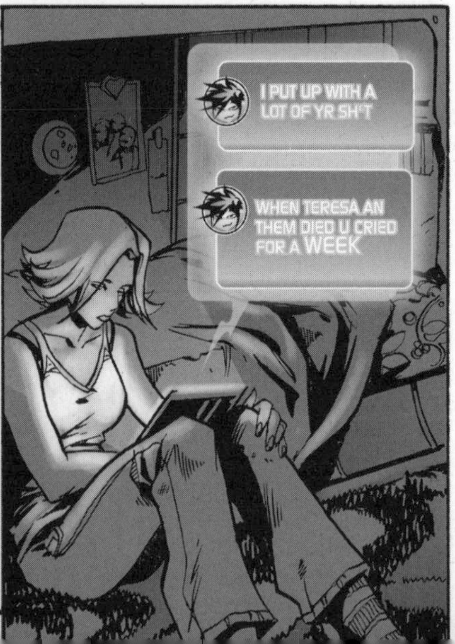
I PUT UP WITH A LOT OF YR SH*T
WHEN TERESA AN THEM DIED U CRIED FOR A WEEK

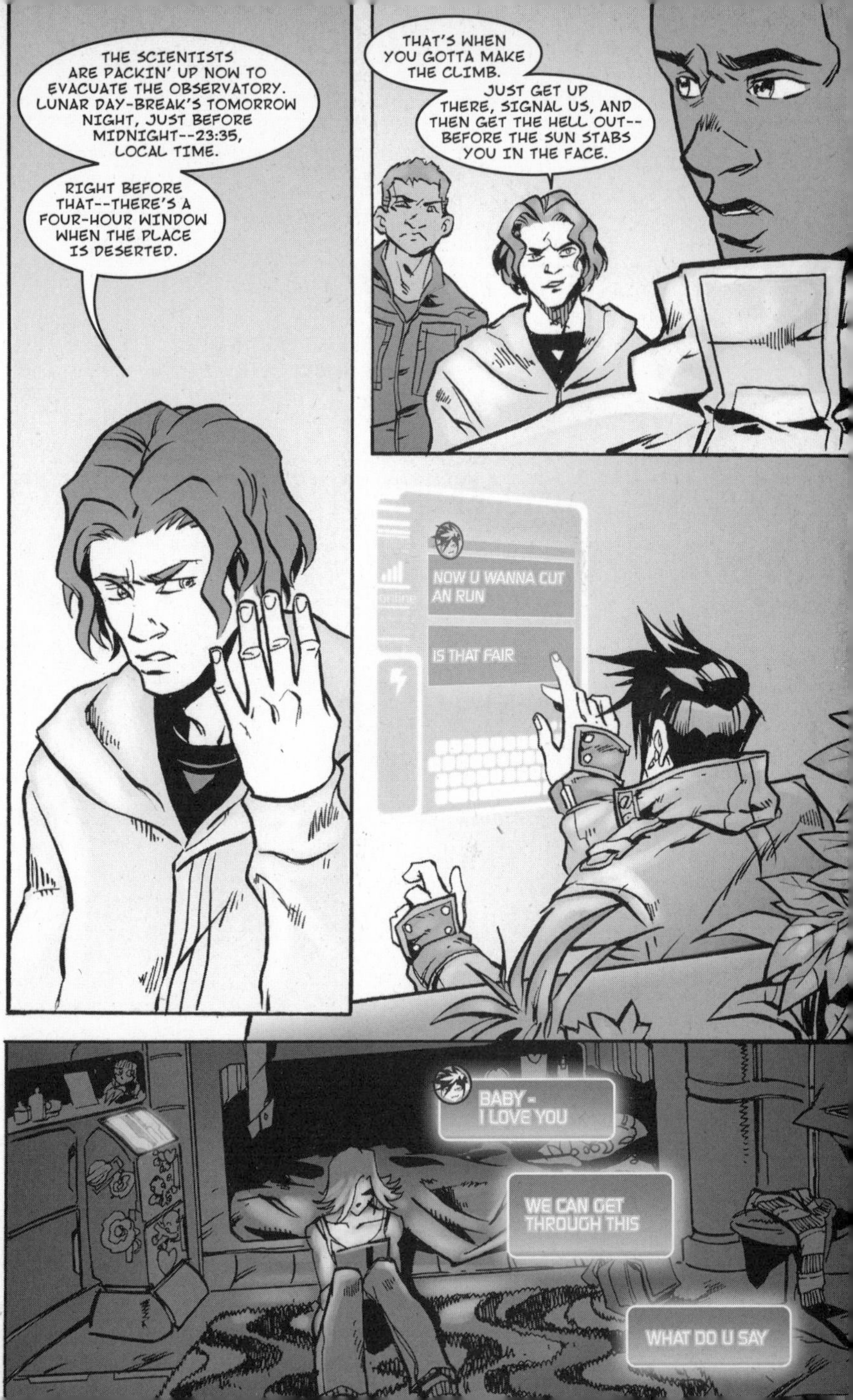
THE SCIENTISTS ARE PACKIN' UP NOW TO EVACUATE THE OBSERVATORY. LUNAR DAY-BREAK'S TOMORROW NIGHT, JUST BEFORE MIDNIGHT--23:35, LOCAL TIME.
RIGHT BEFORE THAT--THERE'S A FOUR-HOUR WINDOW WHEN THE PLACE IS DESERTED.
THAT'S WHEN YOU GOTTA MAKE THE CLIMB.
JUST GET UP THERE, SIGNAL US, AND THEN GET THE HELL OUT--BEFORE THE SUN STABS YOU IN THE FACE.
NOW U WANNA CUT AN RUN
IS THAT FAIR
BABY - I LOVE YOU
WE CAN GET THROUGH THIS
WHAT DO U SAY

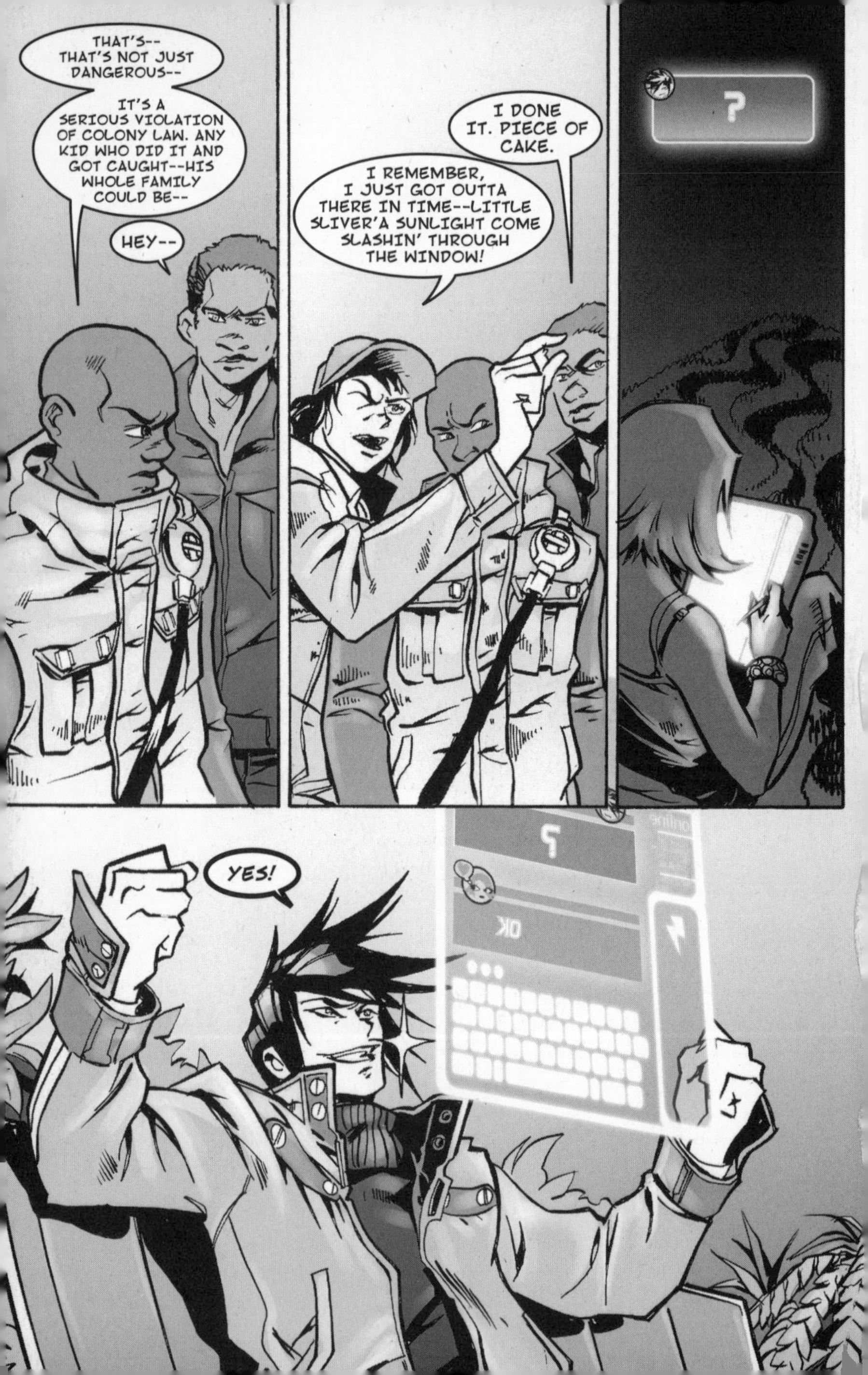
THAT'S-- THAT'S NOT JUST DANGEROUS--
IT'S A SERIOUS VIOLATION OF COLONY LAW. ANY KID WHO DID IT AND GOT CAUGHT--HIS WHOLE FAMILY COULD BE--
HEY--
I REMEMBER, I JUST GOT OUTTA THERE IN TIME--LITTLE SLIVER'A SUNLIGHT COME SLASHIN' THROUGH THE WINDOW!
I DONE IT. PIECE OF CAKE.
?
YES!
?
OK

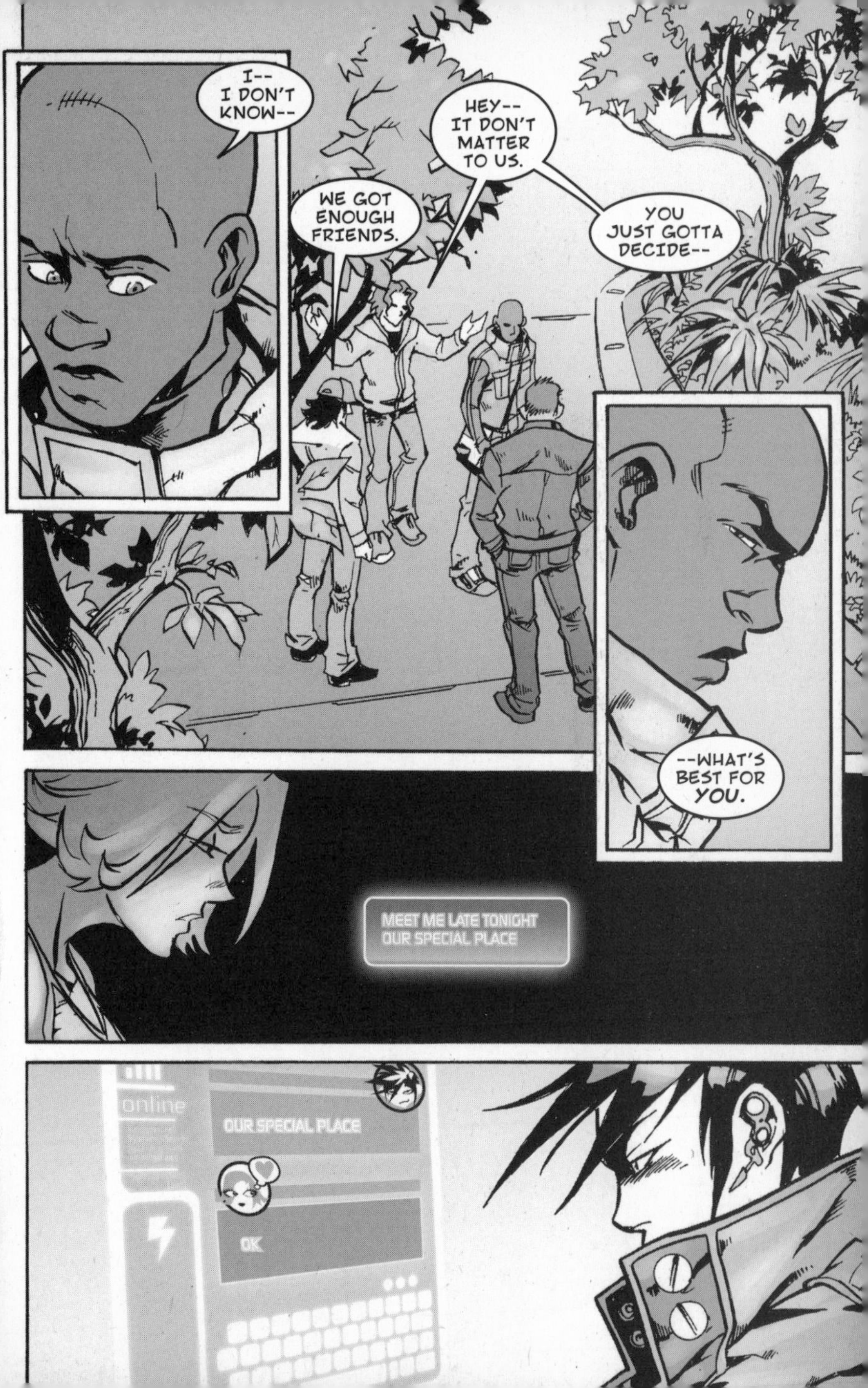

I-- I DON'T KNOW--
HEY-- IT DON'T MATTER TO US.
WE GOT ENOUGH FRIENDS.
YOU JUST GOTTA DECIDE--
--WHAT'S BEST FOR YOU.
MEET ME LATE TONIGHT OUR SPECIAL PLACE
online
OUR SPECIAL PLACE
OK

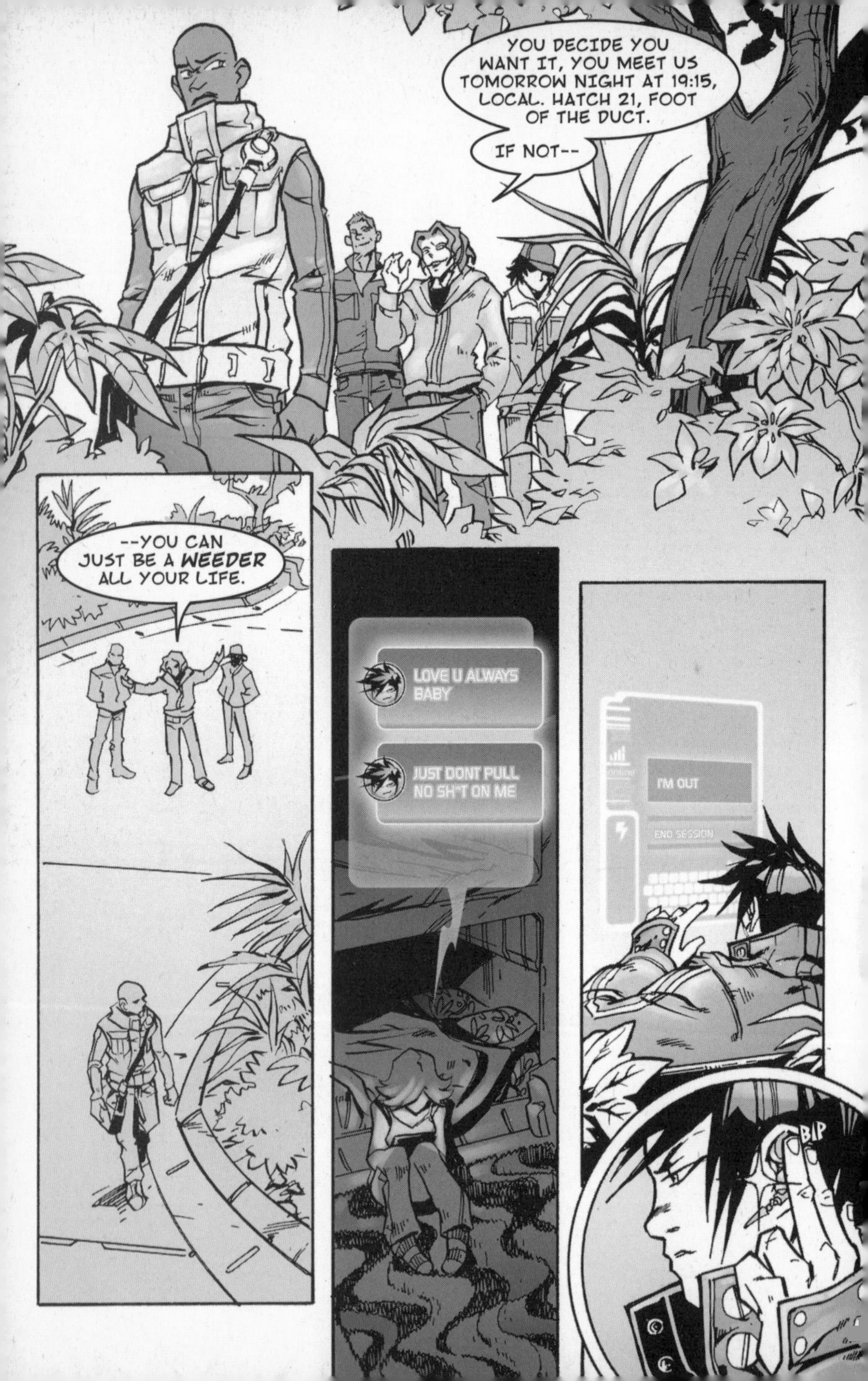
YOU DECIDE YOU WANT IT, YOU MEET US TOMORROW NIGHT AT 19:15, LOCAL. HATCH 21, FOOT OF THE DUCT.
IF NOT--
--YOU CAN JUST BE A **WEEDER** ALL YOUR LIFE.
LOVE U ALWAYS BABY
JUST DONT PULL NO SH*T ON ME
I'M OUT
END SESSION
BIP

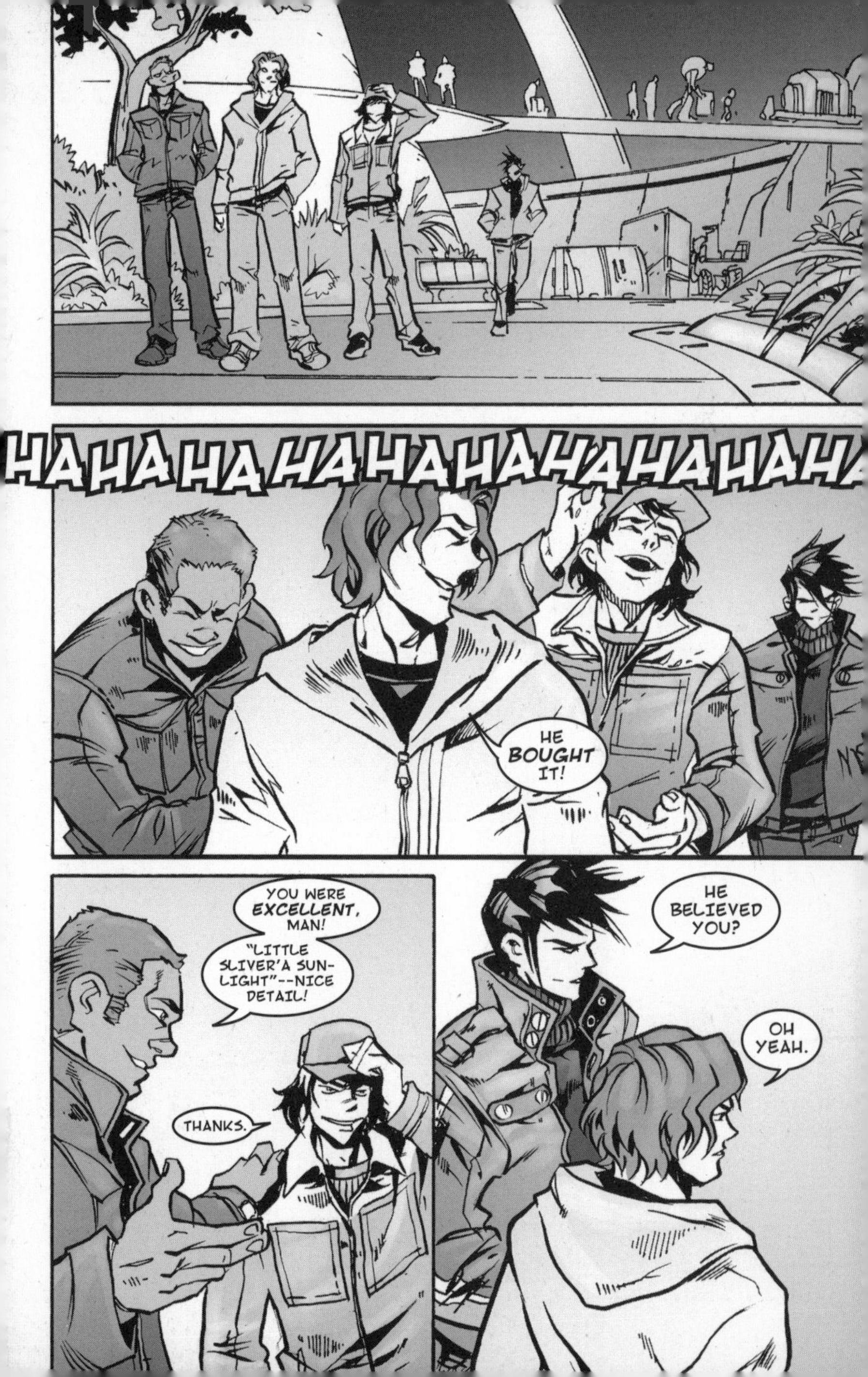
HAHAHAHAHAHAHAHAHAHA
HE BOUGHT IT!
YOU WERE EXCELLENT, MAN!
"LITTLE SLIVER'A SUN-LIGHT"--NICE DETAIL!
THANKS.
HE BELIEVED YOU?
OH YEAH.

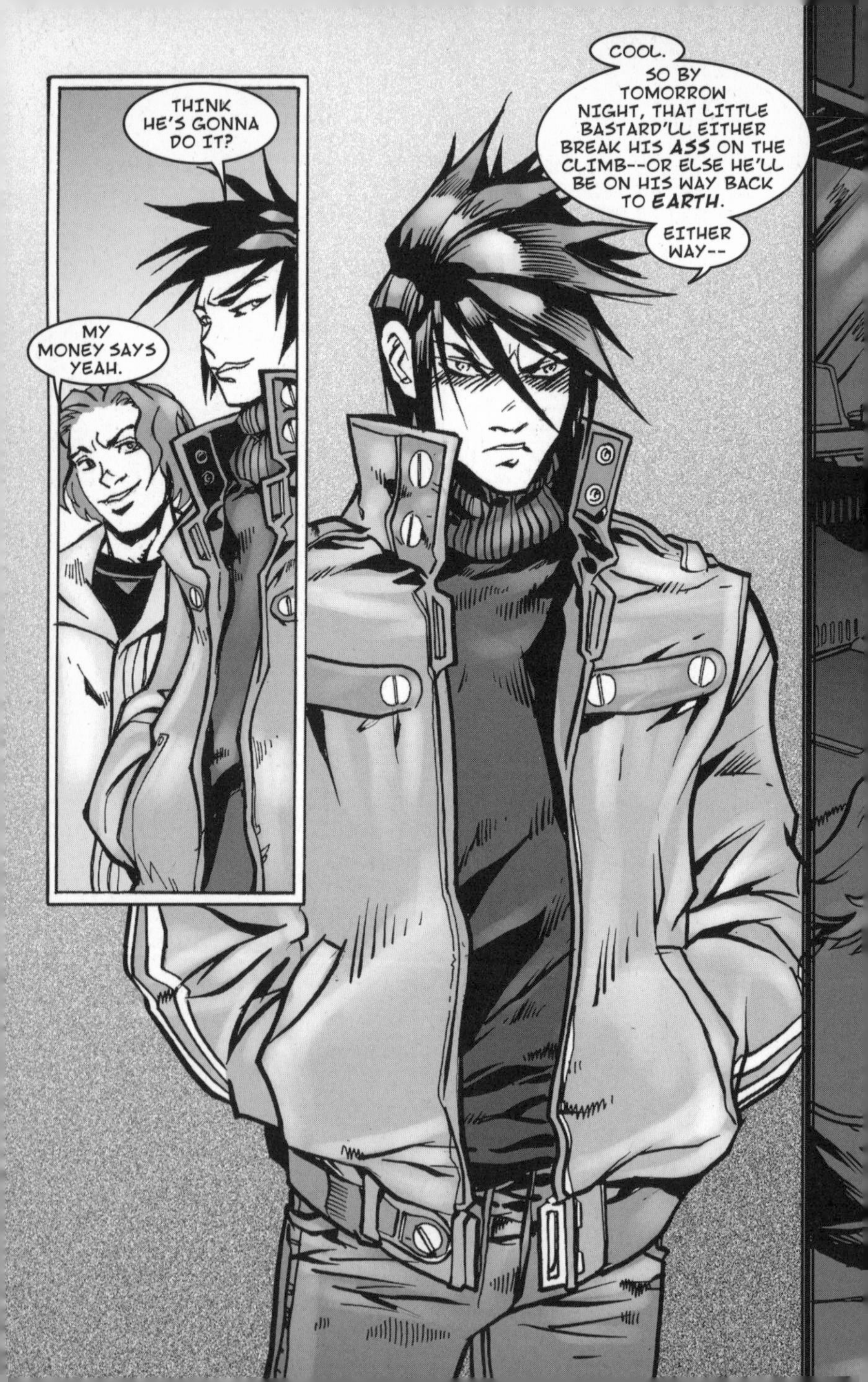
THINK HE'S GONNA DO IT?
MY MONEY SAYS YEAH.
COOL.
SO BY TOMORROW NIGHT, THAT LITTLE BASTARD'LL EITHER BREAK HIS ASS ON THE CLIMB--OR ELSE HE'LL BE ON HIS WAY BACK TO EARTH.
EITHER WAY--

--HE WON'T BE SNIFFIN' AROUND MY PROPERTY ANYMORE.

I'M OUT

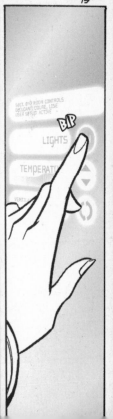

SECT. B12 ROOM CONTROLS
OCCUPANT: EQUIRE, LISE
USER SETUP: ACTIVE

BIP

LIGHTS

TEMPERATI

VENTI

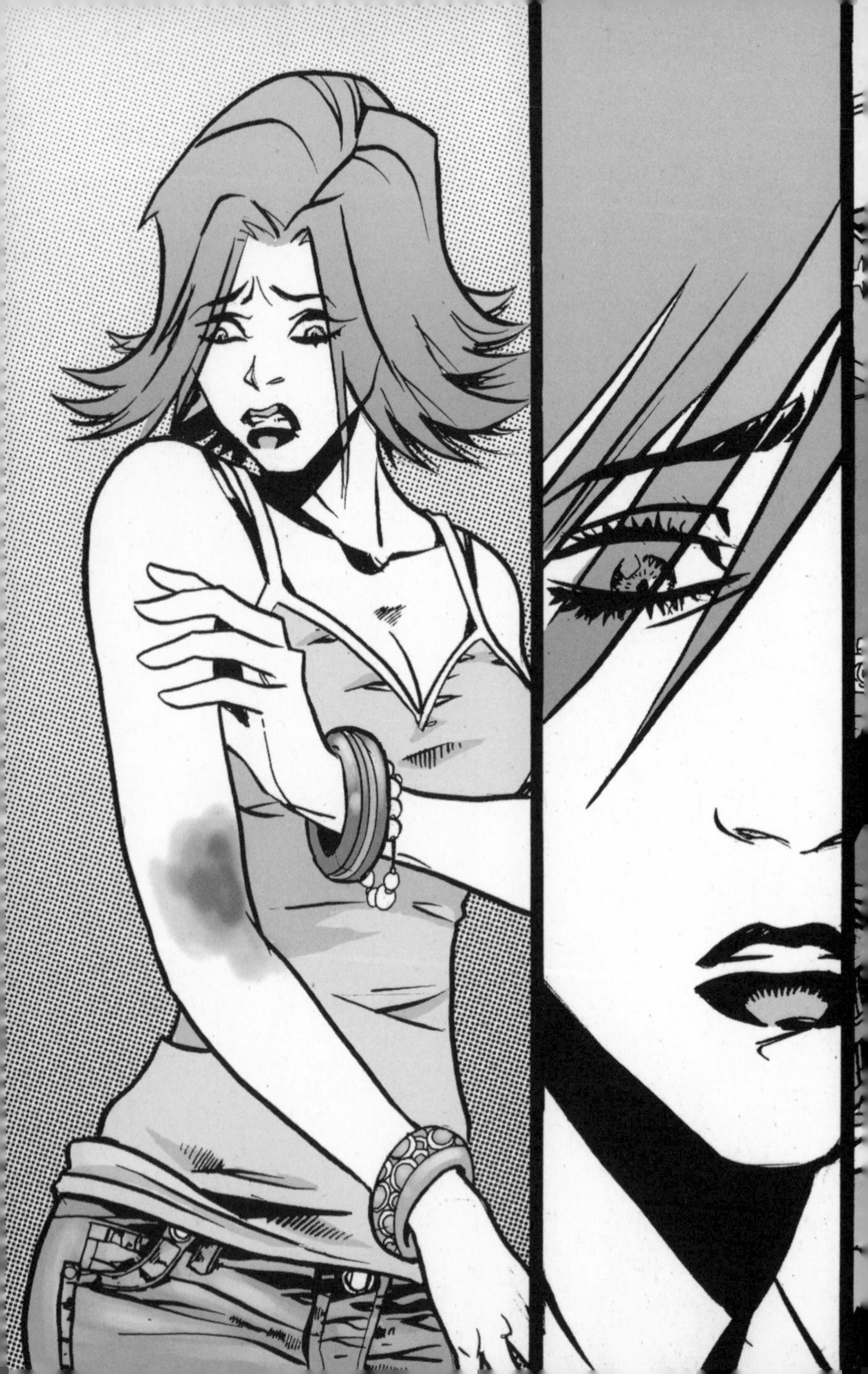

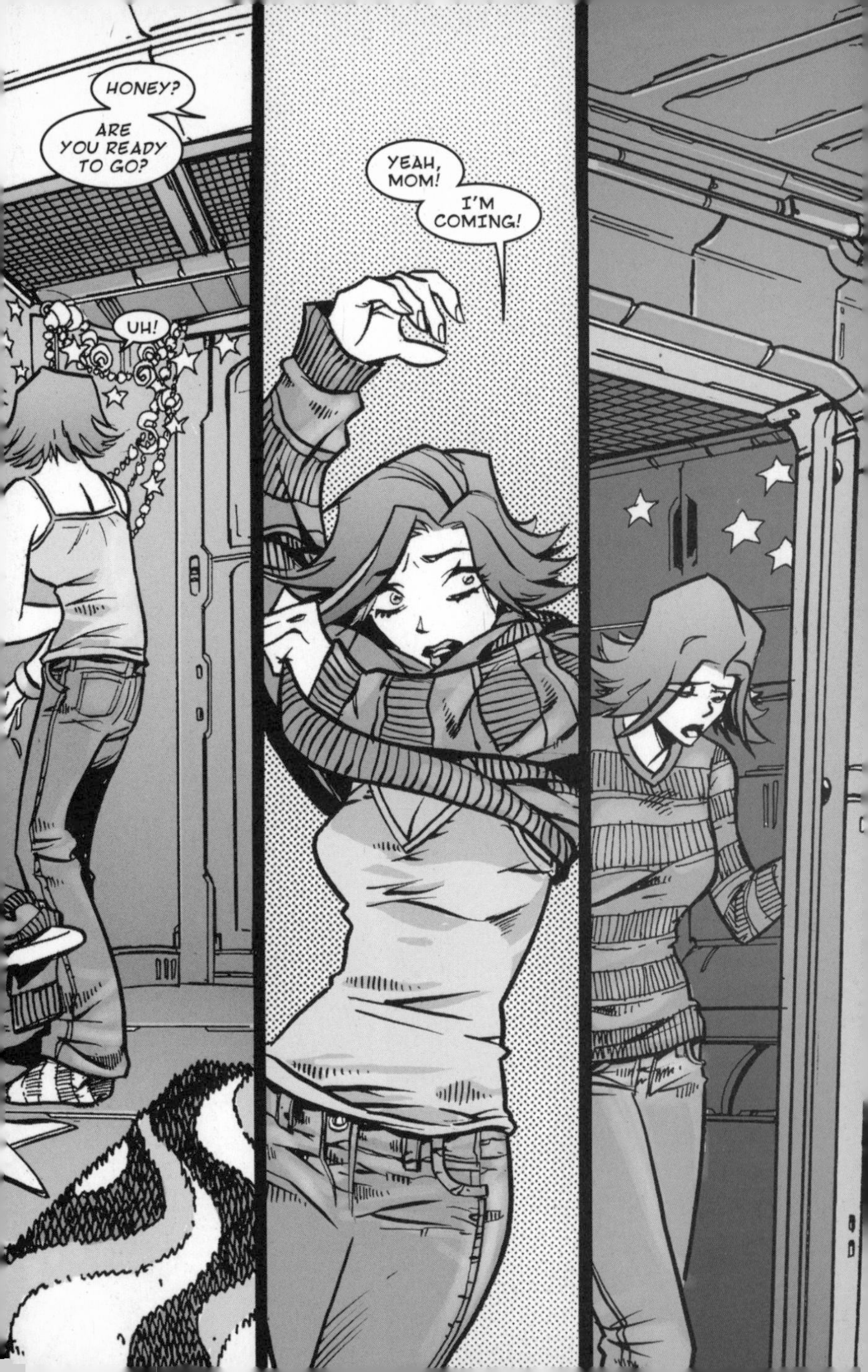
HONEY?
ARE YOU READY TO GO?
UH!
YEAH, MOM!
I'M COMING!

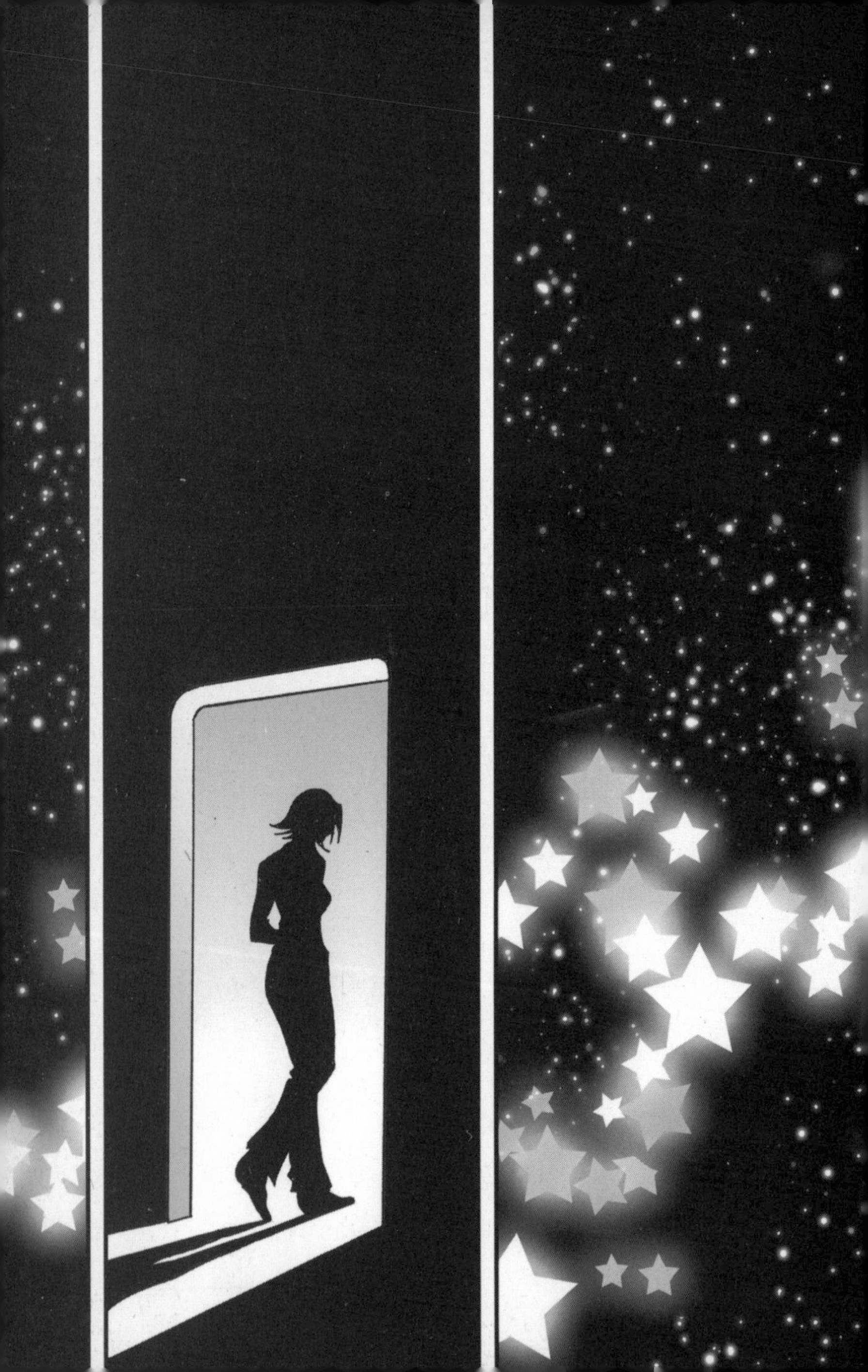

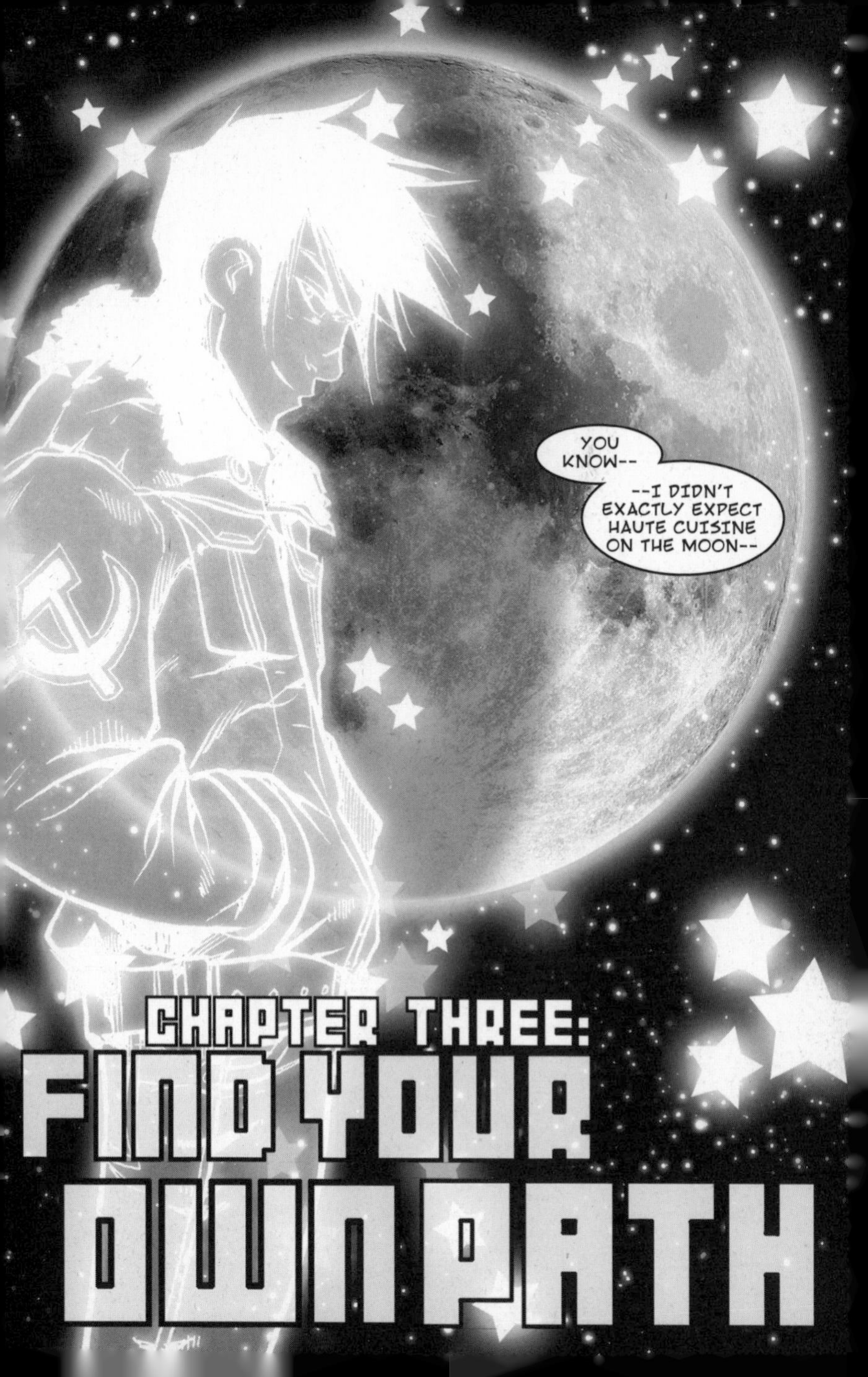
YOU KNOW--
--I DIDN'T EXACTLY EXPECT HAUTE CUISINE ON THE MOON--
CHAPTER THREE:
FIND YOUR OWN PATH

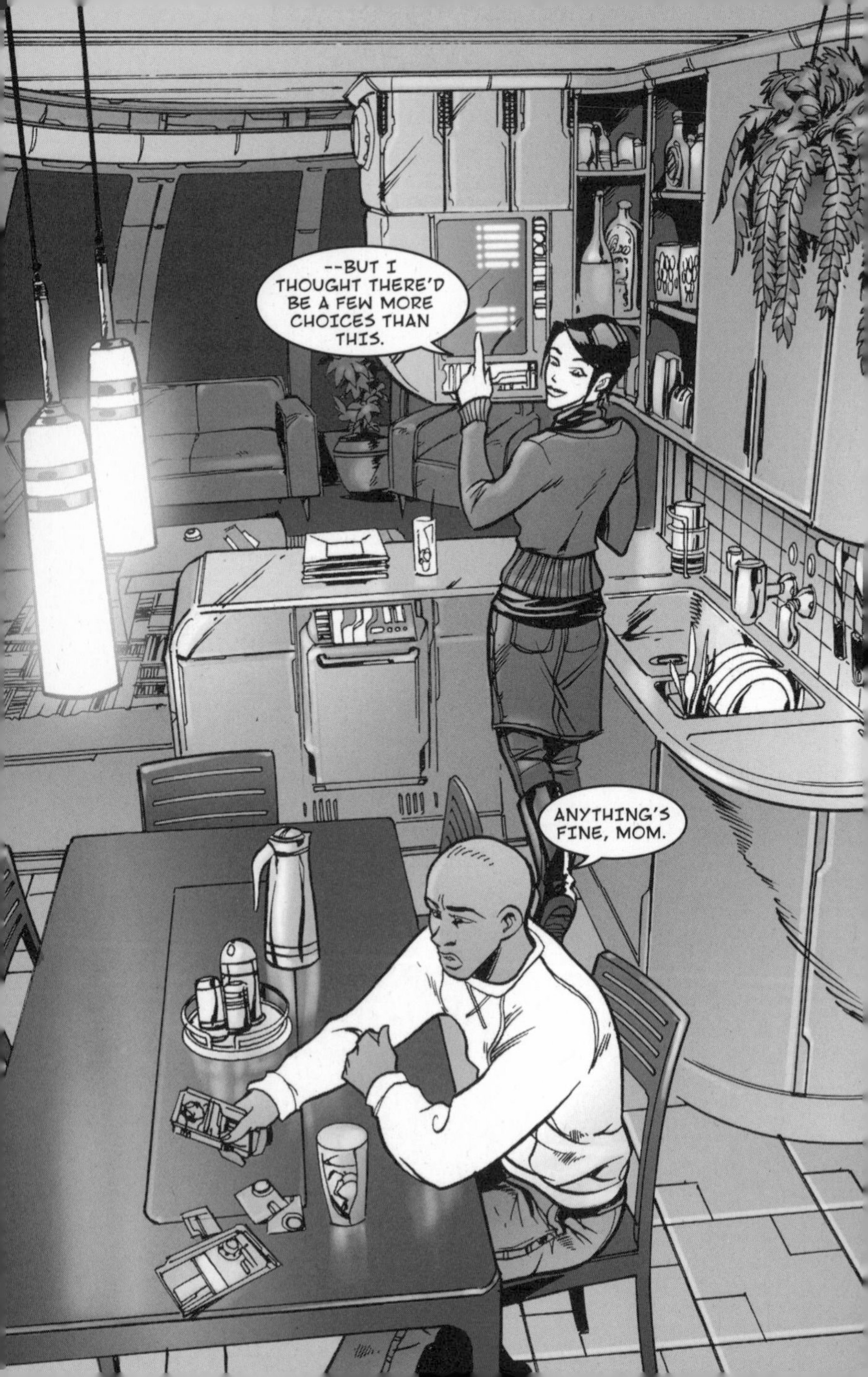
--BUT I THOUGHT THERE'D BE A FEW MORE CHOICES THAN THIS.
ANYTHING'S FINE, MOM.

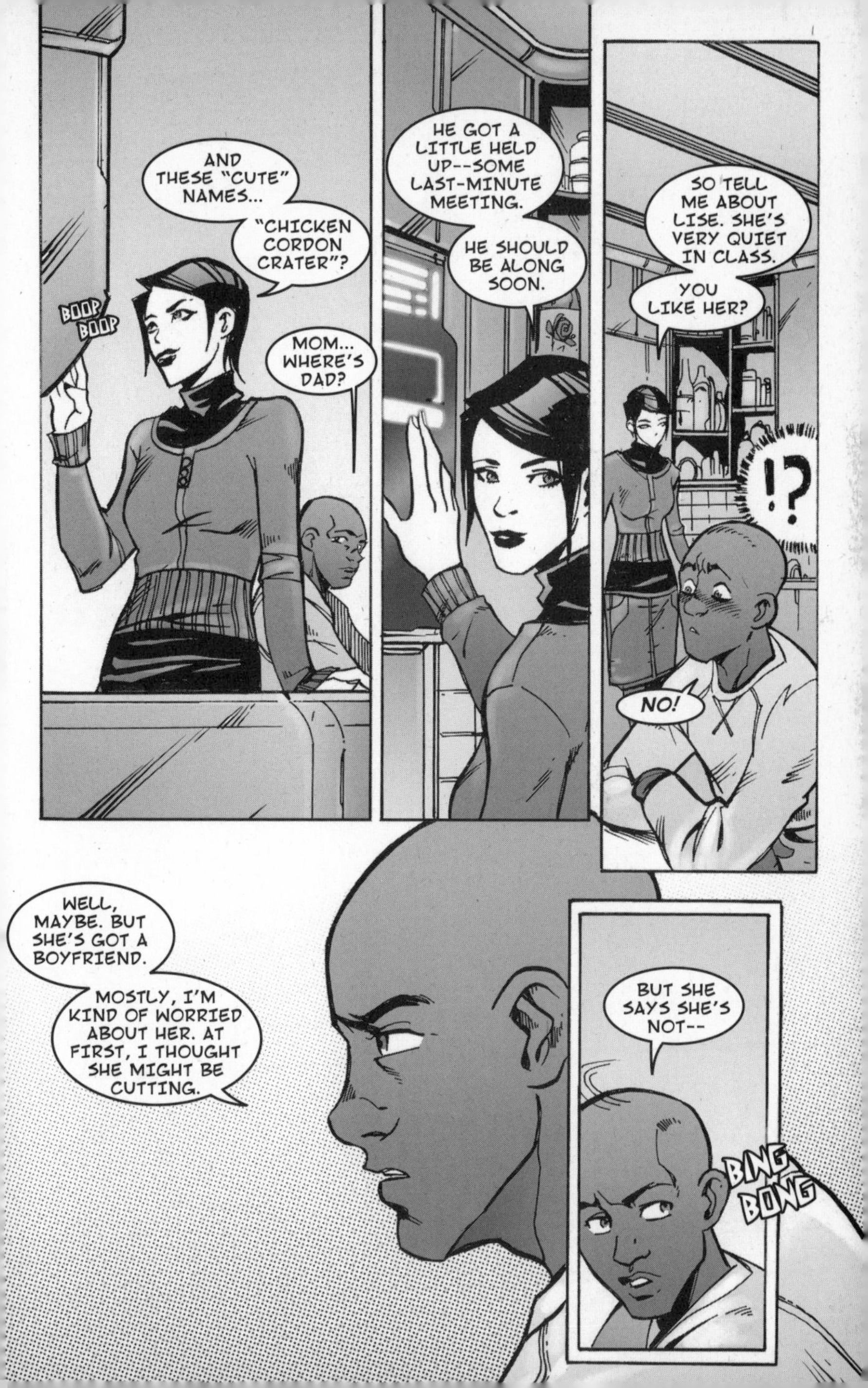
AND THESE "CUTE" NAMES...
"CHICKEN CORDON CRATER"?
BOOP BOOP
MOM... WHERE'S DAD?
HE GOT A LITTLE HELD UP--SOME LAST-MINUTE MEETING.
HE SHOULD BE ALONG SOON.
SO TELL ME ABOUT LISE. SHE'S VERY QUIET IN CLASS.
YOU LIKE HER?
!?
NO!
WELL, MAYBE. BUT SHE'S GOT A BOYFRIEND.
MOSTLY, I'M KIND OF WORRIED ABOUT HER. AT FIRST, I THOUGHT SHE MIGHT BE CUTTING.
BUT SHE SAYS SHE'S NOT--
BING BONG

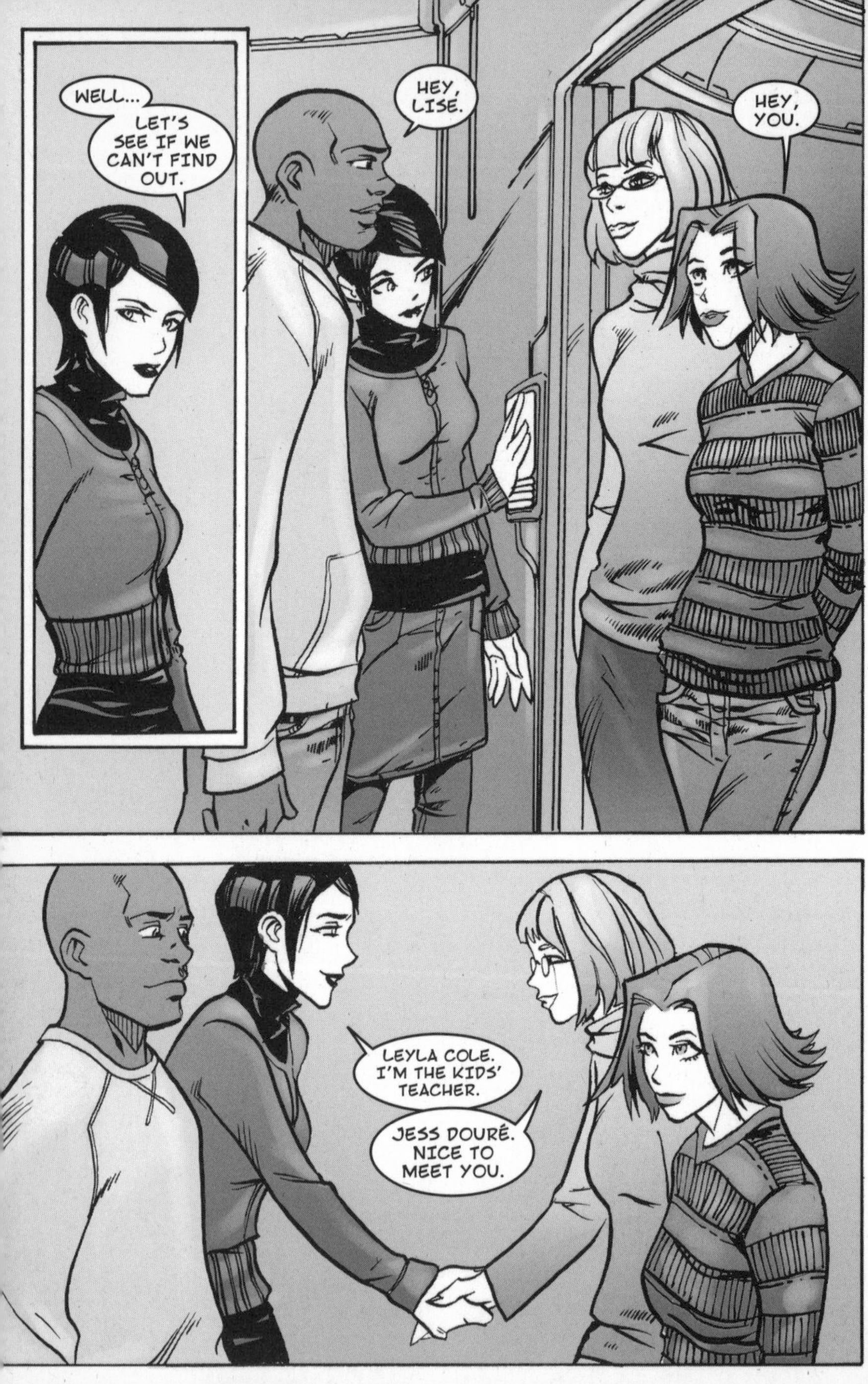
WELL...
LET'S SEE IF WE CAN'T FIND OUT.
HEY, LISE.
HEY, YOU.
LEYLA COLE. I'M THE KIDS' TEACHER.
JESS DOURÉ. NICE TO MEET YOU.

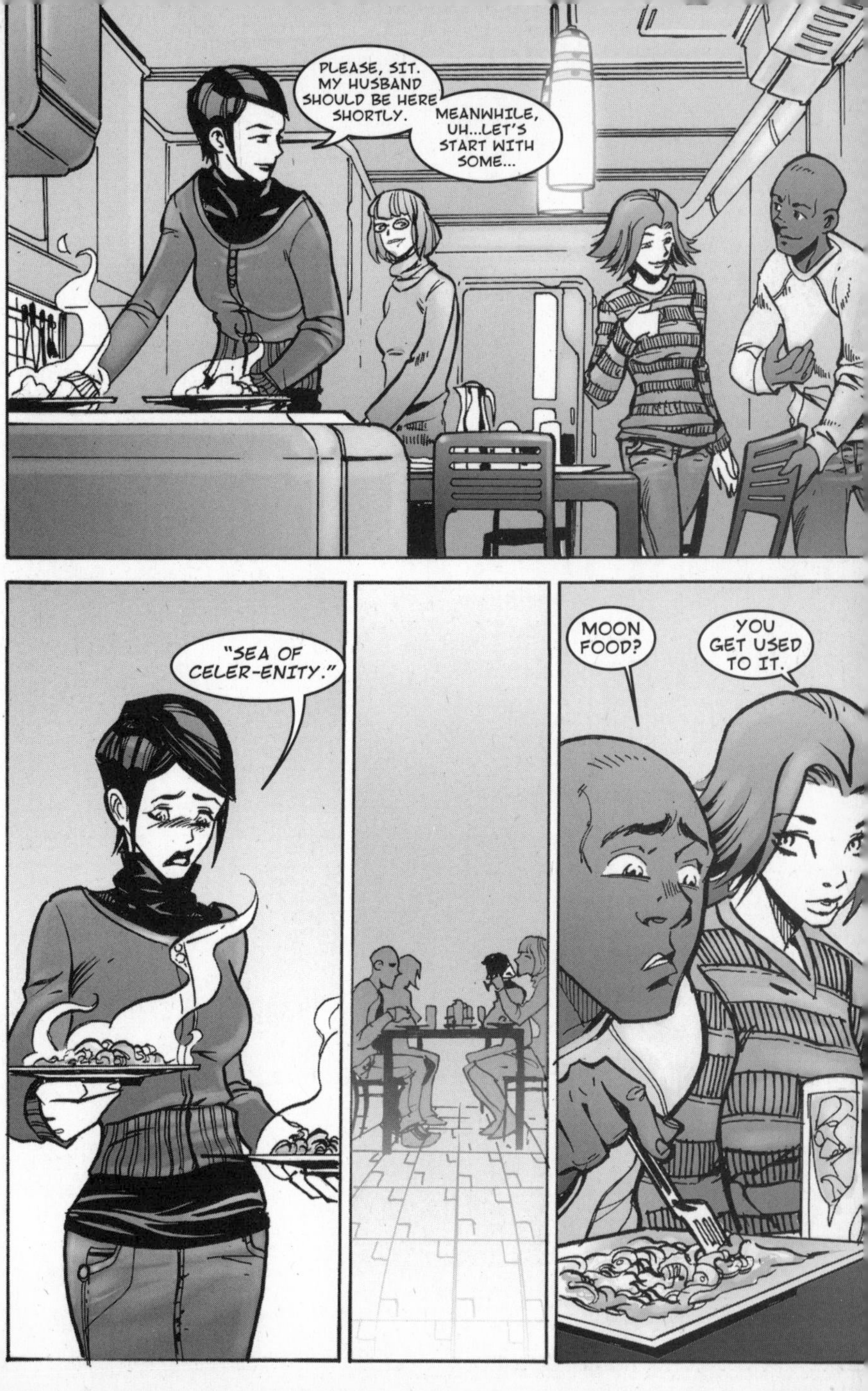
PLEASE, SIT. MY HUSBAND SHOULD BE HERE SHORTLY.
MEANWHILE, UH...LET'S START WITH SOME...
"SEA OF CELER-ENITY."
MOON FOOD?
YOU GET USED TO IT.

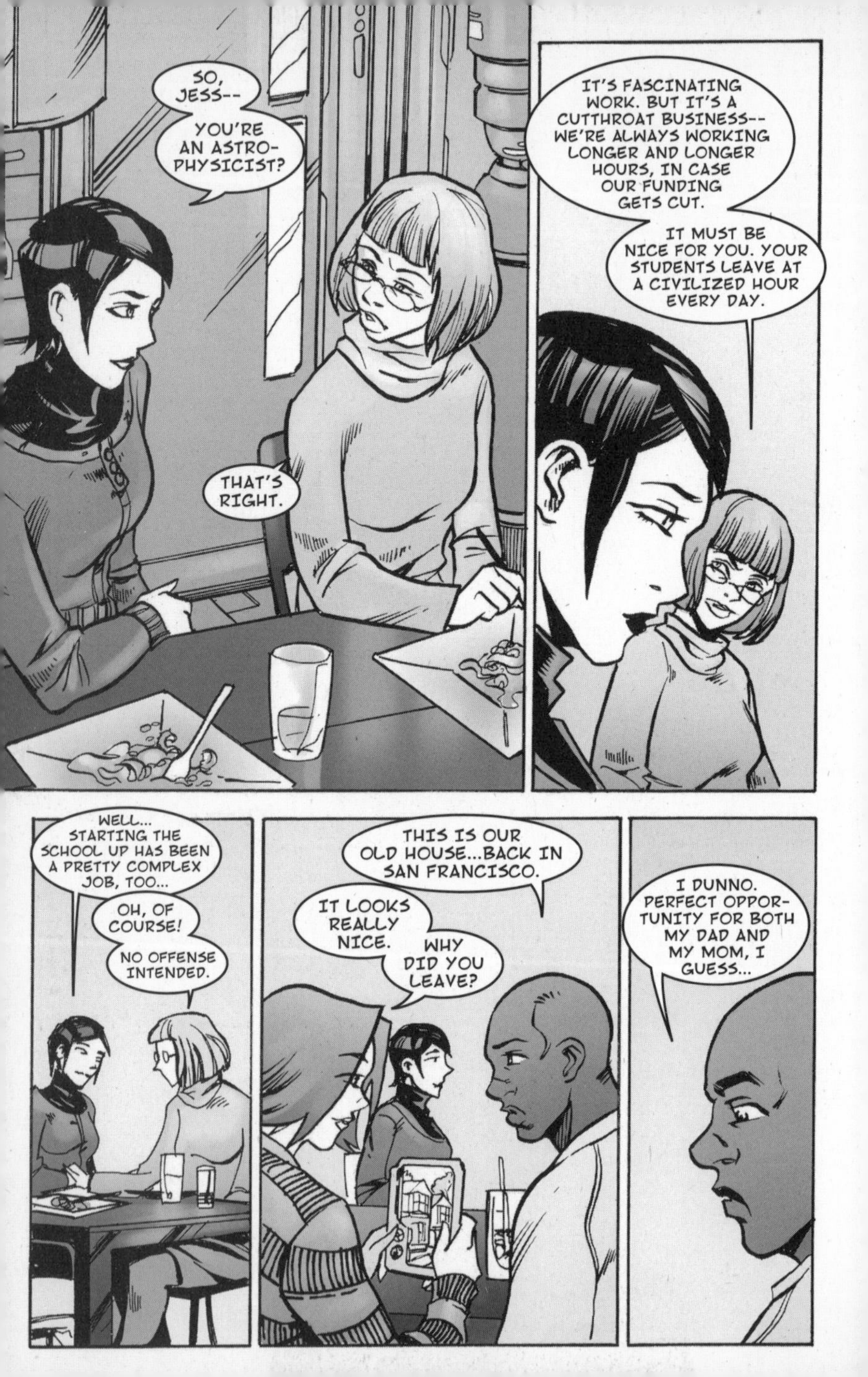
SO, JESS--
YOU'RE AN ASTRO-PHYSICIST?
THAT'S RIGHT.
IT'S FASCINATING WORK. BUT IT'S A CUTTHROAT BUSINESS-- WE'RE ALWAYS WORKING LONGER AND LONGER HOURS, IN CASE OUR FUNDING GETS CUT.
IT MUST BE NICE FOR YOU. YOUR STUDENTS LEAVE AT A CIVILIZED HOUR EVERY DAY.
WELL... STARTING THE SCHOOL UP HAS BEEN A PRETTY COMPLEX JOB, TOO...
OH, OF COURSE!
NO OFFENSE INTENDED.
THIS IS OUR OLD HOUSE...BACK IN SAN FRANCISCO.
IT LOOKS REALLY NICE.
WHY DID YOU LEAVE?
I DUNNO. PERFECT OPPOR-TUNITY FOR BOTH MY DAD AND MY MOM, I GUESS...

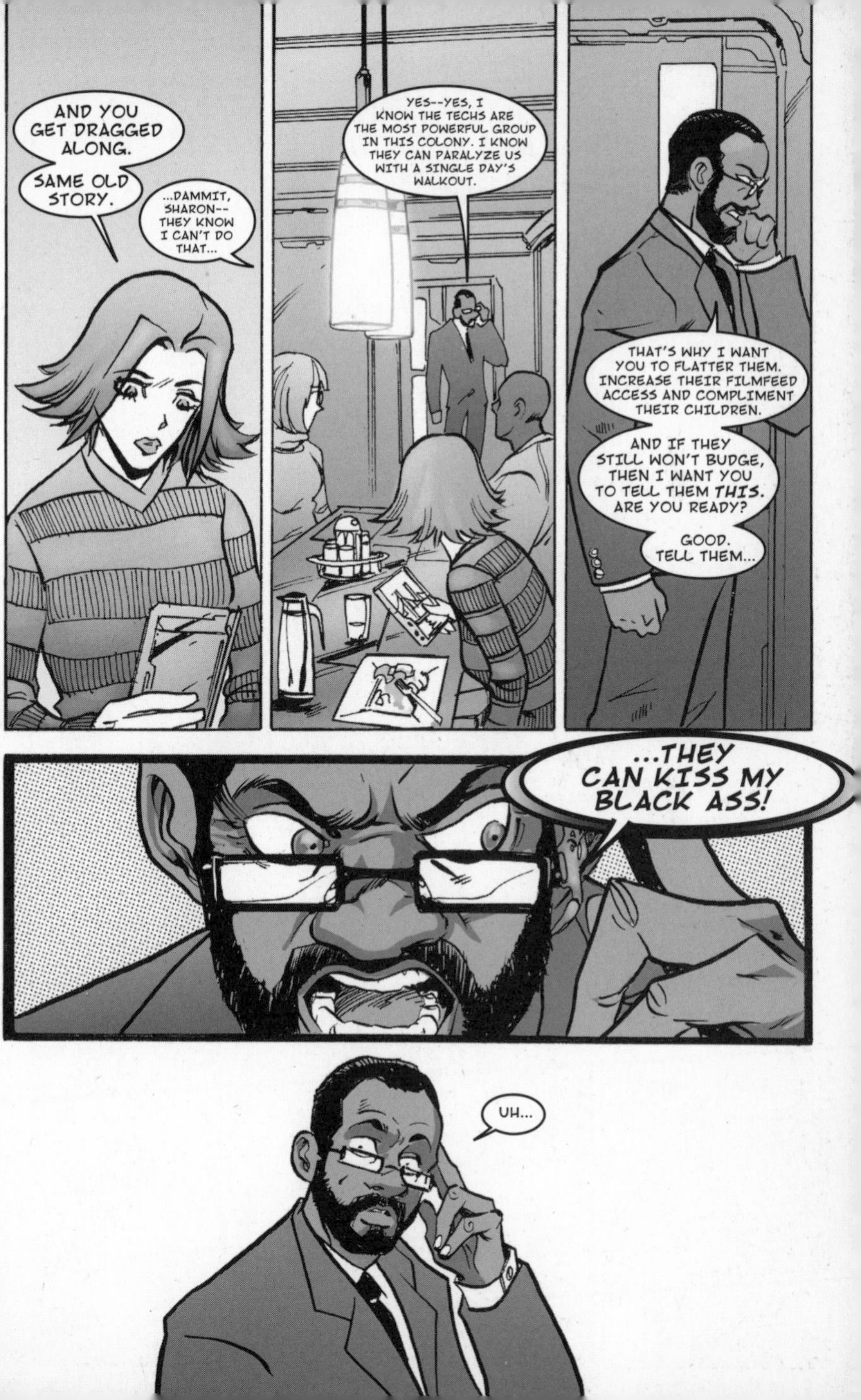
AND YOU GET DRAGGED ALONG.
SAME OLD STORY.
...DAMMIT, SHARON-- THEY KNOW I CAN'T DO THAT...
YES--YES, I KNOW THE TECHS ARE THE MOST POWERFUL GROUP IN THIS COLONY. I KNOW THEY CAN PARALYZE US WITH A SINGLE DAY'S WALKOUT.
THAT'S WHY I WANT YOU TO FLATTER THEM. INCREASE THEIR FILMFEED ACCESS AND COMPLIMENT THEIR CHILDREN.
AND IF THEY STILL WON'T BUDGE, THEN I WANT YOU TO TELL THEM THIS. ARE YOU READY?
GOOD. TELL THEM...
...THEY CAN KISS MY BLACK ASS!
UH...

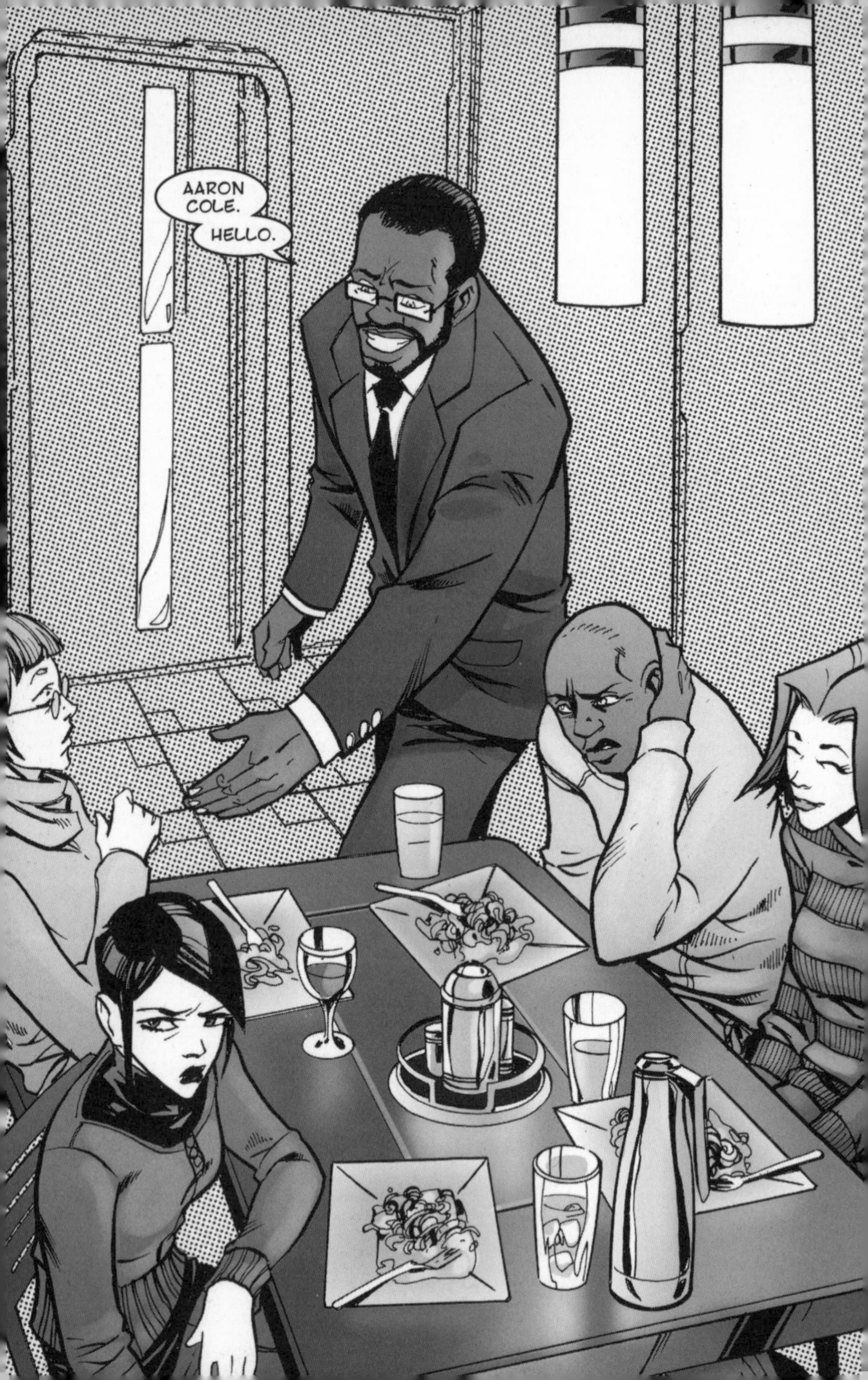
AARON COLE.
HELLO.

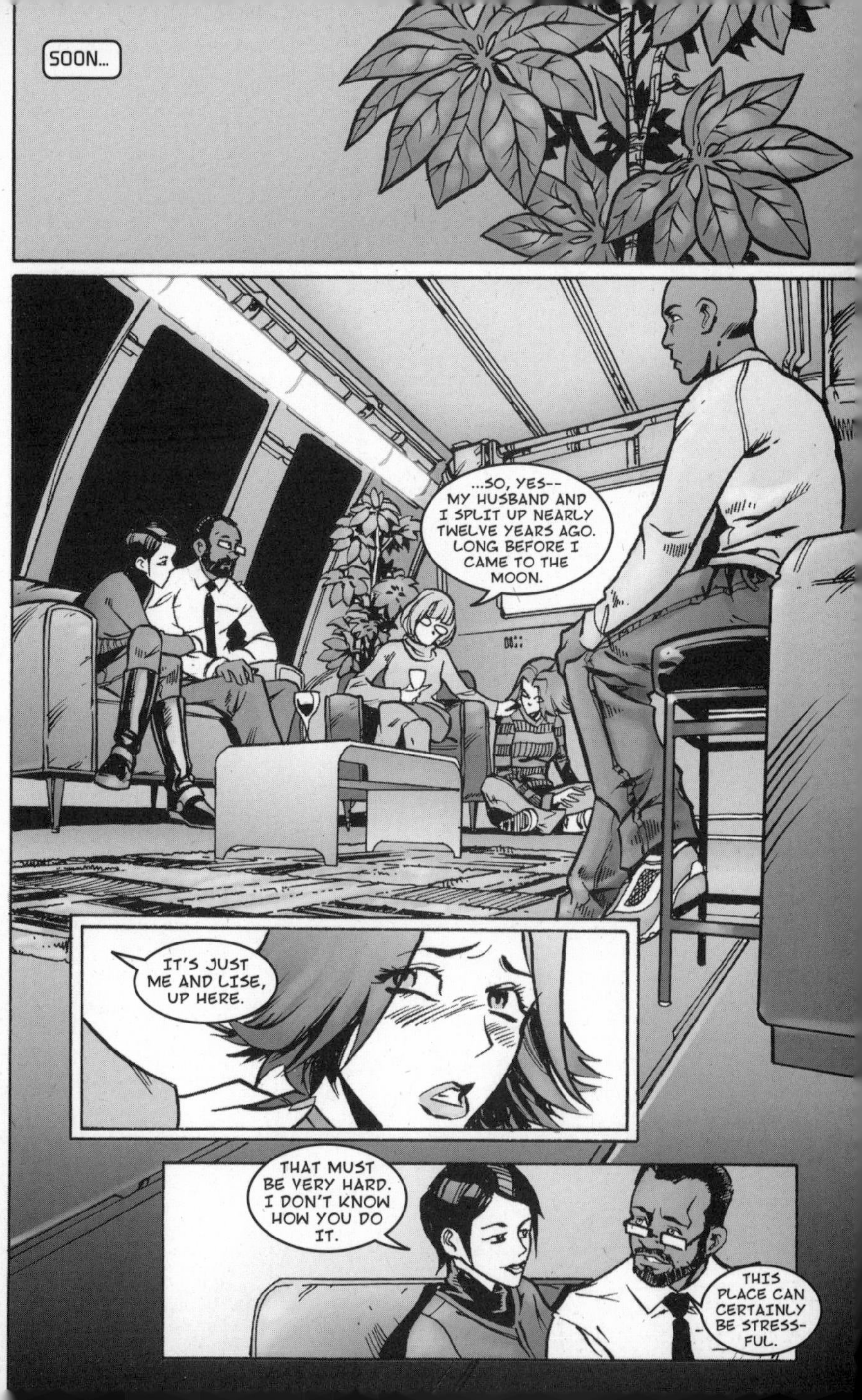
SOON...
...SO, YES-- MY HUSBAND AND I SPLIT UP NEARLY TWELVE YEARS AGO. LONG BEFORE I CAME TO THE MOON.
IT'S JUST ME AND LISE, UP HERE.
THAT MUST BE VERY HARD. I DON'T KNOW HOW YOU DO IT.
THIS PLACE CAN CERTAINLY BE STRESS-FUL.

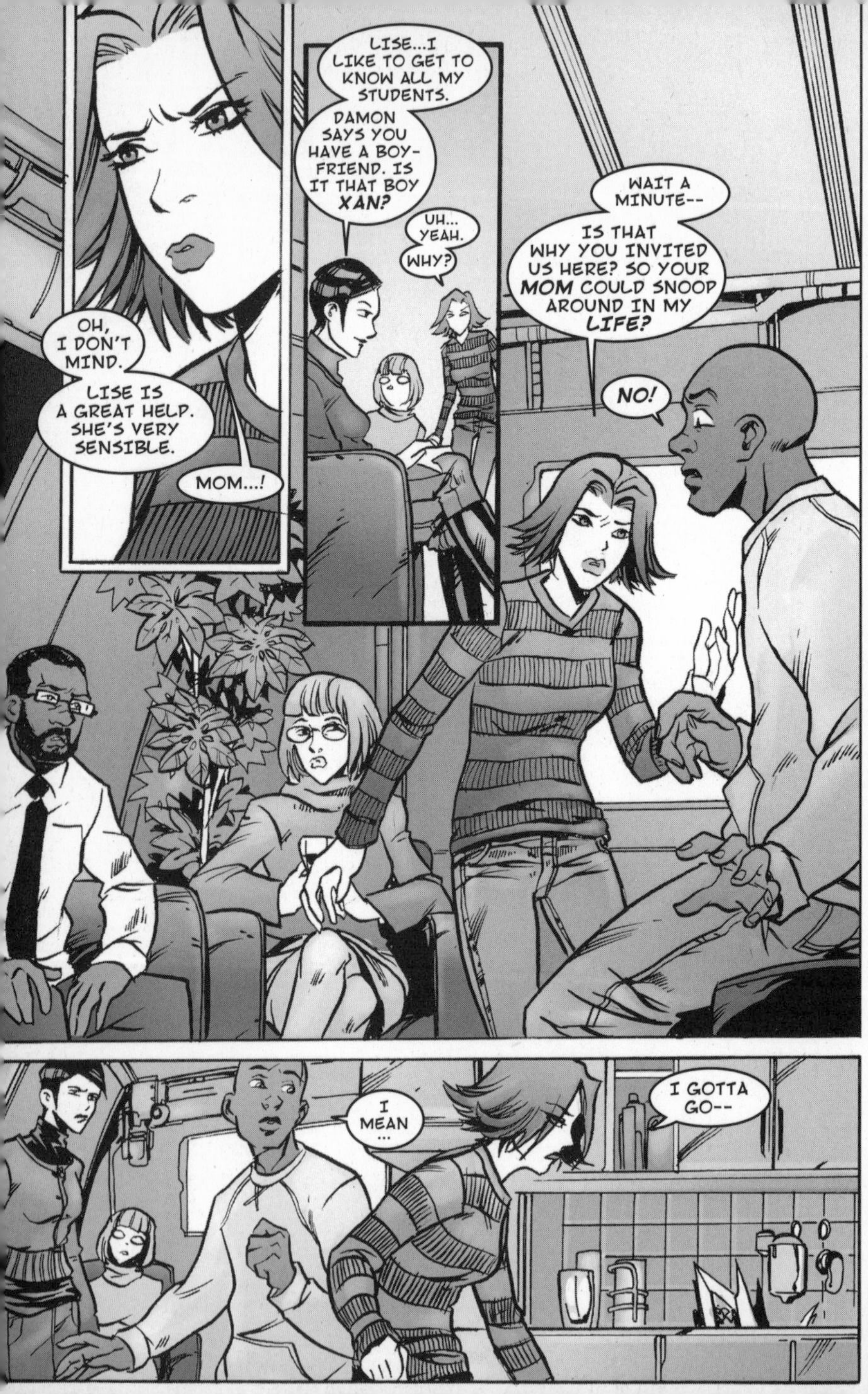

OH, I DON'T MIND.
LISE IS A GREAT HELP. SHE'S VERY SENSIBLE.
MOM...!
LISE...I LIKE TO GET TO KNOW ALL MY STUDENTS.
DAMON SAYS YOU HAVE A BOY-FRIEND. IS IT THAT BOY **XAN?**
UH... YEAH.
WHY?
WAIT A MINUTE--
IS THAT WHY YOU INVITED US HERE? SO YOUR **MOM** COULD SNOOP AROUND IN MY **LIFE?**
NO!
I MEAN ...
I GOTTA GO--

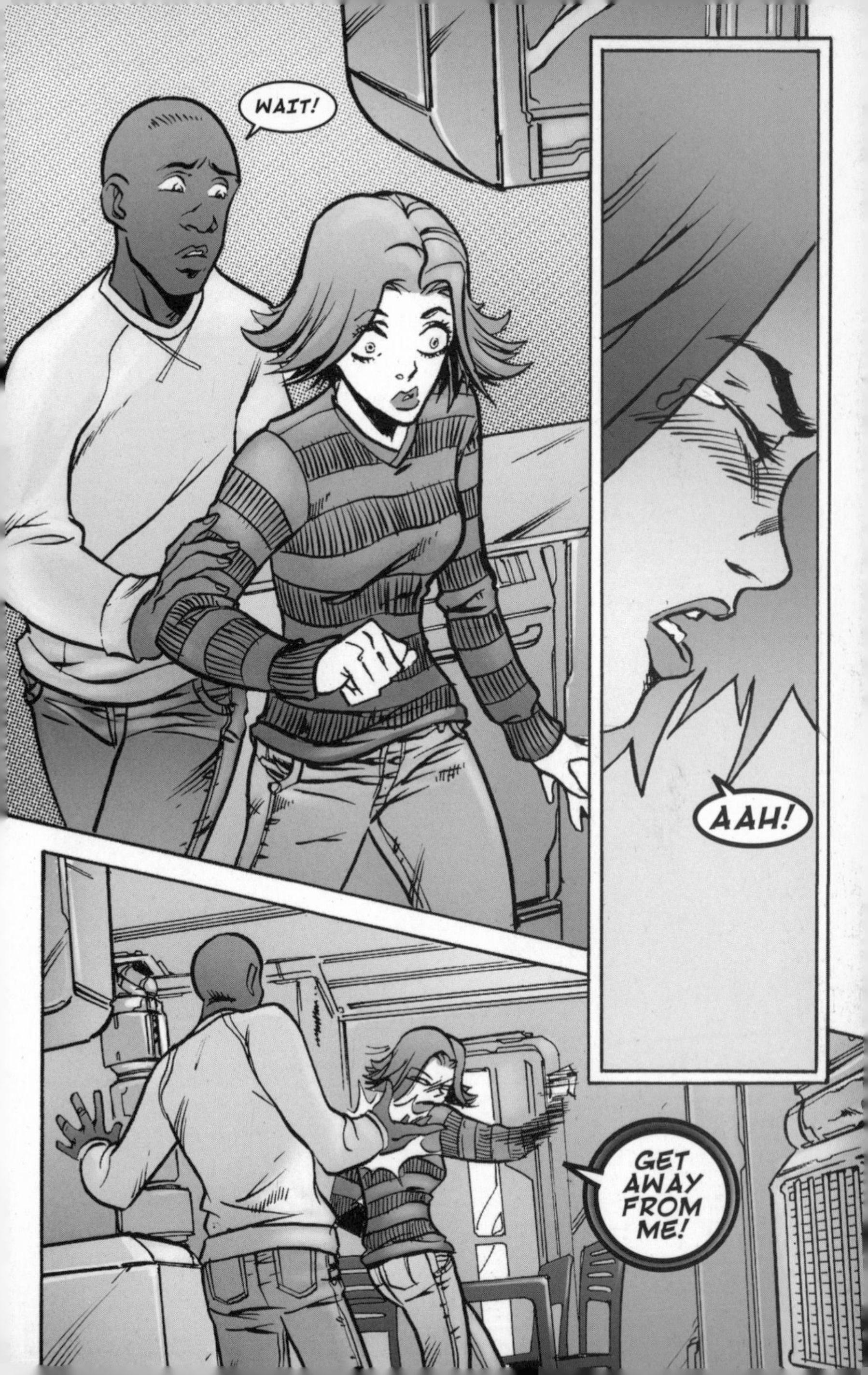
WAIT!
AAH!
GET AWAY FROM ME!

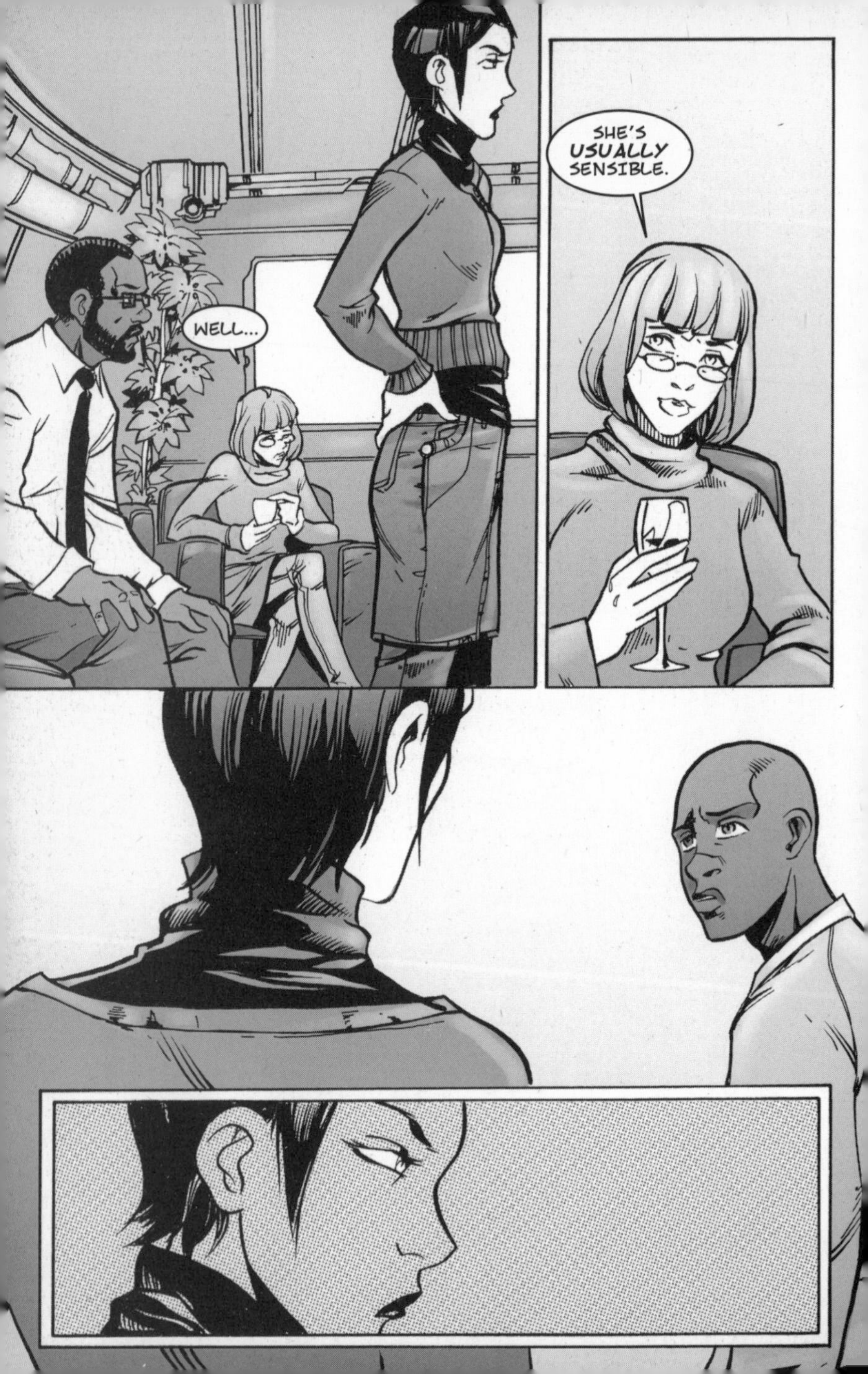
WELL...
SHE'S USUALLY SENSIBLE.

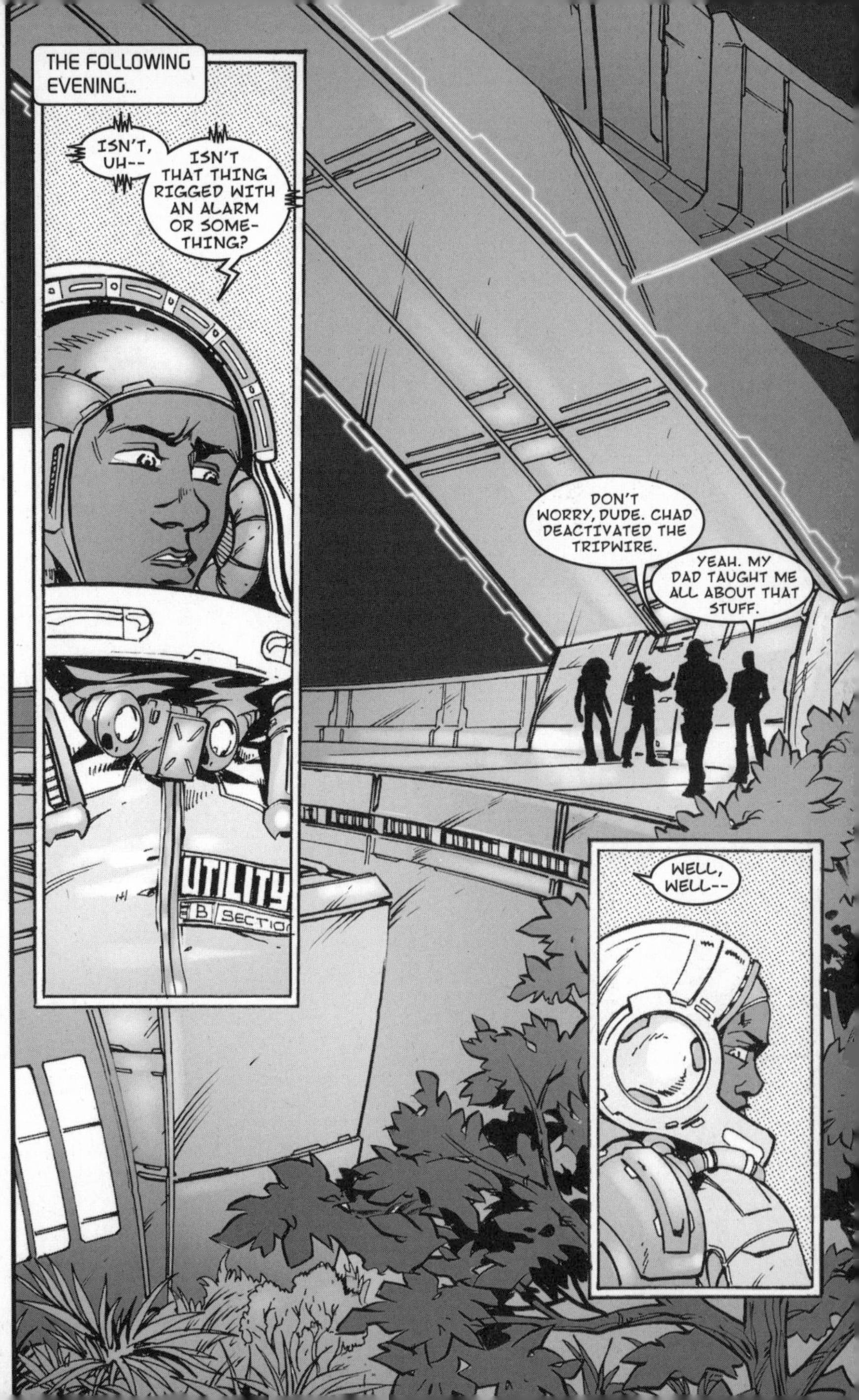
THE FOLLOWING EVENING...
ISN'T, UH--
ISN'T THAT THING RIGGED WITH AN ALARM OR SOME-THING?
UTILITY
B SECTIO
DON'T WORRY, DUDE. CHAD DEACTIVATED THE TRIPWIRE.
YEAH. MY DAD TAUGHT ME ALL ABOUT THAT STUFF.
WELL, WELL--

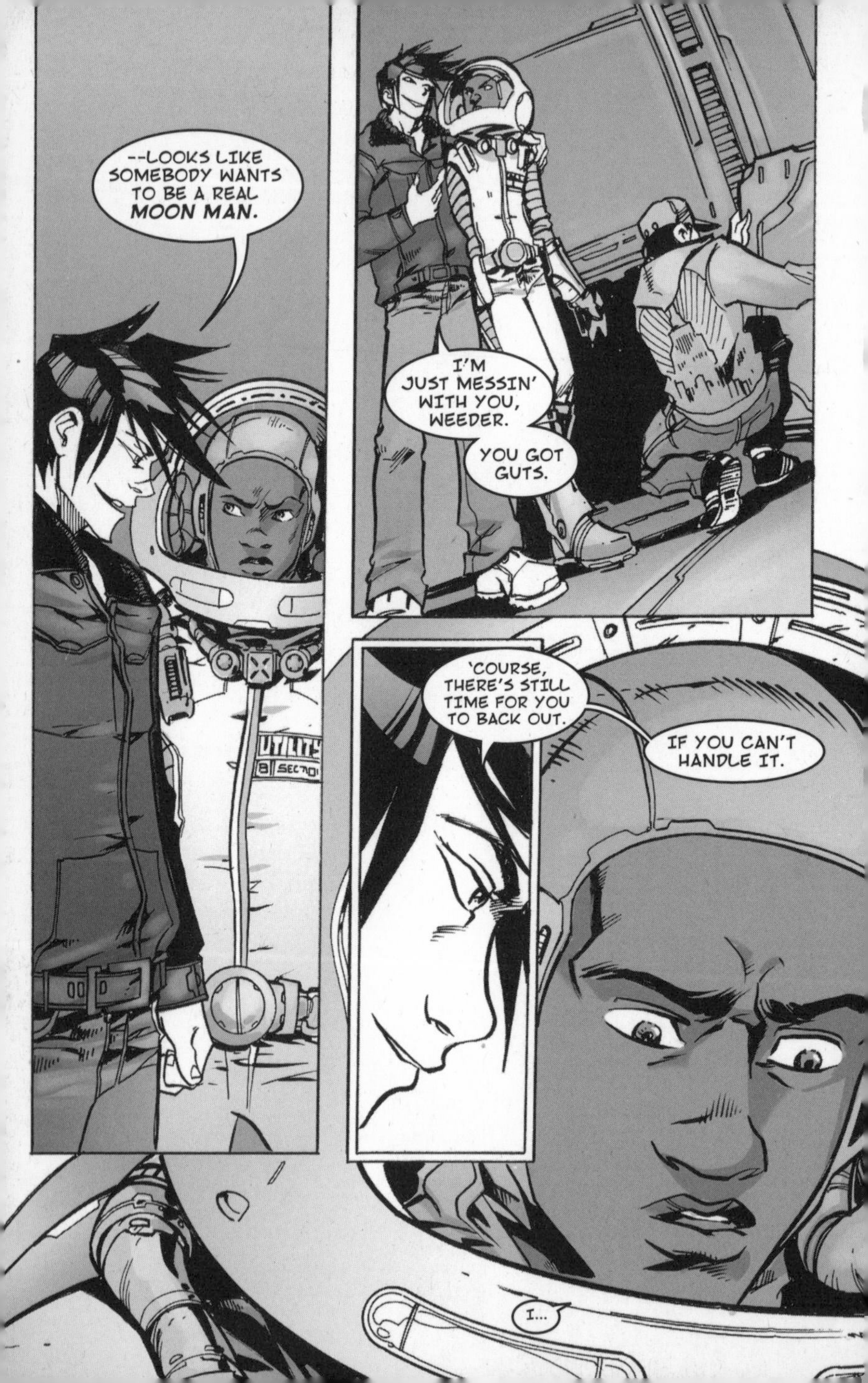
--LOOKS LIKE SOMEBODY WANTS TO BE A REAL **MOON MAN**.
I'M JUST MESSIN' WITH YOU, WEEDER.
YOU GOT GUTS.
'COURSE, THERE'S STILL TIME FOR YOU TO BACK OUT.
IF YOU CAN'T HANDLE IT.
I...

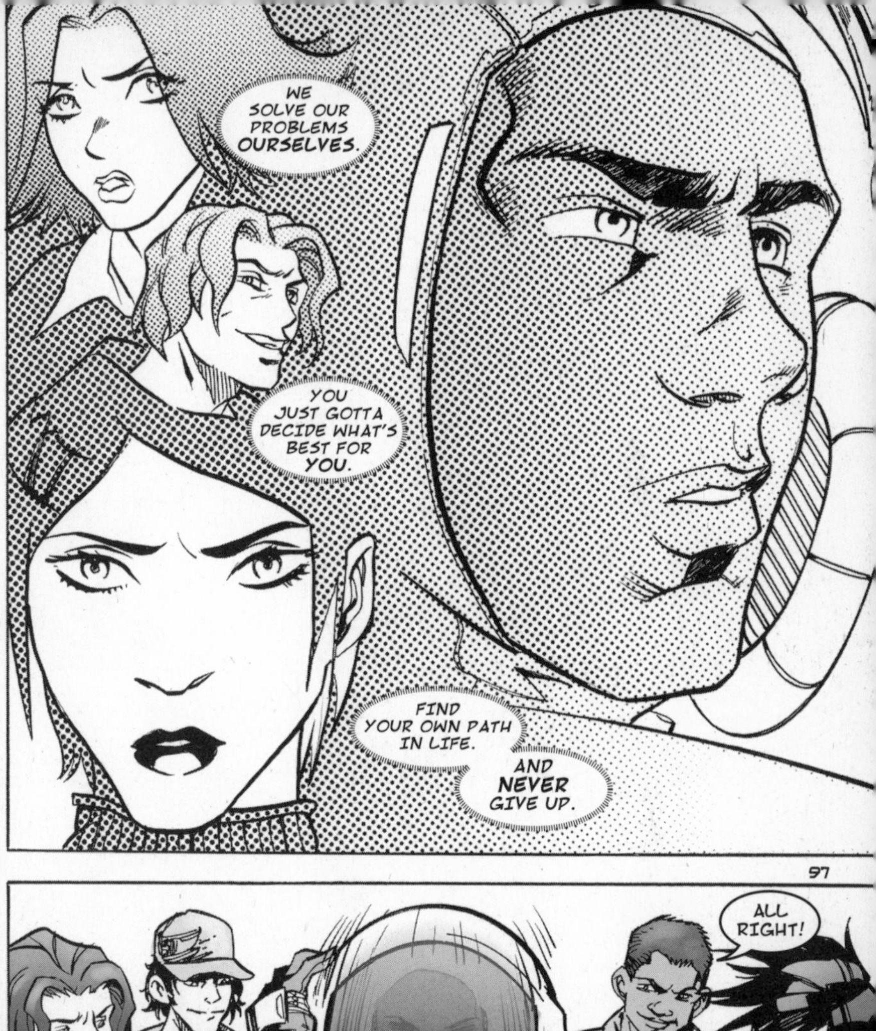
WE SOLVE OUR PROBLEMS **OURSELVES.**
YOU JUST GOTTA DECIDE WHAT'S BEST FOR **YOU.**
FIND YOUR OWN PATH IN LIFE.
AND **NEVER** GIVE UP.

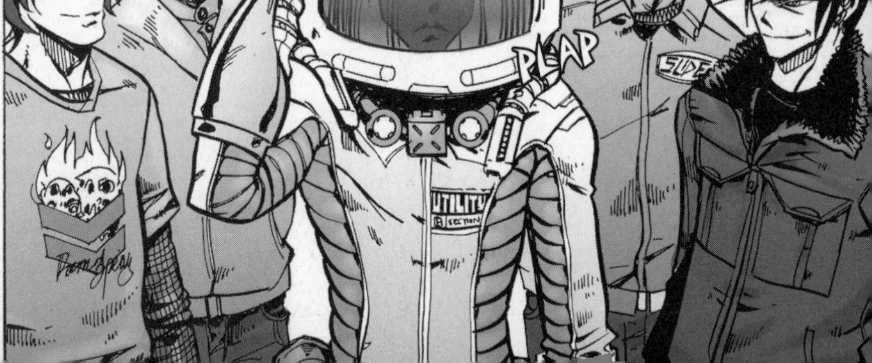
ALL RIGHT!
PLAP

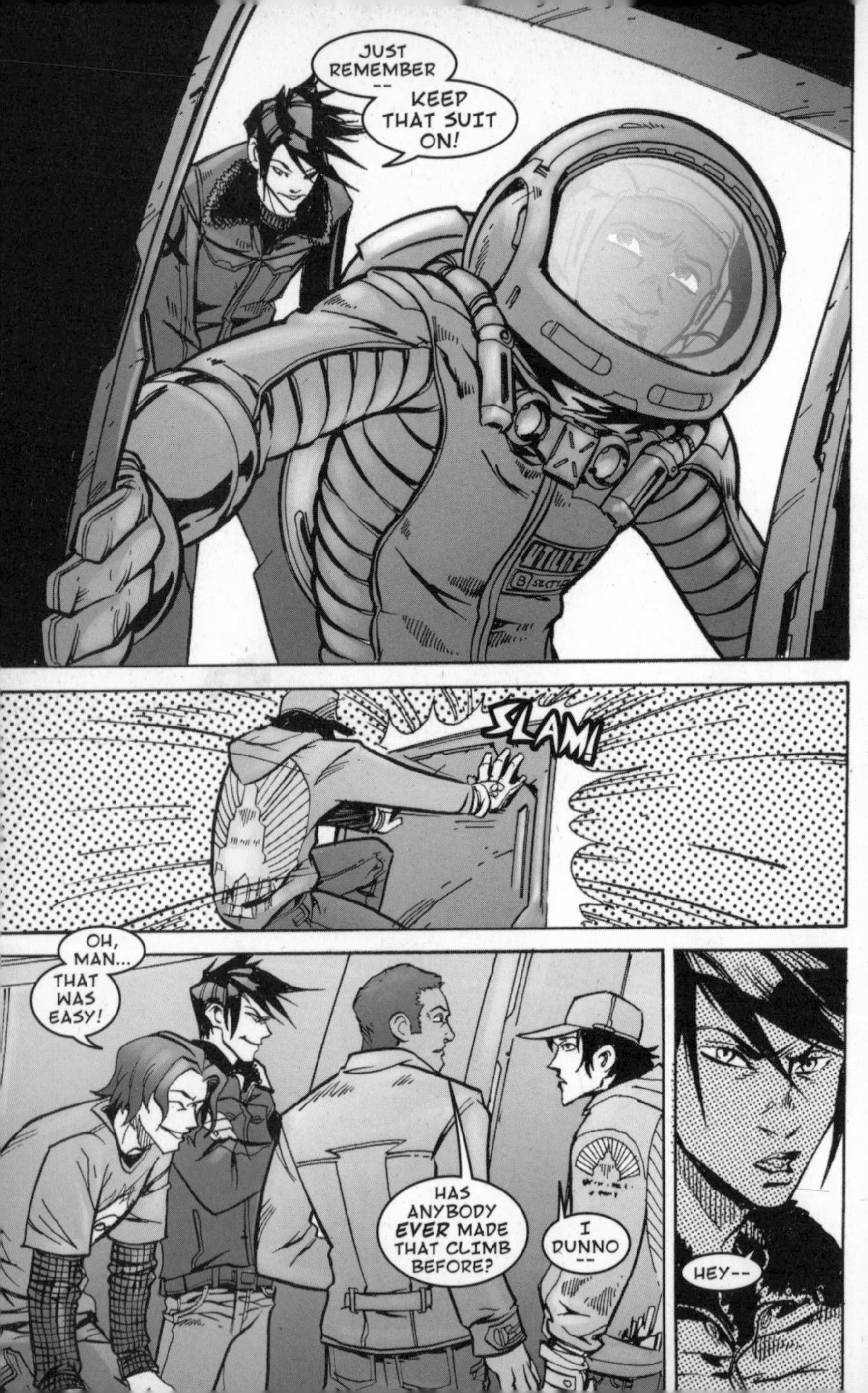

JUST REMEMBER --
KEEP THAT SUIT ON!
SLAM!
OH, MAN... THAT WAS EASY!
HAS ANYBODY **EVER** MADE THAT CLIMB BEFORE?
I DUNNO --
HEY--

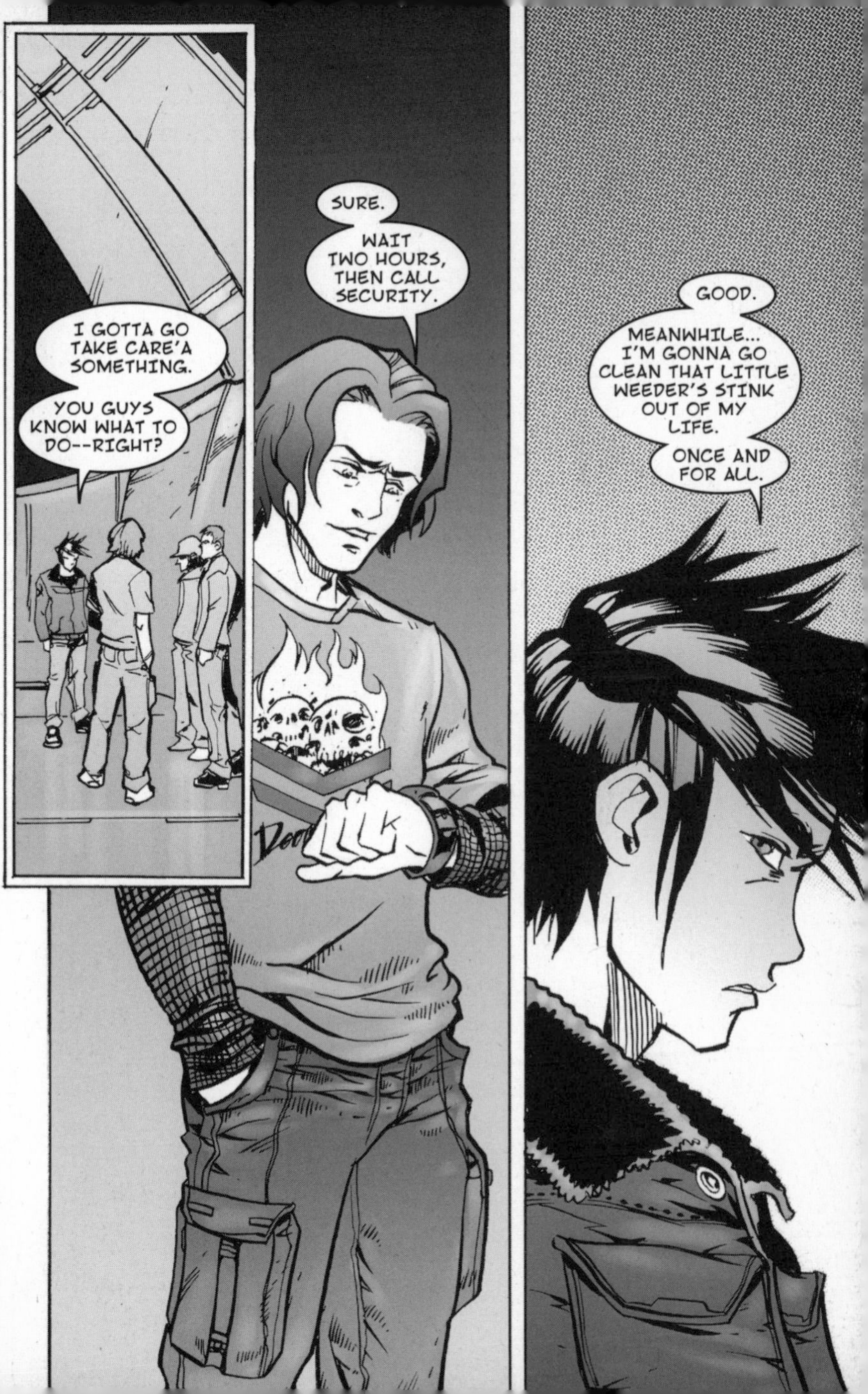

I GOTTA GO TAKE CARE'A SOMETHING.
YOU GUYS KNOW WHAT TO DO--RIGHT?
SURE.
WAIT TWO HOURS, THEN CALL SECURITY.
GOOD.
MEANWHILE... I'M GONNA GO CLEAN THAT LITTLE WEEDER'S STINK OUT OF MY LIFE.
ONCE AND FOR ALL.

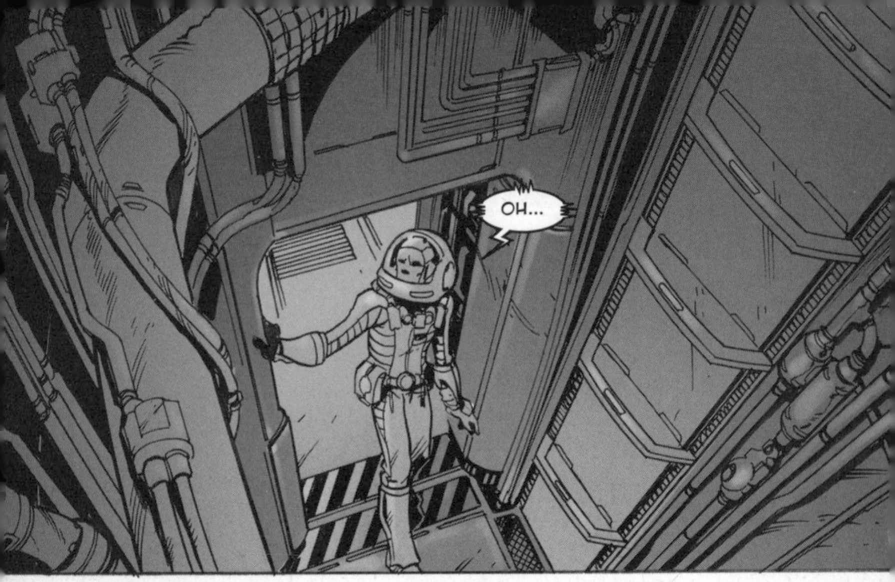
OH...

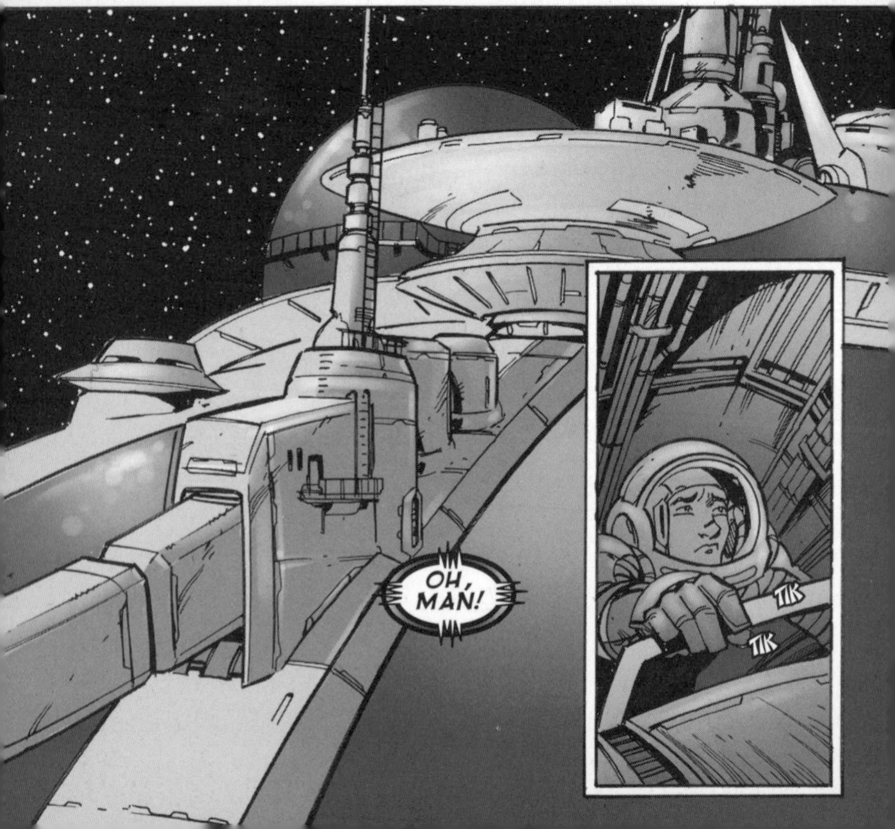
OH, MAN!
TIK
TIK

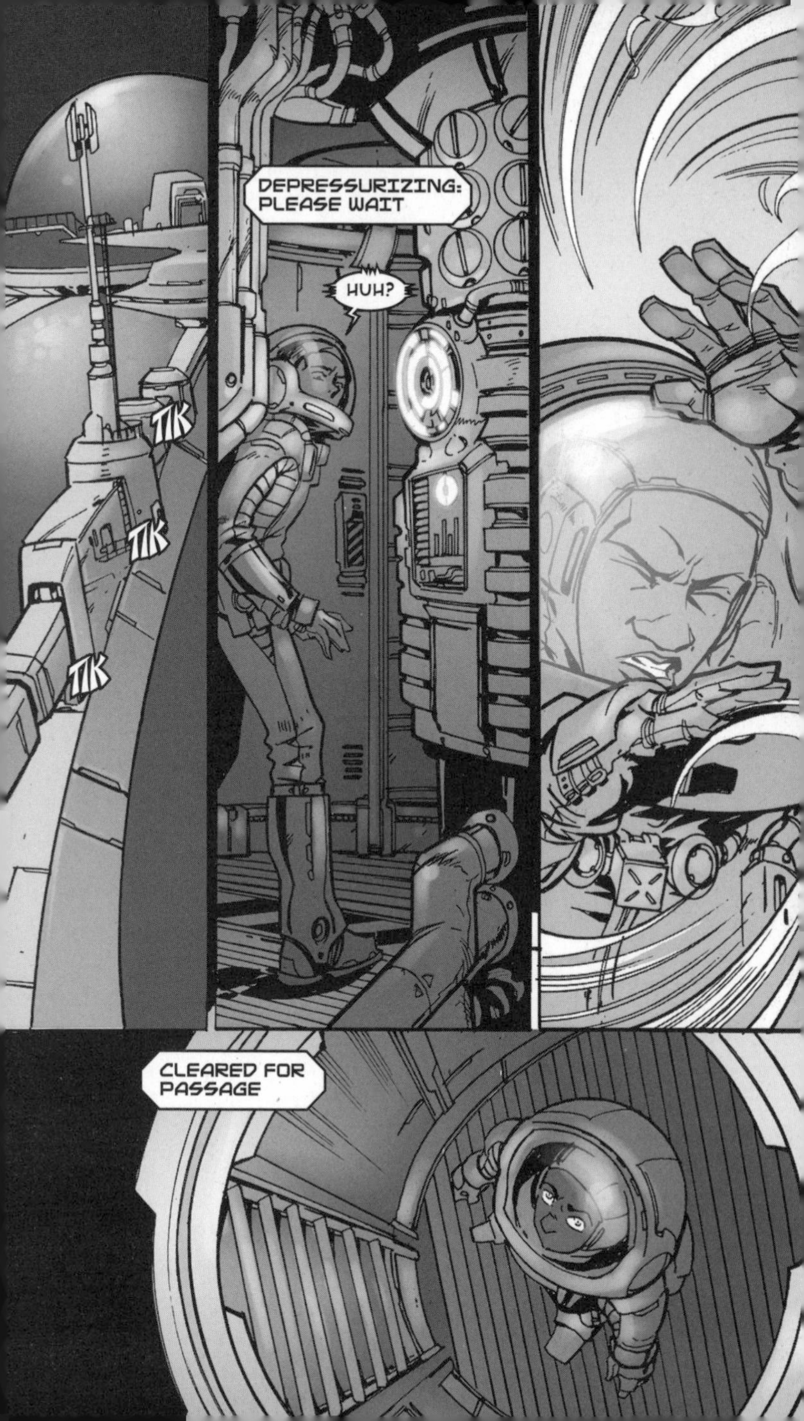
TIK
TIK
TIK
DEPRESSURIZING: PLEASE WAIT
HUH?
CLEARED FOR PASSAGE

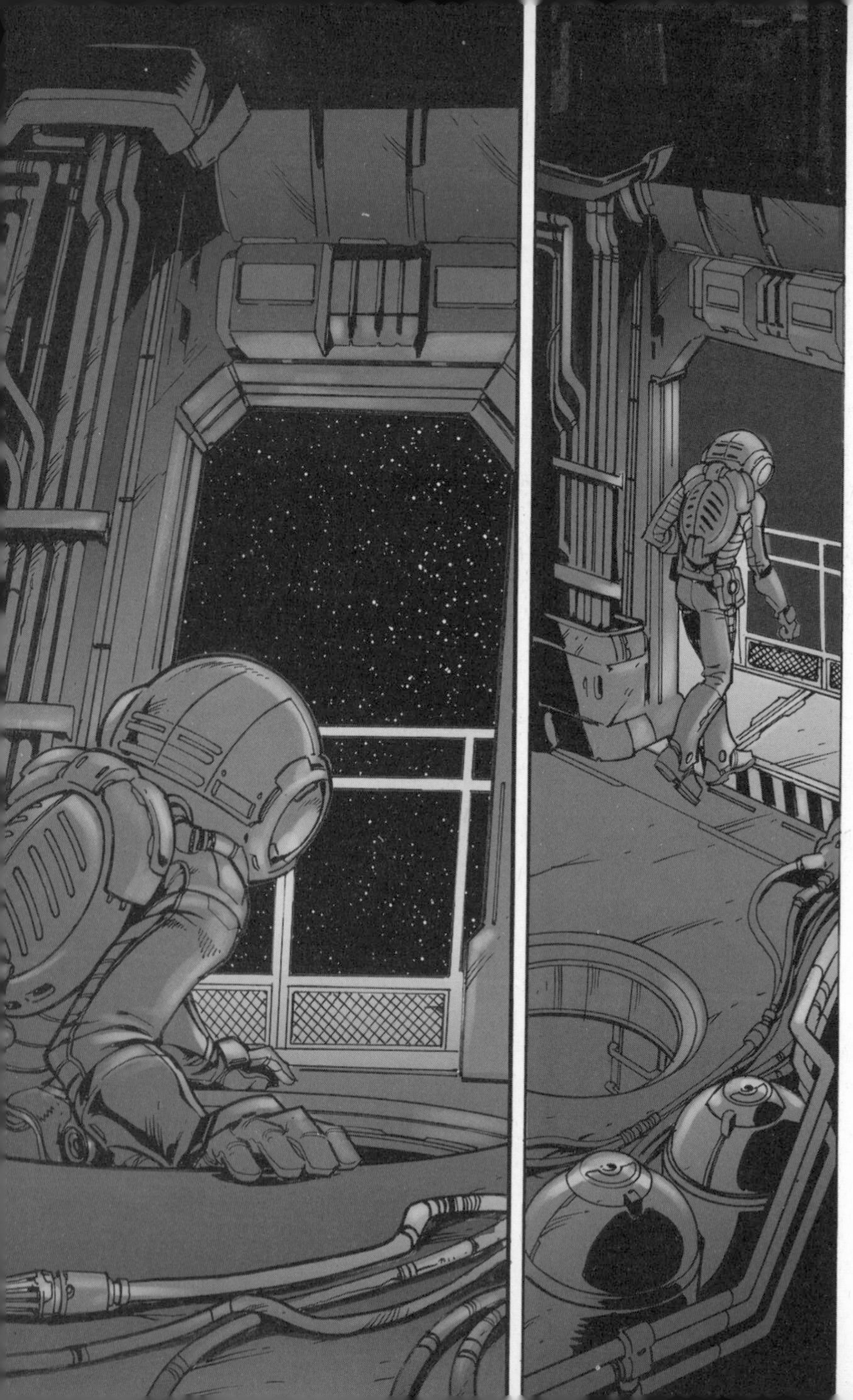

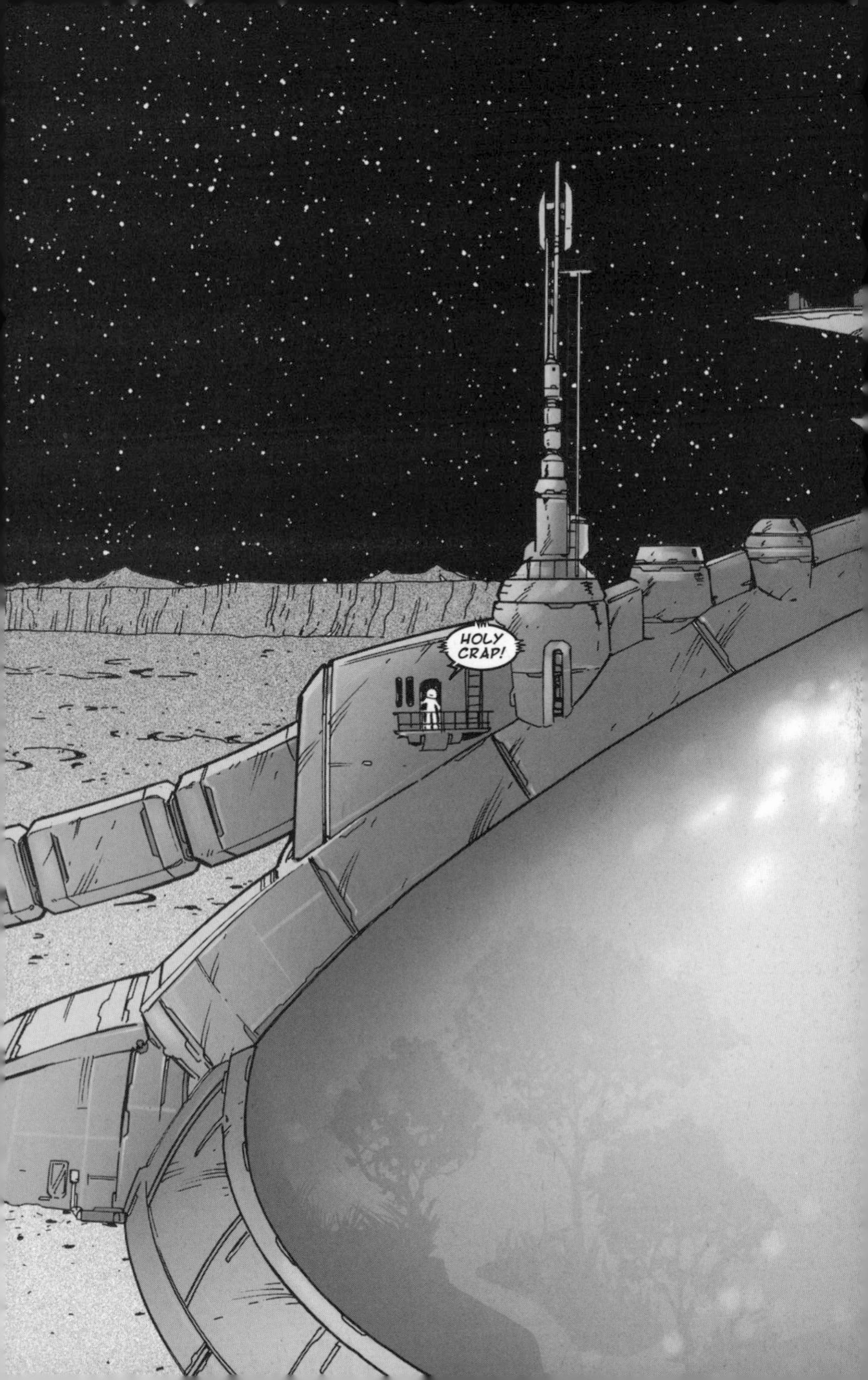
HOLY CRAP!

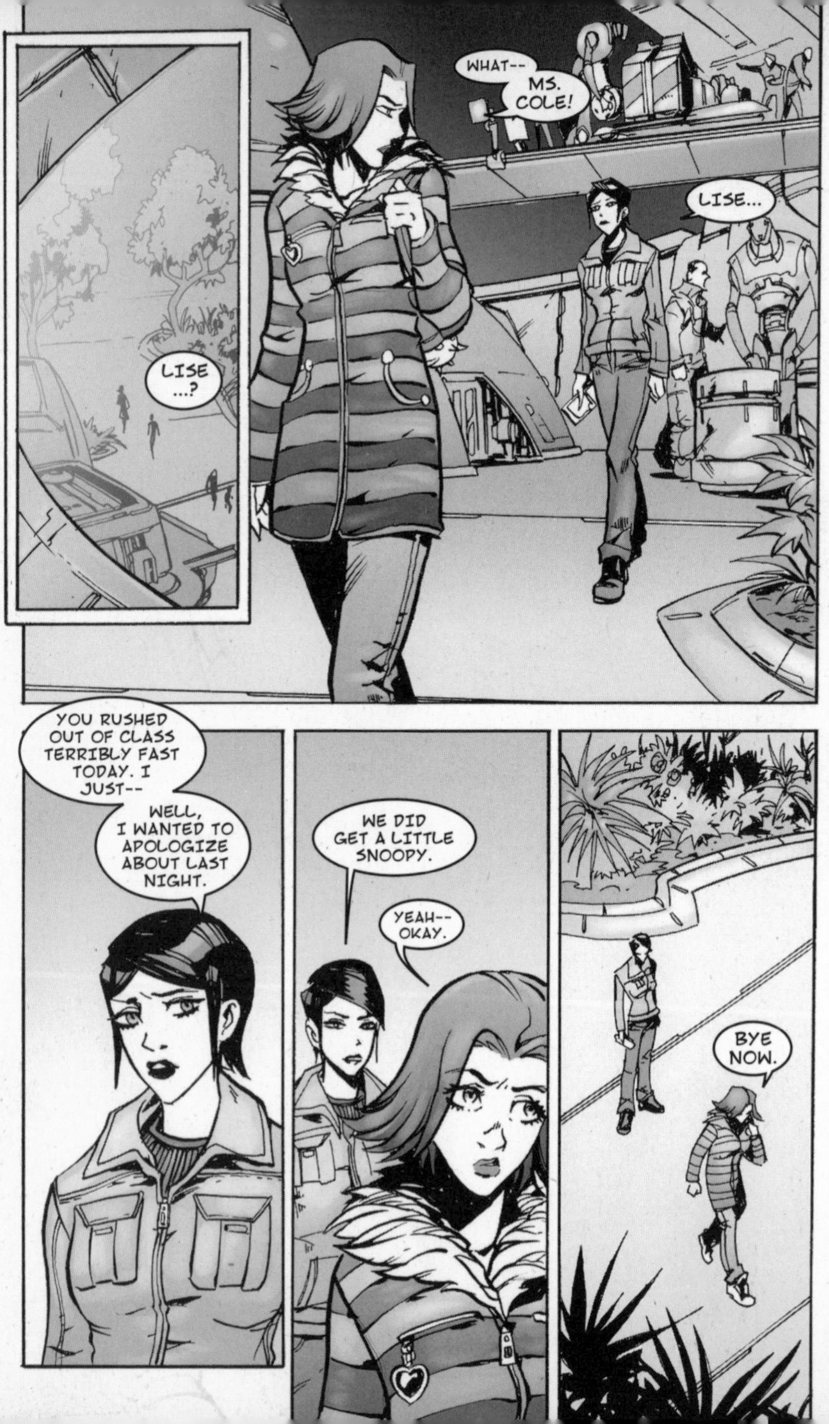
WHAT--
MS. COLE!
LISE...
LISE ...?
YOU RUSHED OUT OF CLASS TERRIBLY FAST TODAY. I JUST--
WELL, I WANTED TO APOLOGIZE ABOUT LAST NIGHT.
WE DID GET A LITTLE SNOOPY.
YEAH-- OKAY.
BYE NOW.

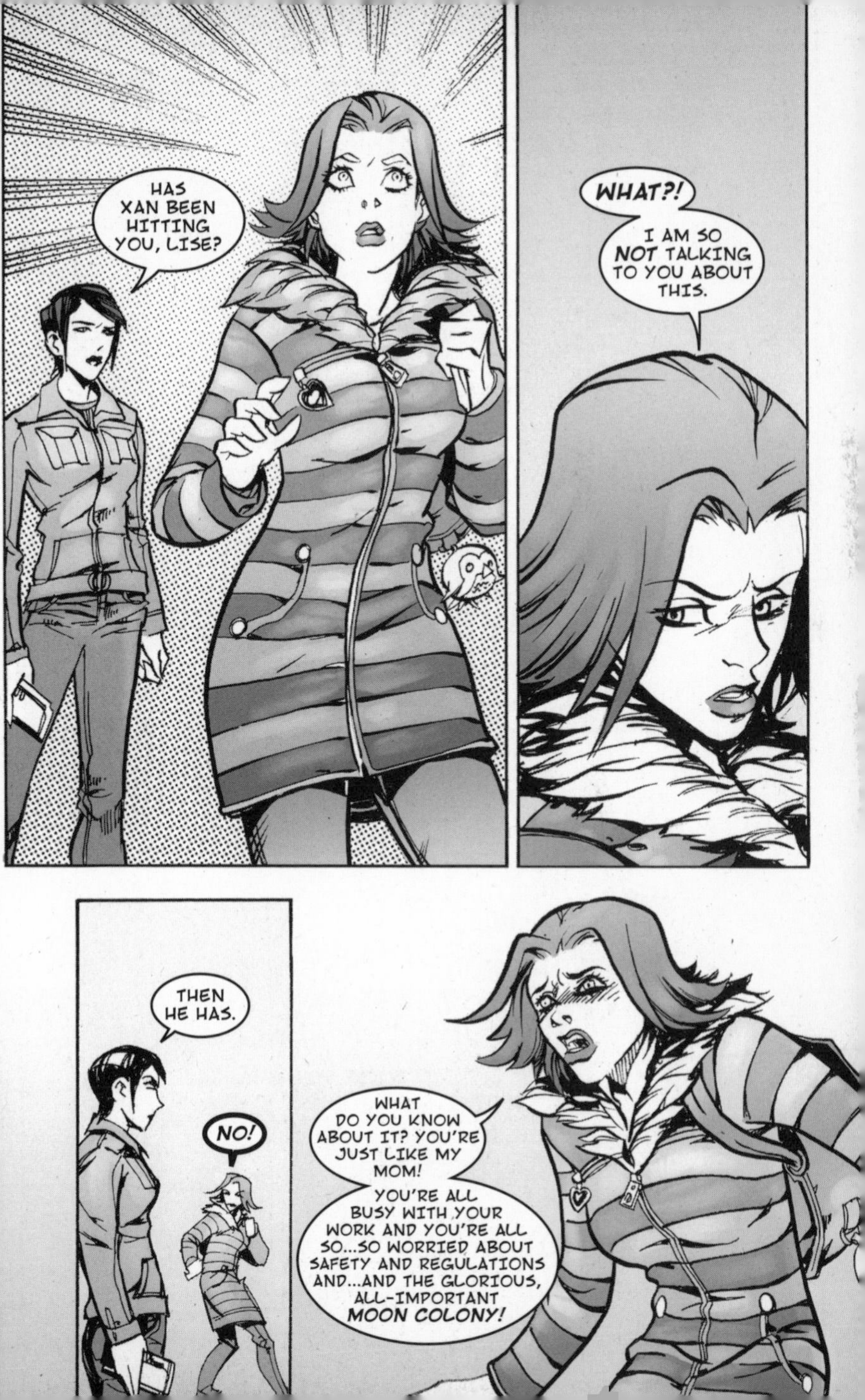
HAS XAN BEEN HITTING YOU, LISE?
WHAT?!
I AM SO **NOT** TALKING TO YOU ABOUT THIS.
THEN HE HAS.
NO!
WHAT DO YOU KNOW ABOUT IT? YOU'RE JUST LIKE MY MOM!
YOU'RE ALL BUSY WITH YOUR WORK AND YOU'RE ALL SO...SO WORRIED ABOUT SAFETY AND REGULATIONS AND...AND THE GLORIOUS, ALL-IMPORTANT **MOON COLONY!**

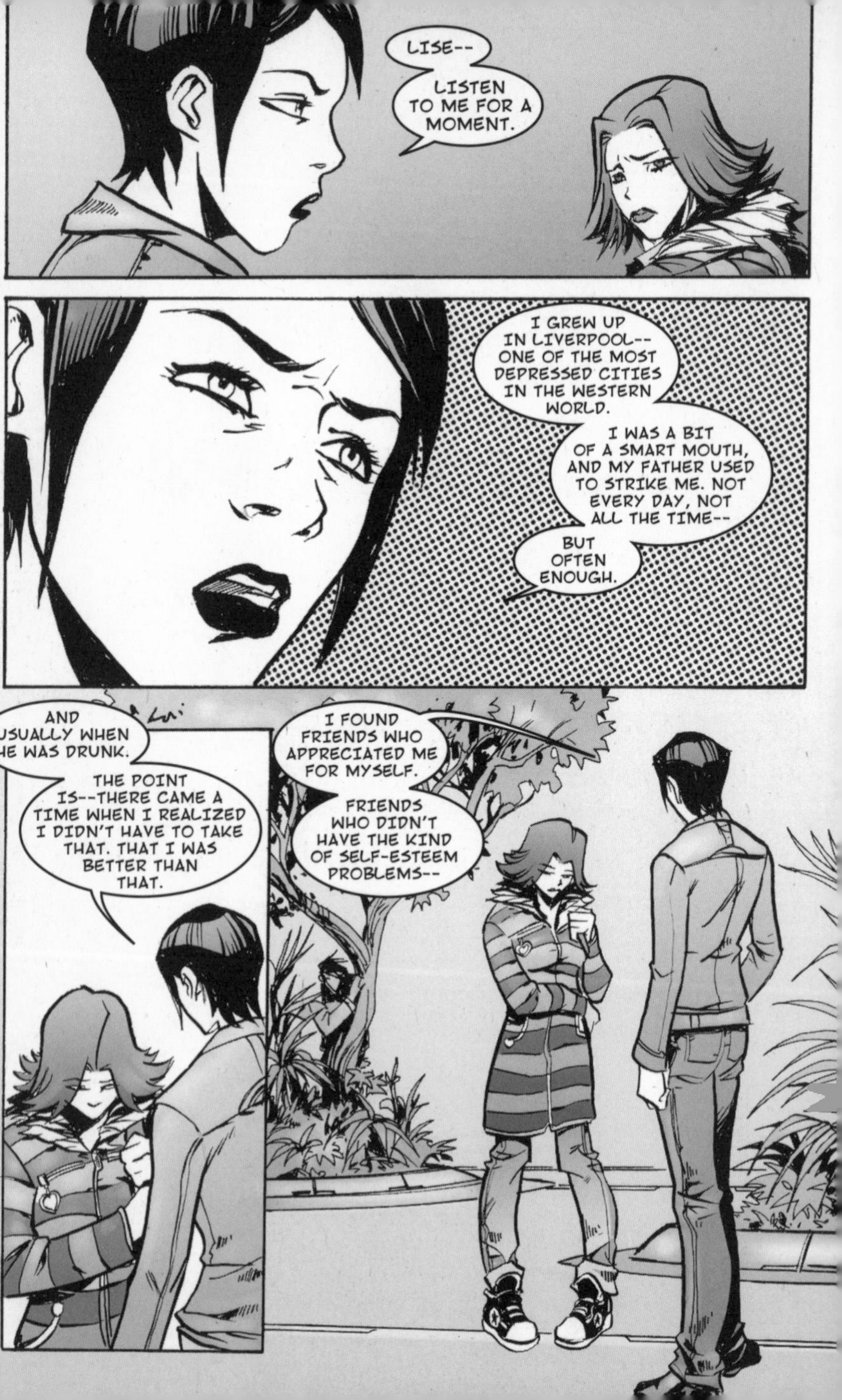

LISE--
LISTEN TO ME FOR A MOMENT.
I GREW UP IN LIVERPOOL-- ONE OF THE MOST DEPRESSED CITIES IN THE WESTERN WORLD.
I WAS A BIT OF A SMART MOUTH, AND MY FATHER USED TO STRIKE ME. NOT EVERY DAY, NOT ALL THE TIME--
BUT OFTEN ENOUGH.
AND USUALLY WHEN HE WAS DRUNK.
THE POINT IS--THERE CAME A TIME WHEN I REALIZED I DIDN'T HAVE TO TAKE THAT. THAT I WAS BETTER THAN THAT.
I FOUND FRIENDS WHO APPRECIATED ME FOR MYSELF.
FRIENDS WHO DIDN'T HAVE THE KIND OF SELF-ESTEEM PROBLEMS--

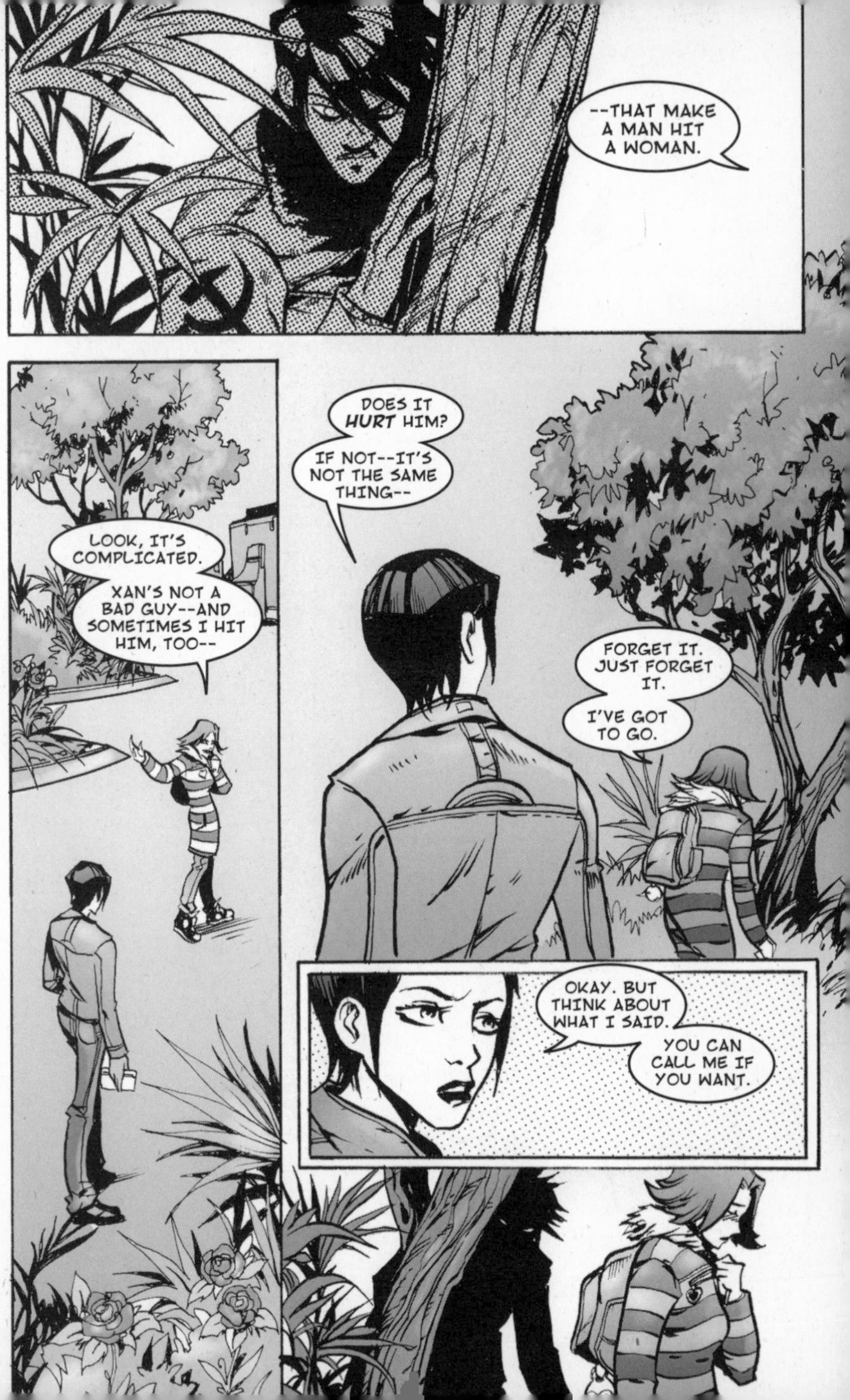
--THAT MAKE A MAN HIT A WOMAN.
LOOK, IT'S COMPLICATED.
XAN'S NOT A BAD GUY--AND SOMETIMES I HIT HIM, TOO--
DOES IT *HURT* HIM?
IF NOT--IT'S NOT THE SAME THING--
FORGET IT. JUST FORGET IT.
I'VE GOT TO GO.
OKAY. BUT THINK ABOUT WHAT I SAID.
YOU CAN CALL ME IF YOU WANT.

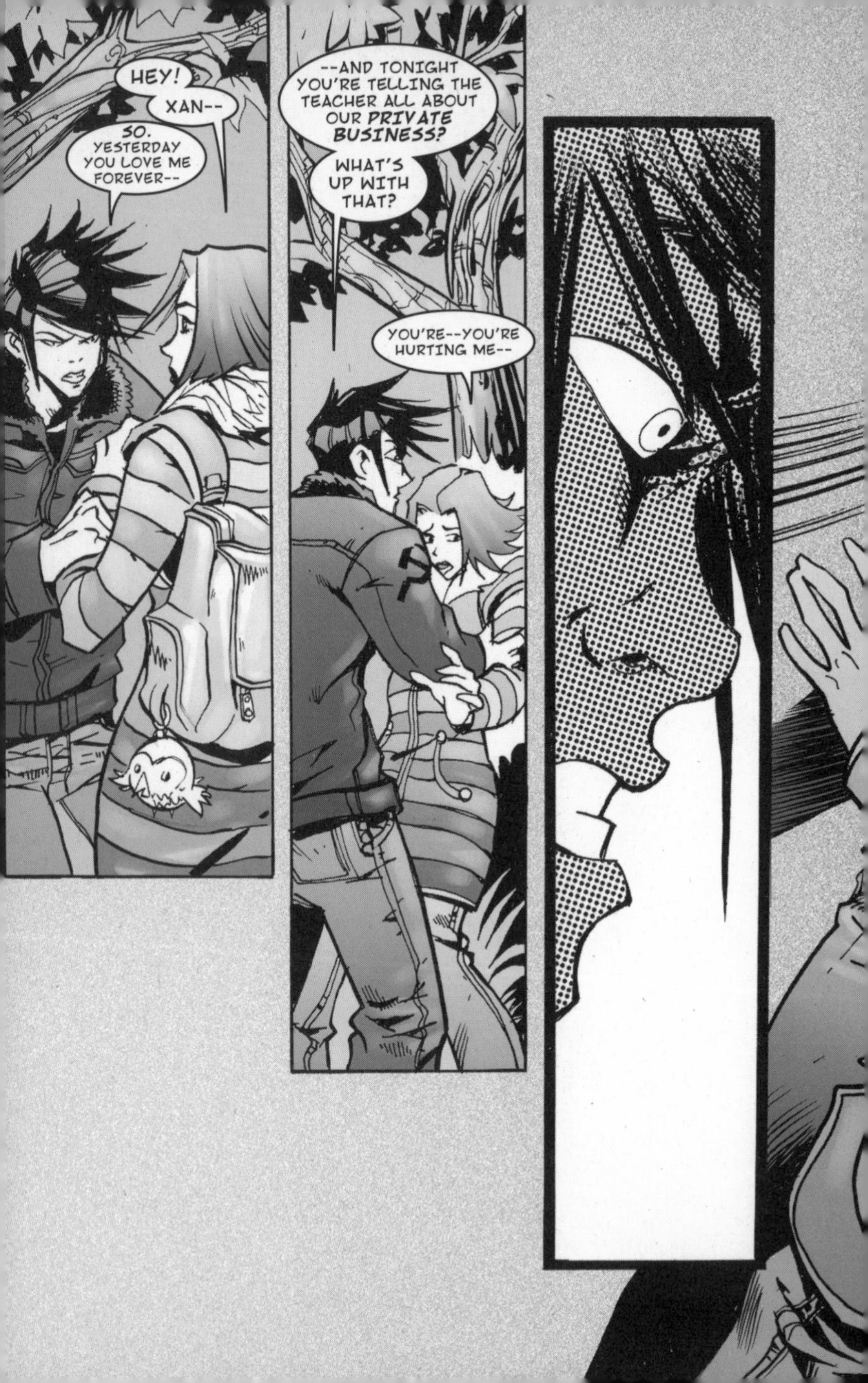
HEY!
XAN--
SO. YESTERDAY YOU LOVE ME FOREVER--
--AND TONIGHT YOU'RE TELLING THE TEACHER ALL ABOUT OUR *PRIVATE BUSINESS?*
WHAT'S UP WITH THAT?
YOU'RE--YOU'RE HURTING ME--

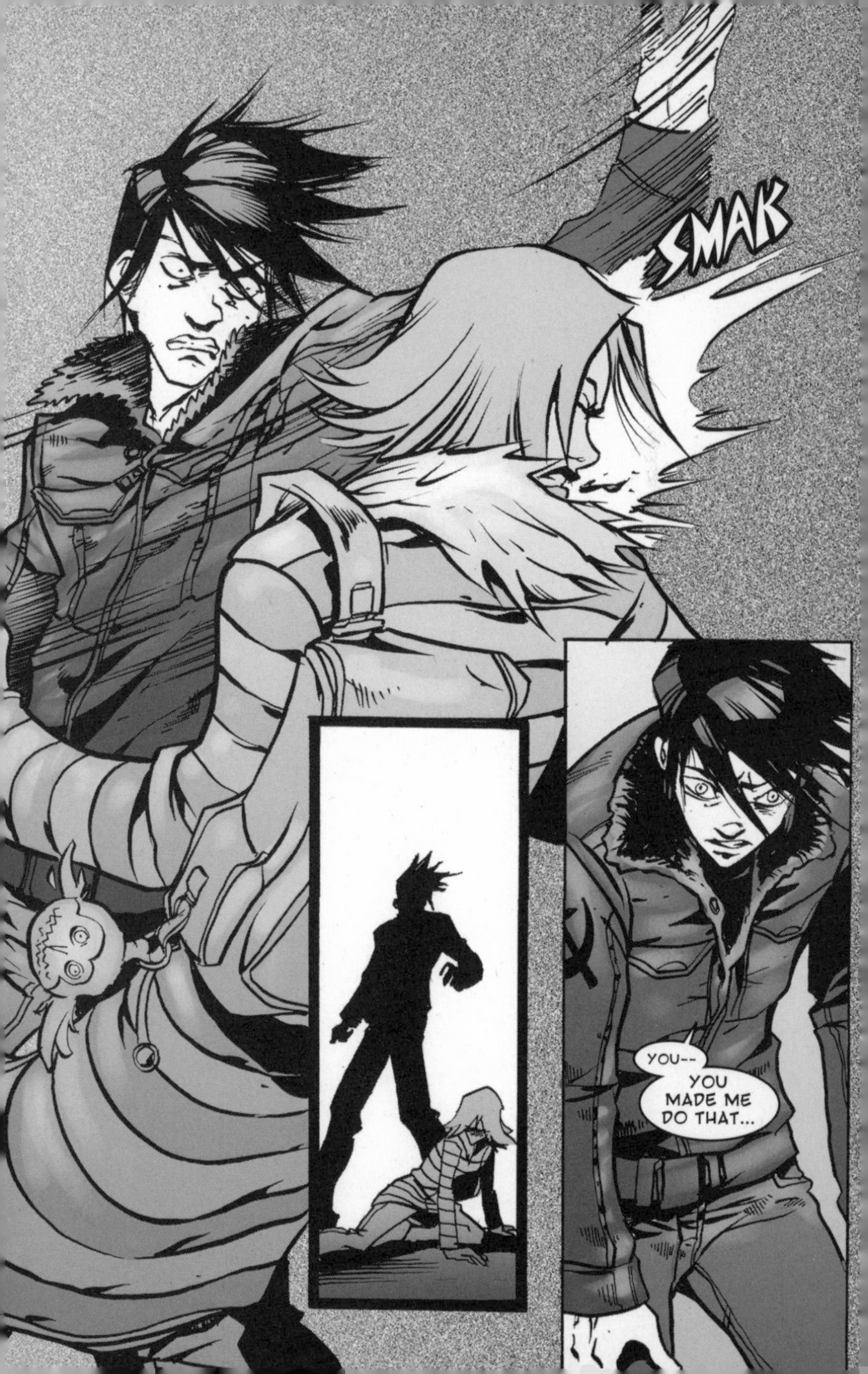
SMAK
YOU--
YOU MADE ME DO THAT...

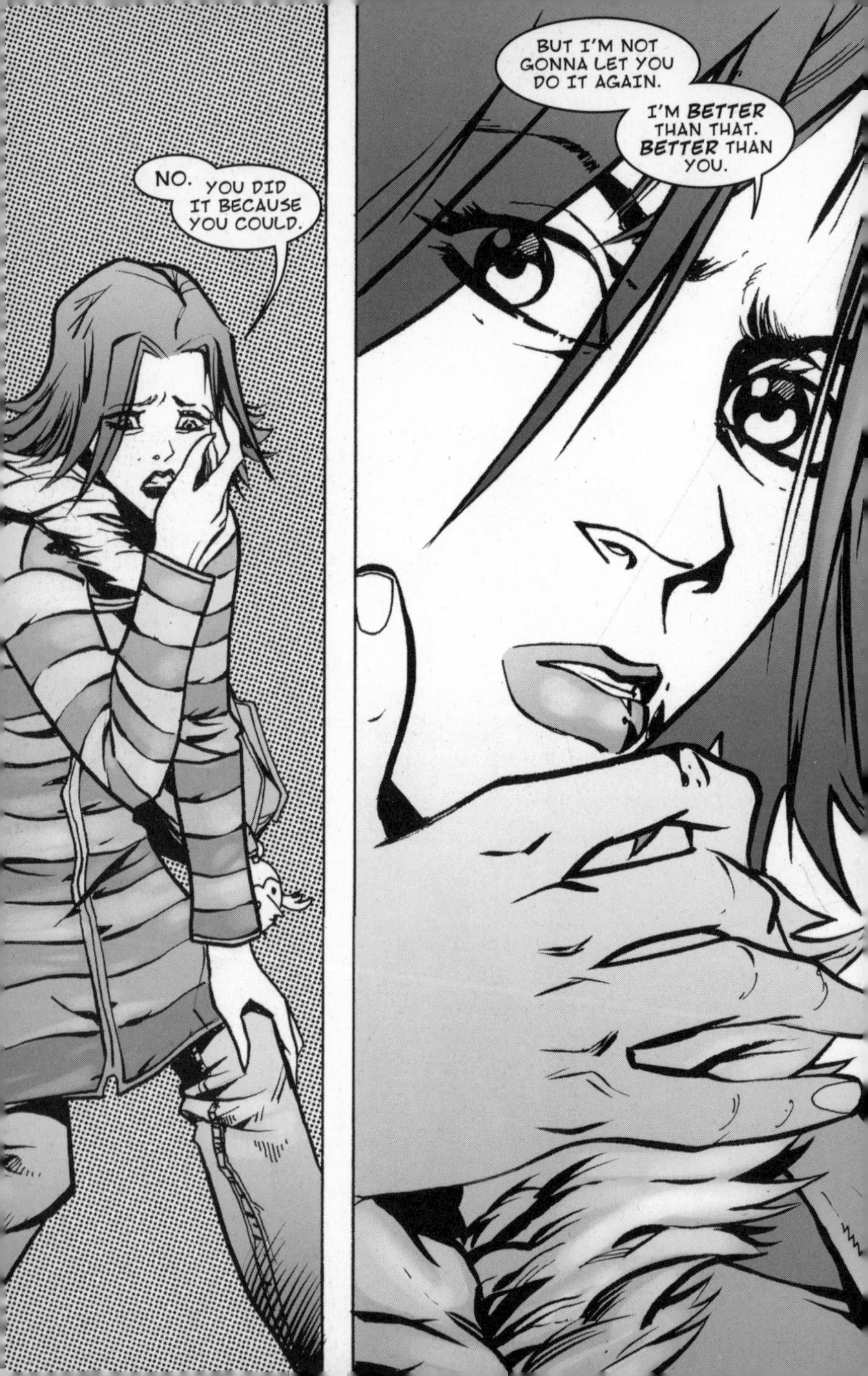
NO.
YOU DID IT BECAUSE YOU COULD.
BUT I'M NOT GONNA LET YOU DO IT AGAIN.
I'M BETTER THAN THAT. BETTER THAN YOU.

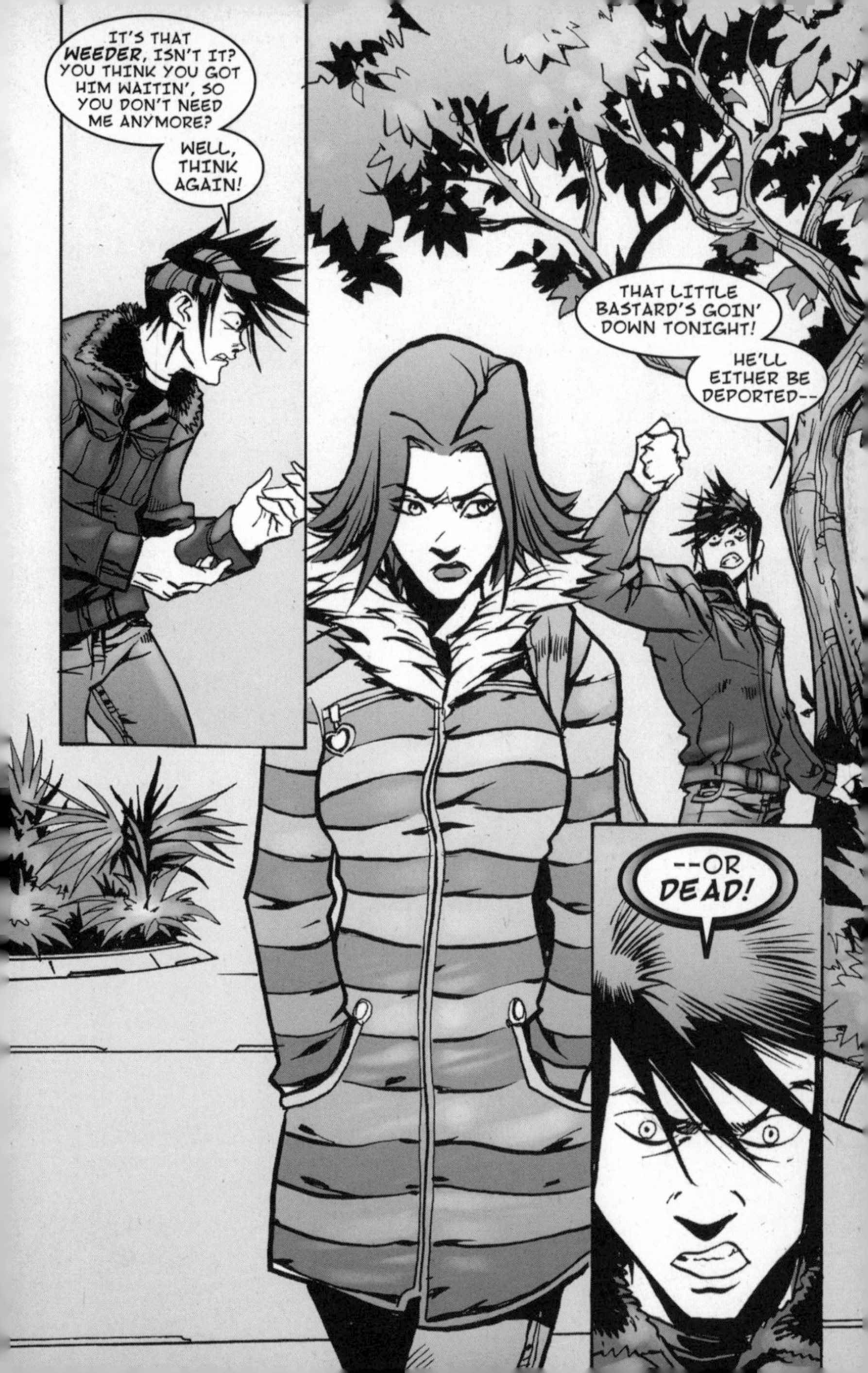
IT'S THAT WEEDER, ISN'T IT? YOU THINK YOU GOT HIM WAITIN', SO YOU DON'T NEED ME ANYMORE?
WELL, THINK AGAIN!
THAT LITTLE BASTARD'S GOIN' DOWN TONIGHT!
HE'LL EITHER BE DEPORTED--
--OR DEAD!

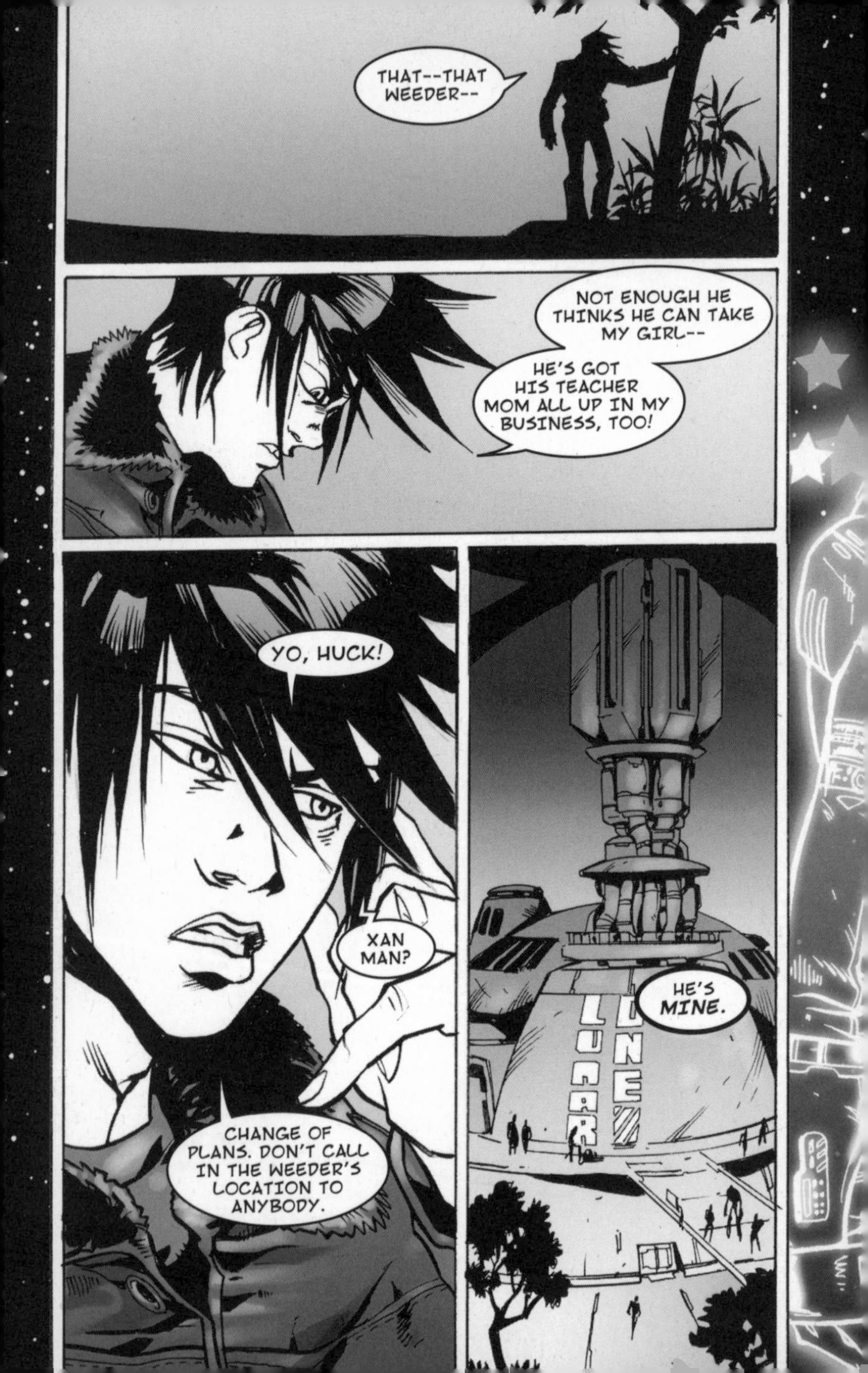
THAT--THAT WEEDER--
NOT ENOUGH HE THINKS HE CAN TAKE MY GIRL--
HE'S GOT HIS TEACHER MOM ALL UP IN MY BUSINESS, TOO!
YO, HUCK!
XAN MAN?
CHANGE OF PLANS. DON'T CALL IN THE WEEDER'S LOCATION TO ANYBODY.
LUNAR
HE'S MINE.

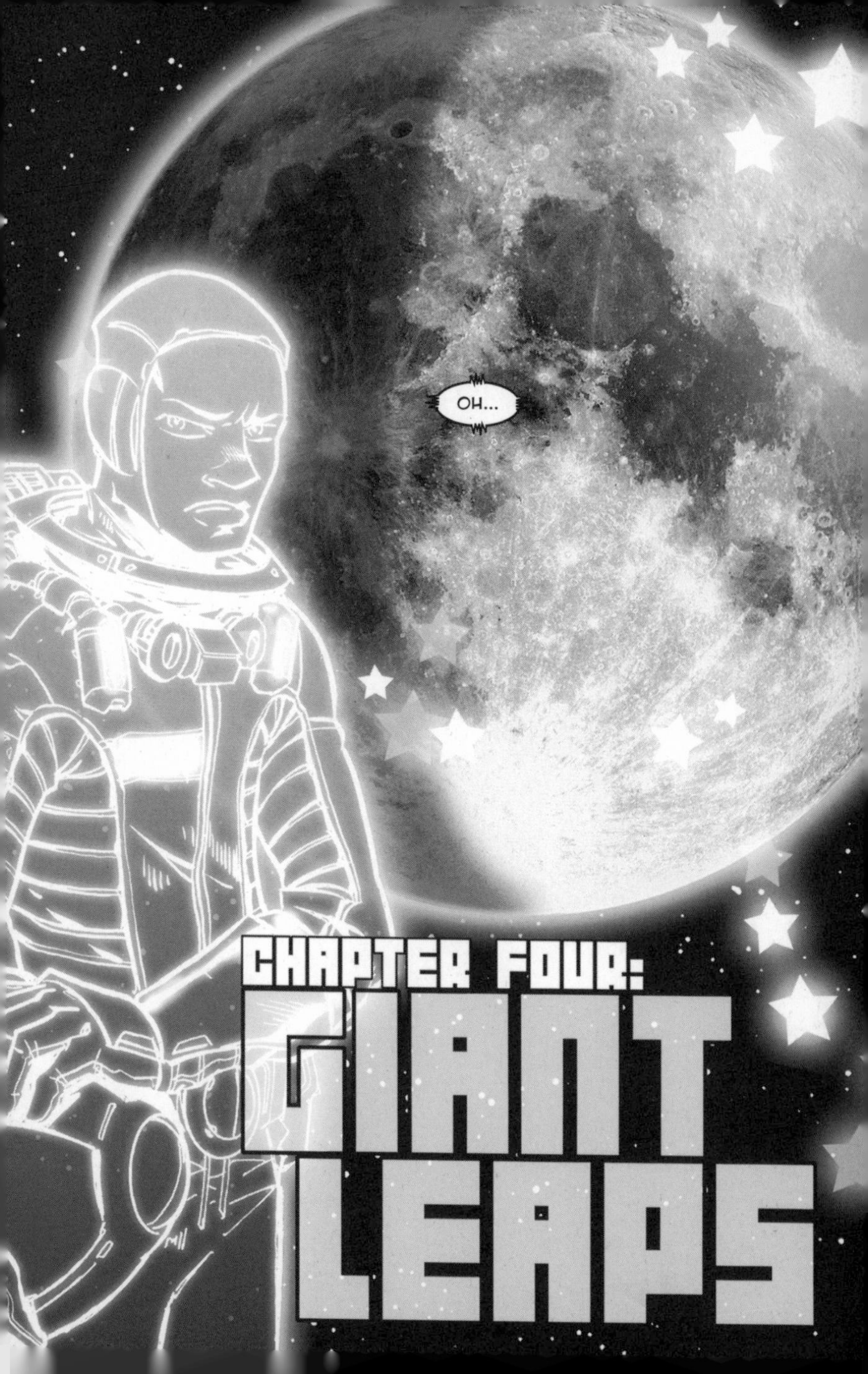
OH...
CHAPTER FOUR:
GIANT
LEAPS

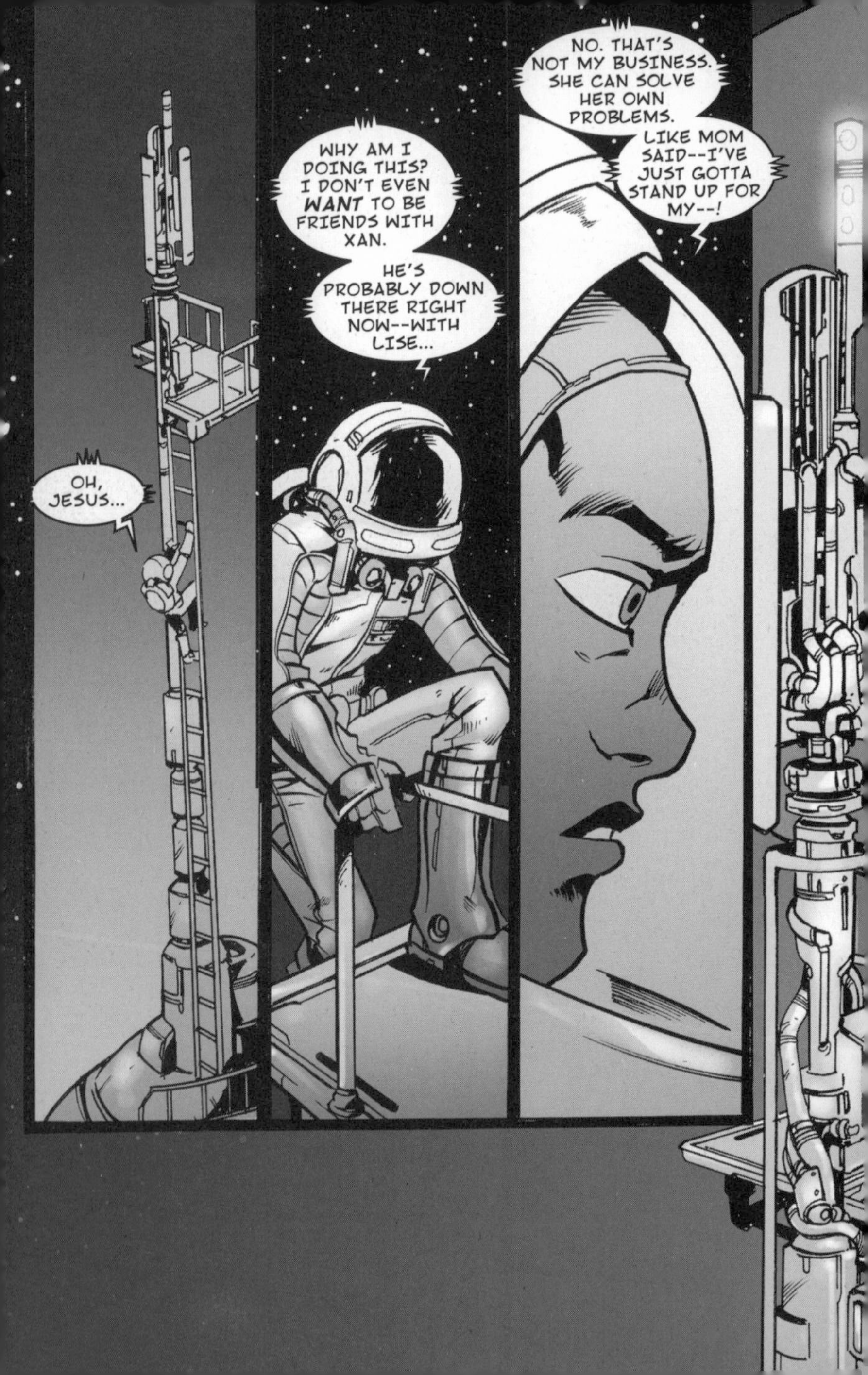
OH, JESUS...
WHY AM I DOING THIS? I DON'T EVEN *WANT* TO BE FRIENDS WITH XAN.
HE'S PROBABLY DOWN THERE RIGHT NOW--WITH LISE...
NO. THAT'S NOT MY BUSINESS. SHE CAN SOLVE HER OWN PROBLEMS.
LIKE MOM SAID--I'VE JUST GOTTA STAND UP FOR MY--!

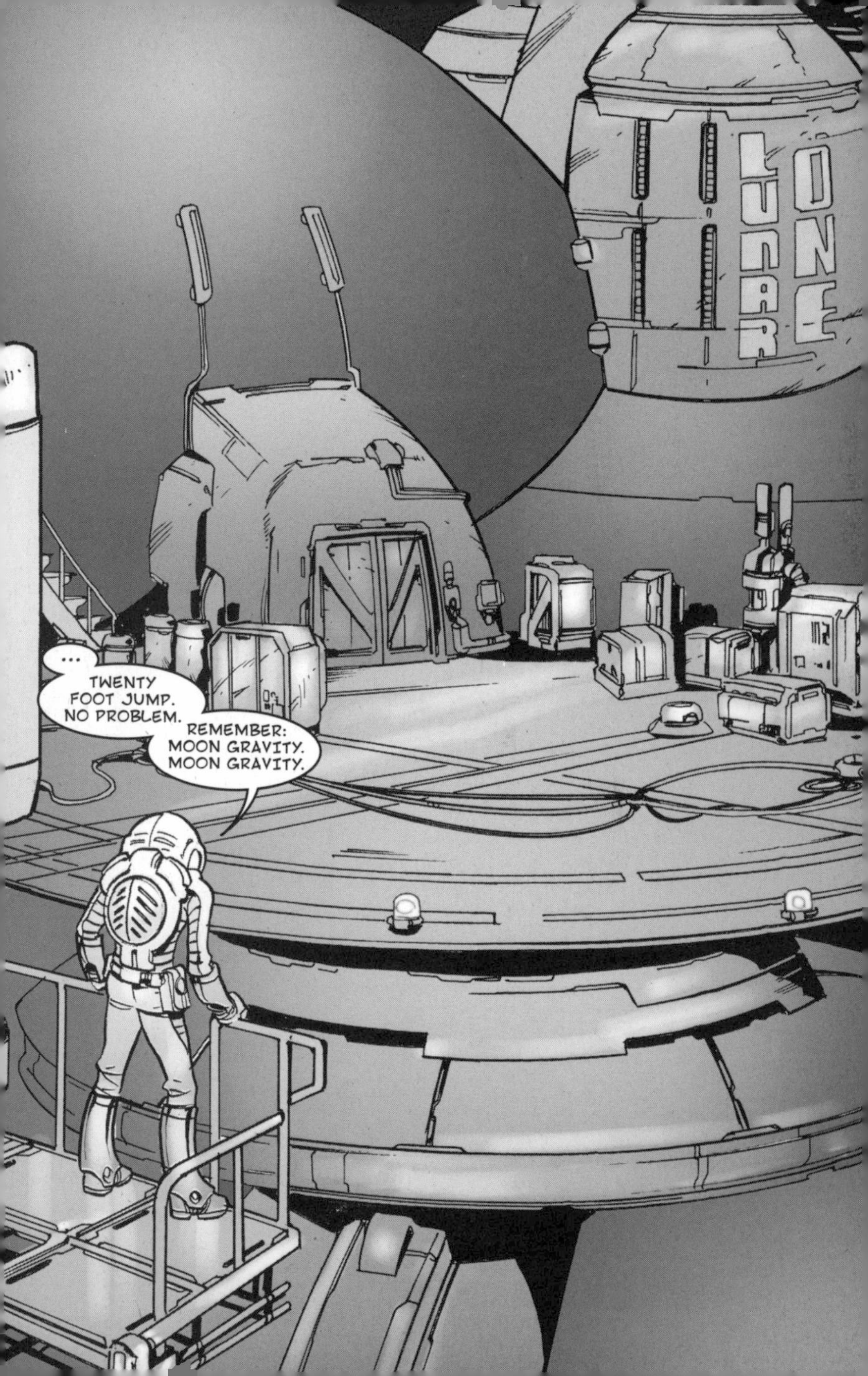
LUNAR ONE
...
TWENTY FOOT JUMP. NO PROBLEM.
REMEMBER: MOON GRAVITY. MOON GRAVITY.

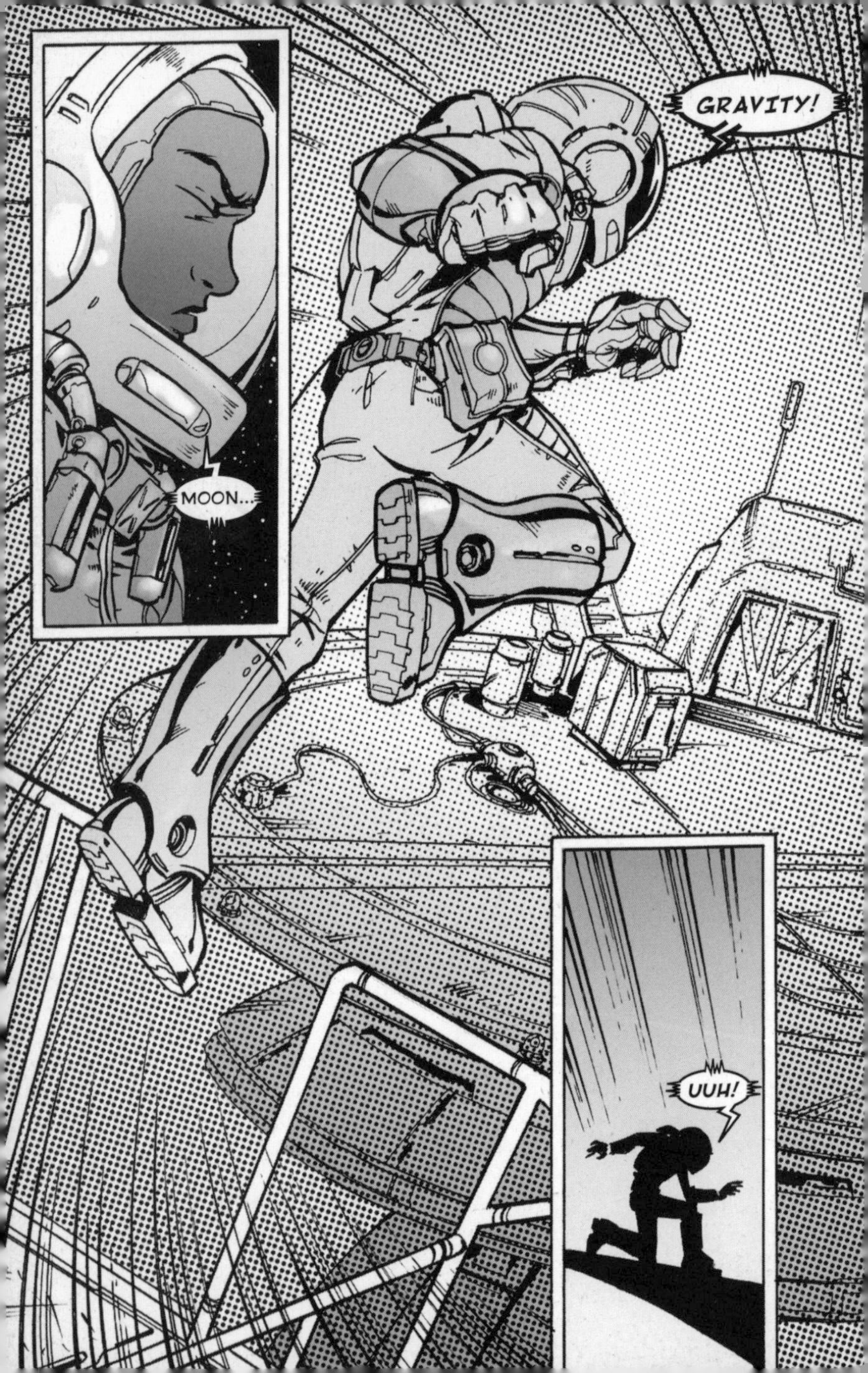
MOON...
GRAVITY!
UUH!

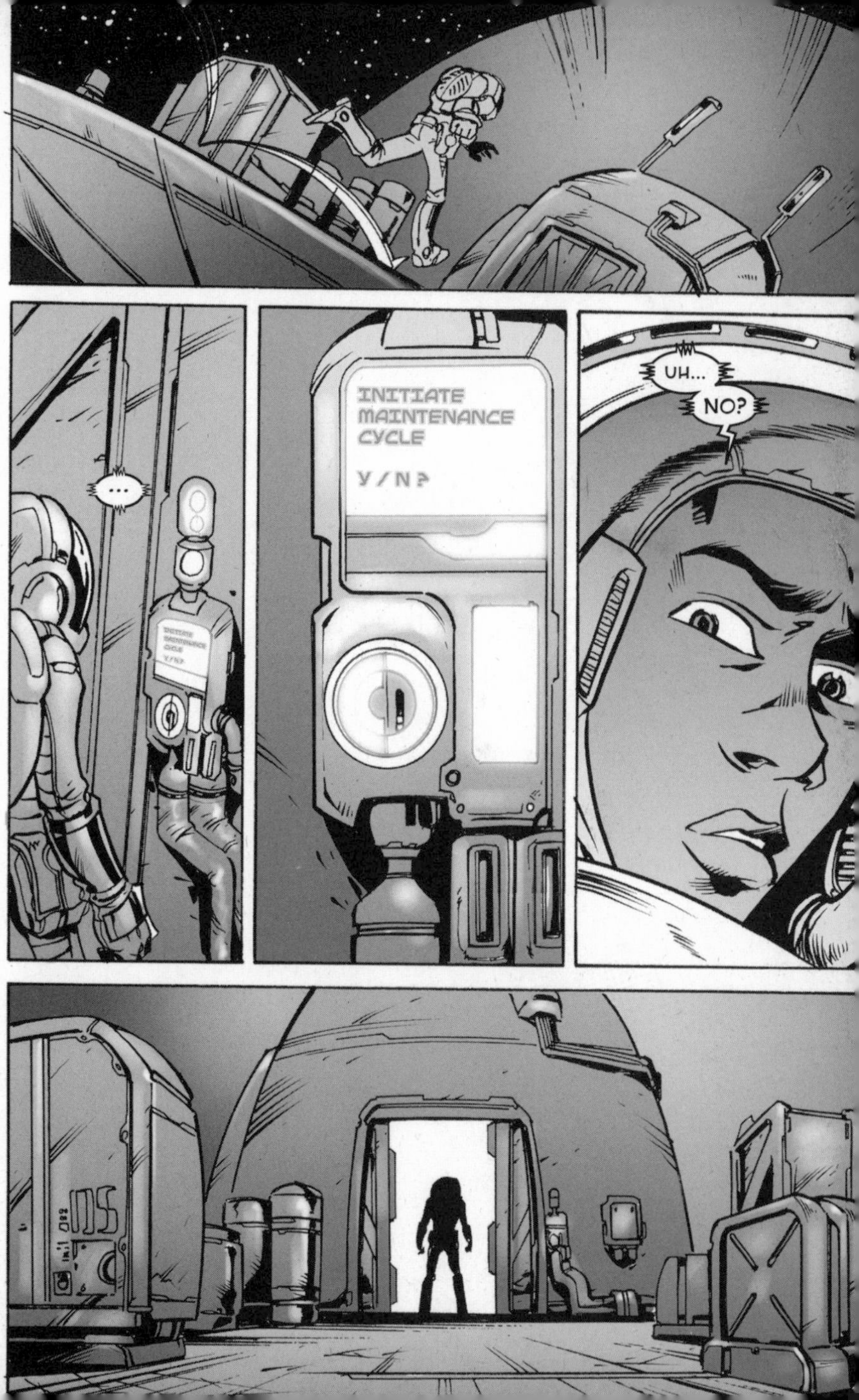
...
INITIATE MAINTENANCE CYCLE Y/N?
UH... NO?

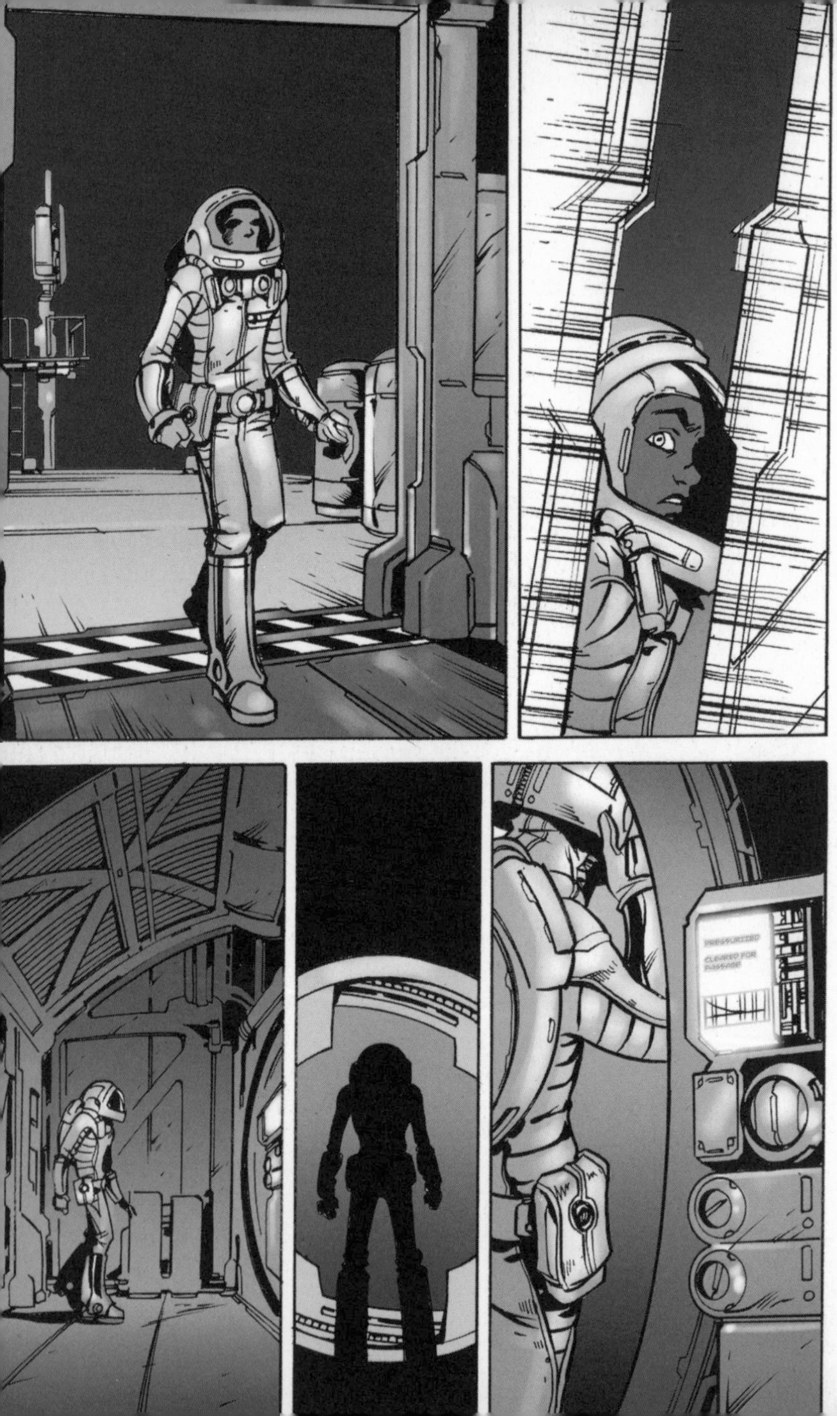
PRESSURIZED
CLEARED FOR PASSAGE

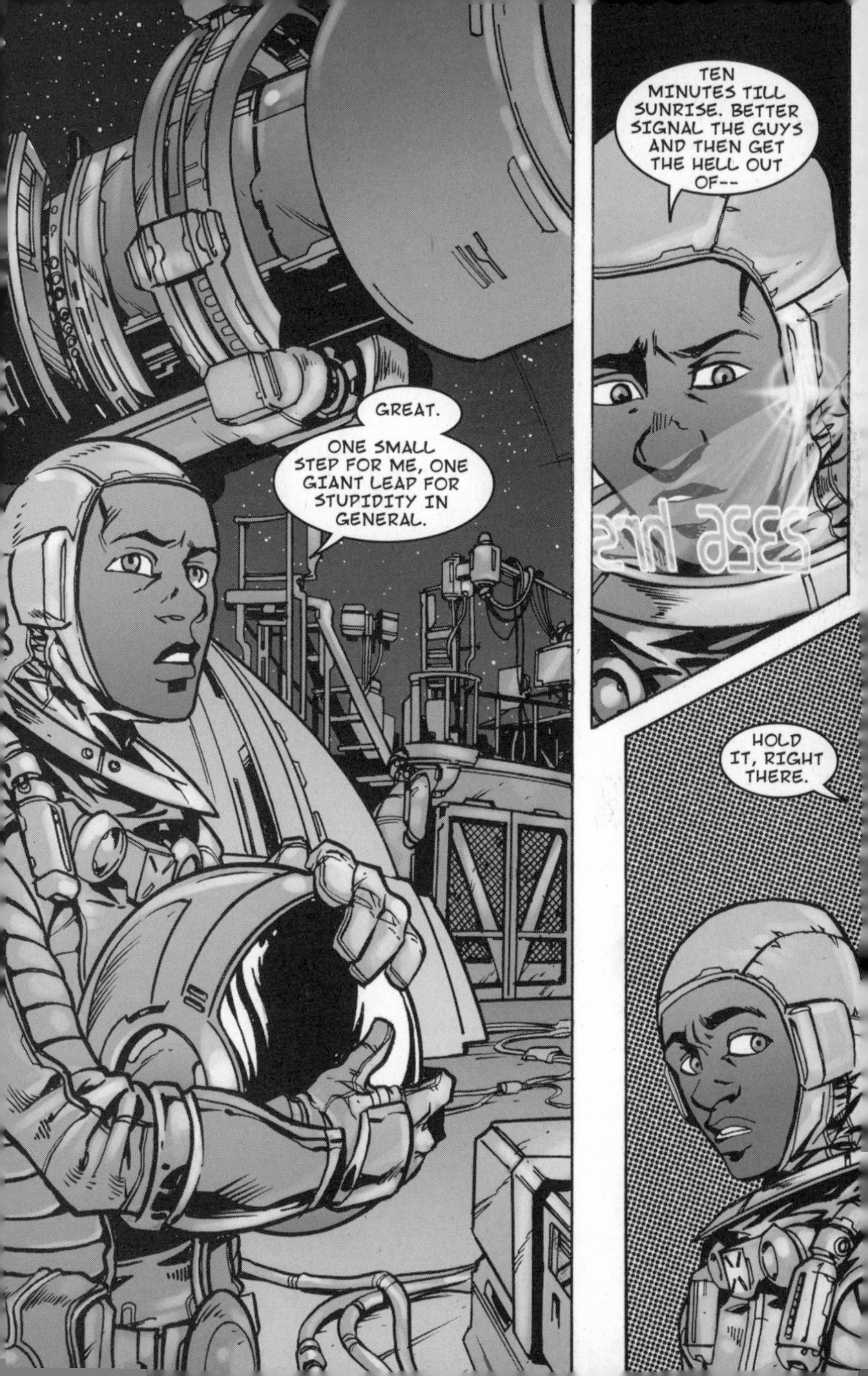
GREAT.
ONE SMALL STEP FOR ME, ONE GIANT LEAP FOR STUPIDITY IN GENERAL.
TEN MINUTES TILL SUNRISE. BETTER SIGNAL THE GUYS AND THEN GET THE HELL OUT OF--
HOLD IT, RIGHT THERE.

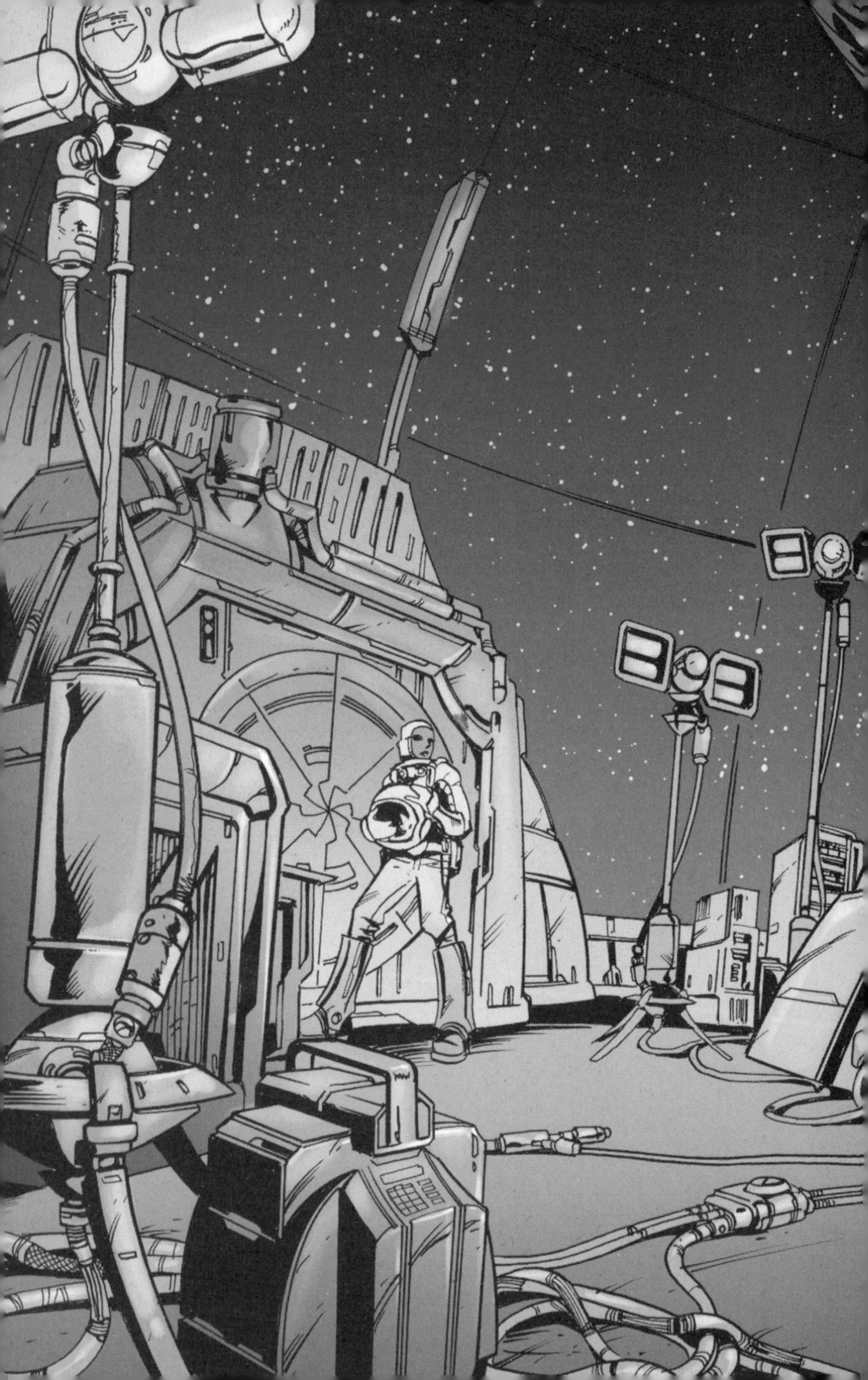

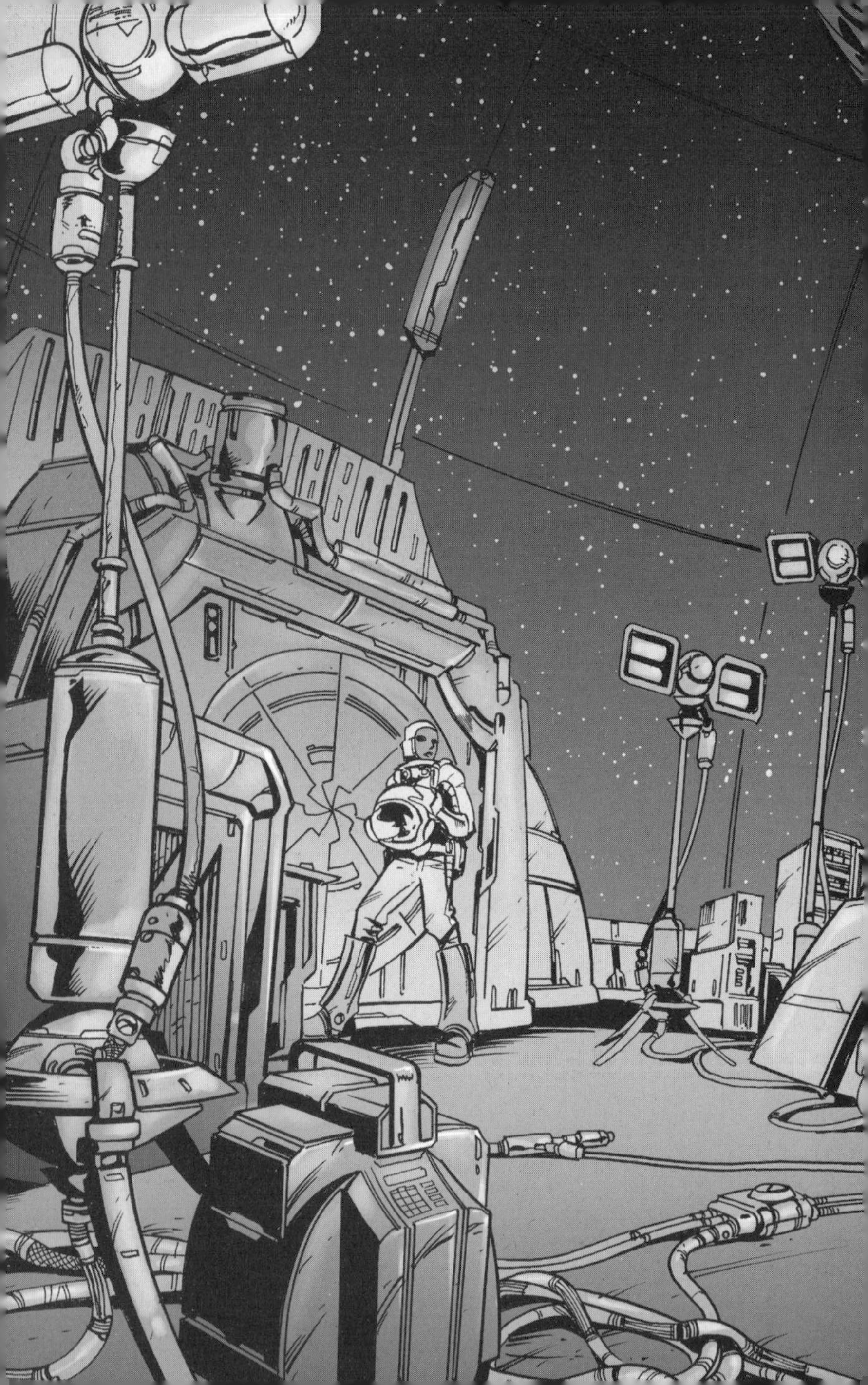

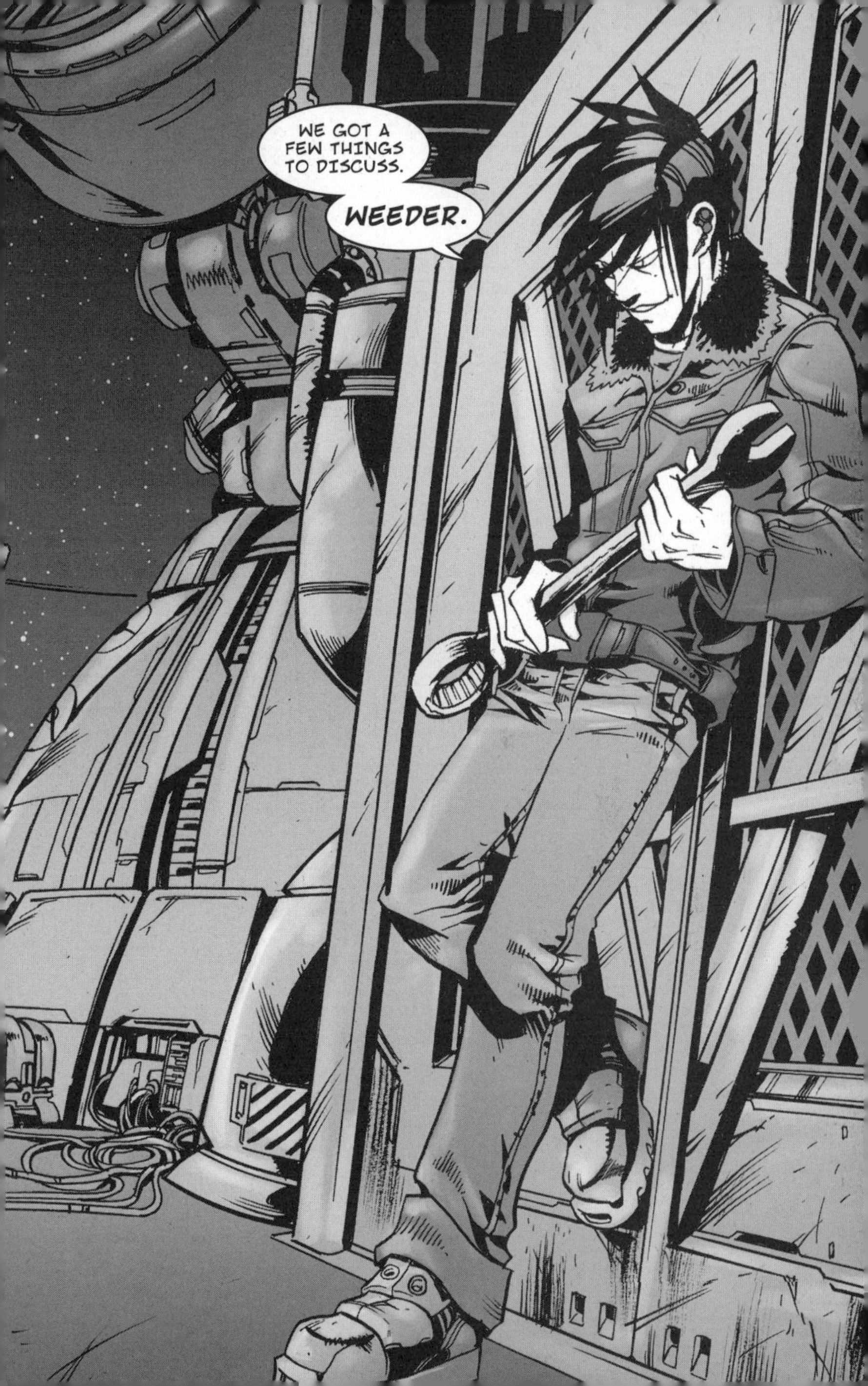
WE GOT A FEW THINGS TO DISCUSS.
WEEDER.

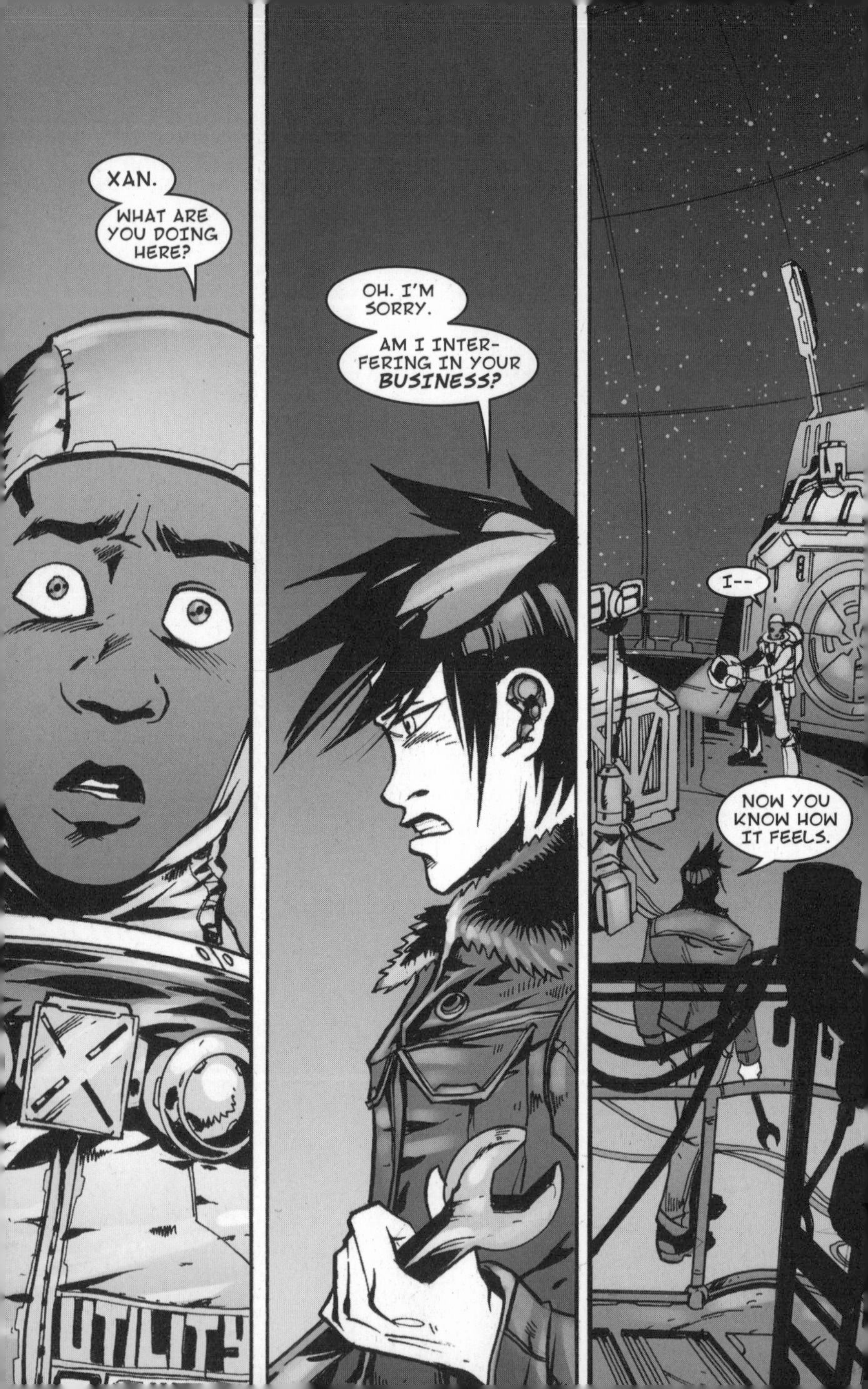
XAN.
WHAT ARE YOU DOING HERE?
UTILITY
OH. I'M SORRY.
AM I INTER-FERING IN YOUR ***BUSINESS?***
I--
NOW YOU KNOW HOW IT FEELS.

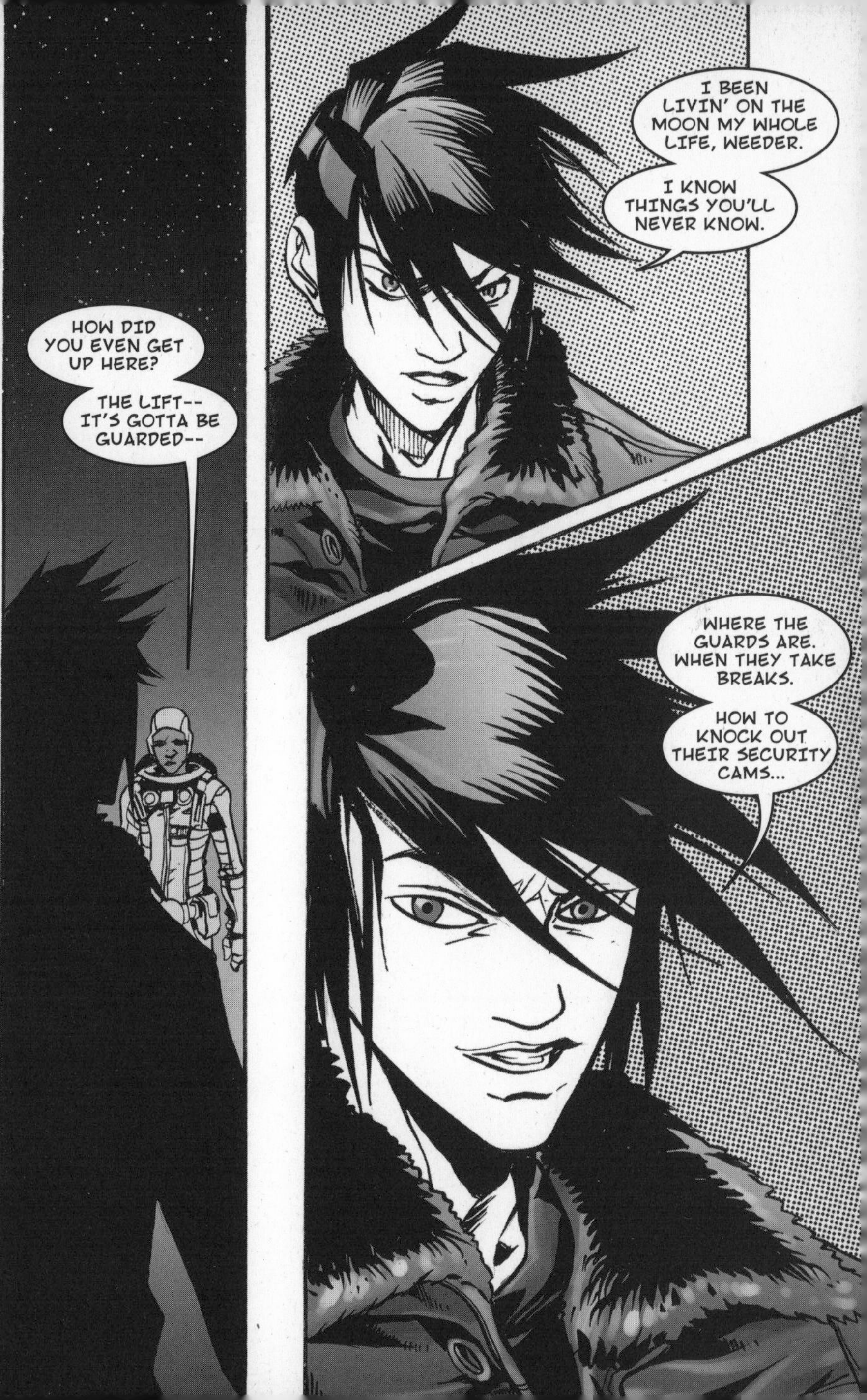
HOW DID YOU EVEN GET UP HERE?
THE LIFT-- IT'S GOTTA BE GUARDED--
I BEEN LIVIN' ON THE MOON MY WHOLE LIFE, WEEDER.
I KNOW THINGS YOU'LL NEVER KNOW.
WHERE THE GUARDS ARE. WHEN THEY TAKE BREAKS.
HOW TO KNOCK OUT THEIR SECURITY CAMS...

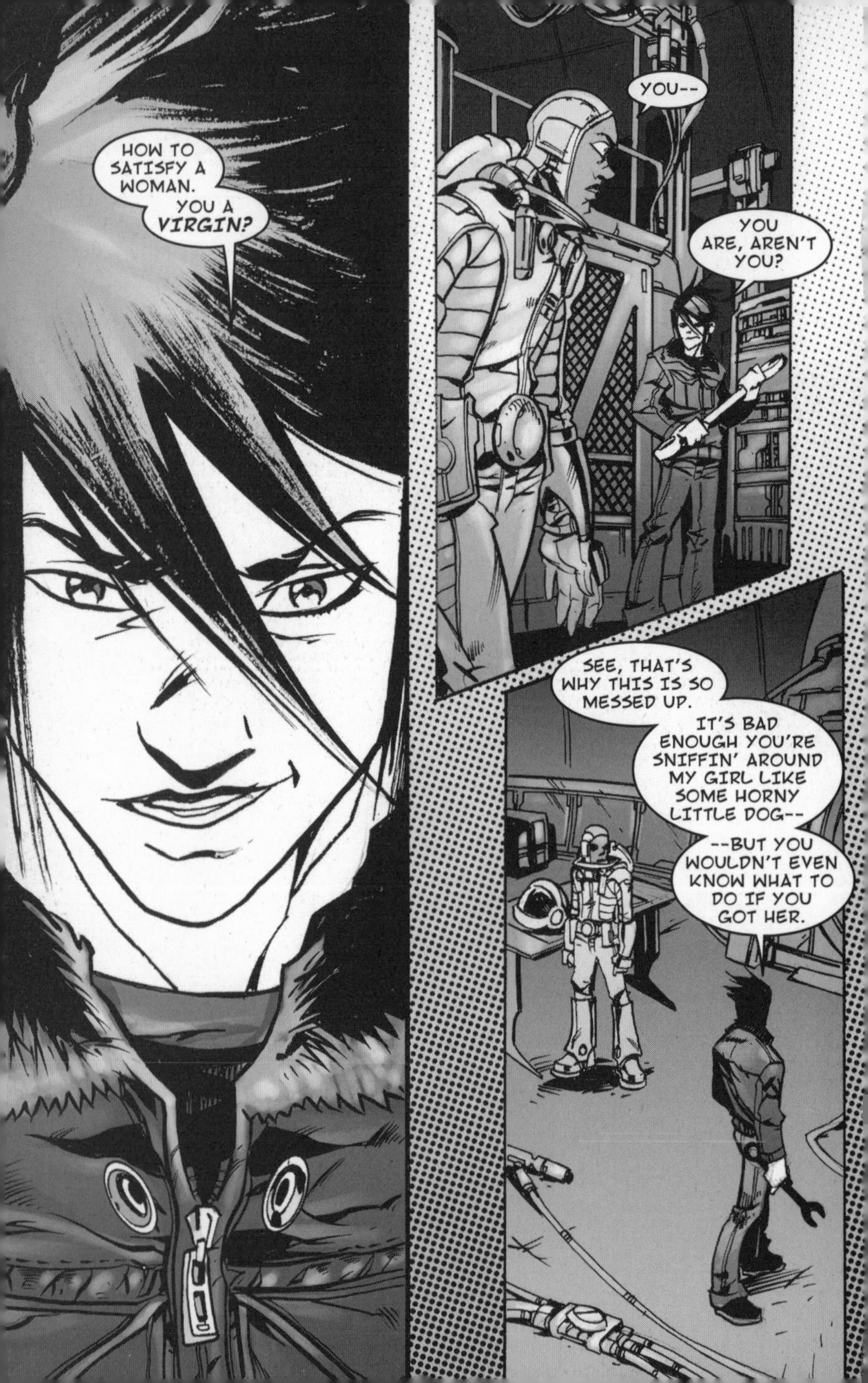
HOW TO SATISFY A WOMAN.
YOU A *VIRGIN?*
YOU--
YOU ARE, AREN'T YOU?
SEE, THAT'S WHY THIS IS SO MESSED UP.
IT'S BAD ENOUGH YOU'RE SNIFFIN' AROUND MY GIRL LIKE SOME HORNY LITTLE DOG--
--BUT YOU WOULDN'T EVEN KNOW WHAT TO DO IF YOU GOT HER.

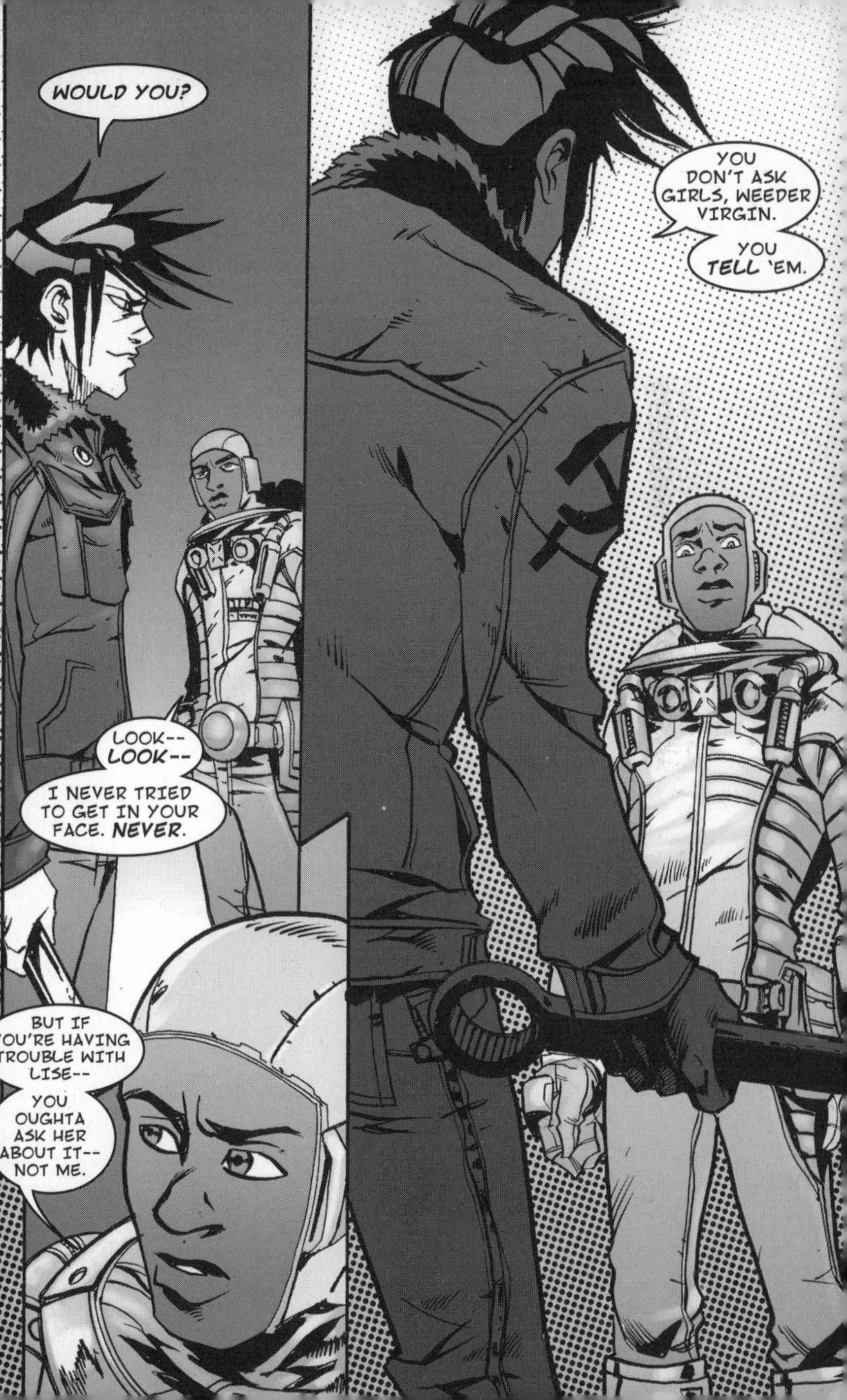
WOULD YOU?
LOOK-- LOOK--
I NEVER TRIED TO GET IN YOUR FACE. NEVER.
BUT IF YOU'RE HAVING TROUBLE WITH LISE--
YOU OUGHTA ASK HER ABOUT IT-- NOT ME.
YOU DON'T ASK GIRLS, WEEDER VIRGIN.
YOU TELL 'EM.

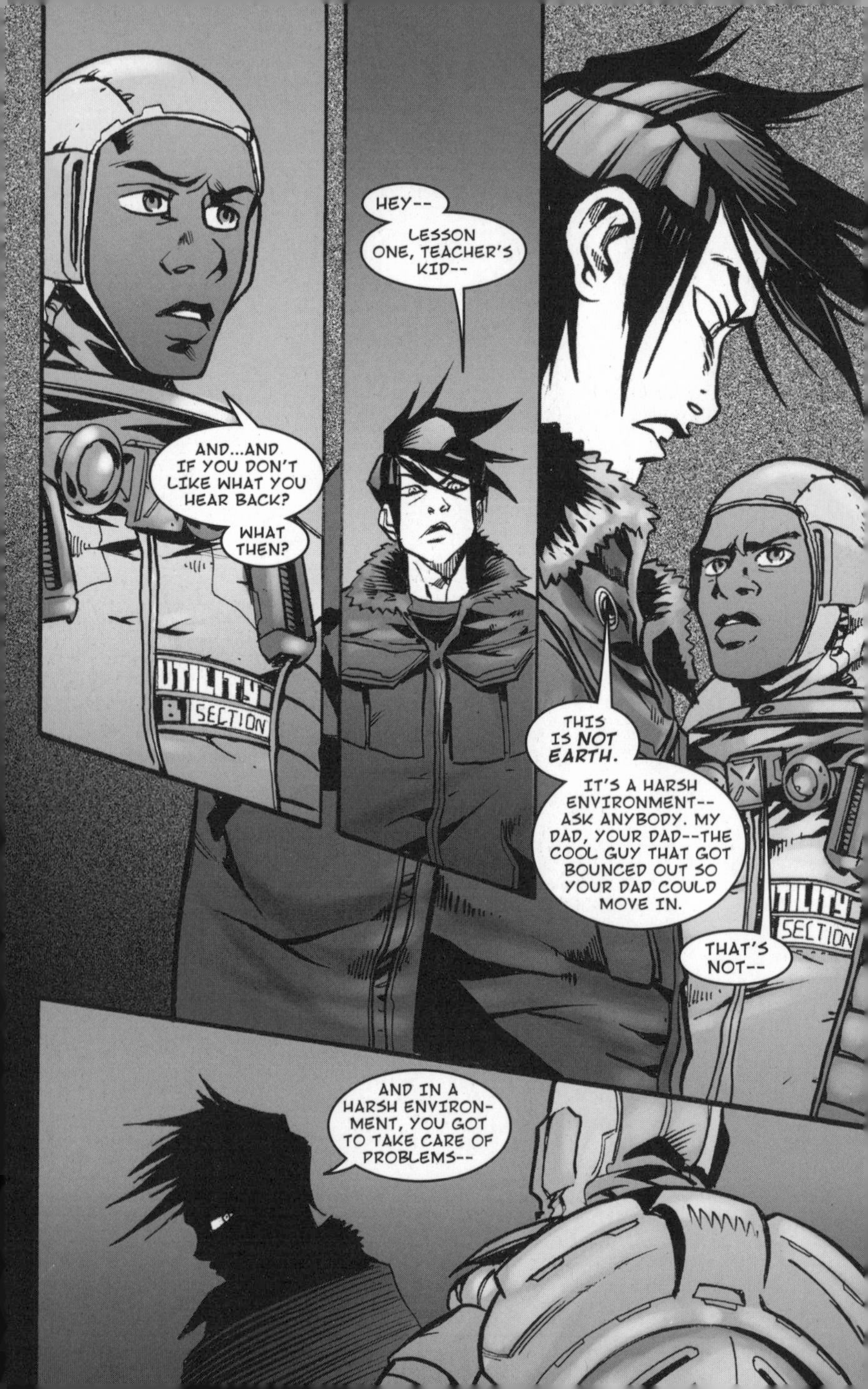
AND...AND IF YOU DON'T LIKE WHAT YOU HEAR BACK?
WHAT THEN?
UTILITY
B SECTION
HEY--
LESSON ONE, TEACHER'S KID--
THIS IS NOT EARTH.
IT'S A HARSH ENVIRONMENT-- ASK ANYBODY. MY DAD, YOUR DAD--THE COOL GUY THAT GOT BOUNCED OUT SO YOUR DAD COULD MOVE IN.
UTILITY
SECTION
THAT'S NOT--
AND IN A HARSH ENVIRONMENT, YOU GOT TO TAKE CARE OF PROBLEMS--

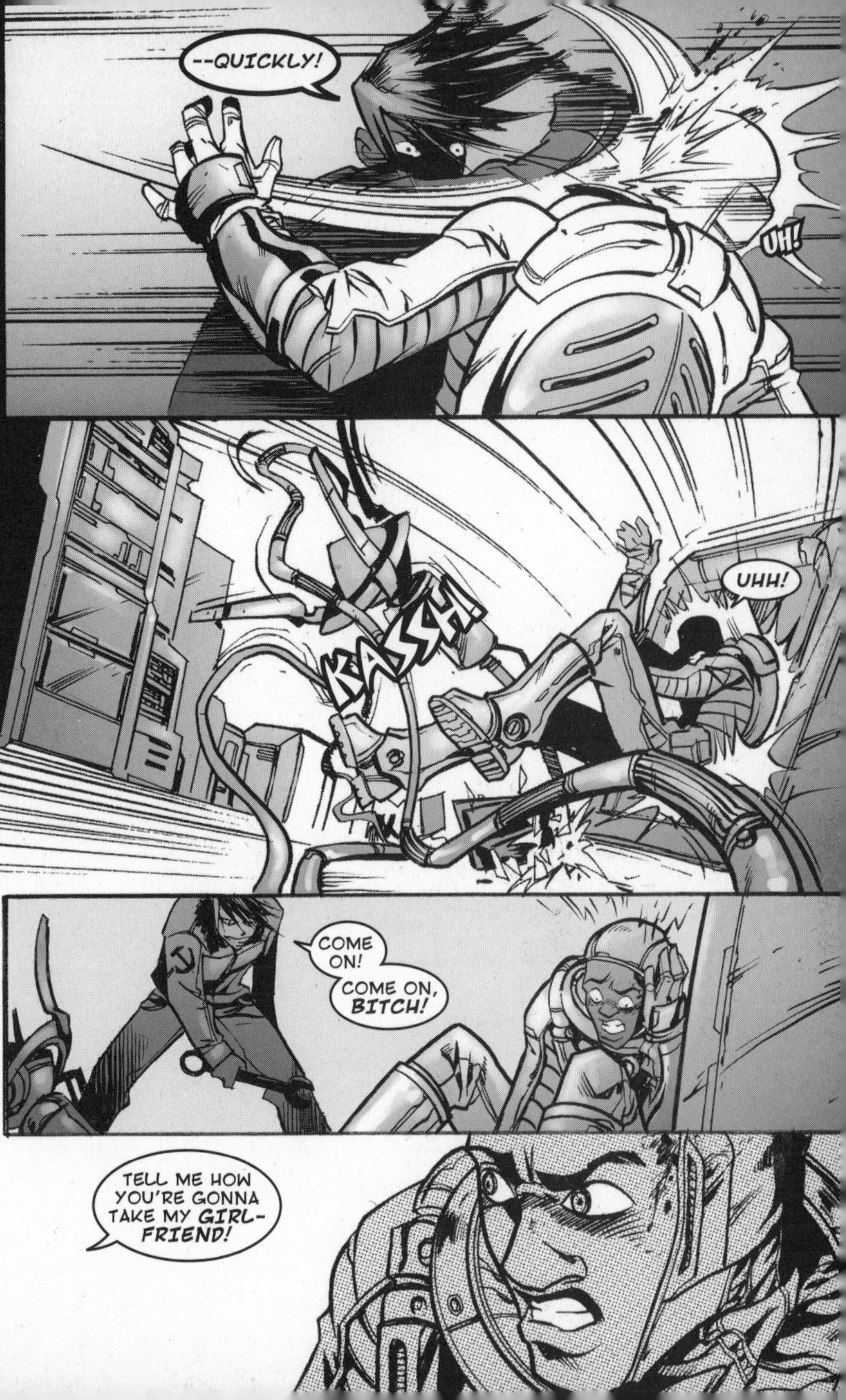
--QUICKLY!
UH!
KASSH!
UHH!
COME ON!
COME ON, BITCH!
TELL ME HOW YOU'RE GONNA TAKE MY GIRL-FRIEND!

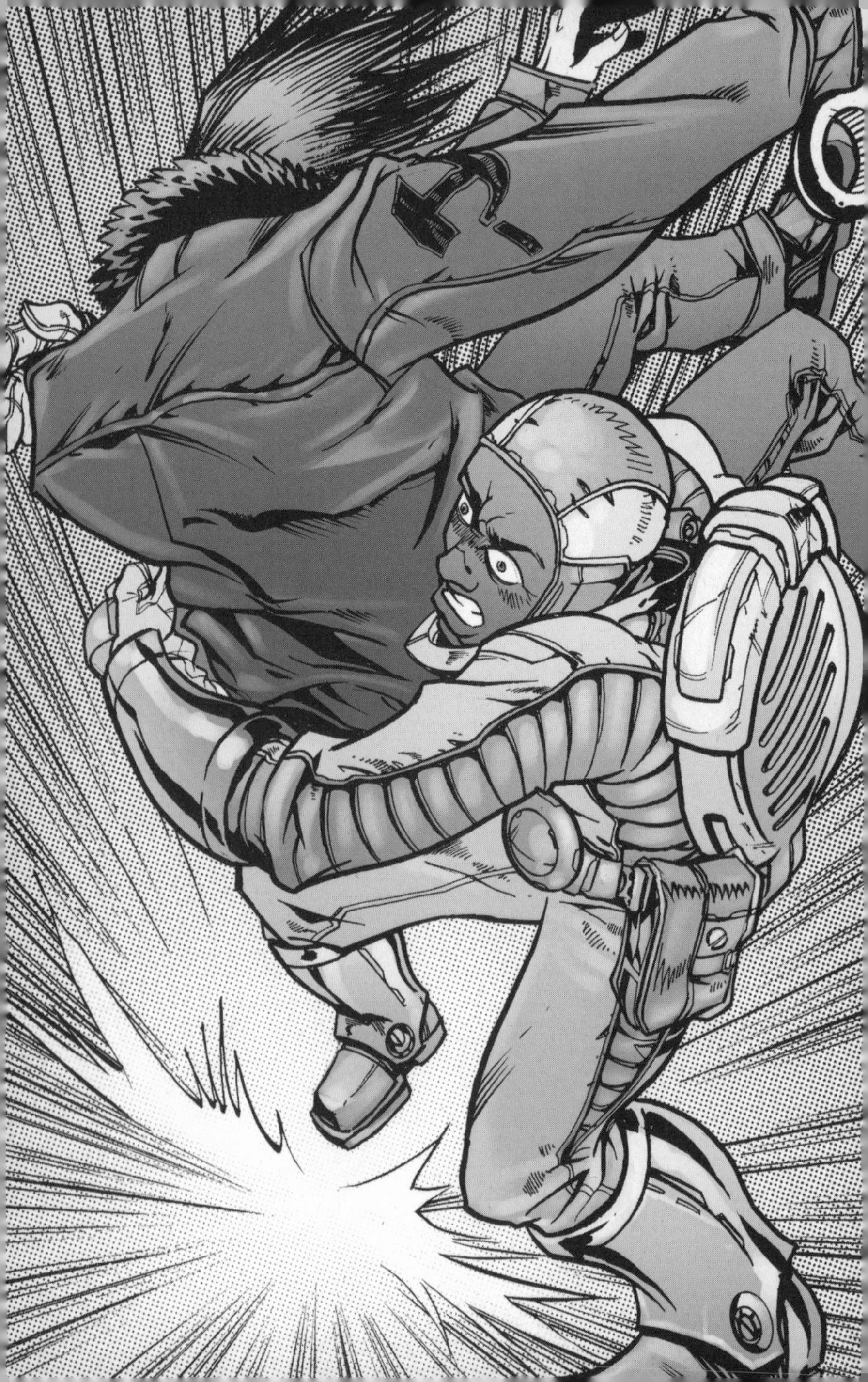

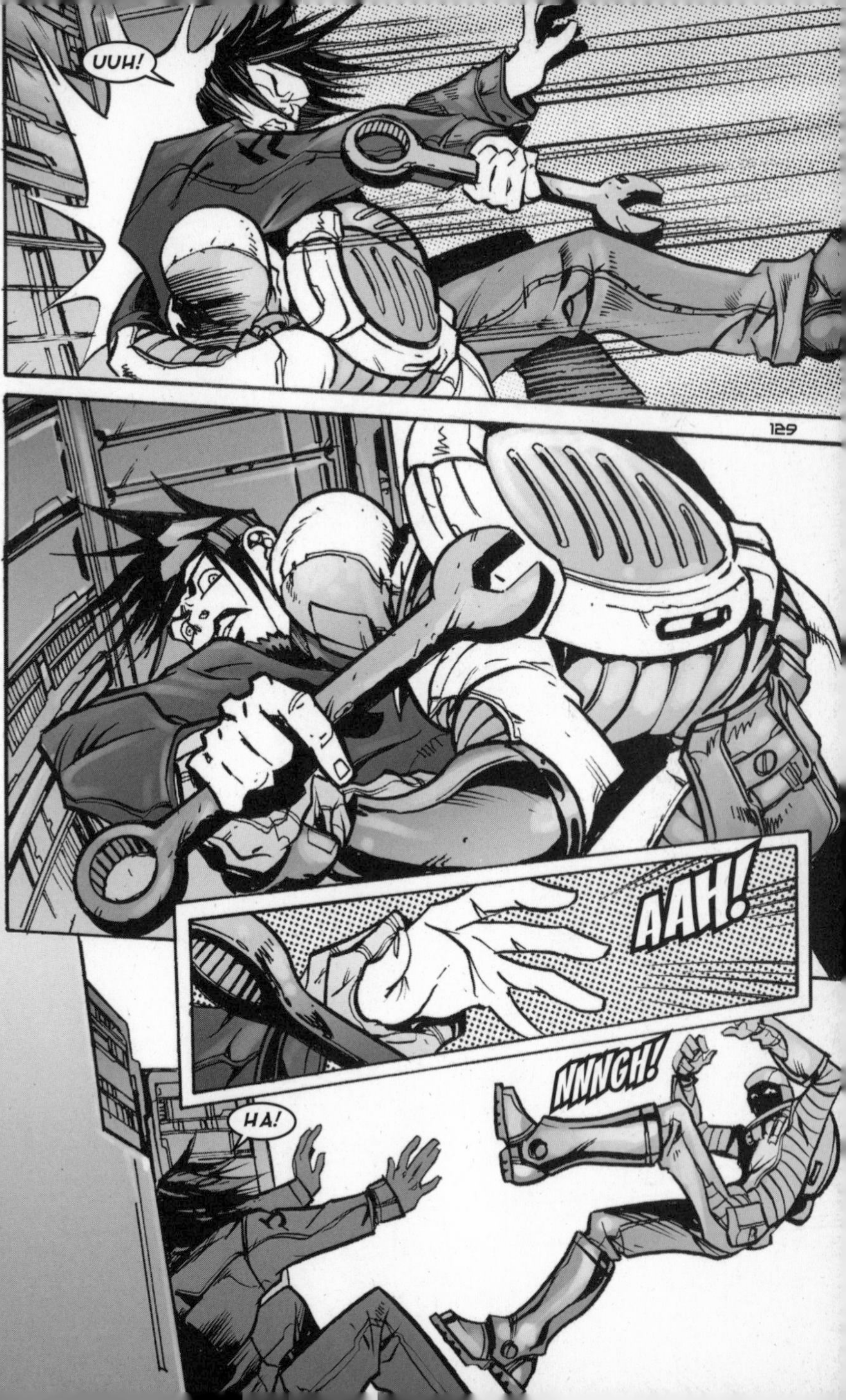
UUH!
AAH!
NNNGH!
HA!

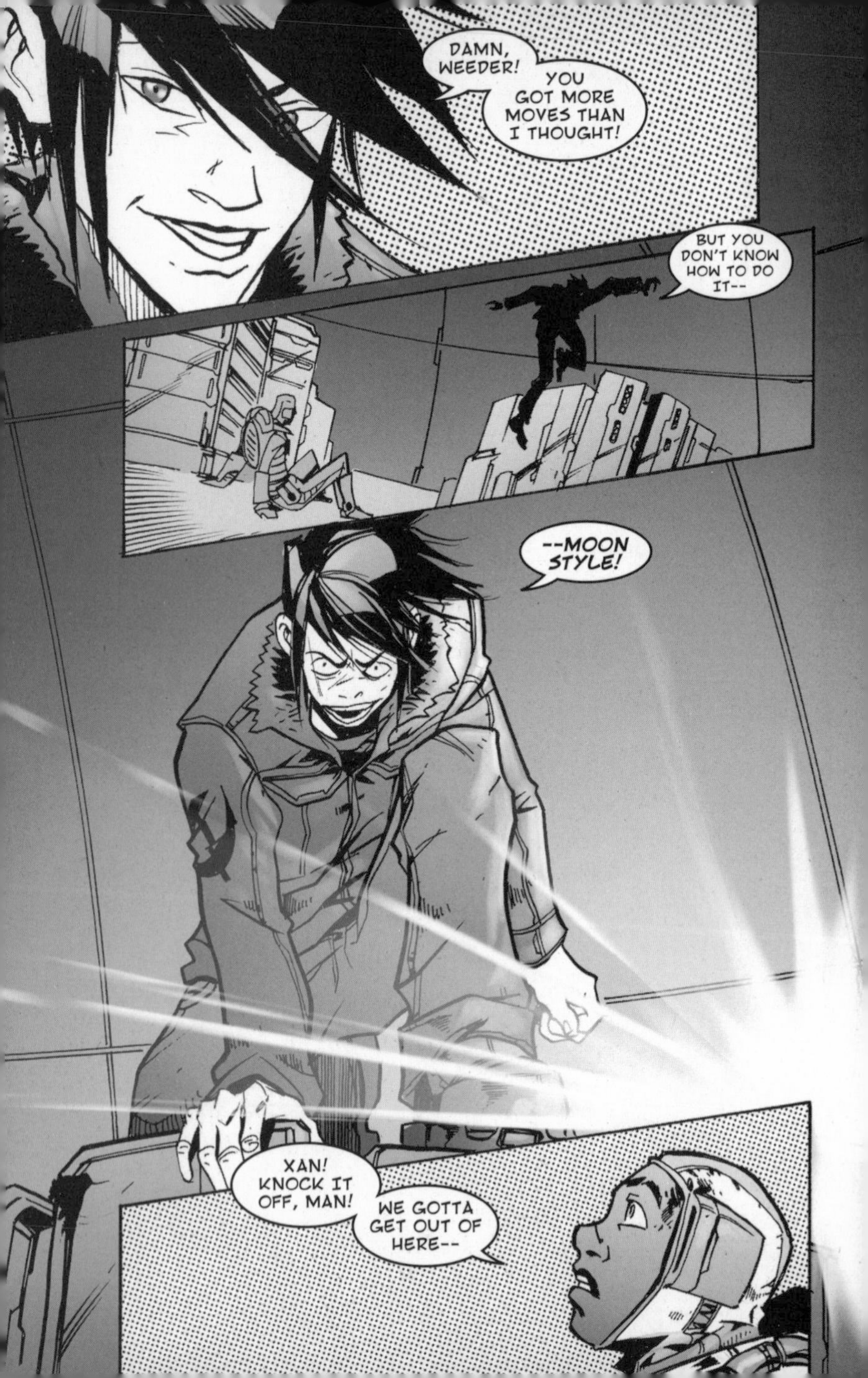
DAMN, WEEDER!
YOU GOT MORE MOVES THAN I THOUGHT!
BUT YOU DON'T KNOW HOW TO DO IT--
--MOON STYLE!
XAN! KNOCK IT OFF, MAN!
WE GOTTA GET OUT OF HERE--

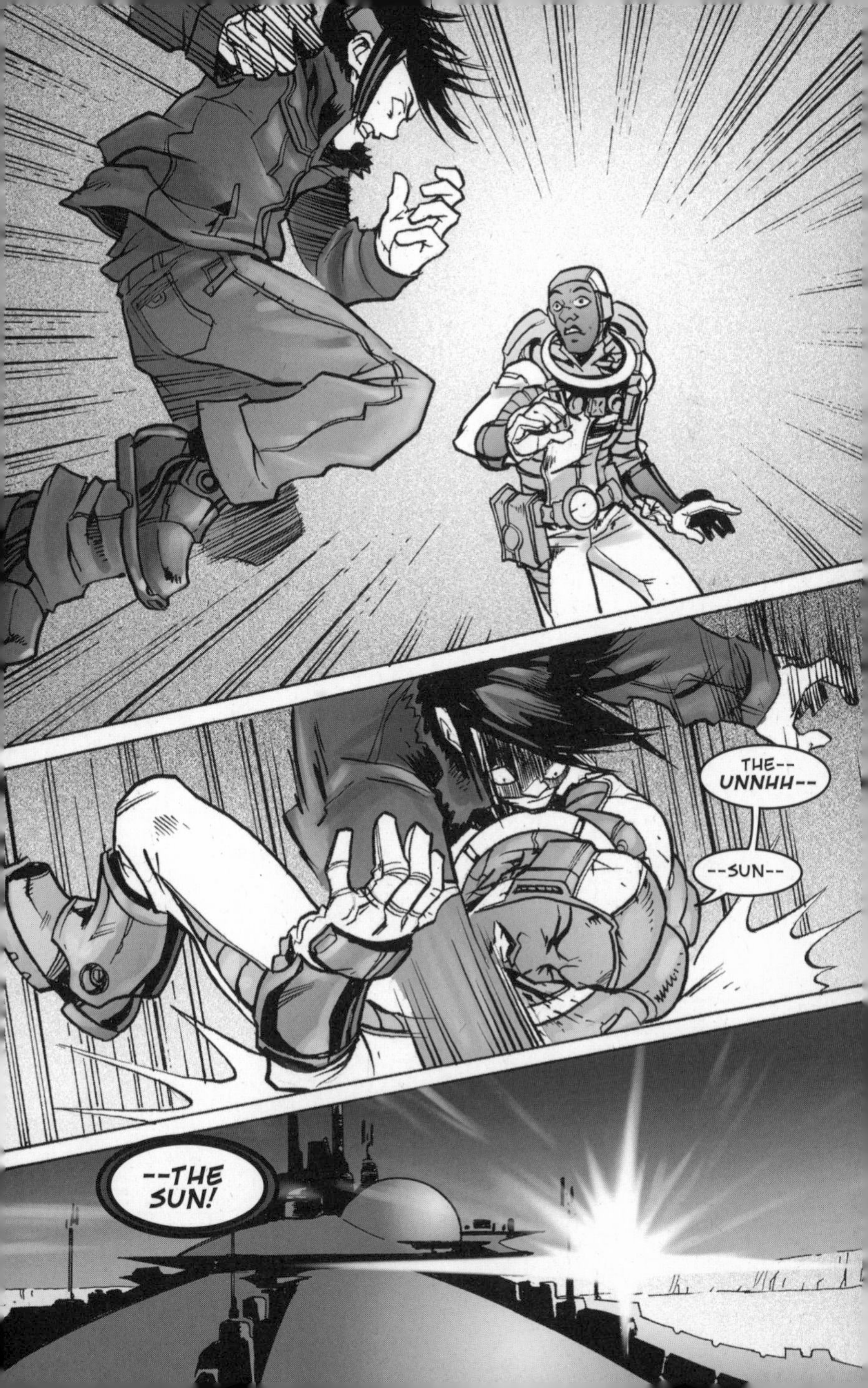
THE--
UNNHH--
--SUN--
--THE SUN!

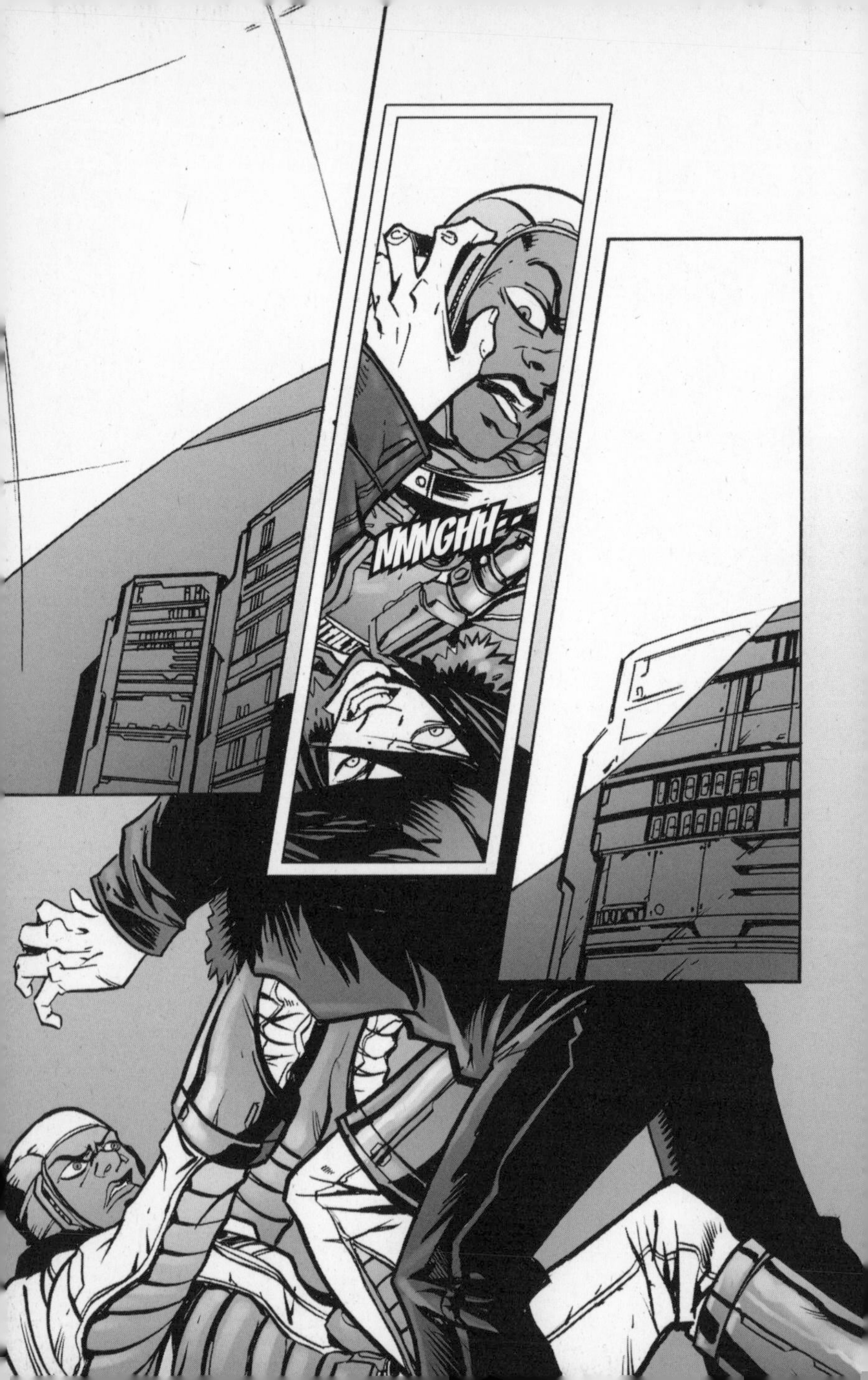
NNNGHH--

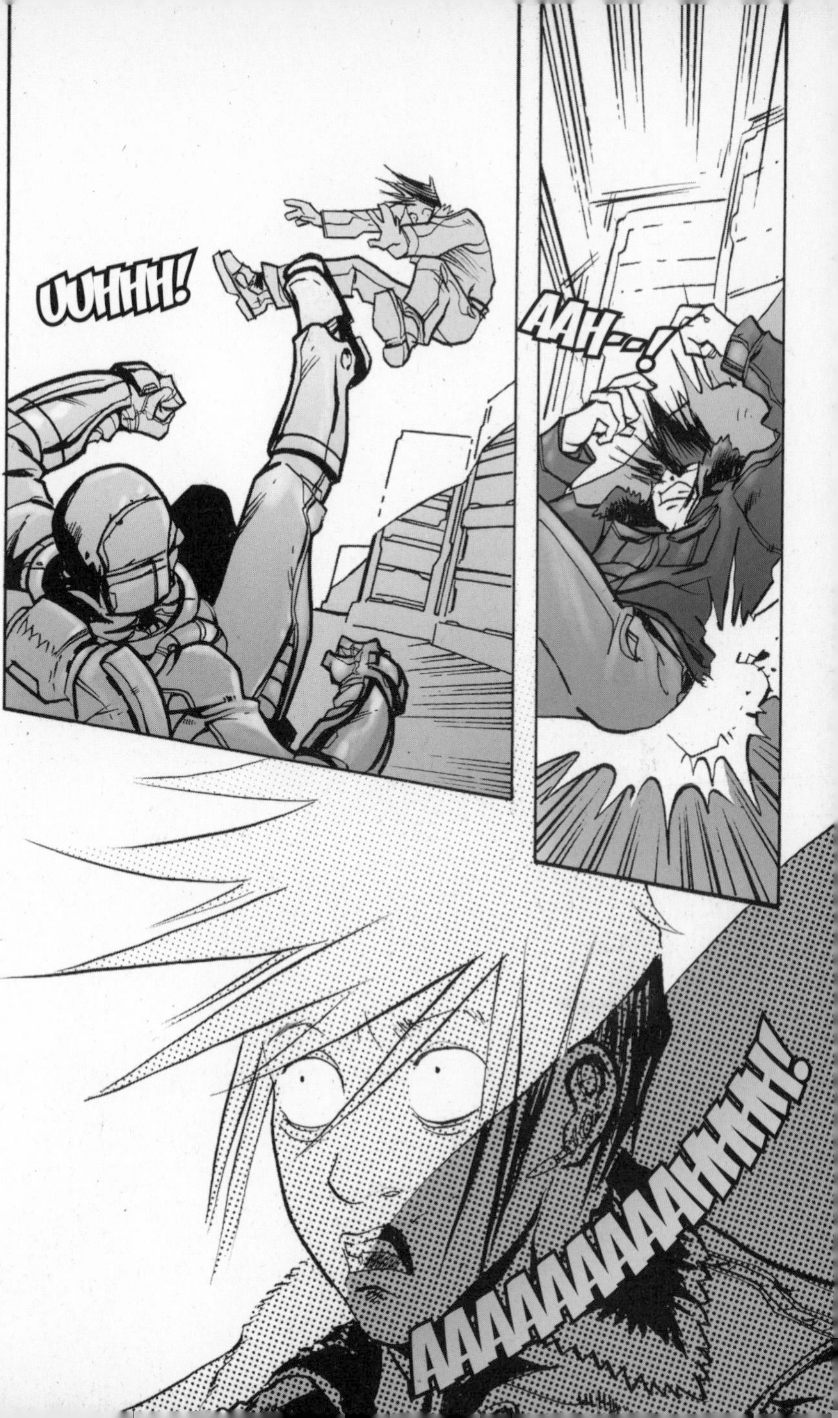
AAH--!
UUHHH!
AAAAAAAAAAHHHHH!

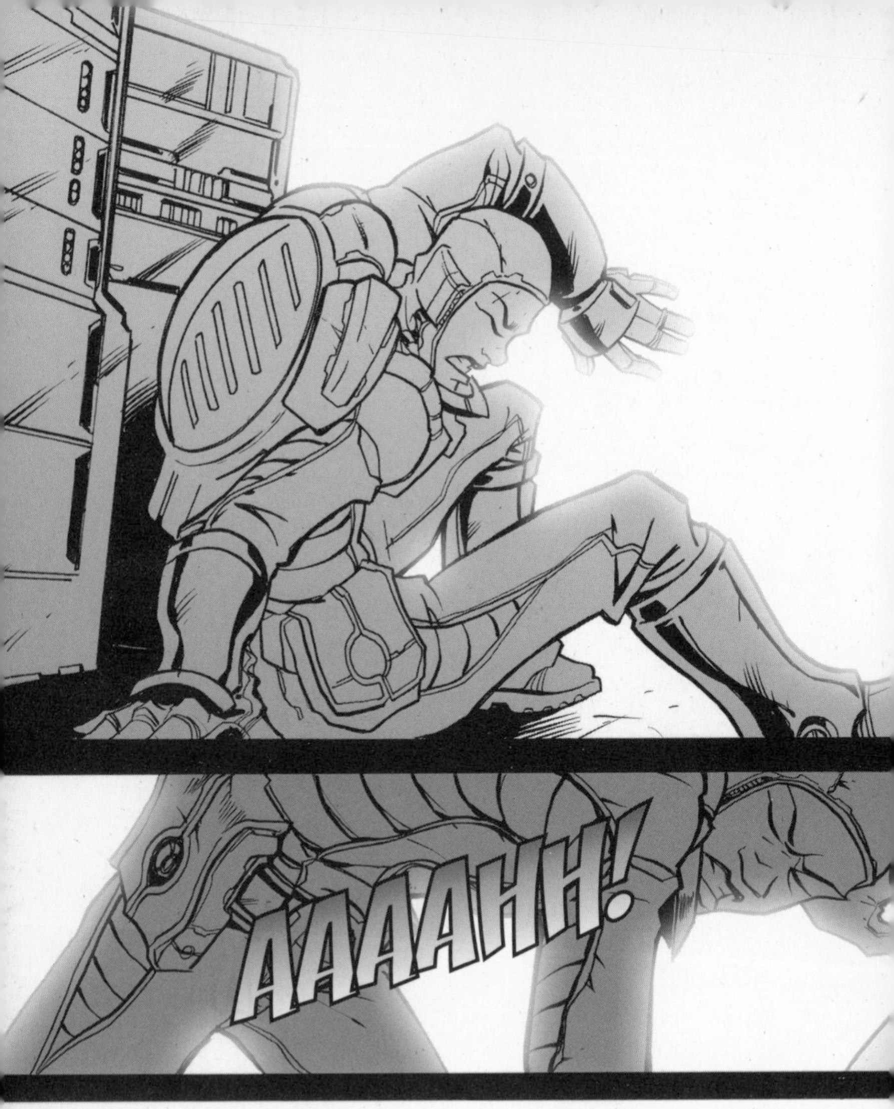
AAAAAHH!

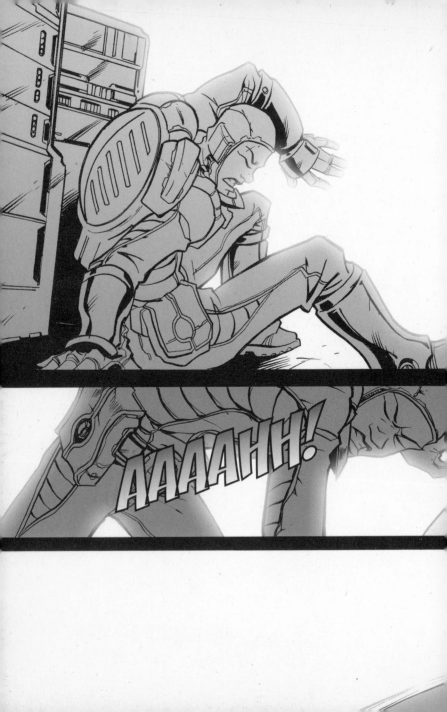

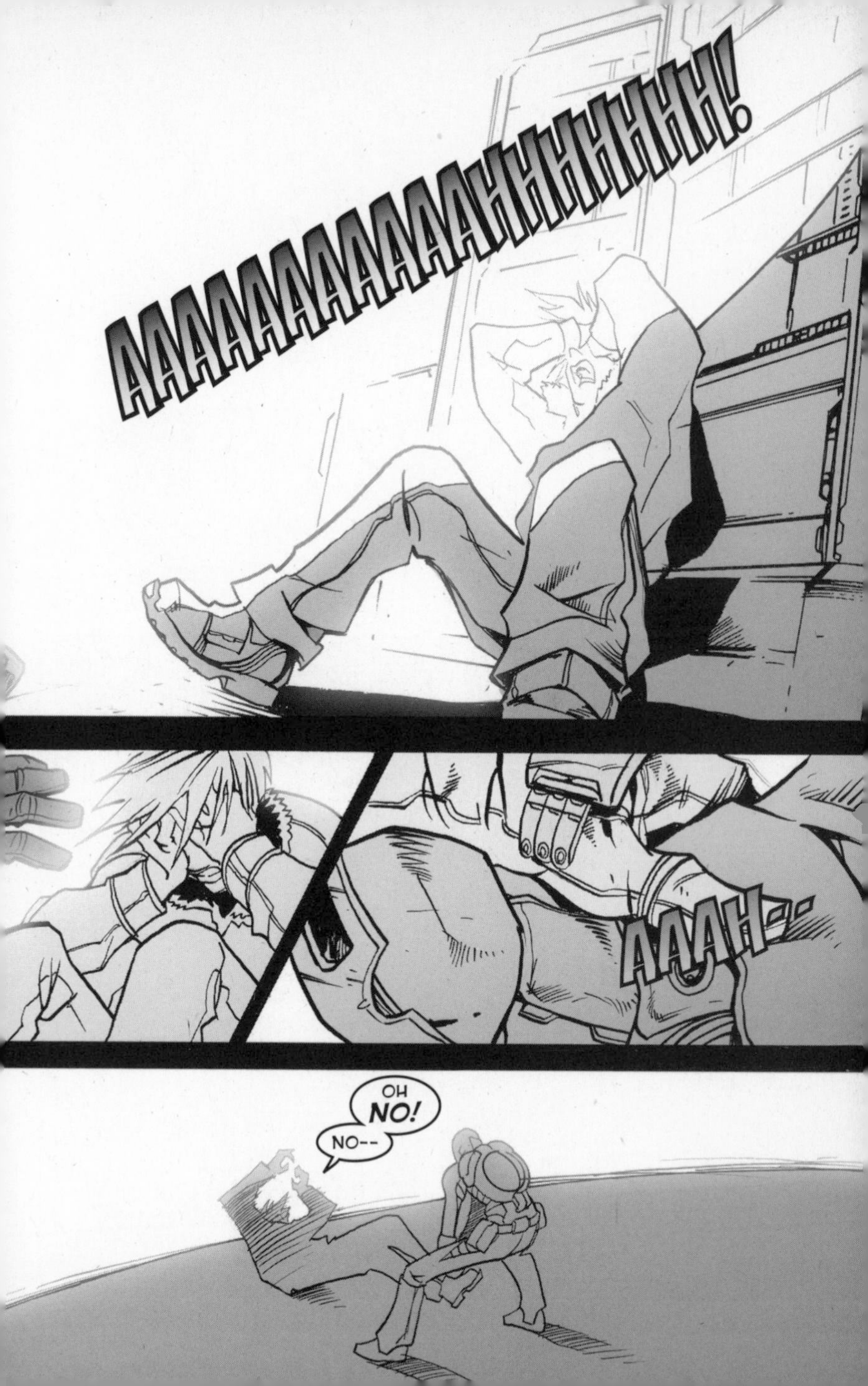
AAAAAAAAAAAHHHHHHH!
AAAH--
OH NO!
NO--

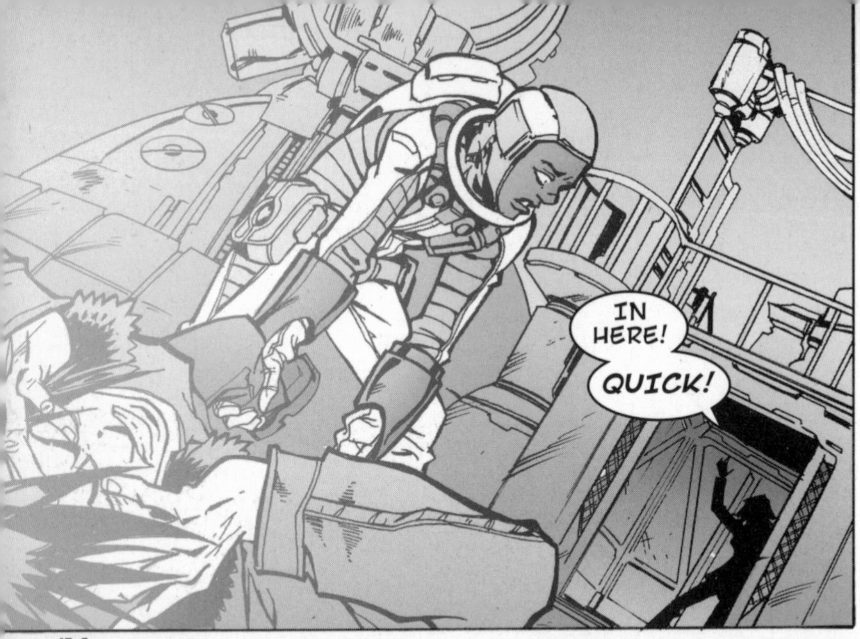
IN HERE!
QUICK!

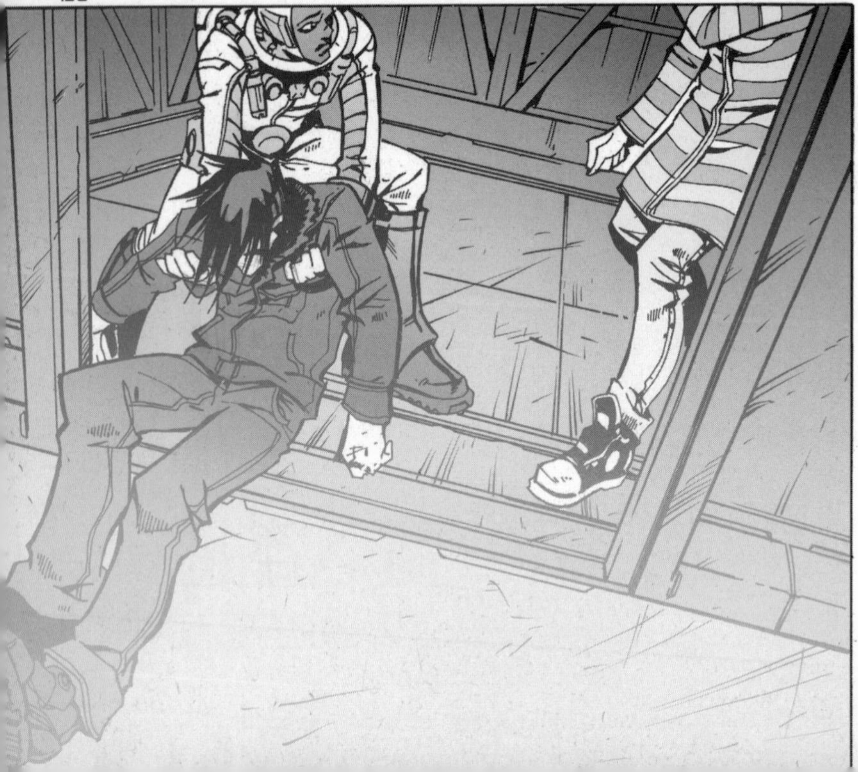

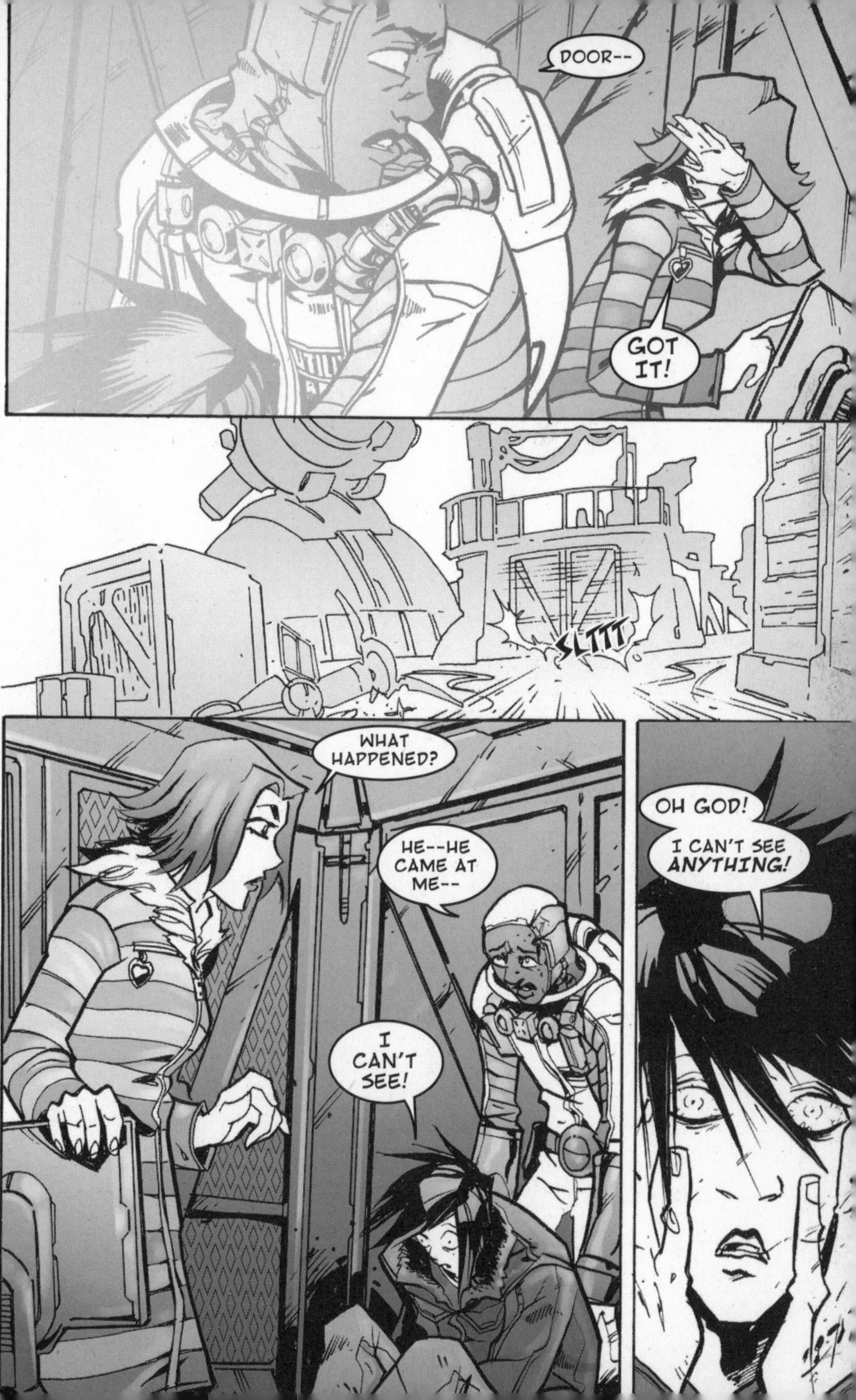
DOOR--
GOT IT!
SLTTT
WHAT HAPPENED?
HE--HE CAME AT ME--
I CAN'T SEE!
OH GOD!
I CAN'T SEE *ANYTHING!*

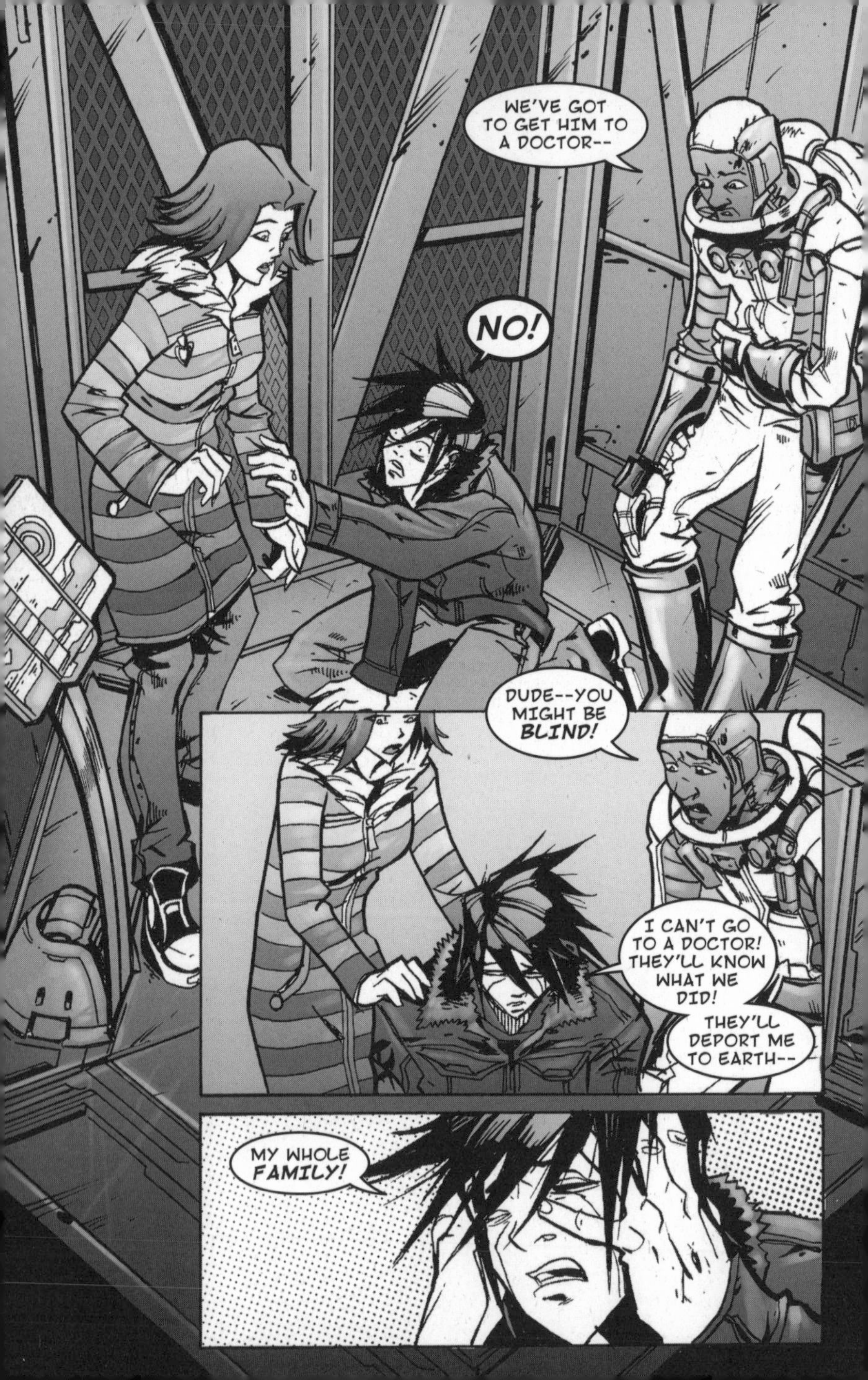
WE'VE GOT TO GET HIM TO A DOCTOR--
NO!
DUDE--YOU MIGHT BE BLIND!
I CAN'T GO TO A DOCTOR! THEY'LL KNOW WHAT WE DID!
THEY'LL DEPORT ME TO EARTH--
MY WHOLE FAMILY!

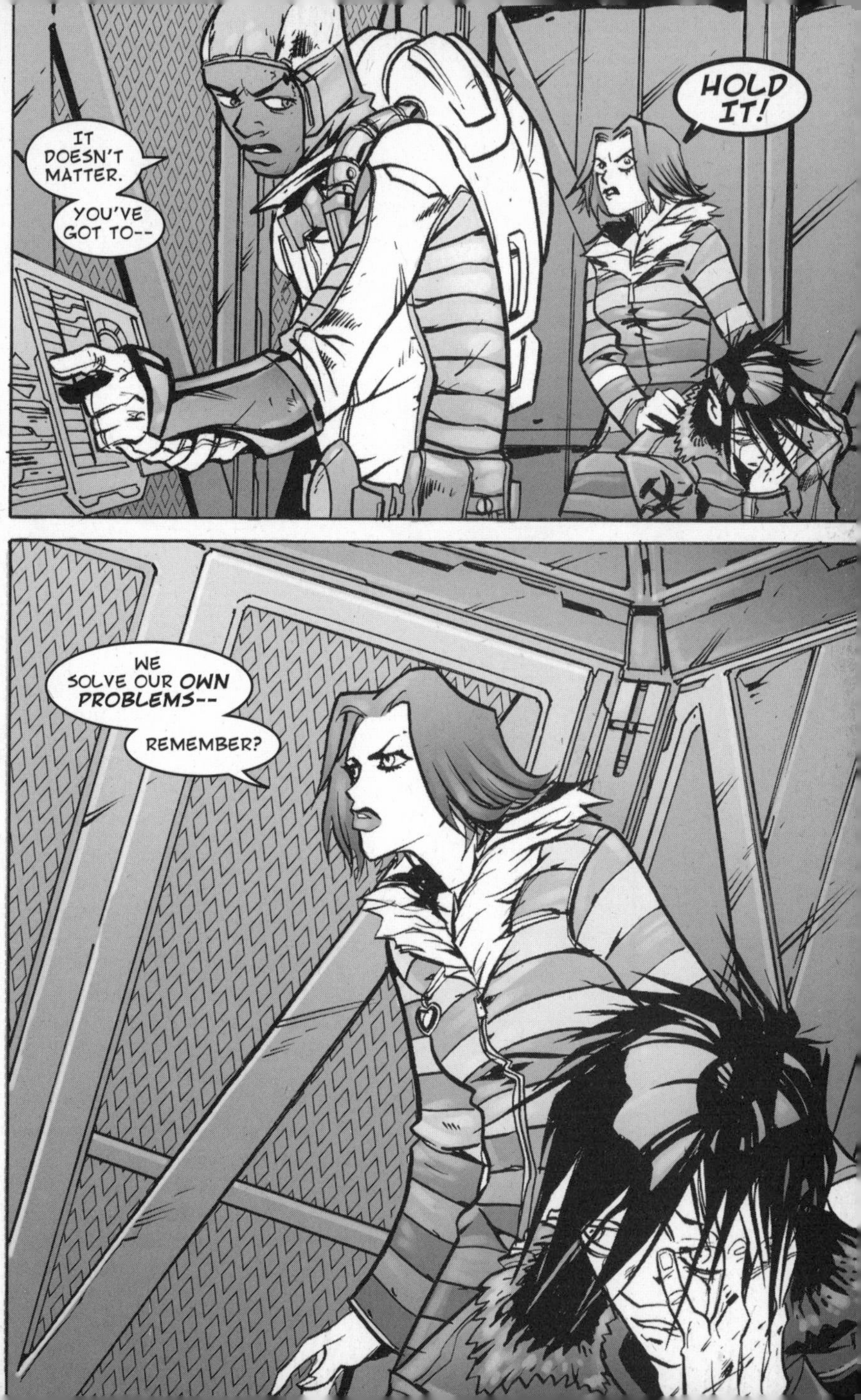
IT DOESN'T MATTER.
YOU'VE GOT TO--
HOLD IT!
WE SOLVE OUR OWN PROBLEMS--
REMEMBER?

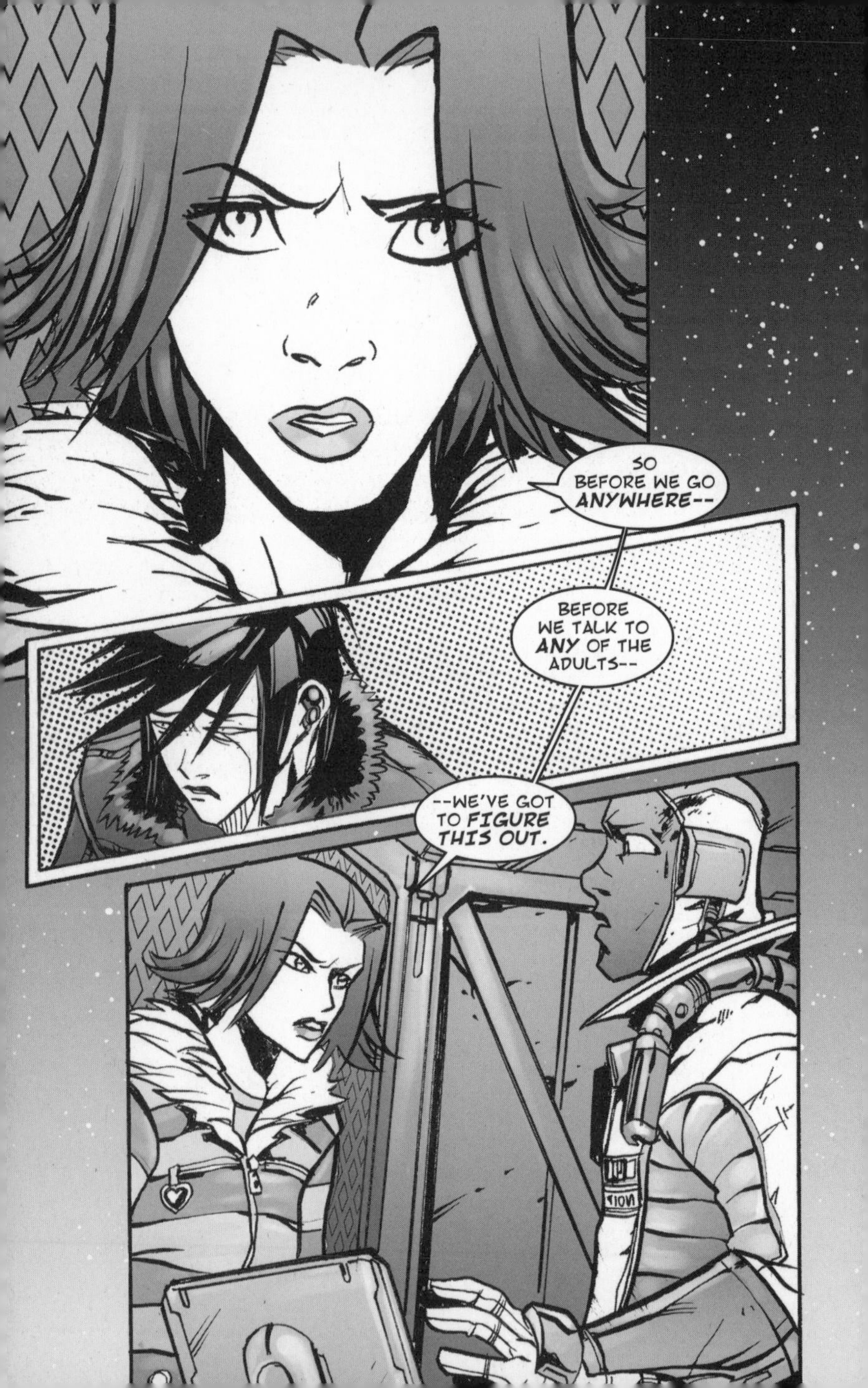
SO BEFORE WE GO ANYWHERE--
BEFORE WE TALK TO ANY OF THE ADULTS--
--WE'VE GOT TO FIGURE THIS OUT.

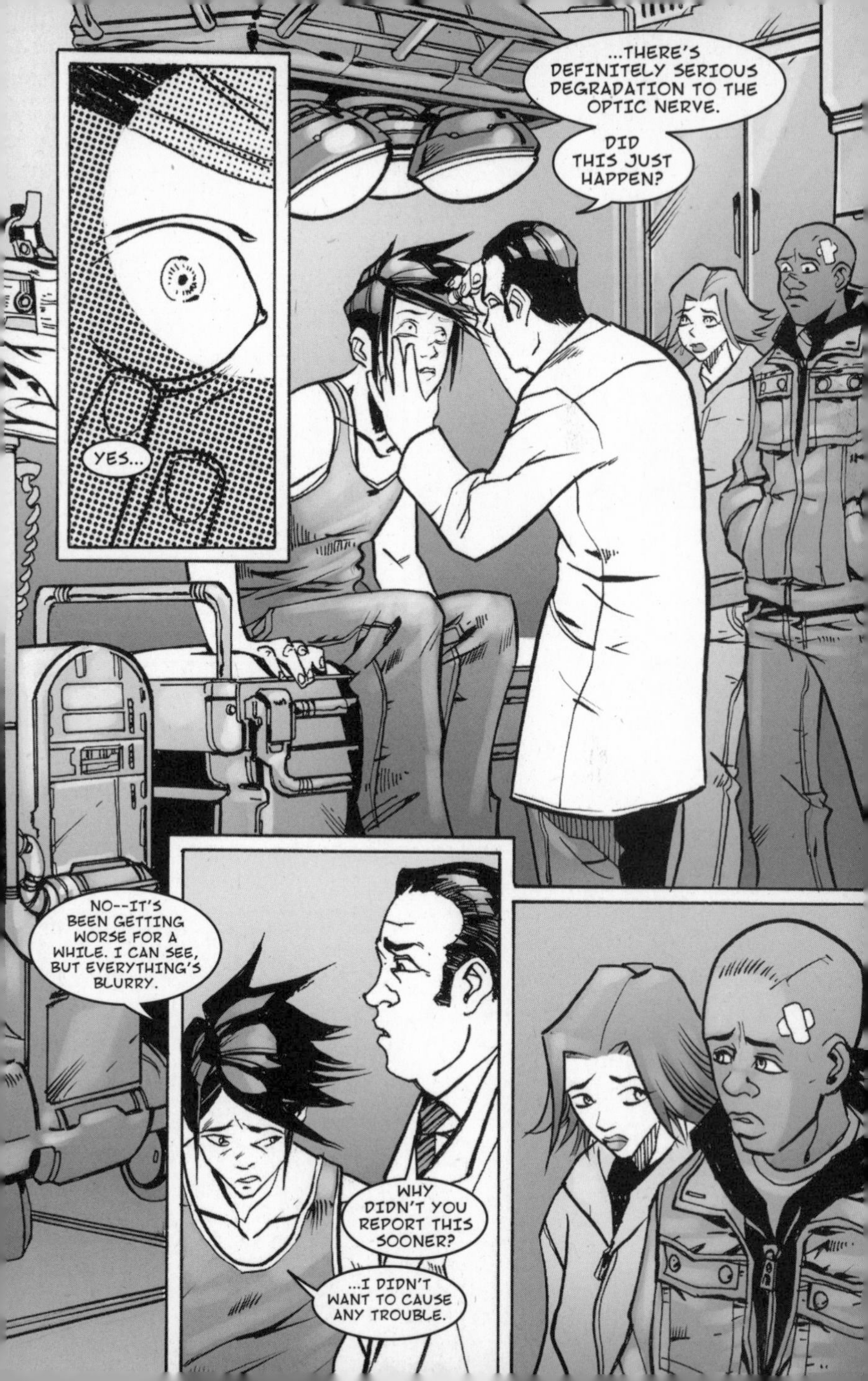
...THERE'S DEFINITELY SERIOUS DEGRADATION TO THE OPTIC NERVE.
DID THIS JUST HAPPEN?
YES...
NO--IT'S BEEN GETTING WORSE FOR A WHILE. I CAN SEE, BUT EVERYTHING'S BLURRY.
WHY DIDN'T YOU REPORT THIS SOONER?
...I DIDN'T WANT TO CAUSE ANY TROUBLE.

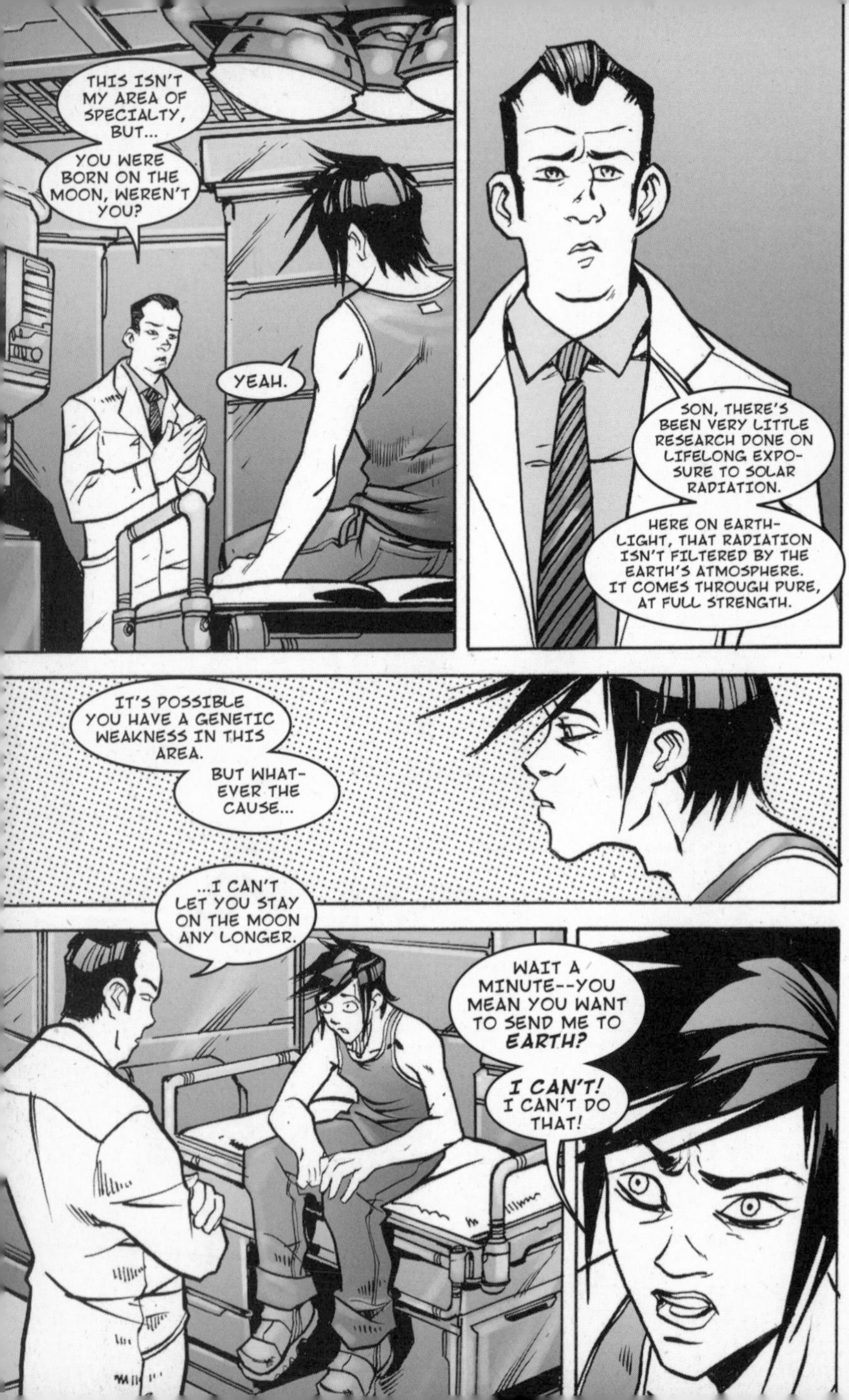
THIS ISN'T MY AREA OF SPECIALTY, BUT...
YOU WERE BORN ON THE MOON, WEREN'T YOU?
YEAH.
SON, THERE'S BEEN VERY LITTLE RESEARCH DONE ON LIFELONG EXPO- SURE TO SOLAR RADIATION.
HERE ON EARTH- LIGHT, THAT RADIATION ISN'T FILTERED BY THE EARTH'S ATMOSPHERE. IT COMES THROUGH PURE, AT FULL STRENGTH.
IT'S POSSIBLE YOU HAVE A GENETIC WEAKNESS IN THIS AREA.
BUT WHAT- EVER THE CAUSE...
...I CAN'T LET YOU STAY ON THE MOON ANY LONGER.
WAIT A MINUTE--YOU MEAN YOU WANT TO SEND ME TO *EARTH?*
I CAN'T! I CAN'T DO THAT!

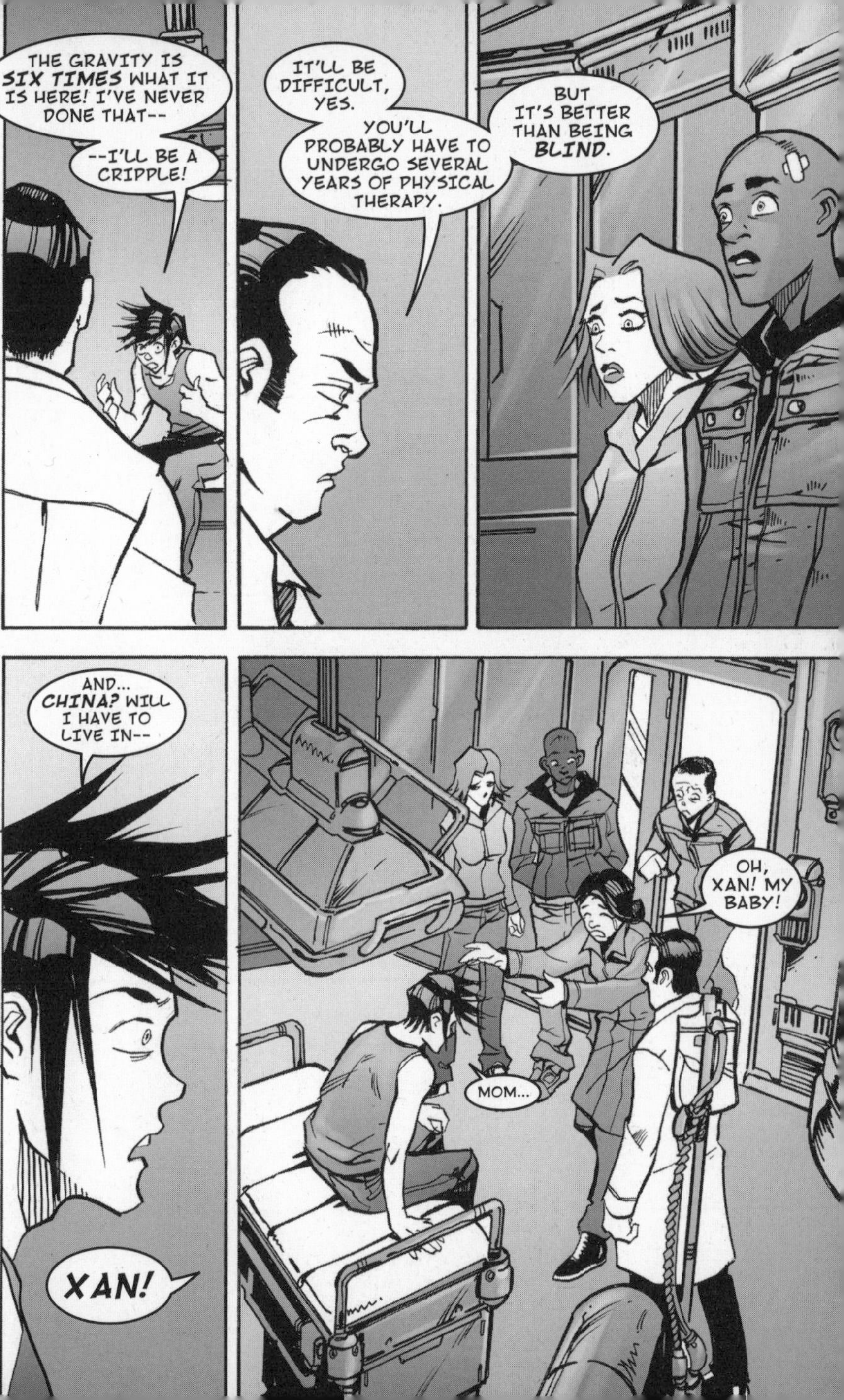
THE GRAVITY IS SIX TIMES WHAT IT IS HERE! I'VE NEVER DONE THAT--
--I'LL BE A CRIPPLE!
IT'LL BE DIFFICULT, YES.
YOU'LL PROBABLY HAVE TO UNDERGO SEVERAL YEARS OF PHYSICAL THERAPY.
BUT IT'S BETTER THAN BEING BLIND.
AND... CHINA? WILL I HAVE TO LIVE IN--
XAN!
OH, XAN! MY BABY!
MOM...

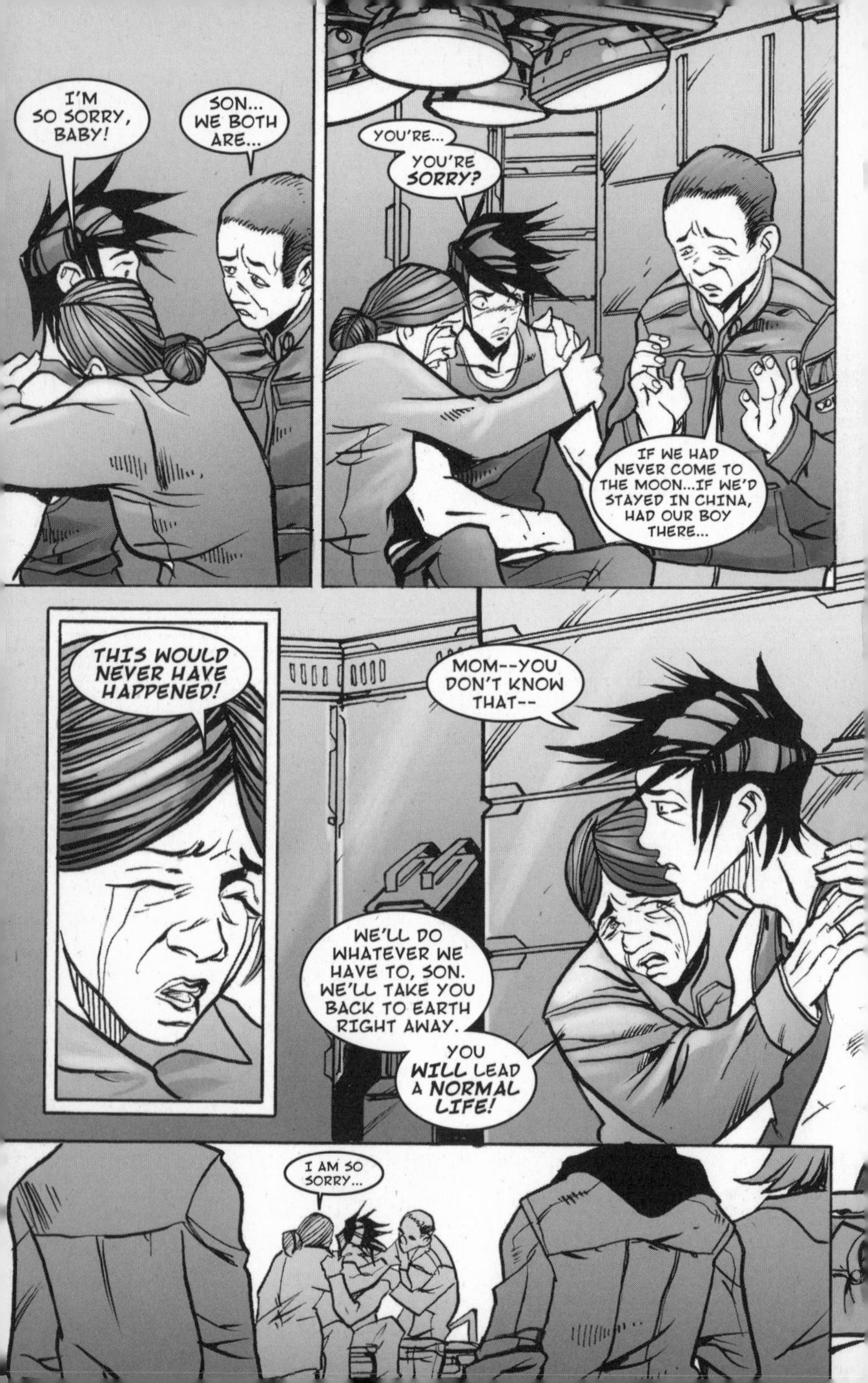
I'M SO SORRY, BABY!
SON... WE BOTH ARE...
YOU'RE...
YOU'RE SORRY?
IF WE HAD NEVER COME TO THE MOON...IF WE'D STAYED IN CHINA, HAD OUR BOY THERE...
THIS WOULD NEVER HAVE HAPPENED!
MOM--YOU DON'T KNOW THAT--
WE'LL DO WHATEVER WE HAVE TO, SON. WE'LL TAKE YOU BACK TO EARTH RIGHT AWAY.
YOU WILL LEAD A NORMAL LIFE!
I AM SO SORRY...

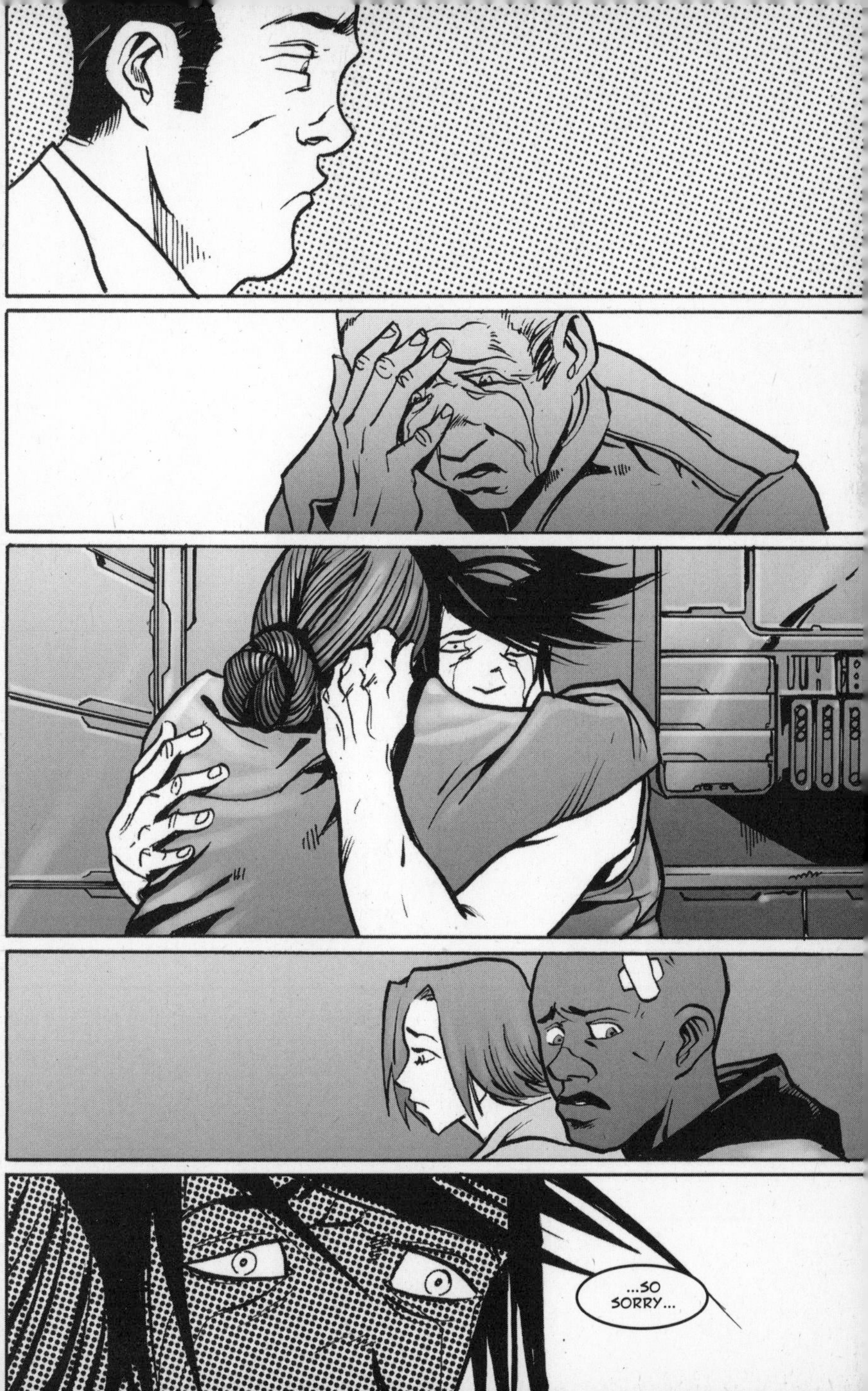
...SO SORRY...

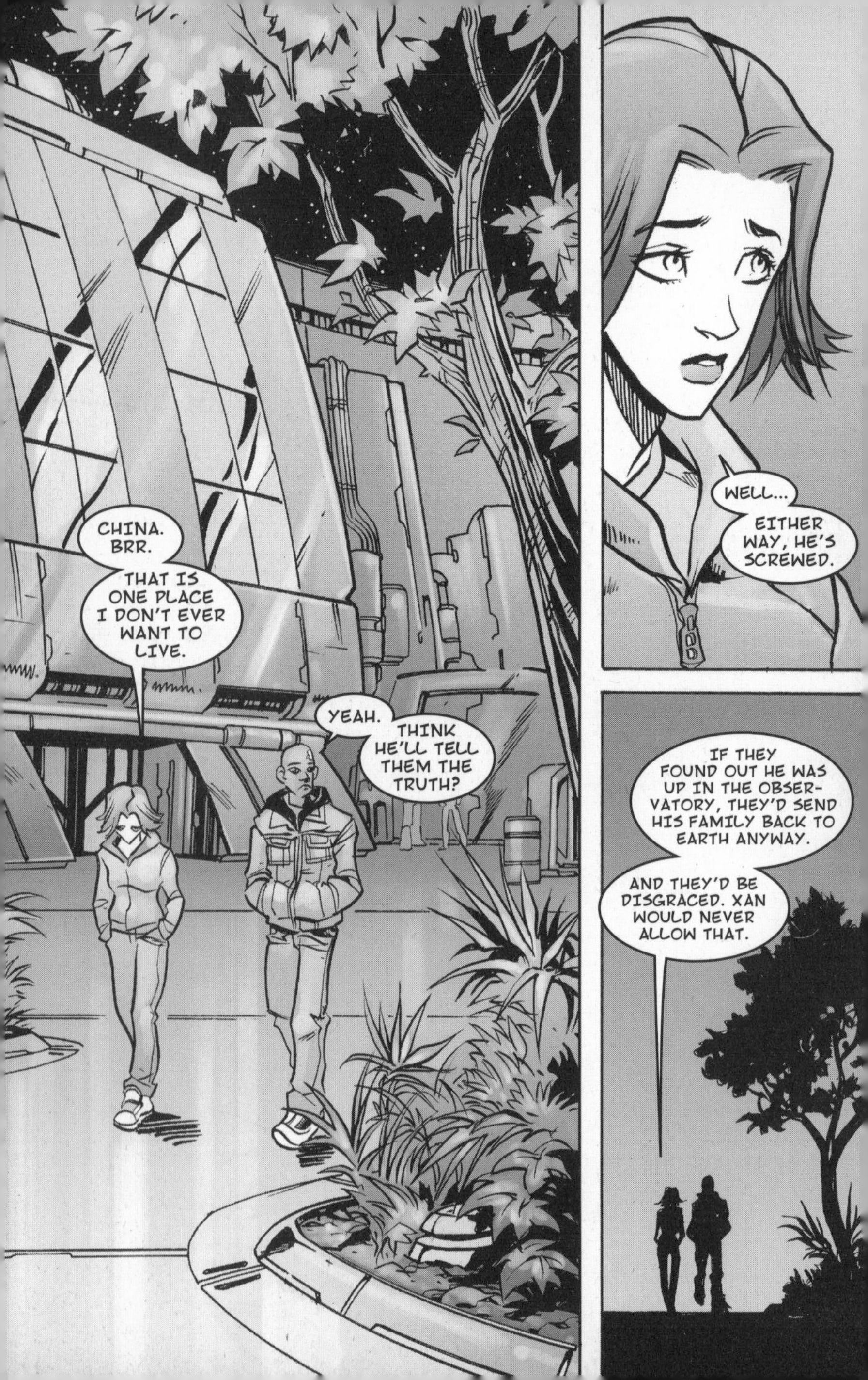
CHINA. BRR.
THAT IS ONE PLACE I DON'T EVER WANT TO LIVE.
YEAH.
THINK HE'LL TELL THEM THE TRUTH?
WELL...
EITHER WAY, HE'S SCREWED.
IF THEY FOUND OUT HE WAS UP IN THE OBSERVATORY, THEY'D SEND HIS FAMILY BACK TO EARTH ANYWAY.
AND THEY'D BE DISGRACED. XAN WOULD NEVER ALLOW THAT.

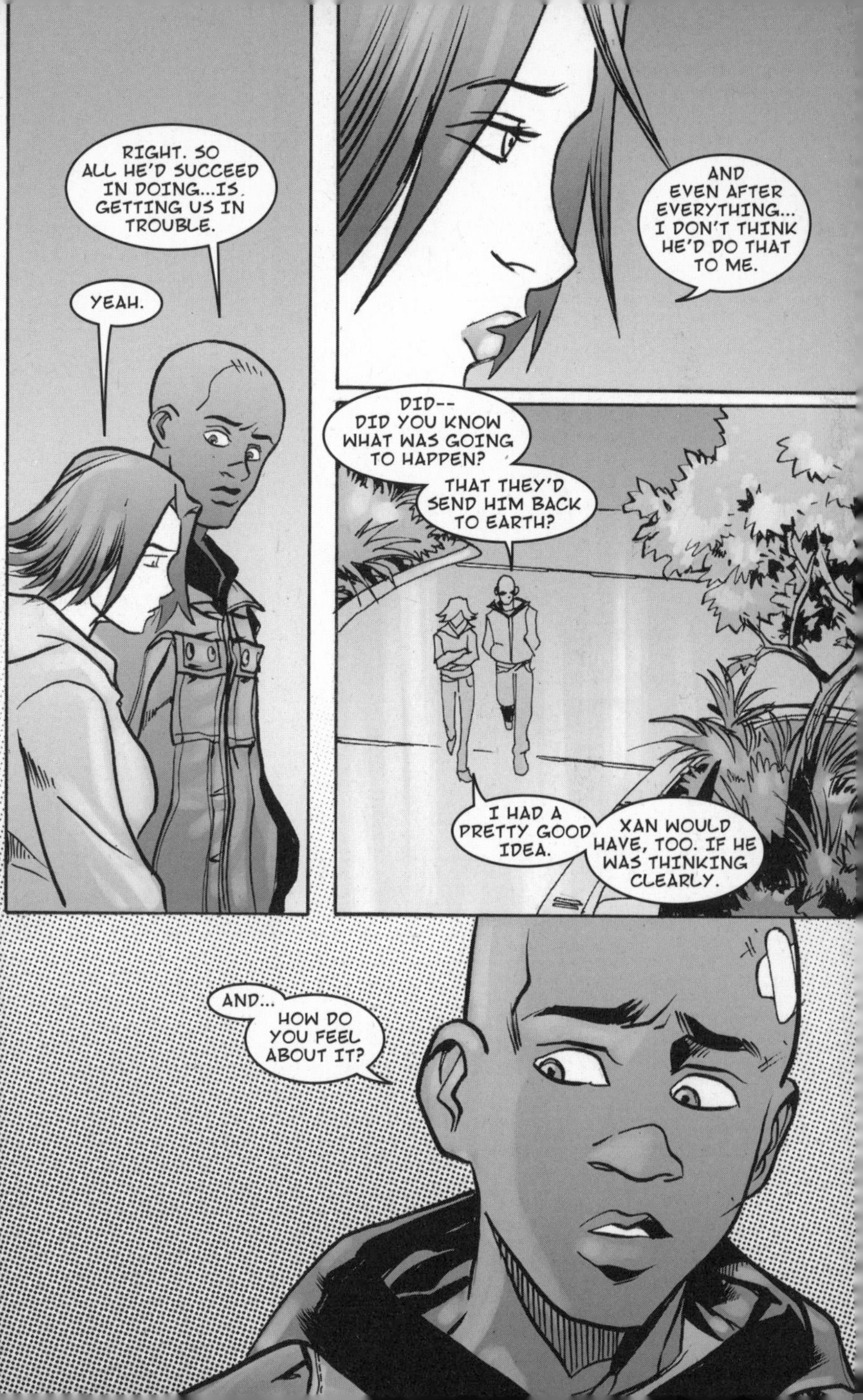
RIGHT. SO ALL HE'D SUCCEED IN DOING...IS. GETTING US IN TROUBLE.
YEAH.
AND EVEN AFTER EVERYTHING... I DON'T THINK HE'D DO THAT TO ME.
DID-- DID YOU KNOW WHAT WAS GOING TO HAPPEN?
THAT THEY'D SEND HIM BACK TO EARTH?
I HAD A PRETTY GOOD IDEA.
XAN WOULD HAVE, TOO. IF HE WAS THINKING CLEARLY.
AND... HOW DO YOU FEEL ABOUT IT?

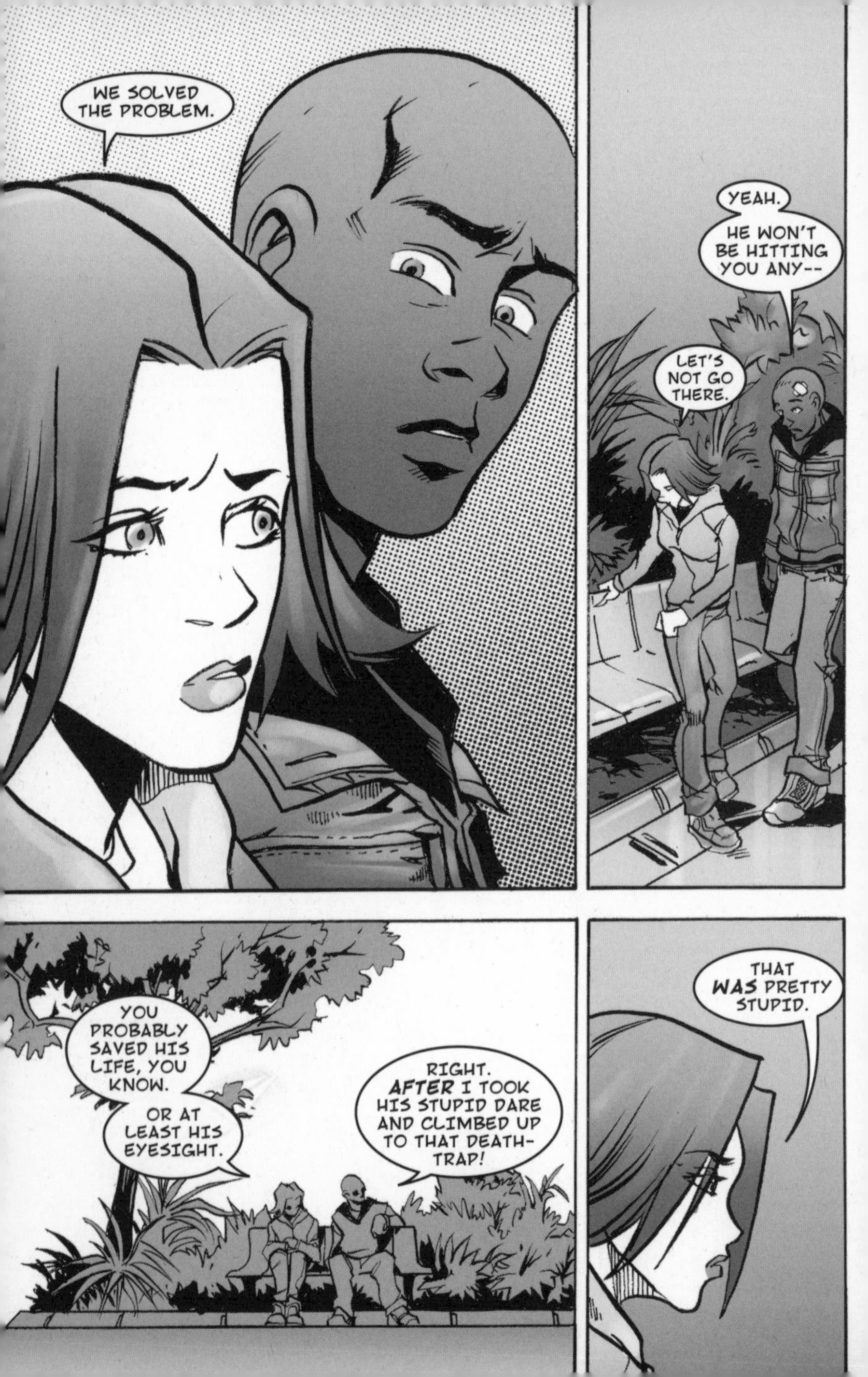
WE SOLVED THE PROBLEM.
YEAH.
HE WON'T BE HITTING YOU ANY--
LET'S NOT GO THERE.
YOU PROBABLY SAVED HIS LIFE, YOU KNOW.
OR AT LEAST HIS EYESIGHT.
RIGHT. **AFTER** I TOOK HIS STUPID DARE AND CLIMBED UP TO THAT DEATH-TRAP!
THAT **WAS** PRETTY STUPID.

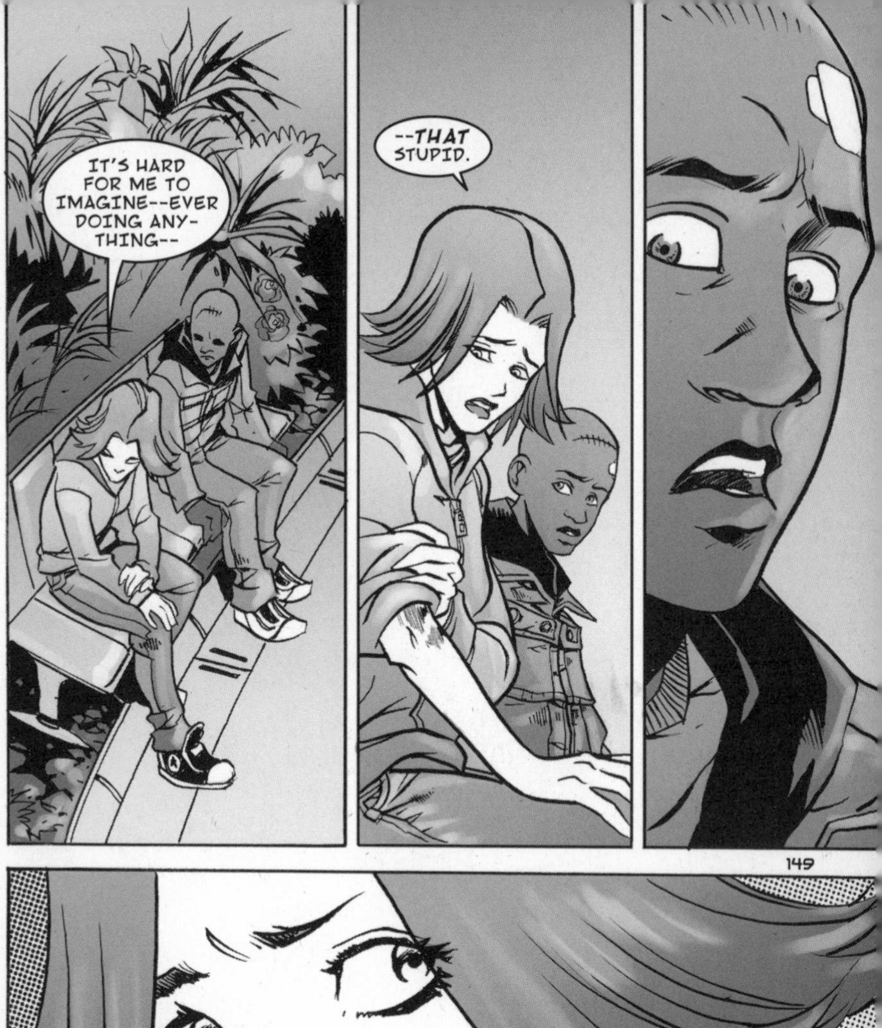
IT'S HARD FOR ME TO IMAGINE--EVER DOING ANY-THING--
--THAT STUPID.

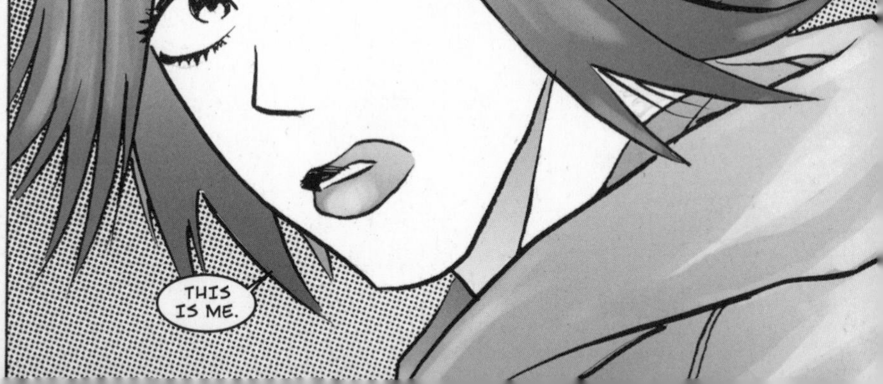
THIS IS ME.

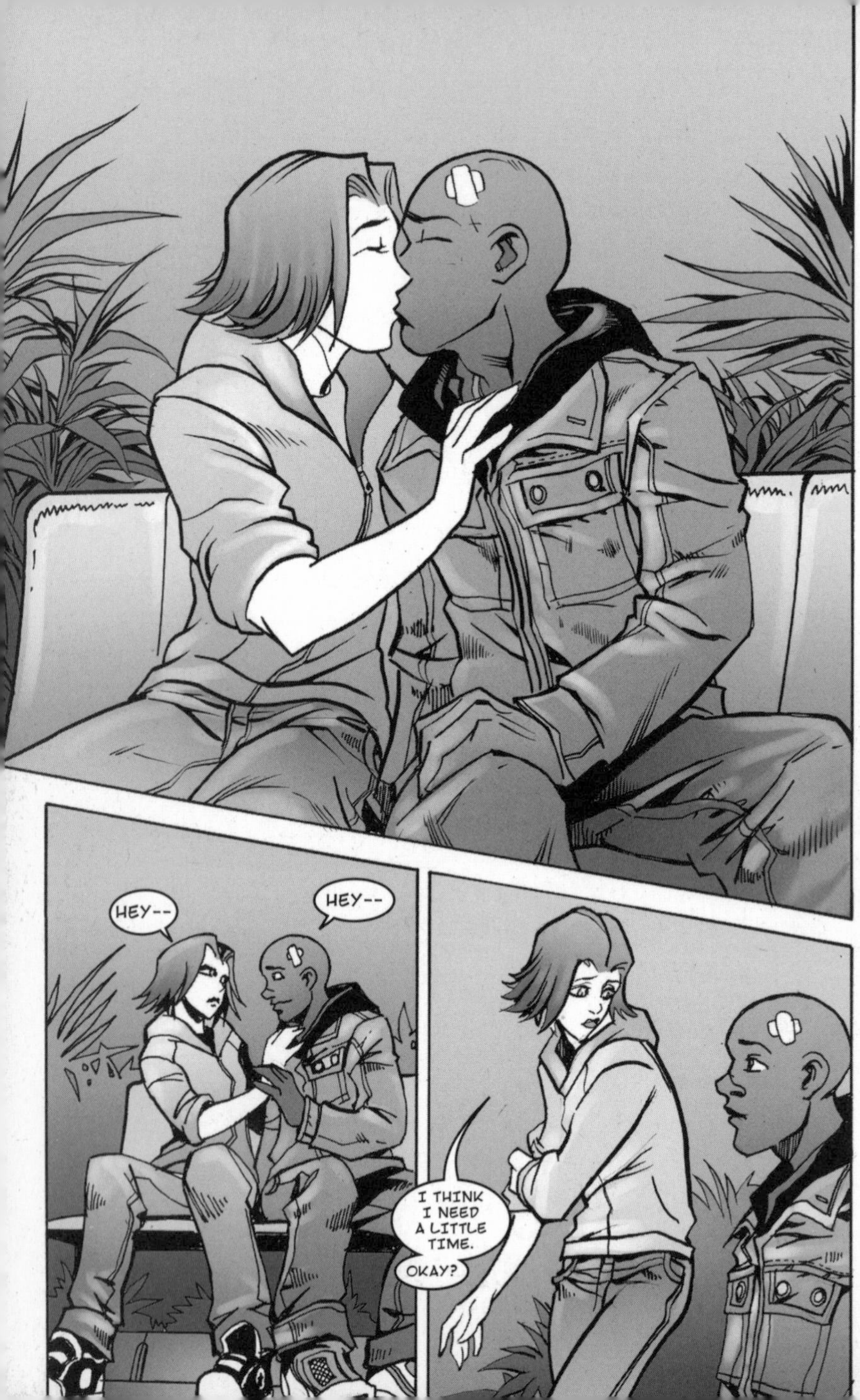
HEY--
HEY--
I THINK I NEED A LITTLE TIME.
OKAY?

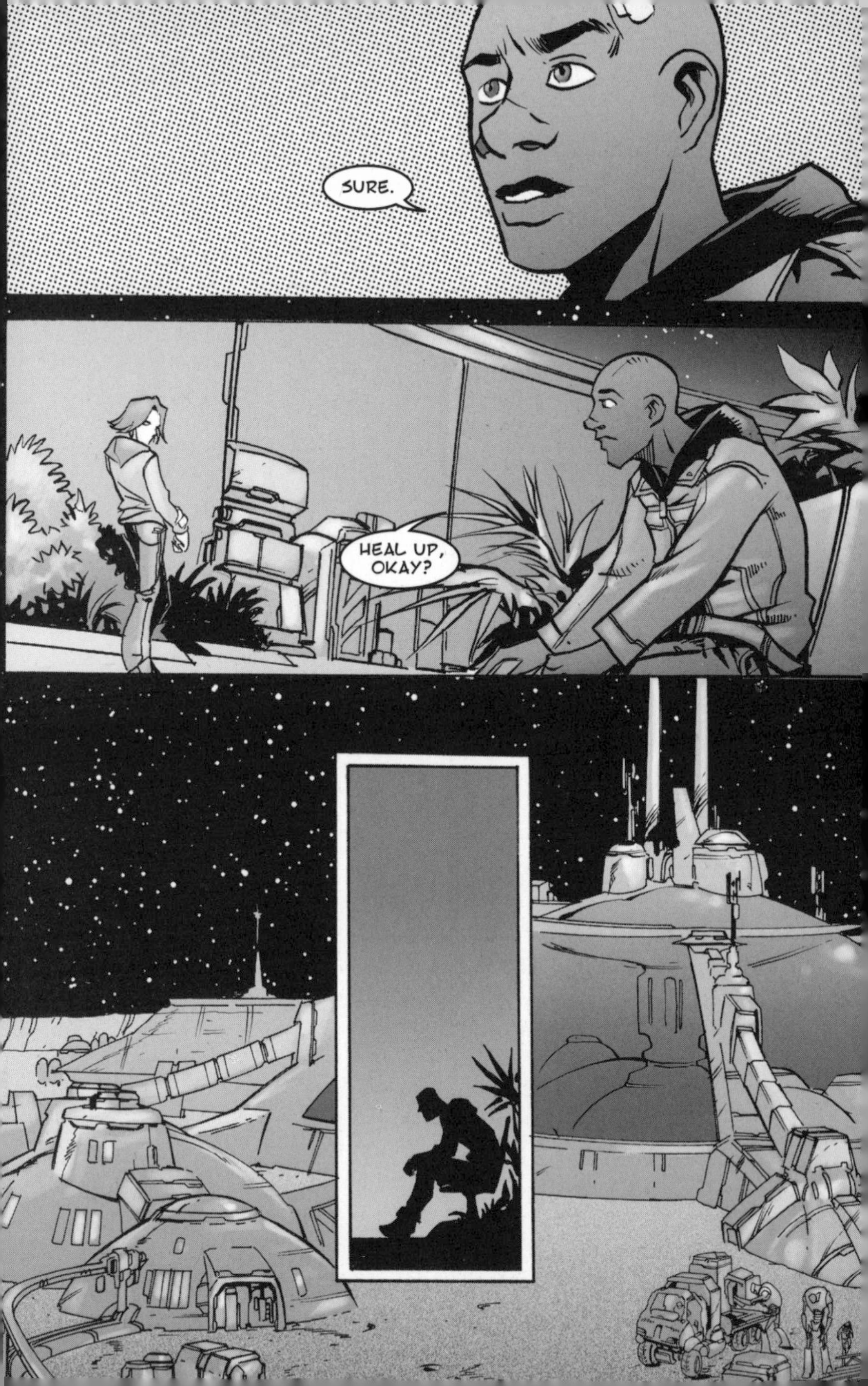
SURE.
HEAL UP, OKAY?

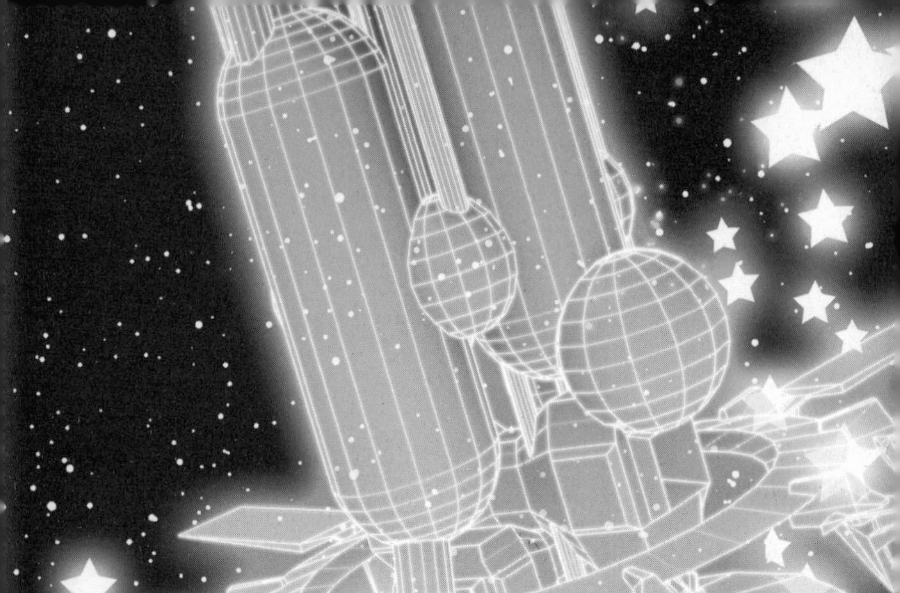
CHAPTER FIVE:
ALL THINGS
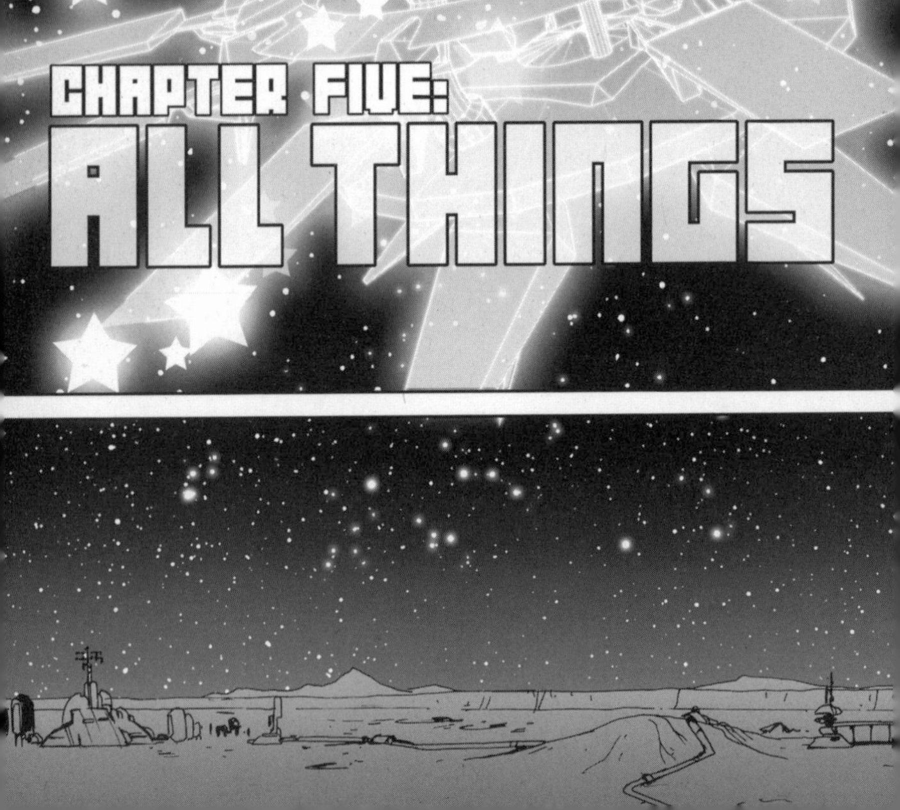

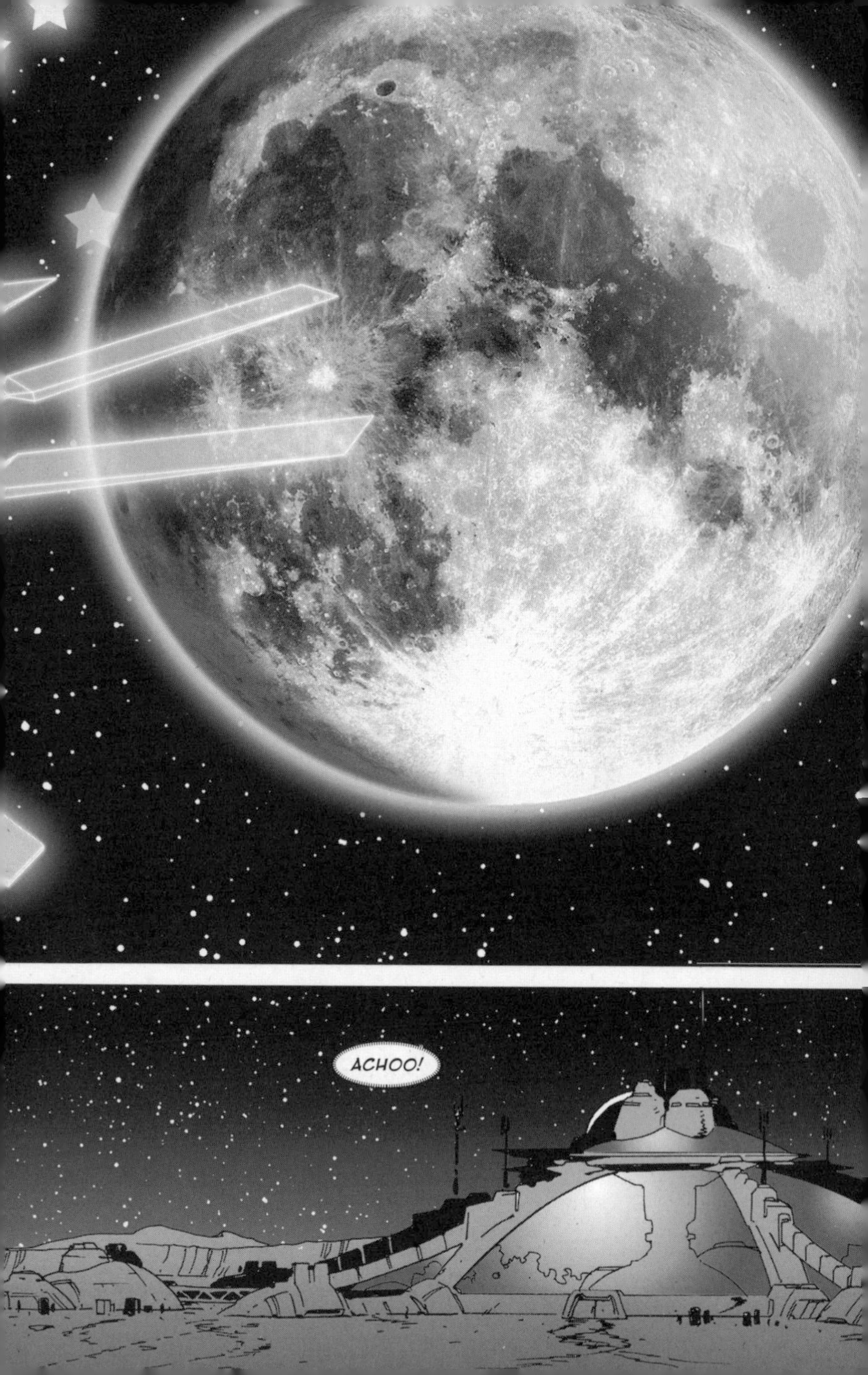
ACHOO!

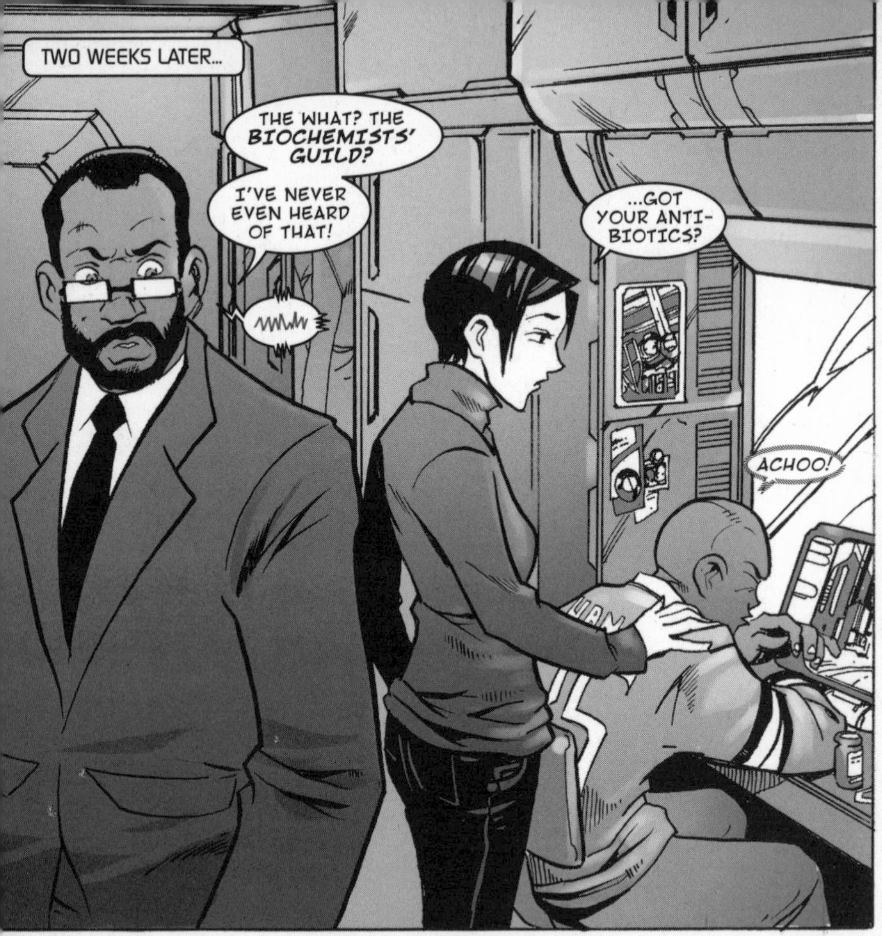
TWO WEEKS LATER...
THE WHAT? THE BIOCHEMISTS' GUILD?
I'VE NEVER EVEN HEARD OF THAT!
...GOT YOUR ANTI-BIOTICS?
ACHOO!
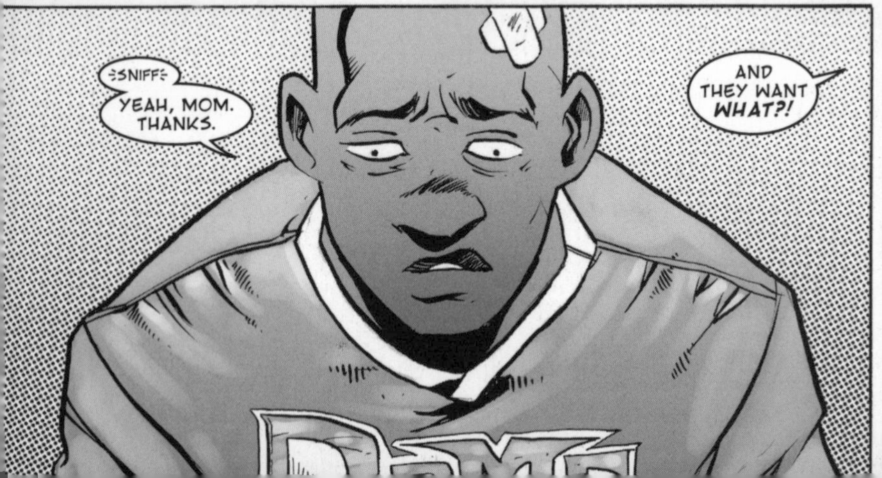
SNIFF
YEAH, MOM. THANKS.
AND THEY WANT WHAT?!

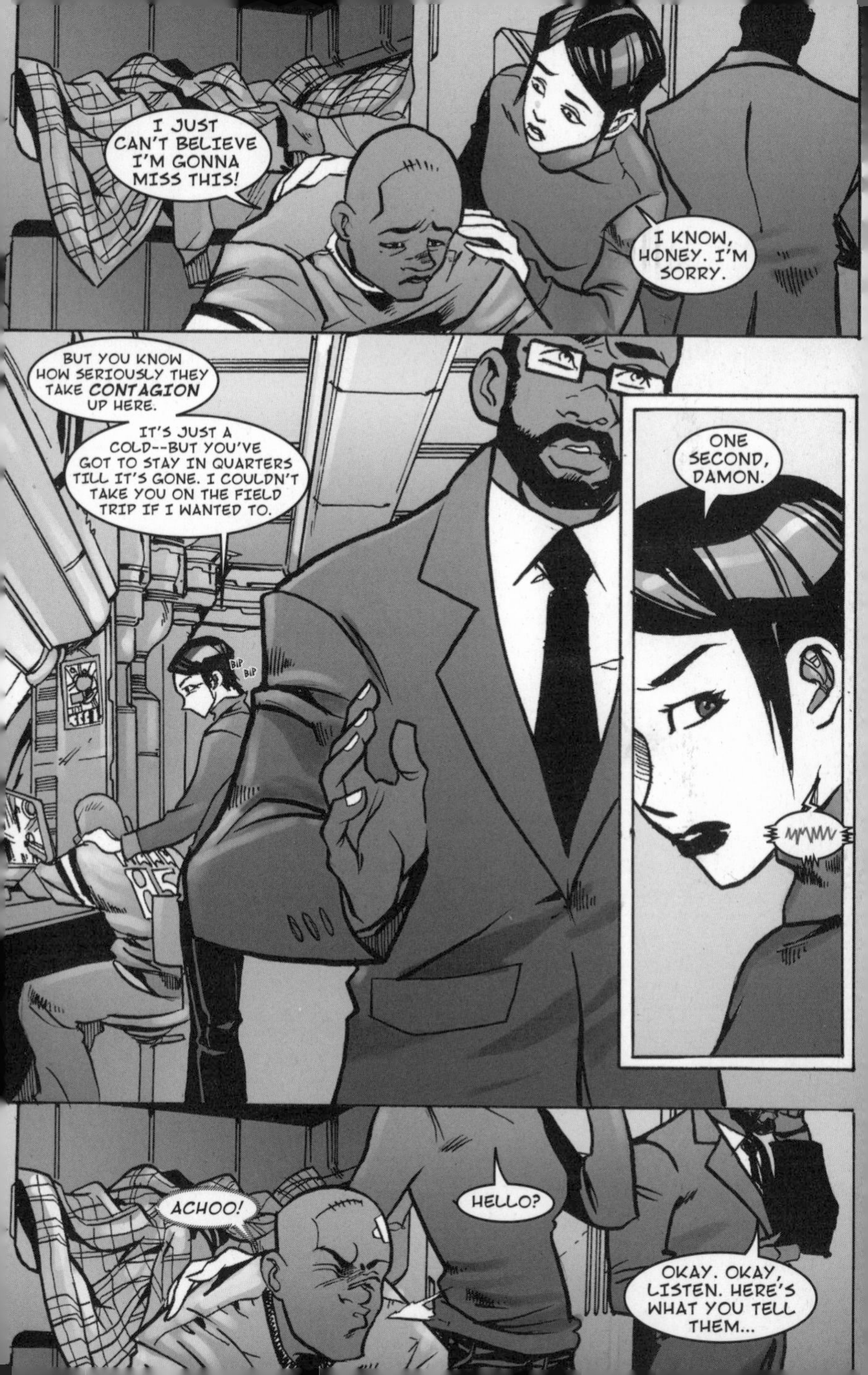
I JUST CAN'T BELIEVE I'M GONNA MISS THIS!
I KNOW, HONEY. I'M SORRY.
BUT YOU KNOW HOW SERIOUSLY THEY TAKE CONTAGION UP HERE.
IT'S JUST A COLD--BUT YOU'VE GOT TO STAY IN QUARTERS TILL IT'S GONE. I COULDN'T TAKE YOU ON THE FIELD TRIP IF I WANTED TO.
BIP BIP
ONE SECOND, DAMON.
MMWWV
ACHOO!
HELLO?
OKAY. OKAY, LISTEN. HERE'S WHAT YOU TELL THEM...

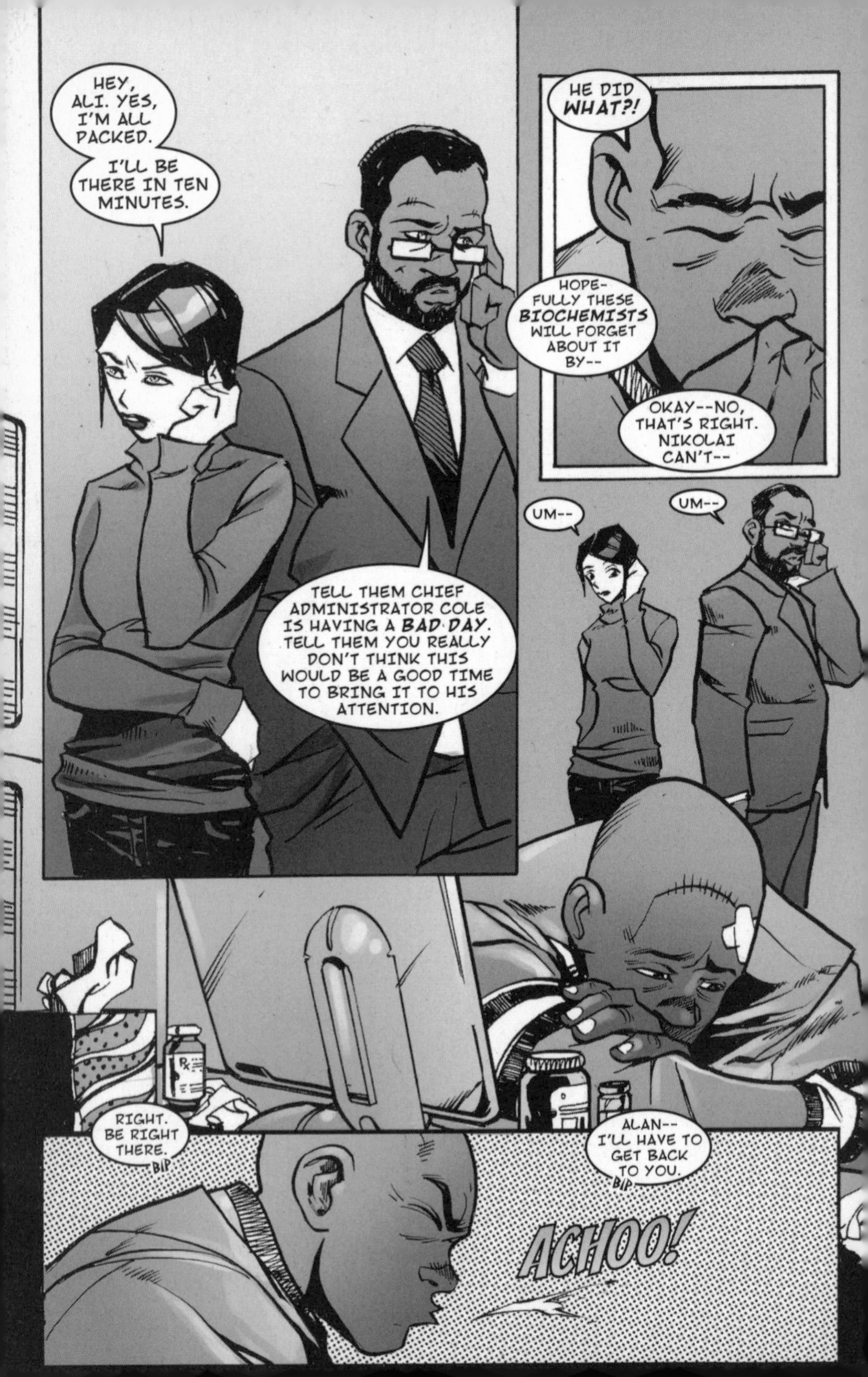
HEY, ALI. YES, I'M ALL PACKED.
I'LL BE THERE IN TEN MINUTES.
TELL THEM CHIEF ADMINISTRATOR COLE IS HAVING A BAD DAY. TELL THEM YOU REALLY DON'T THINK THIS WOULD BE A GOOD TIME TO BRING IT TO HIS ATTENTION.
HE DID WHAT?!
HOPE-FULLY THESE BIOCHEMISTS WILL FORGET ABOUT IT BY--
OKAY--NO, THAT'S RIGHT. NIKOLAI CAN'T--
UM--
UM--
RIGHT. BE RIGHT THERE.
BIP
ALAN-- I'LL HAVE TO GET BACK TO YOU.
BIP
ACHOO!

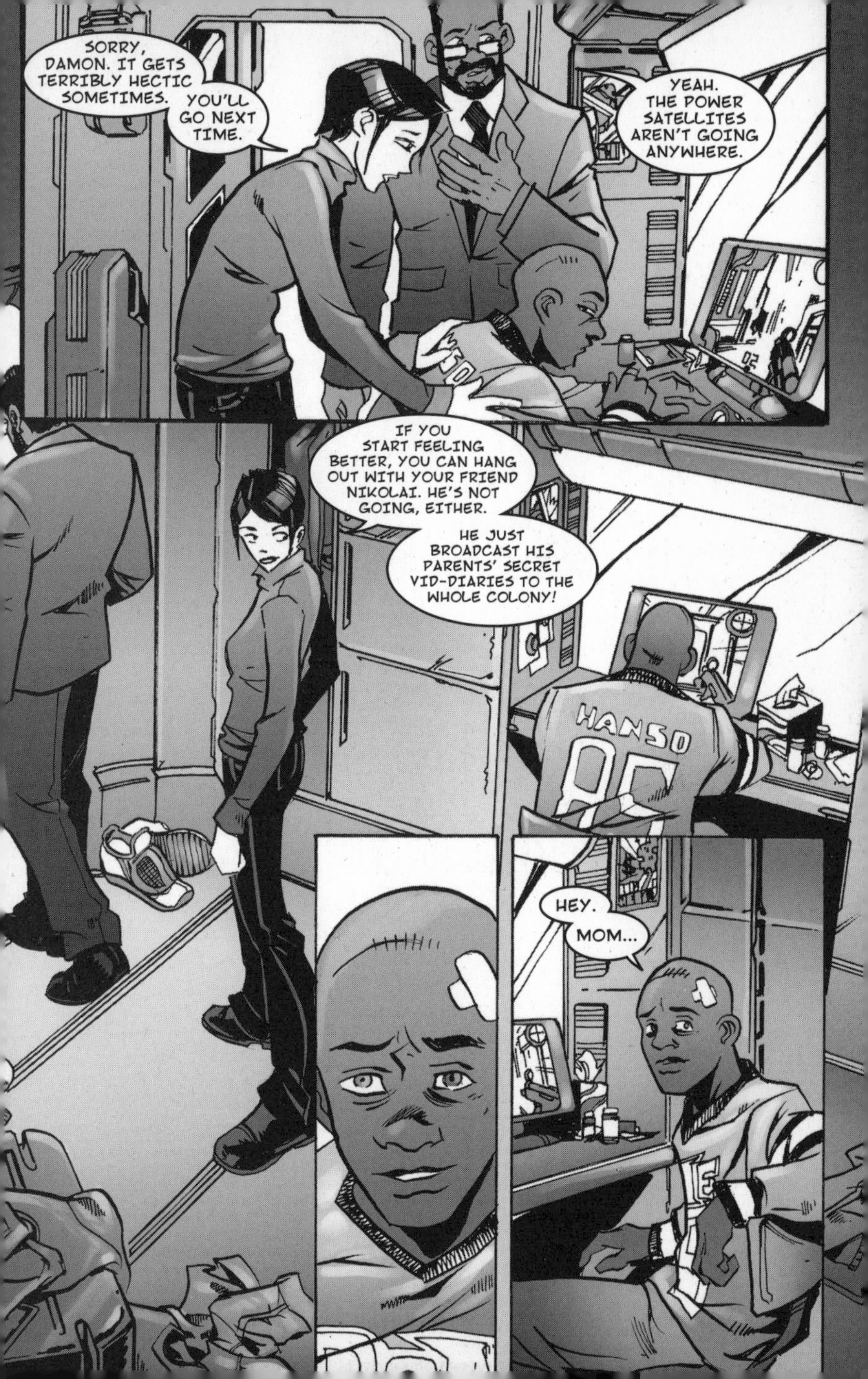
SORRY, DAMON. IT GETS TERRIBLY HECTIC SOMETIMES.
YOU'LL GO NEXT TIME.
YEAH. THE POWER SATELLITES AREN'T GOING ANYWHERE.
IF YOU START FEELING BETTER, YOU CAN HANG OUT WITH YOUR FRIEND NIKOLAI. HE'S NOT GOING, EITHER.
HE JUST BROADCAST HIS PARENTS' SECRET VID-DIARIES TO THE WHOLE COLONY!
HANSO
HEY.
MOM...

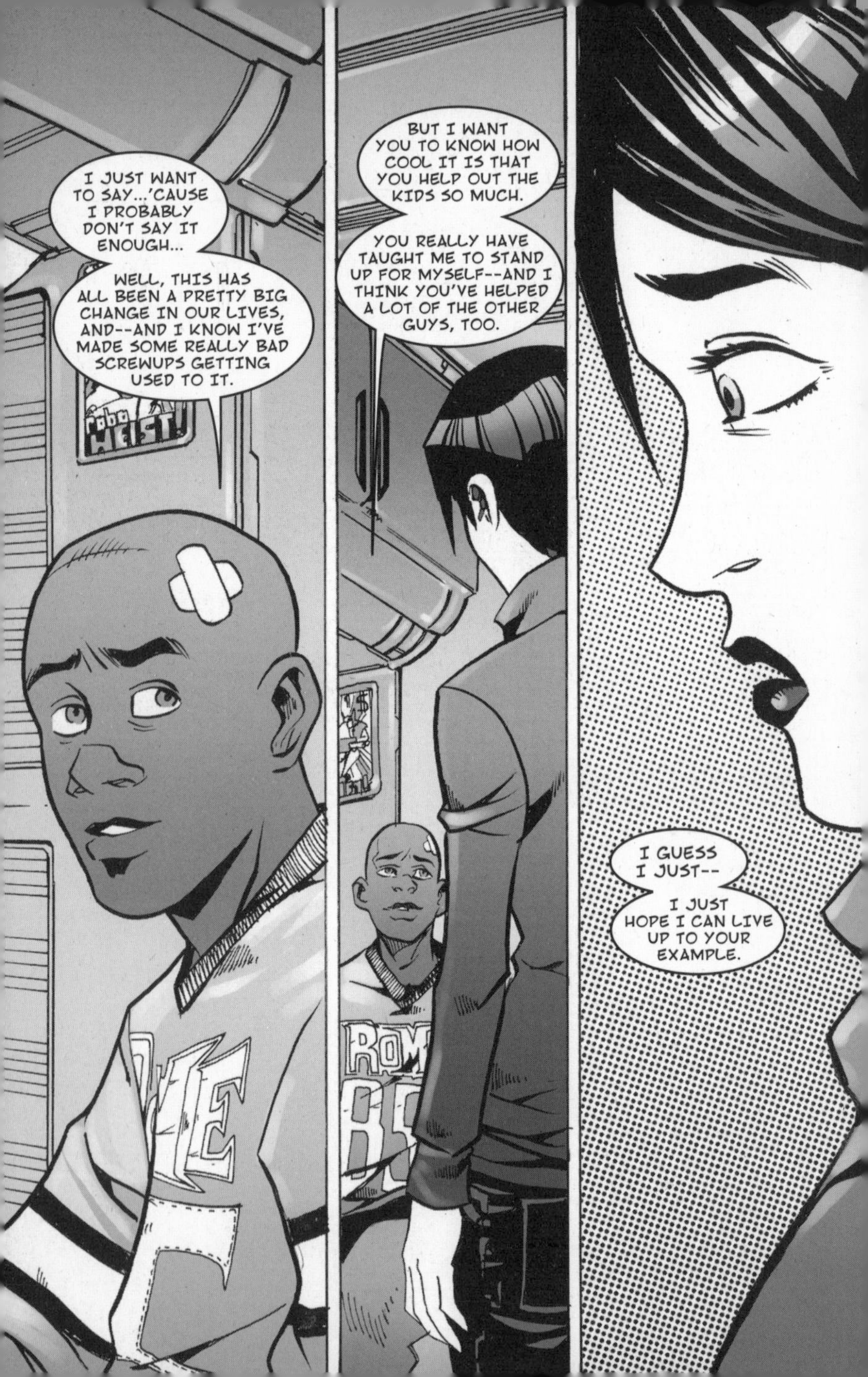
I JUST WANT TO SAY...'CAUSE I PROBABLY DON'T SAY IT ENOUGH...
WELL, THIS HAS ALL BEEN A PRETTY BIG CHANGE IN OUR LIVES, AND--AND I KNOW I'VE MADE SOME REALLY BAD SCREWUPS GETTING USED TO IT.
robo HEIST!
BUT I WANT YOU TO KNOW HOW COOL IT IS THAT YOU HELP OUT THE KIDS SO MUCH.
YOU REALLY HAVE TAUGHT ME TO STAND UP FOR MYSELF--AND I THINK YOU'VE HELPED A LOT OF THE OTHER GUYS, TOO.
I GUESS I JUST--
I JUST HOPE I CAN LIVE UP TO YOUR EXAMPLE.

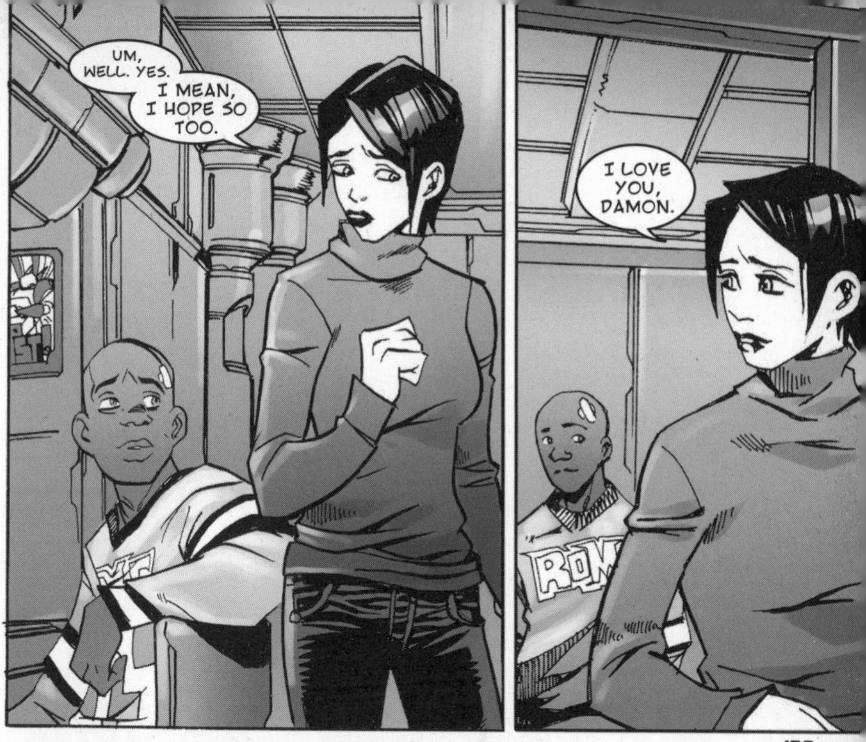
UM, WELL. YES.
I MEAN, I HOPE SO TOO.
I LOVE YOU, DAMON.

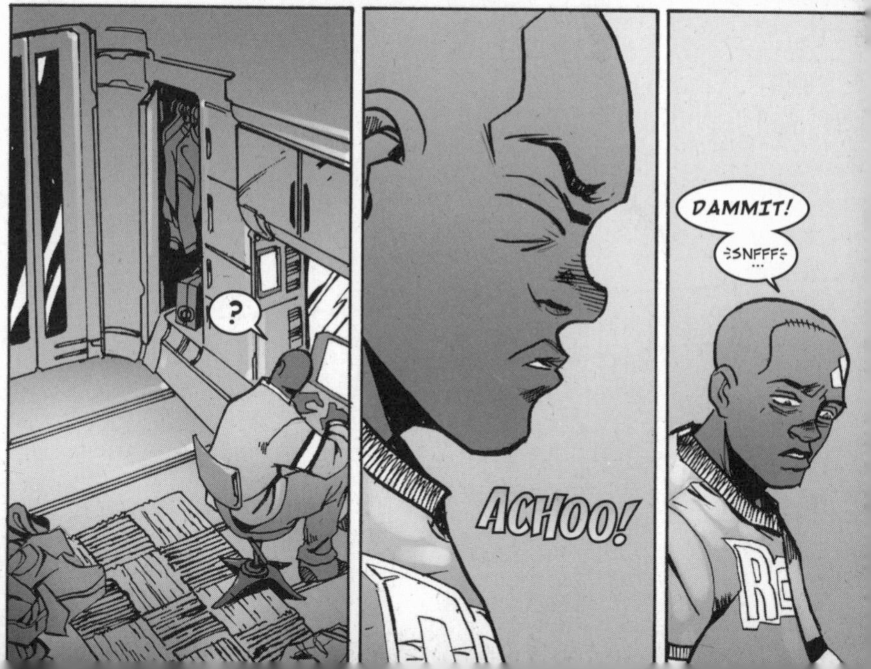
?
ACHOO!
DAMMIT!
SNFFF...

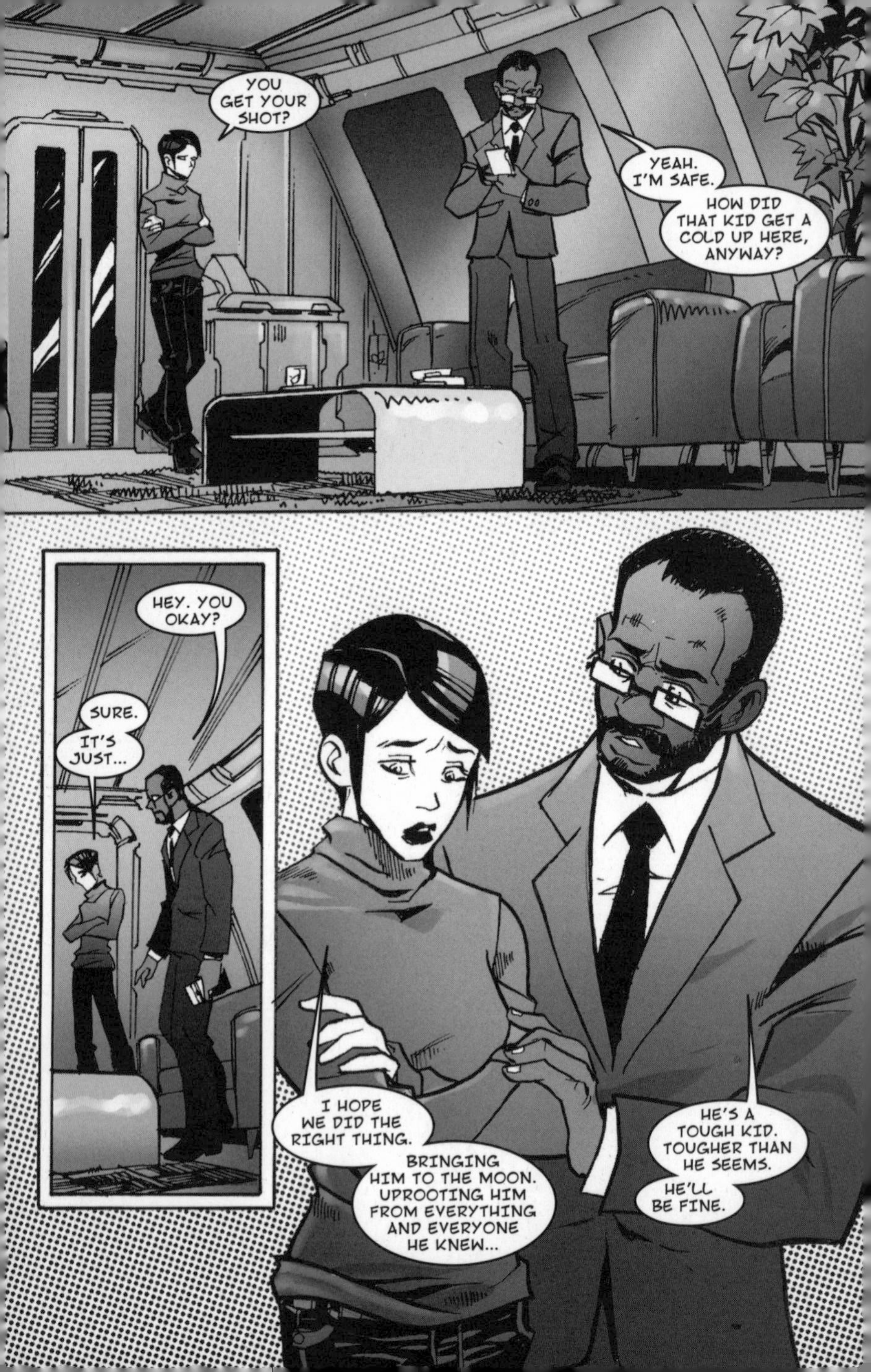
YOU GET YOUR SHOT?
YEAH. I'M SAFE.
HOW DID THAT KID GET A COLD UP HERE, ANYWAY?
HEY. YOU OKAY?
SURE.
IT'S JUST...
I HOPE WE DID THE RIGHT THING.
BRINGING HIM TO THE MOON. UPROOTING HIM FROM EVERYTHING AND EVERYONE HE KNEW...
HE'S A TOUGH KID. TOUGHER THAN HE SEEMS.
HE'LL BE FINE.

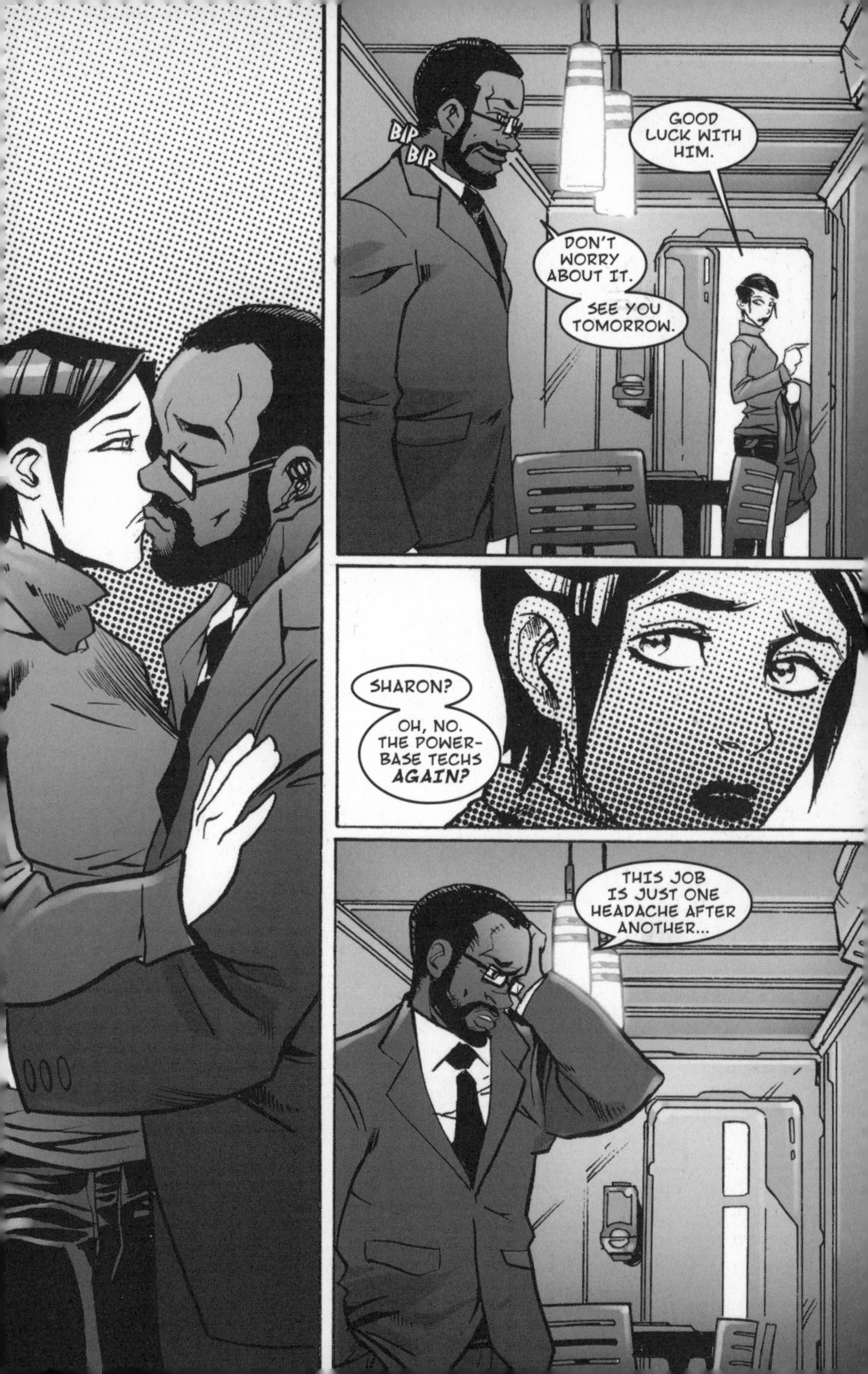
BIP
BIP
GOOD LUCK WITH HIM.
DON'T WORRY ABOUT IT.
SEE YOU TOMORROW.
SHARON?
OH, NO. THE POWER-BASE TECHS AGAIN?
THIS JOB IS JUST ONE HEADACHE AFTER ANOTHER...

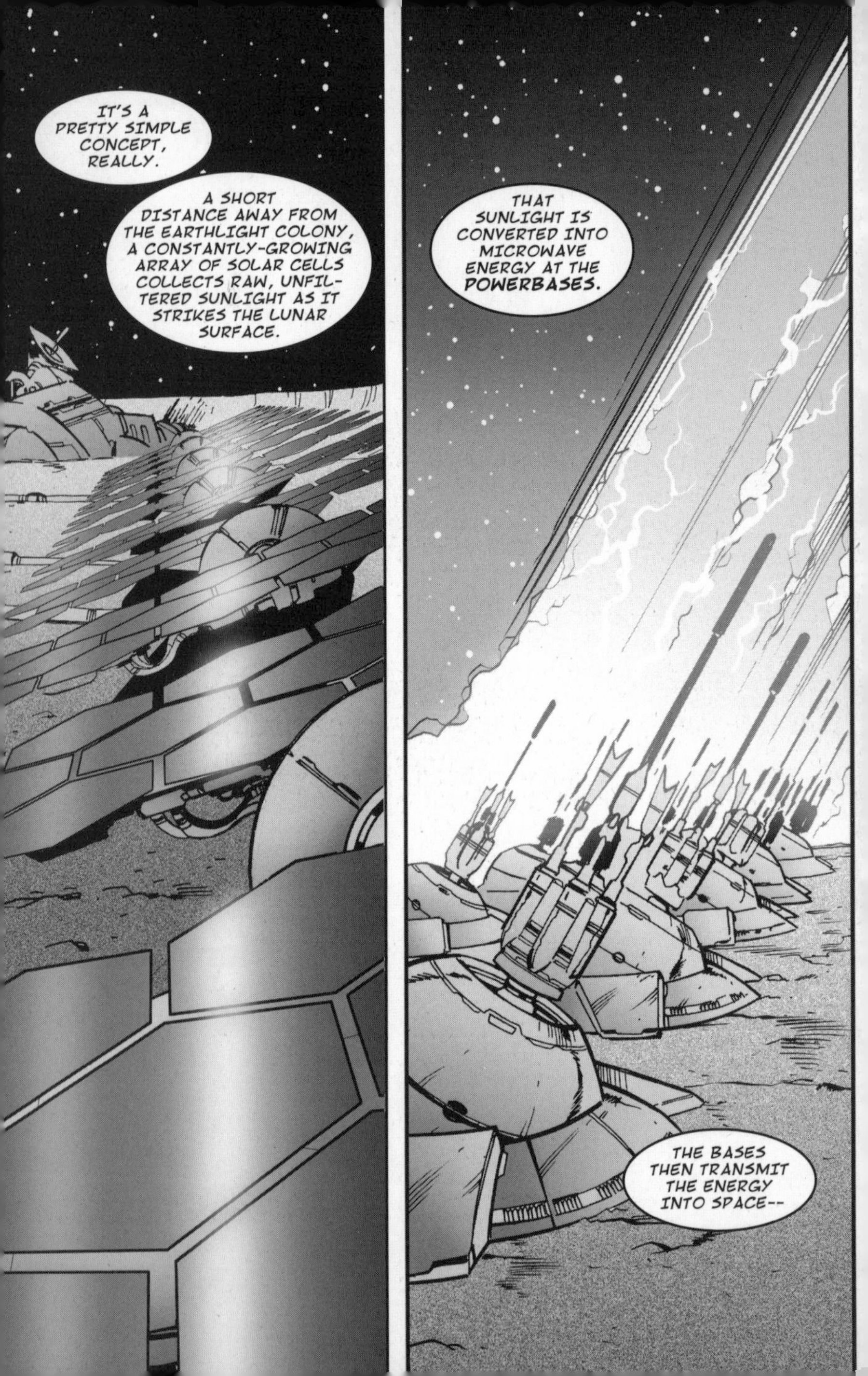
IT'S A PRETTY SIMPLE CONCEPT, REALLY.
A SHORT DISTANCE AWAY FROM THE EARTHLIGHT COLONY, A CONSTANTLY-GROWING ARRAY OF SOLAR CELLS COLLECTS RAW, UNFIL-TERED SUNLIGHT AS IT STRIKES THE LUNAR SURFACE.
THAT SUNLIGHT IS CONVERTED INTO MICROWAVE ENERGY AT THE POWERBASES.
THE BASES THEN TRANSMIT THE ENERGY INTO SPACE--

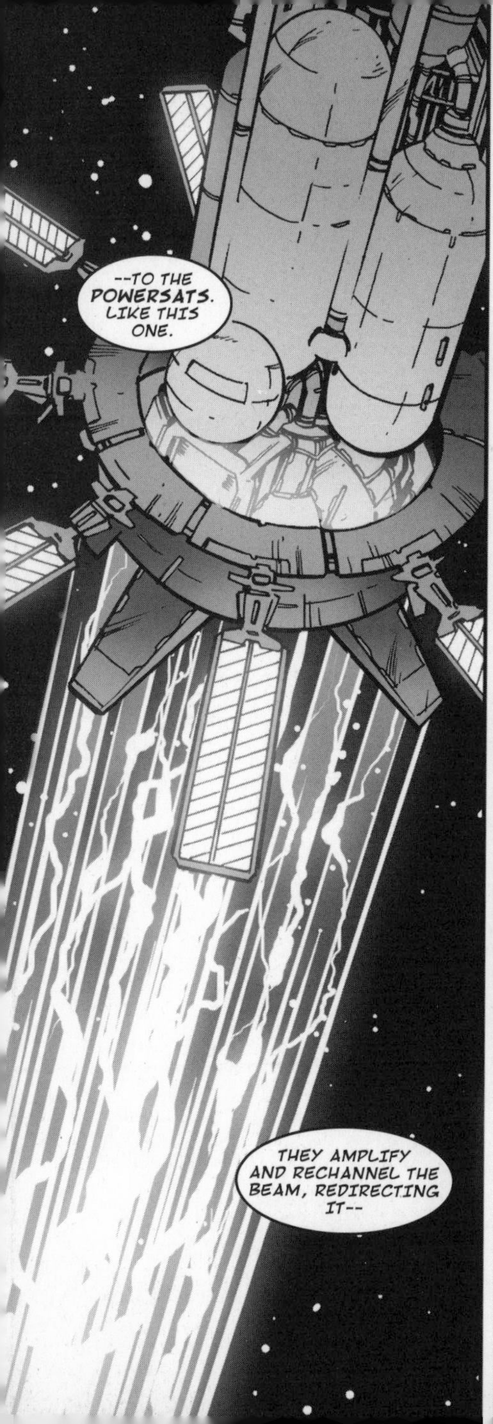
--TO THE POWERSATS. LIKE THIS ONE.
THEY AMPLIFY AND RECHANNEL THE BEAM, REDIRECTING IT--
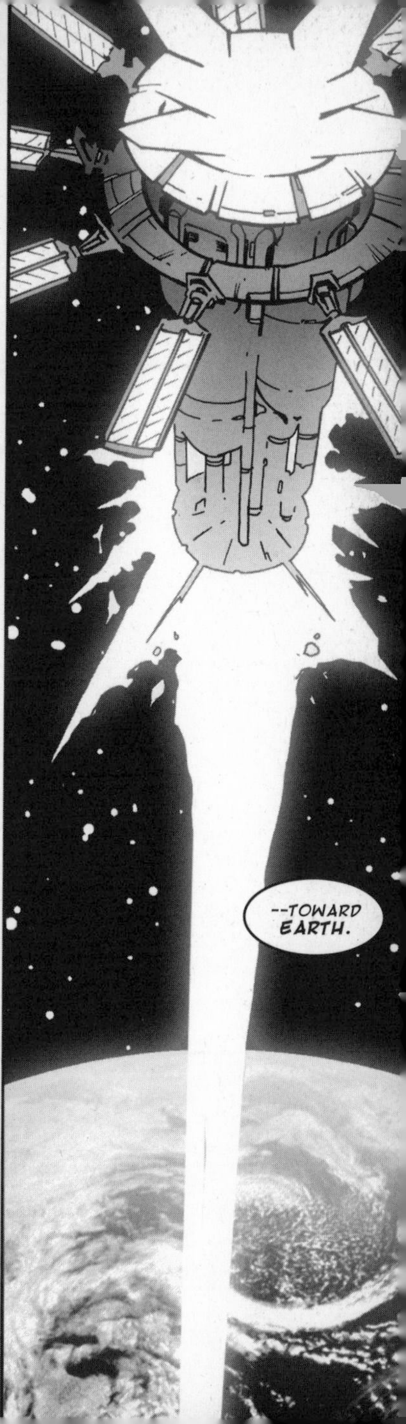
--TOWARD EARTH.

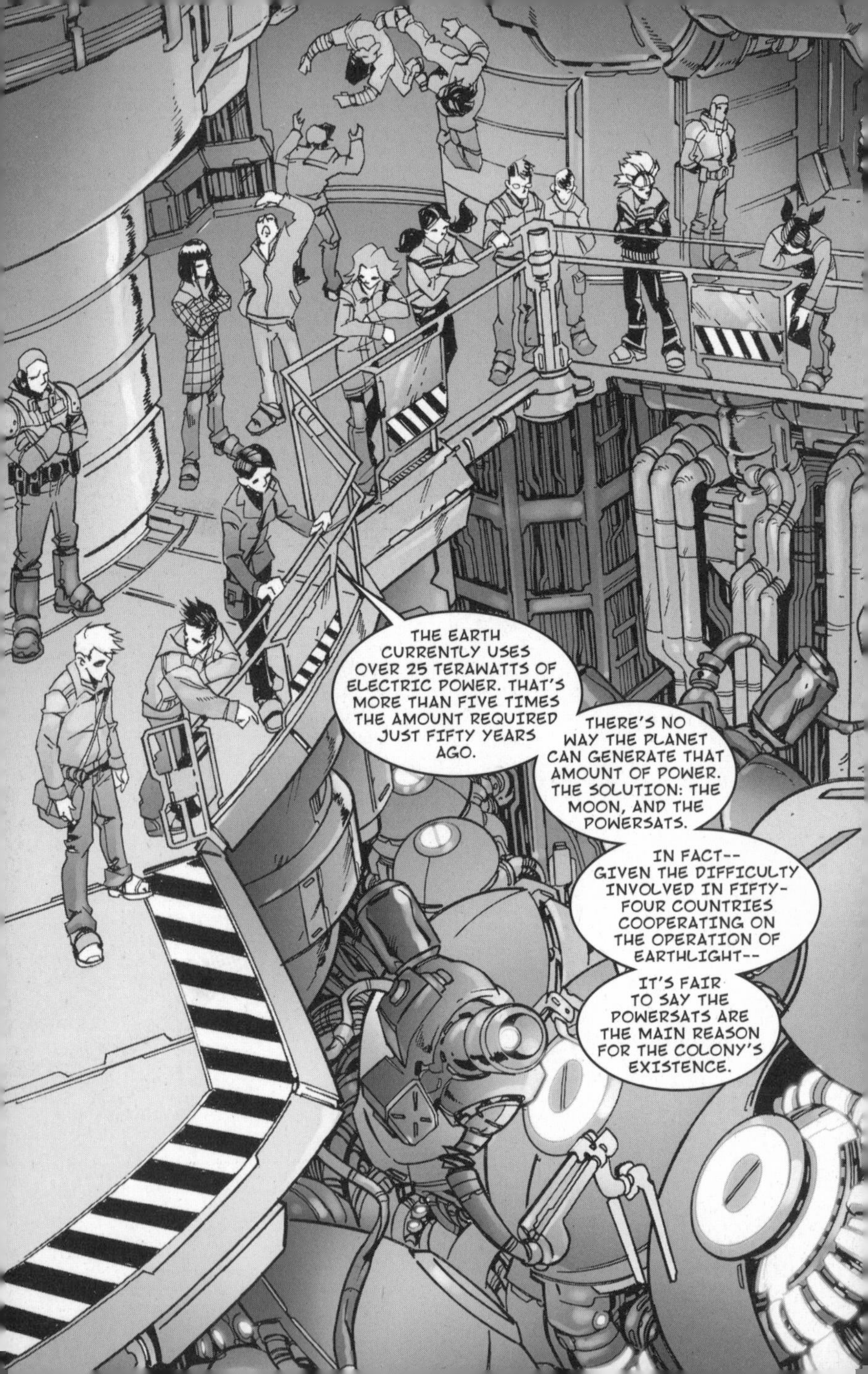
THE EARTH CURRENTLY USES OVER 25 TERAWATTS OF ELECTRIC POWER. THAT'S MORE THAN FIVE TIMES THE AMOUNT REQUIRED JUST FIFTY YEARS AGO.
THERE'S NO WAY THE PLANET CAN GENERATE THAT AMOUNT OF POWER. THE SOLUTION: THE MOON, AND THE POWERSATS.
IN FACT-- GIVEN THE DIFFICULTY INVOLVED IN FIFTY-FOUR COUNTRIES COOPERATING ON THE OPERATION OF EARTHLIGHT--
IT'S FAIR TO SAY THE POWERSATS ARE THE MAIN REASON FOR THE COLONY'S EXISTENCE.

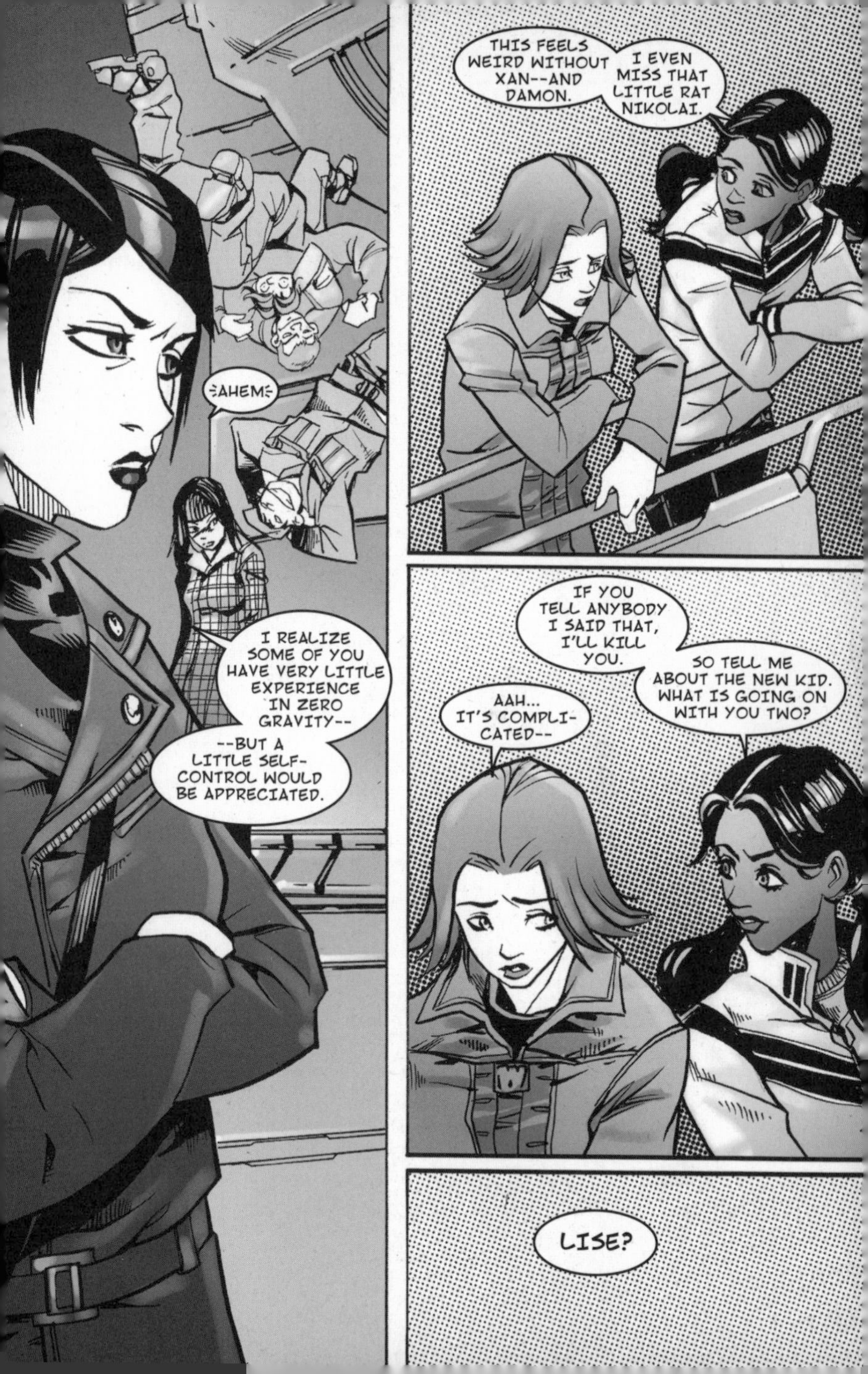
AHEM
I REALIZE SOME OF YOU HAVE VERY LITTLE EXPERIENCE IN ZERO GRAVITY--
--BUT A LITTLE SELF-CONTROL WOULD BE APPRECIATED.
THIS FEELS WEIRD WITHOUT XAN--AND DAMON.
I EVEN MISS THAT LITTLE RAT NIKOLAI.
IF YOU TELL ANYBODY I SAID THAT, I'LL KILL YOU.
SO TELL ME ABOUT THE NEW KID. WHAT IS GOING ON WITH YOU TWO?
AAH... IT'S COMPLI-CATED--
LISE?

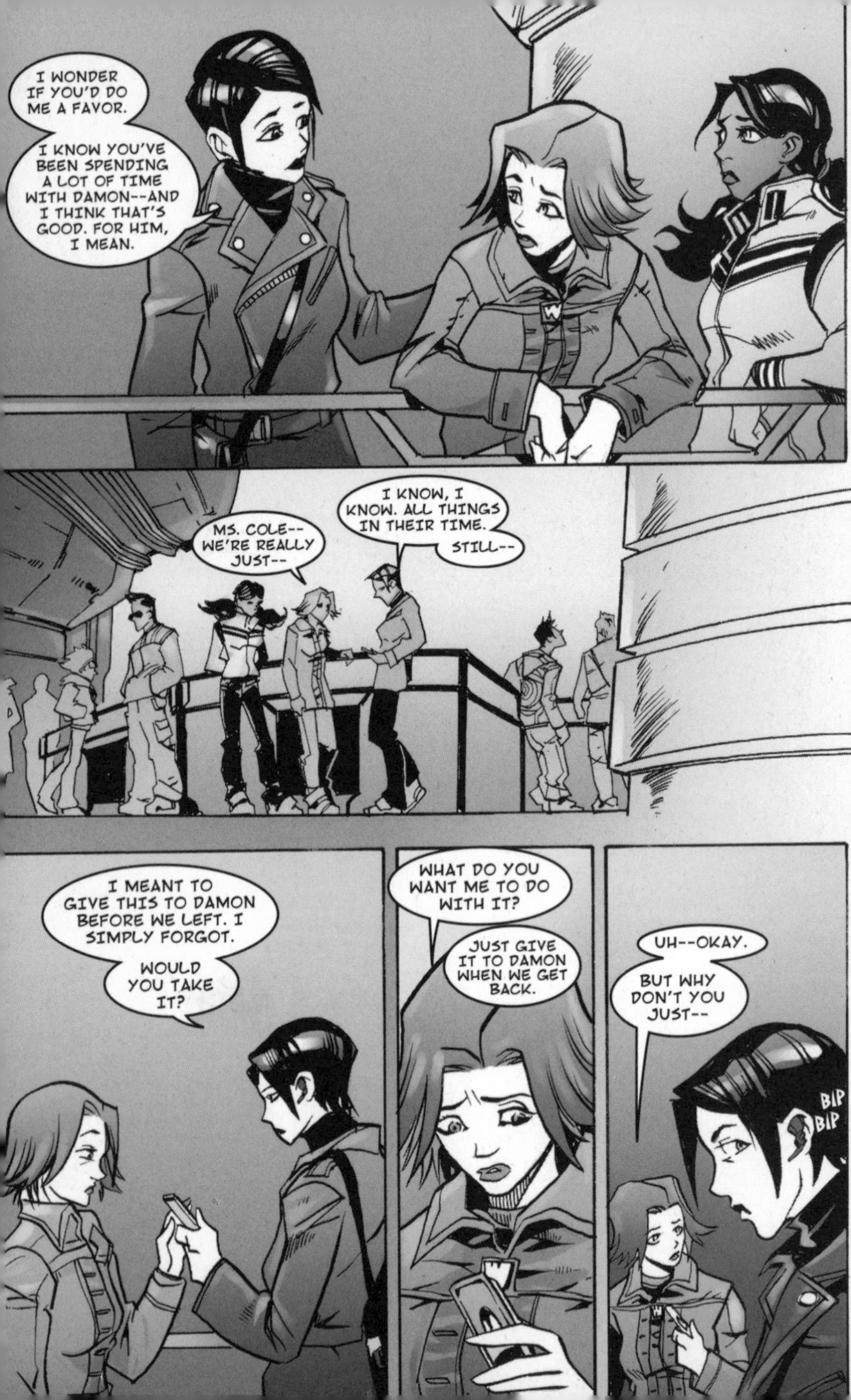
I WONDER IF YOU'D DO ME A FAVOR.
I KNOW YOU'VE BEEN SPENDING A LOT OF TIME WITH DAMON--AND I THINK THAT'S GOOD. FOR HIM, I MEAN.
MS. COLE--WE'RE REALLY JUST--
I KNOW, I KNOW. ALL THINGS IN THEIR TIME.
STILL--
I MEANT TO GIVE THIS TO DAMON BEFORE WE LEFT. I SIMPLY FORGOT.
WOULD YOU TAKE IT?
WHAT DO YOU WANT ME TO DO WITH IT?
JUST GIVE IT TO DAMON WHEN WE GET BACK.
UH--OKAY.
BUT WHY DON'T YOU JUST--
BIP BIP

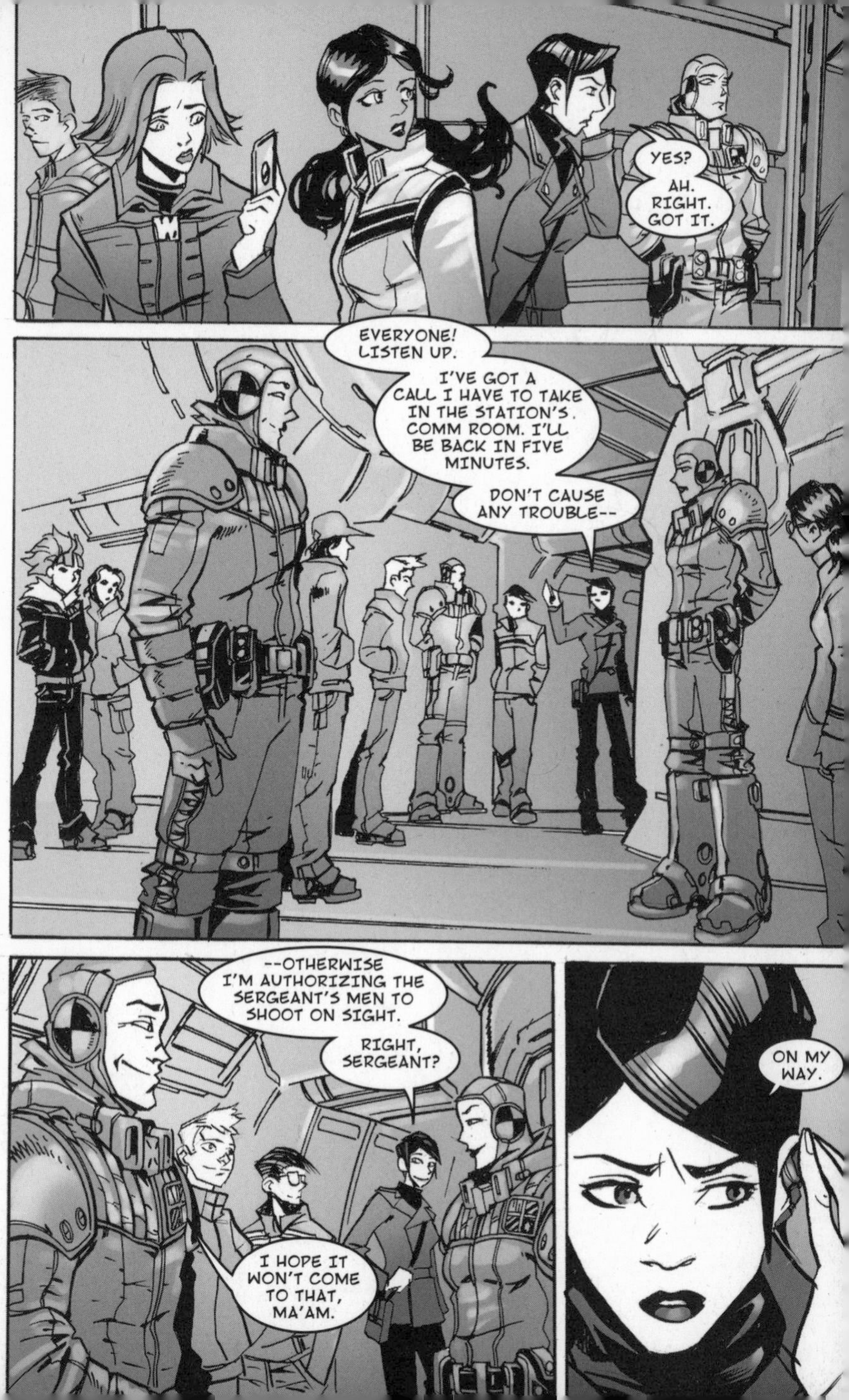
YES?
AH. RIGHT. GOT IT.
EVERYONE! LISTEN UP.
I'VE GOT A CALL I HAVE TO TAKE IN THE STATION'S COMM ROOM. I'LL BE BACK IN FIVE MINUTES.
DON'T CAUSE ANY TROUBLE--
--OTHERWISE I'M AUTHORIZING THE SERGEANT'S MEN TO SHOOT ON SIGHT.
RIGHT, SERGEANT?
I HOPE IT WON'T COME TO THAT, MA'AM.
ON MY WAY.

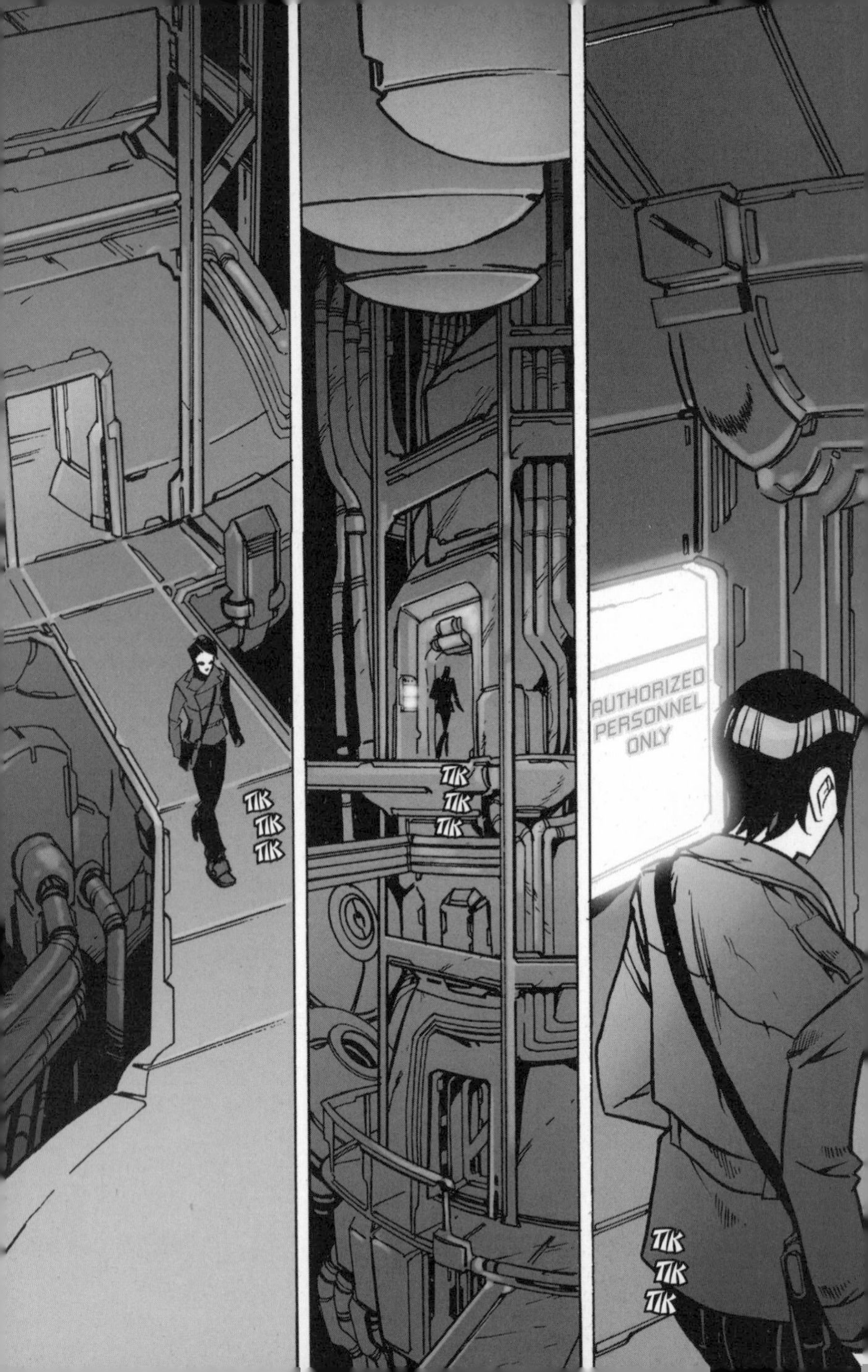
TIK
TIK
TIK
TIK
TIK
TIK
AUTHORIZED
PERSONNEL
ONLY
TIK
TIK
TIK

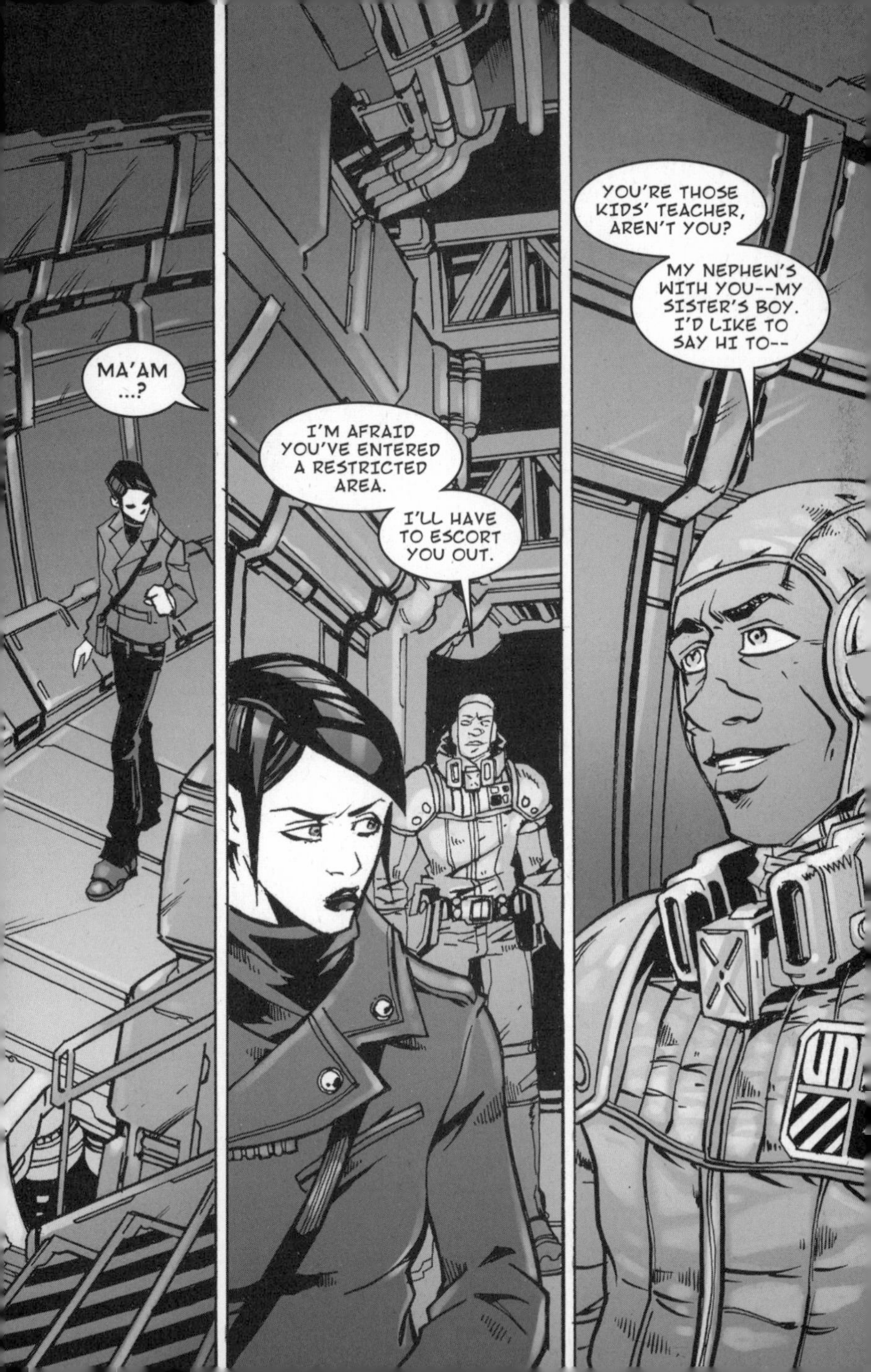
MA'AM ...?
I'M AFRAID YOU'VE ENTERED A RESTRICTED AREA.
I'LL HAVE TO ESCORT YOU OUT.
YOU'RE THOSE KIDS' TEACHER, AREN'T YOU?
MY NEPHEW'S WITH YOU--MY SISTER'S BOY. I'D LIKE TO SAY HI TO--

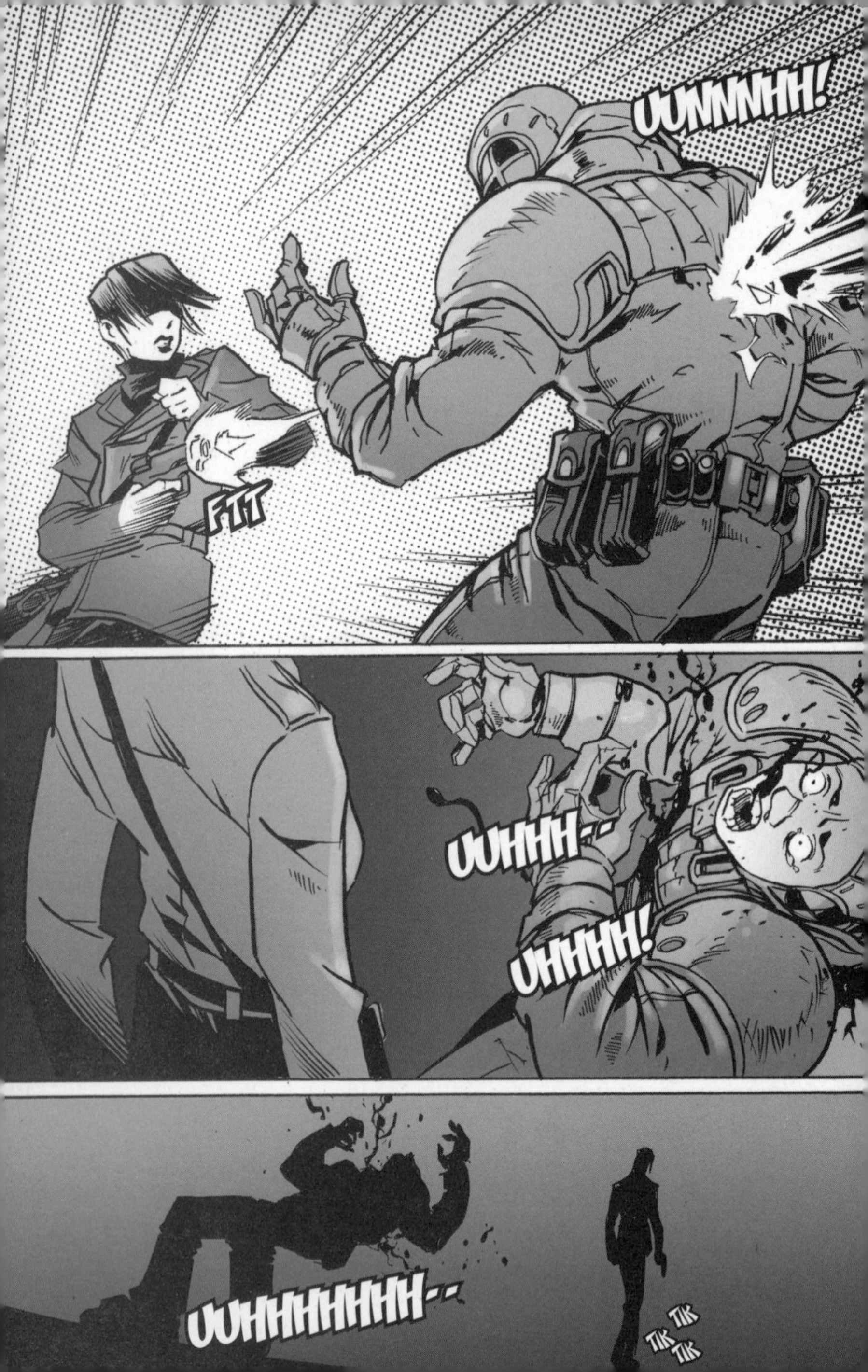
UUNNNHH!
FTT
UUHHH- -
UHHHH!
UUHHHHHHH- -
TIK
TIK
TIK

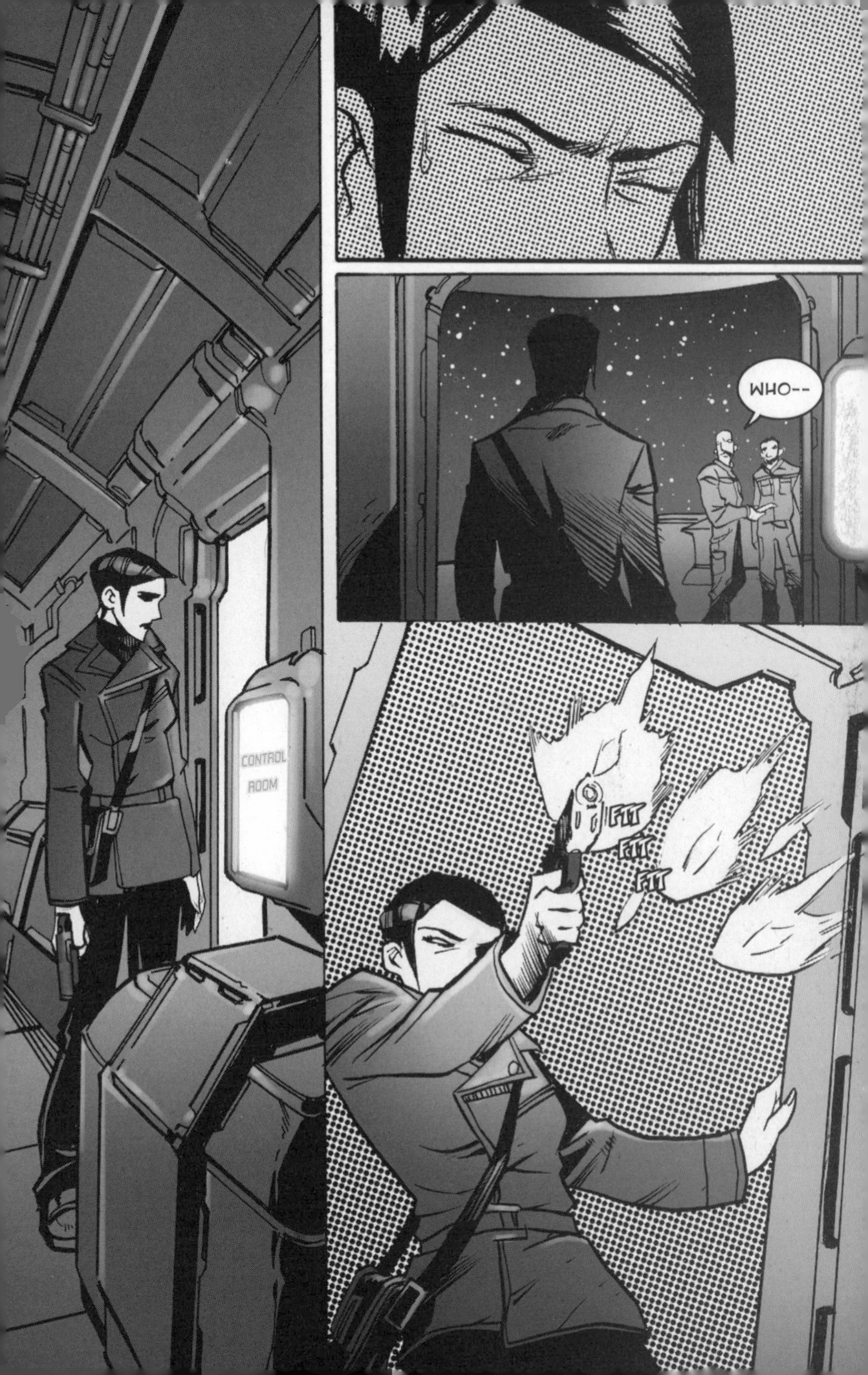
CONTROL ROOM
WHO--
FTT
FTT
FTT

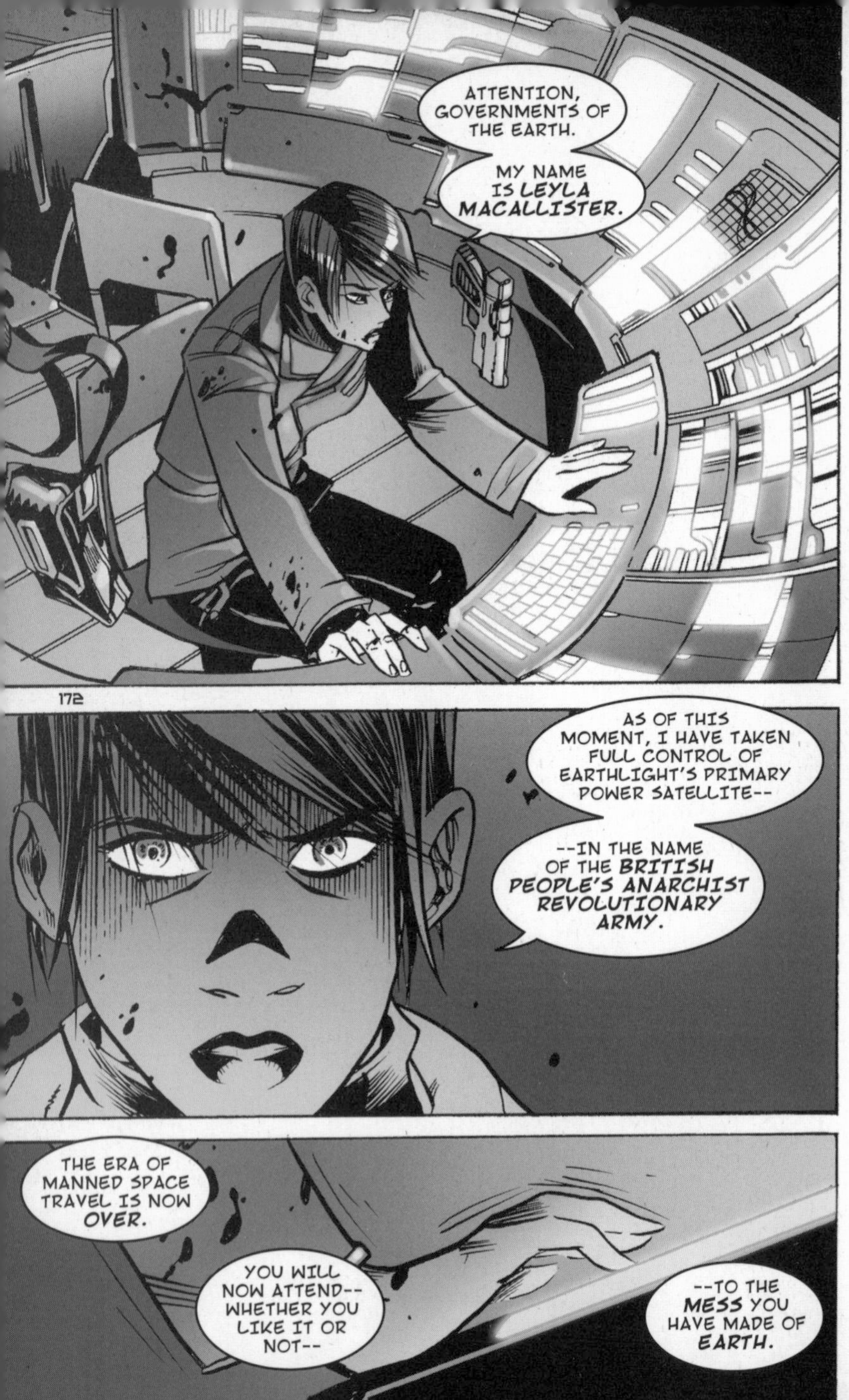
ATTENTION, GOVERNMENTS OF THE EARTH.
MY NAME IS LEYLA MACALLISTER.
AS OF THIS MOMENT, I HAVE TAKEN FULL CONTROL OF EARTHLIGHT'S PRIMARY POWER SATELLITE--
--IN THE NAME OF THE BRITISH PEOPLE'S ANARCHIST REVOLUTIONARY ARMY.
THE ERA OF MANNED SPACE TRAVEL IS NOW OVER.
YOU WILL NOW ATTEND--WHETHER YOU LIKE IT OR NOT--
--TO THE MESS YOU HAVE MADE OF EARTH.

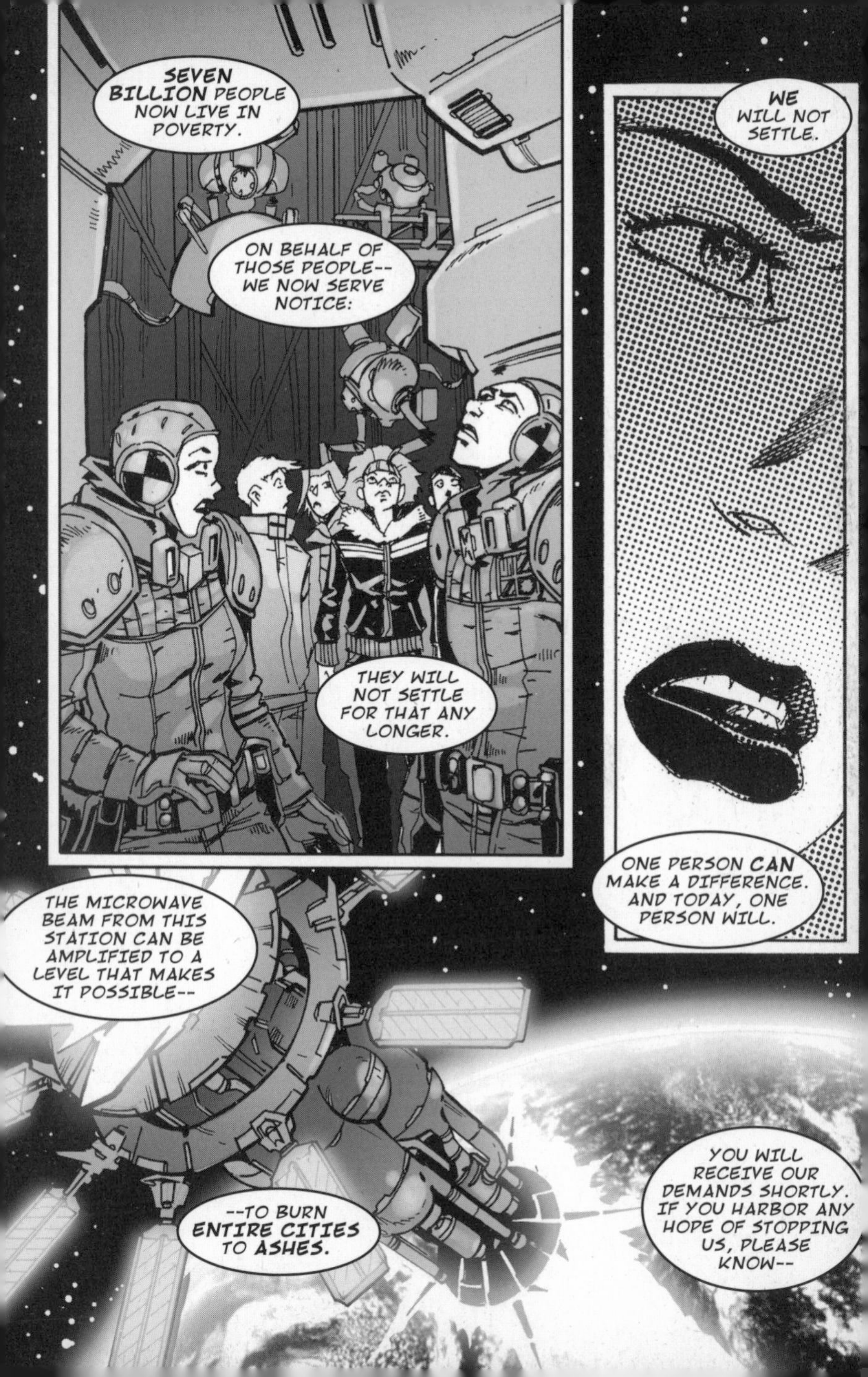
SEVEN BILLION PEOPLE NOW LIVE IN POVERTY.
ON BEHALF OF THOSE PEOPLE-- WE NOW SERVE NOTICE:
THEY WILL NOT SETTLE FOR THAT ANY LONGER.
WE WILL NOT SETTLE.
ONE PERSON CAN MAKE A DIFFERENCE. AND TODAY, ONE PERSON WILL.
THE MICROWAVE BEAM FROM THIS STATION CAN BE AMPLIFIED TO A LEVEL THAT MAKES IT POSSIBLE--
--TO BURN ENTIRE CITIES TO ASHES.
YOU WILL RECEIVE OUR DEMANDS SHORTLY. IF YOU HARBOR ANY HOPE OF STOPPING US, PLEASE KNOW--

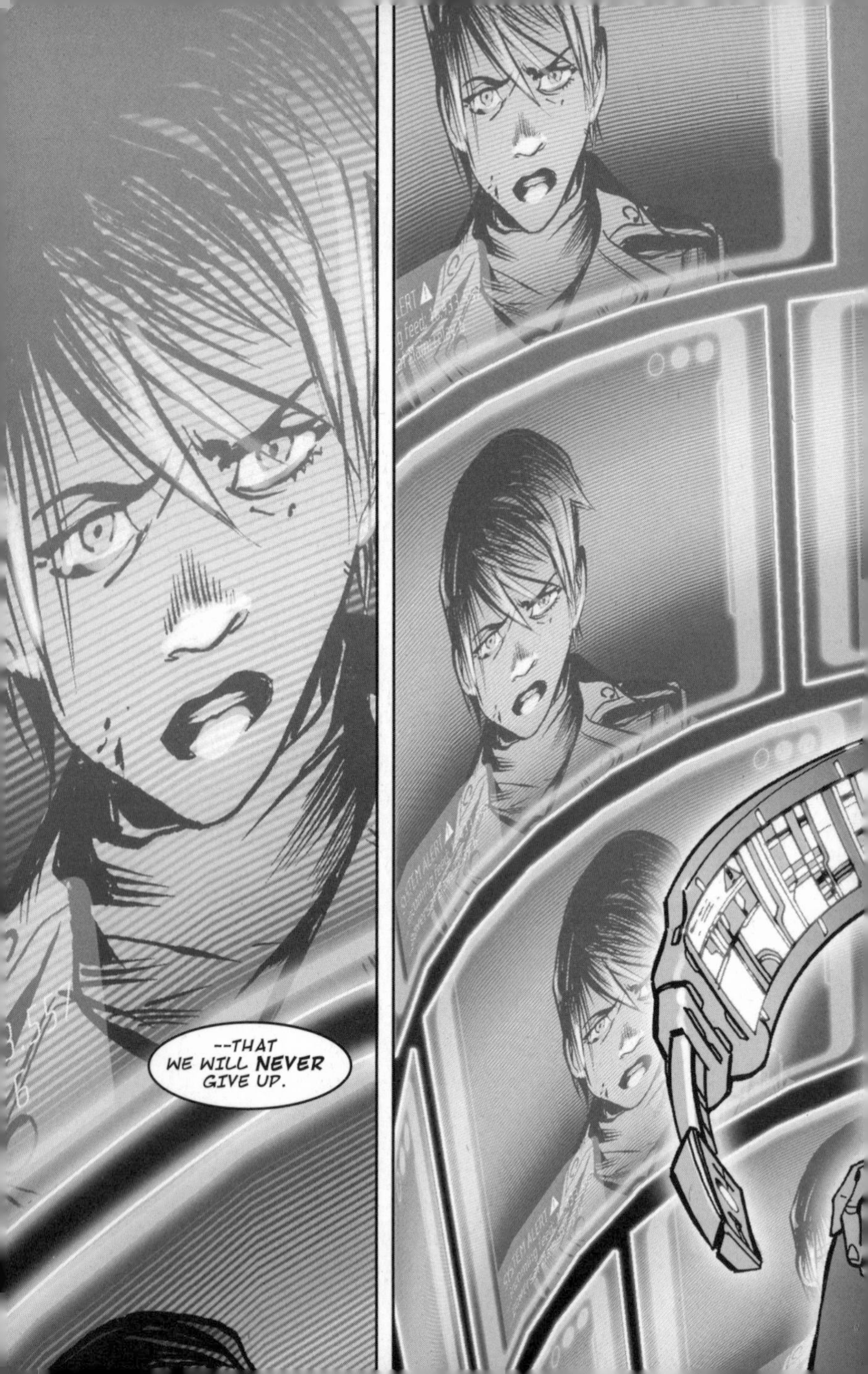
--THAT WE WILL NEVER GIVE UP.

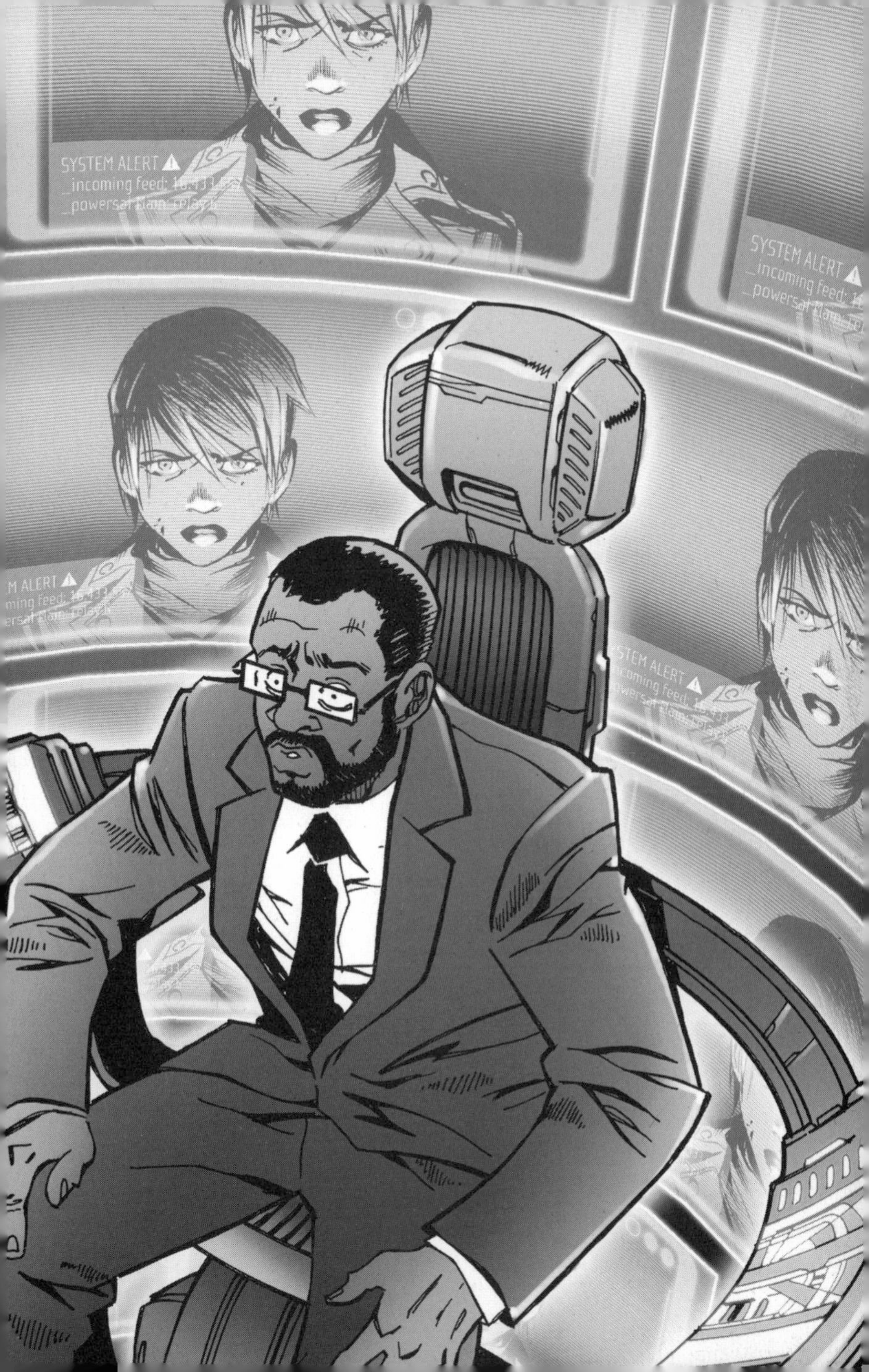
SYSTEM ALERT
_incoming feed:

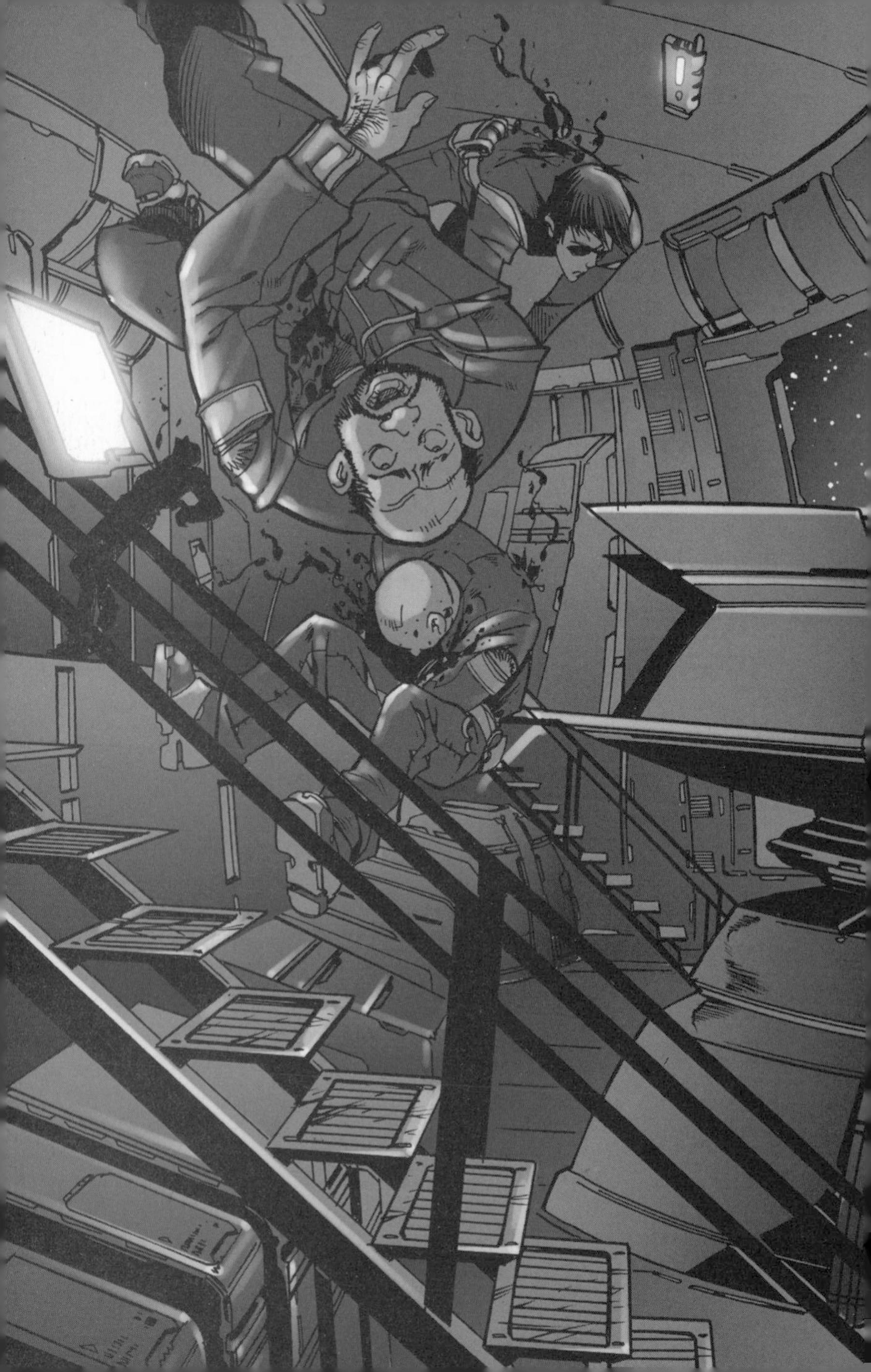

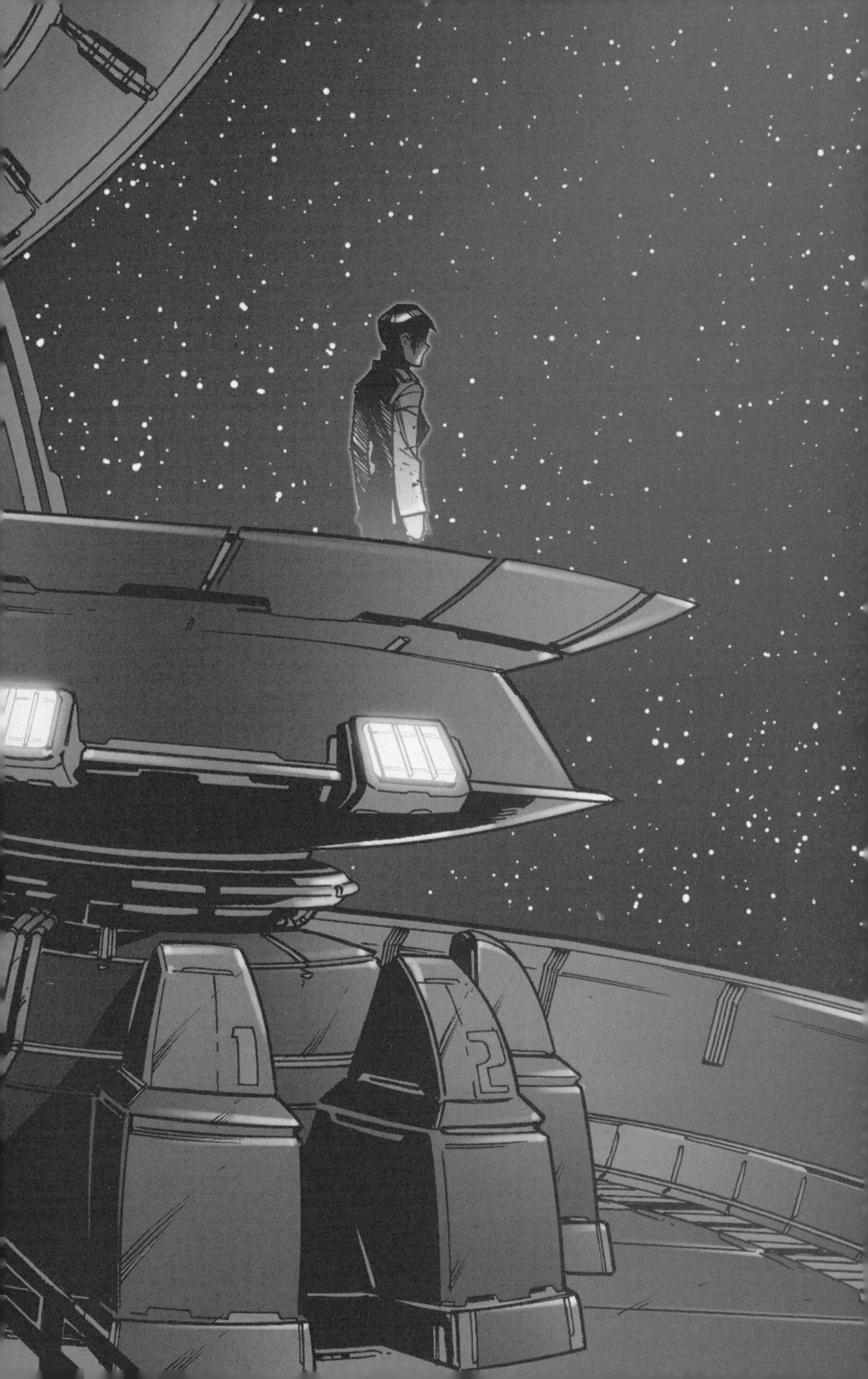
1
2

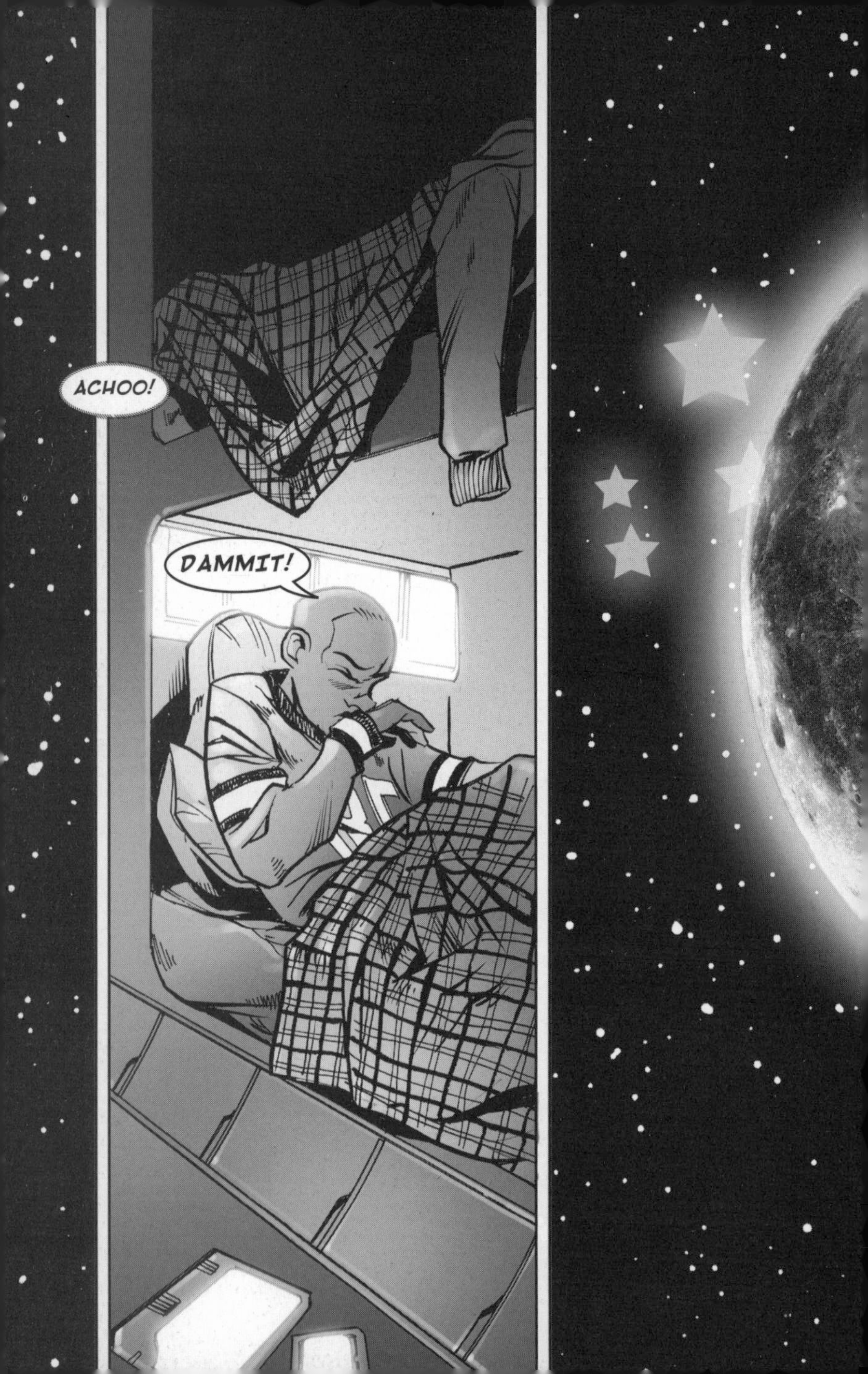
ACHOO!
DAMMIT!

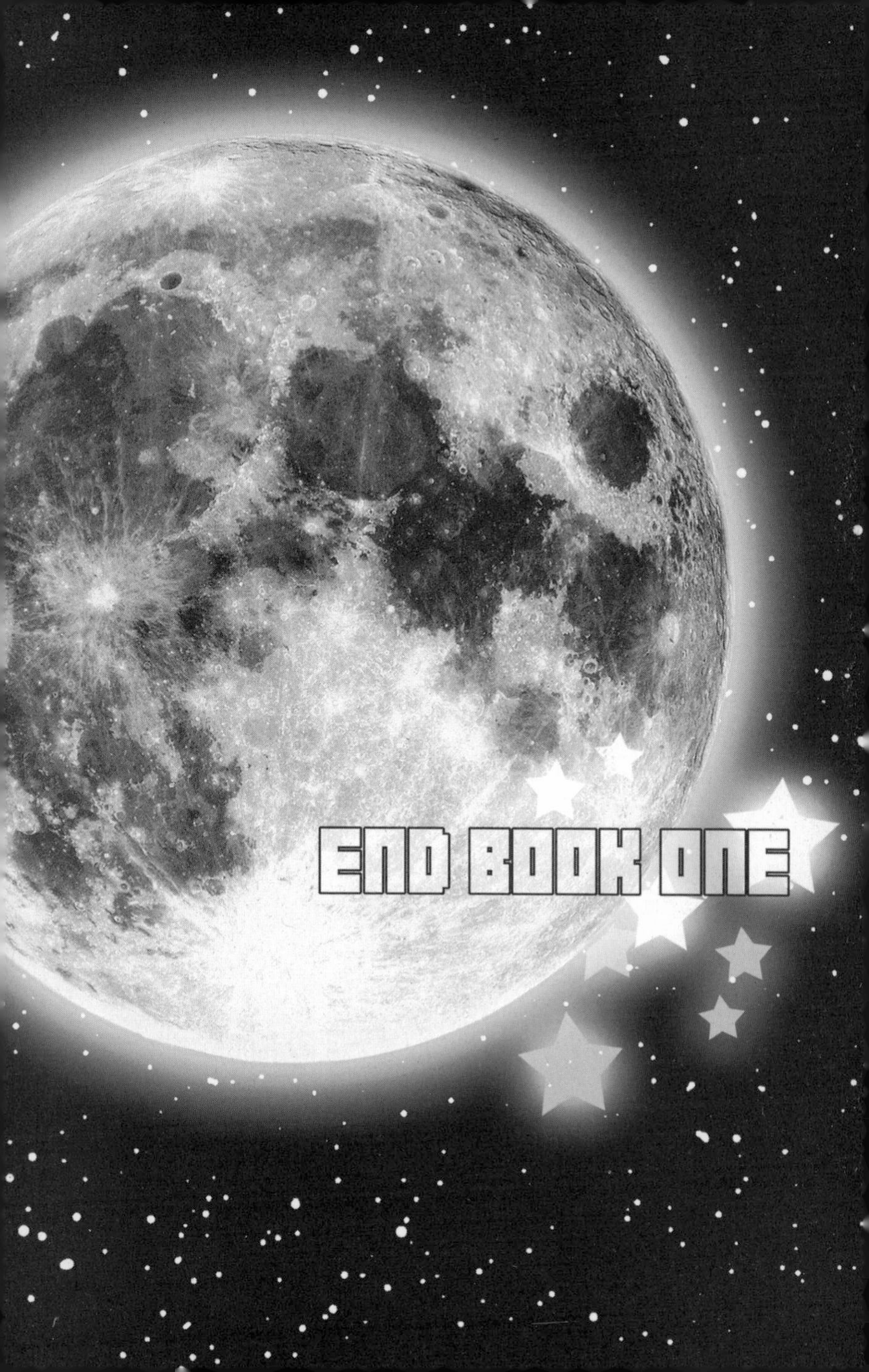
END BOOK ONE

IN THE NEXT VOLUME OF

EARTHLIGHT

Aaron Cole desperately tries to control the crisis aboard the satellite, even as he reels under the overwhelming realization that his loving wife is actually a dangerous terrorist. Meanwhile, unaware of the impending disaster, Damon and Nikolai inadvertently begin to uncover evidence of a wider-ranging conspiracy than first suspected.

The entire world awaits Leyla's demands, left to contemplate the terrible destruction she is capable of should they not be met.

Will the Earthlight colony survive?

To be continued in
EARTHLIGHT Vol. 2
Coming soon!

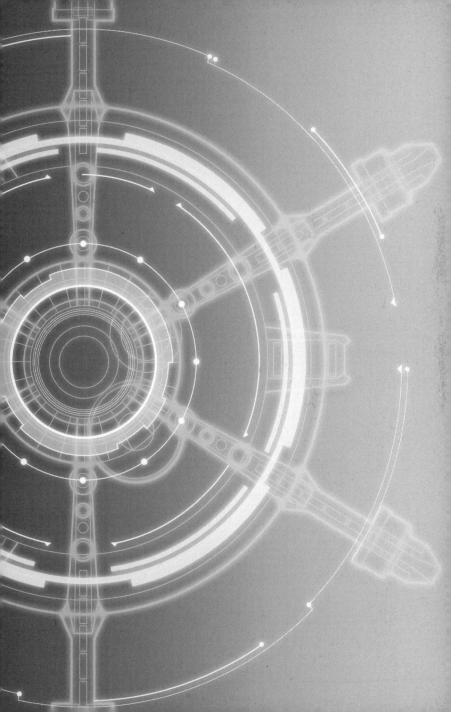

EARLY DESIGNS: EARTHLIGHT VOLUME I

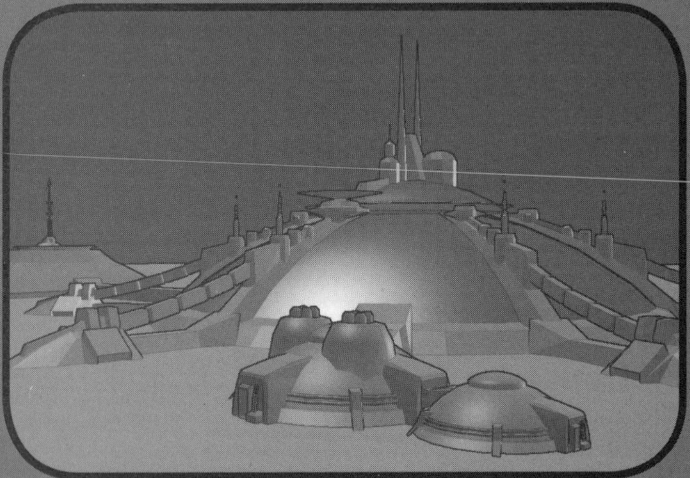

During the design process, Chris Schons uses the 3-D design software "Blender" to help visualize technical environments, such as the colony dome structure and the power satellite

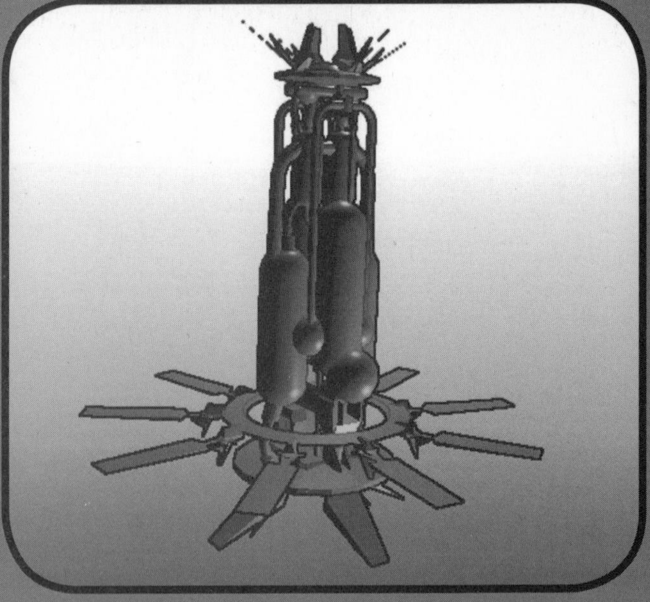

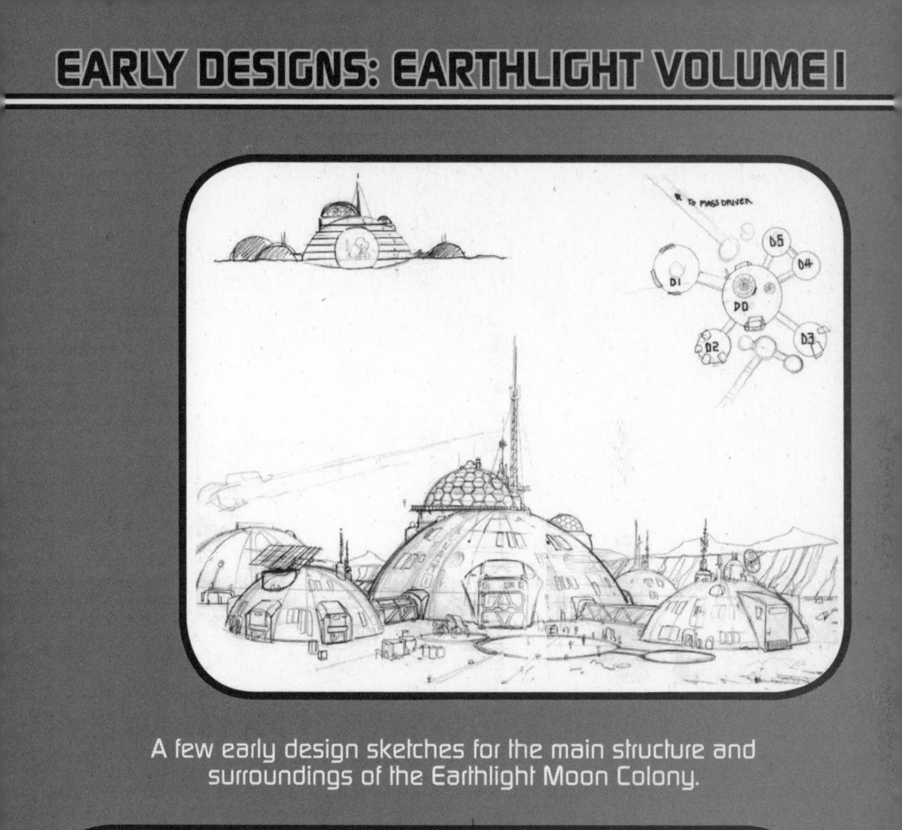
TO MASS DRIVER
D5
D4
D1
D0
D2
D3

A few early design sketches for the main structure and surroundings of the Earthlight Moon Colony.

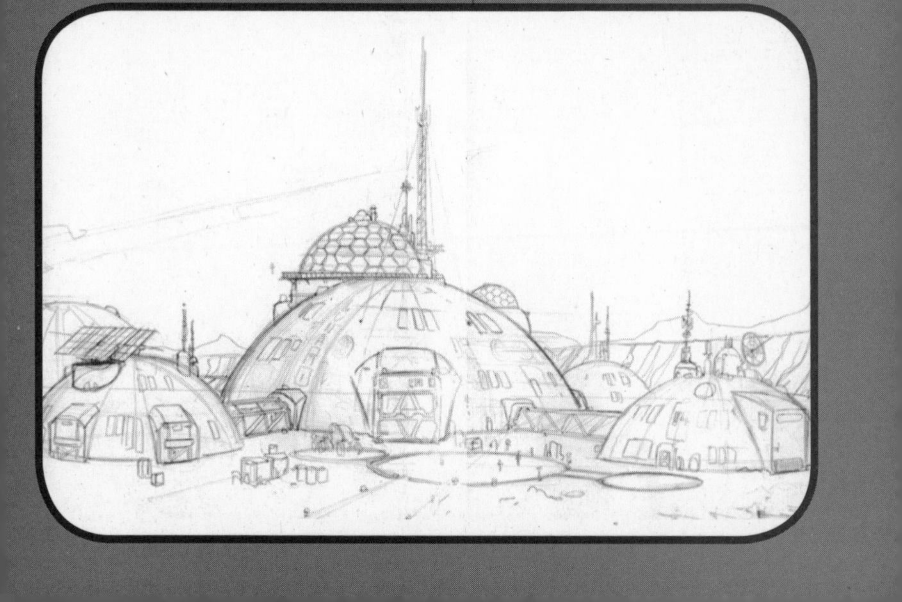

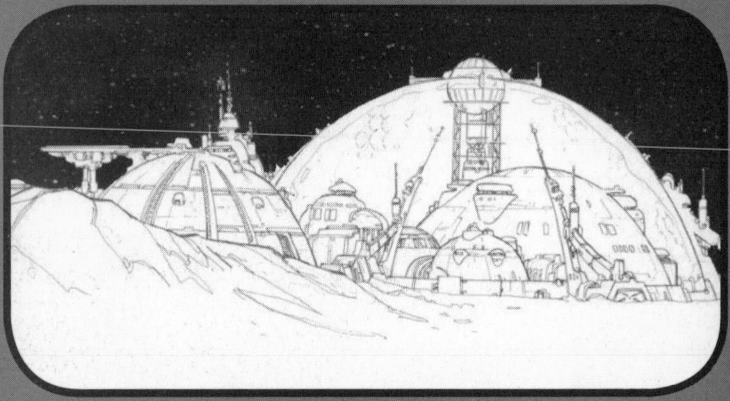

More detailed designs of the main dome and the shuttle landing pad. Notice that Chris has added a starscape in the background to help with the visualization.

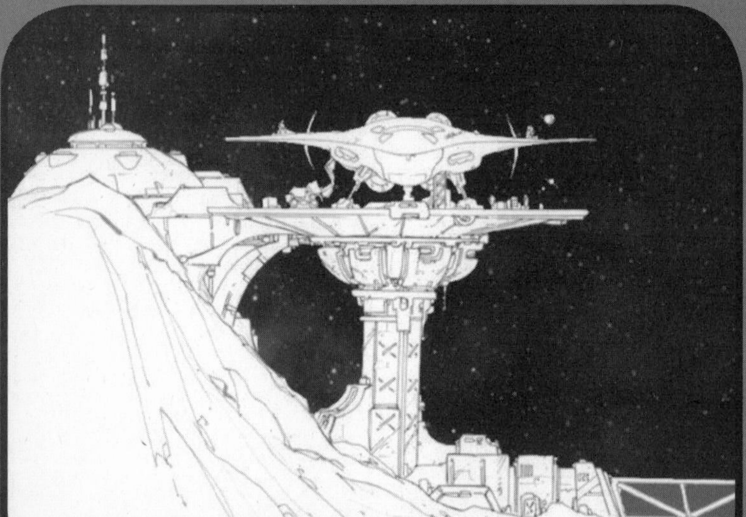

EARLY DESIGNS: EARTHLIGHT VOLUME I

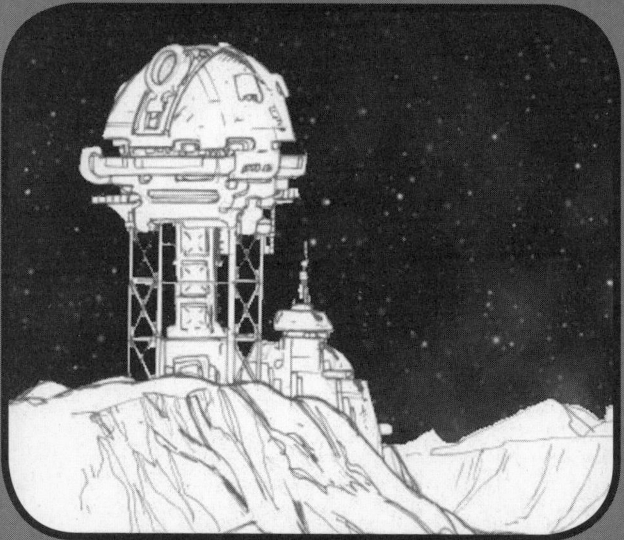

The ill-fated observatory and a closer look at the mass driver; barely mentioned in the actual book, but a crucial part of realizing the details of *Earthlight*.

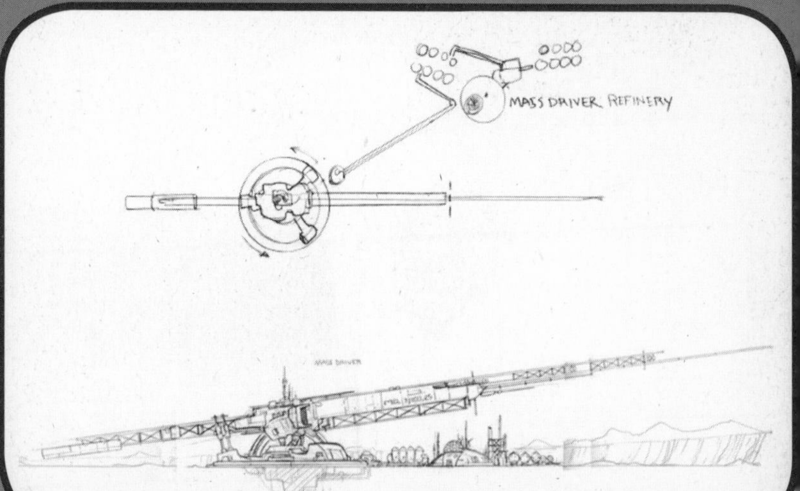
MASS DRIVER REFINERY

EARLY DESIGNS: EARTHLIGHT VOLUME I

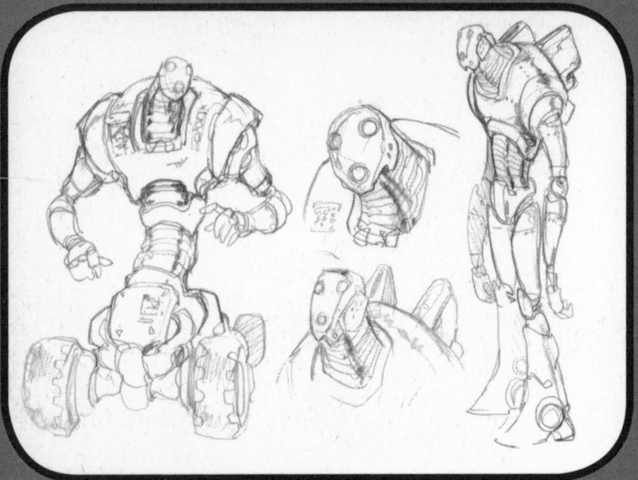

Chris' robot and spiderbot designs manage to look both utilitarian and unsettling at the same time, perfectly capturing the ominous mood of the book's prologue.

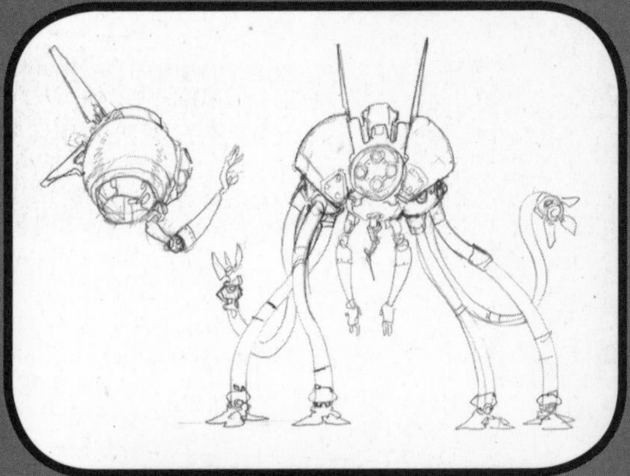

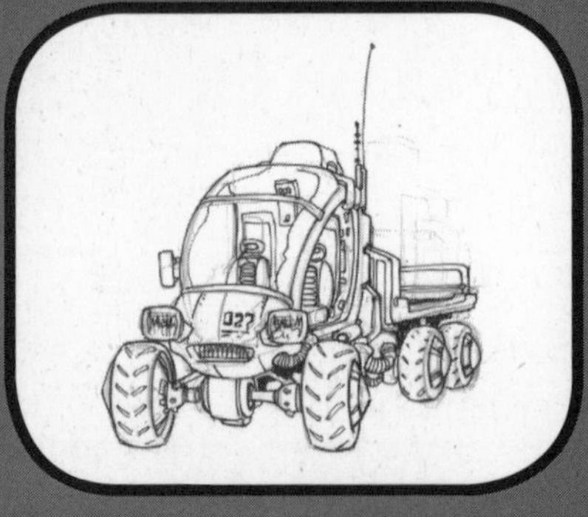

EARLY DESIGNS: EARTHLIGHT VOLUME I

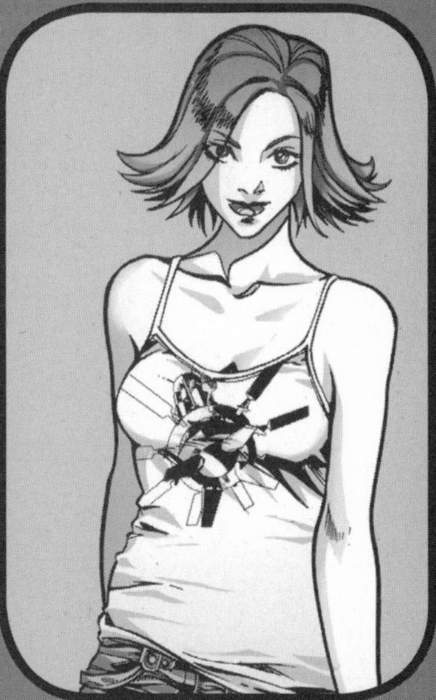

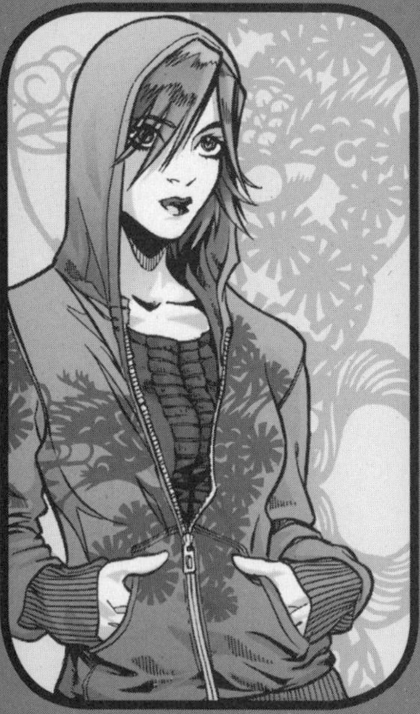

Unused character art, originally intended for use on the cover. Chris has done an exceptional job of giving the teenagers of *Earthlight* a sense of style and individuality.

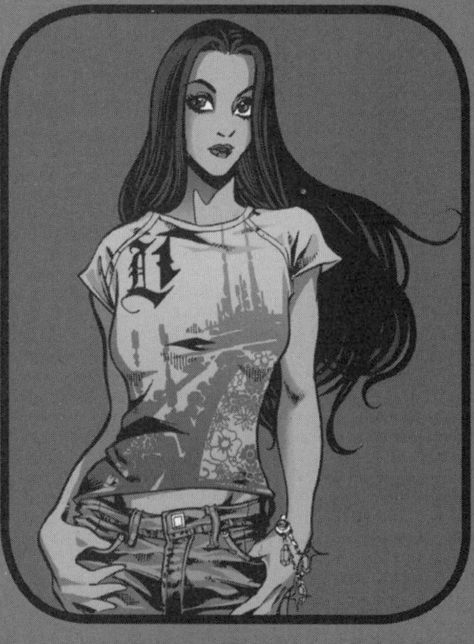

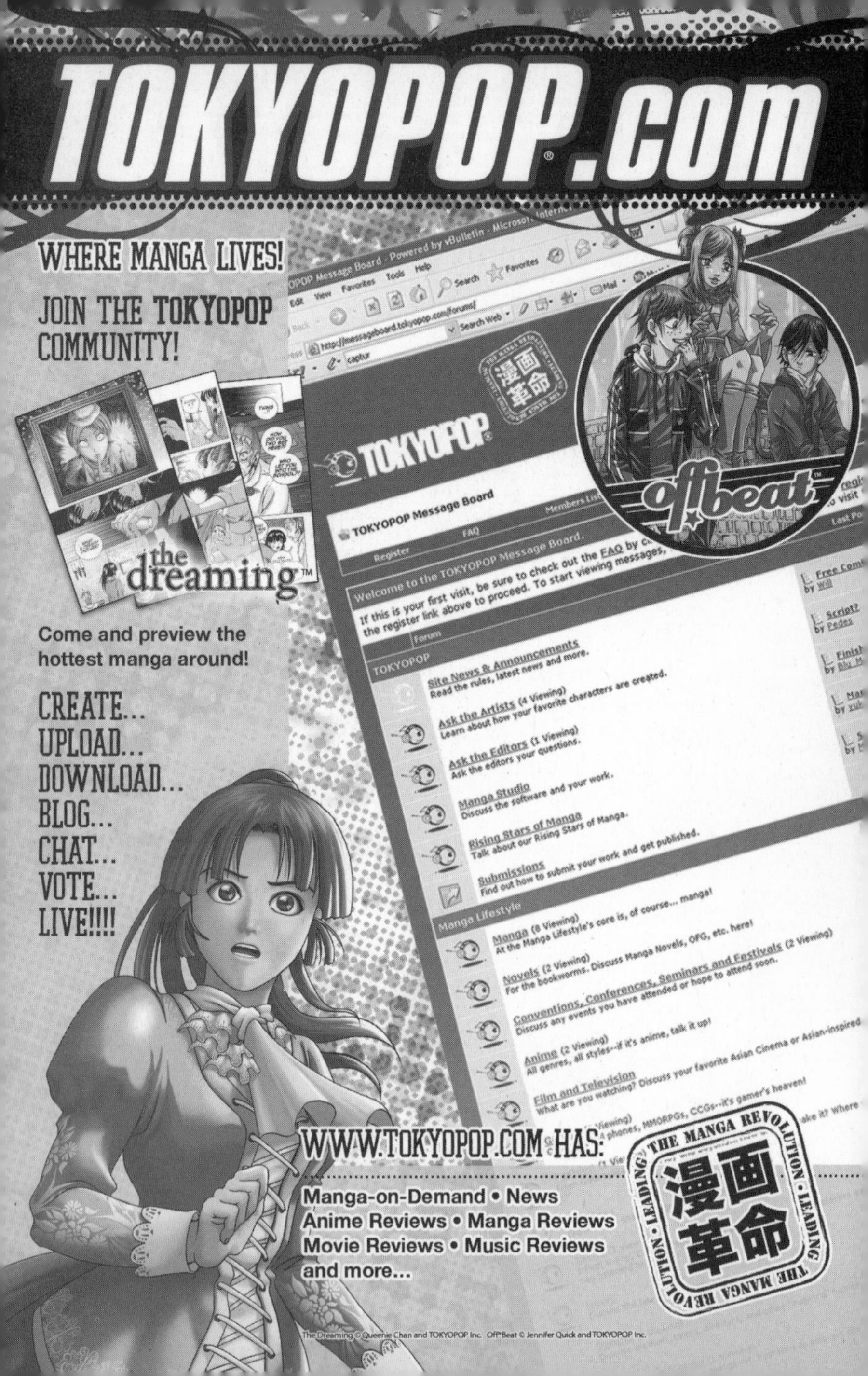
TOKYOPOP.com
WHERE MANGA LIVES!
JOIN THE TOKYOPOP COMMUNITY!
the dreaming
Come and preview the hottest manga around!
CREATE...
UPLOAD...
DOWNLOAD...
BLOG...
CHAT...
VOTE...
LIVE!!!!
TOKYOPOP
TOKYOPOP Message Board
offbeat
WWW.TOKYOPOP.COM HAS:
Manga-on-Demand • News
Anime Reviews • Manga Reviews
Movie Reviews • Music Reviews
and more...
THE MANGA REVOLUTION • LEADING
漫画革命
The Dreaming © Queenie Chan and TOKYOPOP Inc. Off*Beat © Jennifer Quick and TOKYOPOP Inc.

THE QUICK AND UNDEAD IN ONE MACABRE MANGA.

PRIEST™

Ivan Isaacs was a devoted priest until tragic events set him on a path to Hell. Now, he's back for vengeance! With the priesthood corrupted by demons, black prayers and the undead, Ivan returns with help from the devil Belial. He vows a baptism of blood on his pilgrimage for humanity's redemption.

FEATURE FILM IN DEVELOPMENT!

HORROR

OT OLDER TEEN AGE 16+

© MIN-WOO HYUNG, DAIWON C.I. Inc.

EDITORS' PICKS TOKYOPOP MANGA SUPPLEMENT

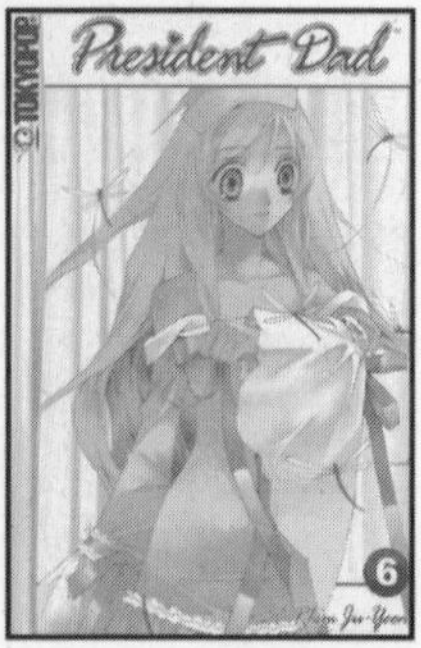
TOKYOPOP
President Dad
6
Rhim Ju-Yeon

COMEDY

TEEN AGE 13+

PRESIDENT DAD

BY JU-YEON RHIM

In spite of the kind of dorky title, this book is tremendously fun and stylish. The mix of romance and truly bizarre comedy won me over in a heartbeat. When young Ami's father becomes the new president of South Korea, suddenly she is forced into a limelight that she never looked for and isn't particularly excited about. She's got your typical teenage crushes on pop idols (and a mysterious boy from her past who may be a North Korean spy! Who'd have thought there'd be global politics thrown into a shojo series?!), and more than her fair share of crazy relatives, but now she's also got a super-tough bodyguard who can disguise himself as anyone you can possibly imagine, and the eyes of the nation are upon her! This underrated manhwa totally deserves a second look!

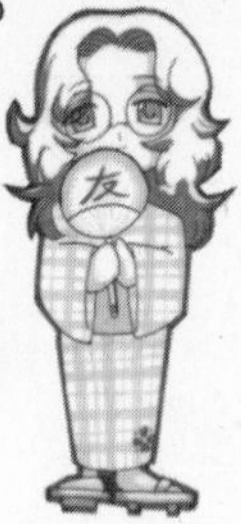

~Lillian Diaz-Pryzbyl, Editor

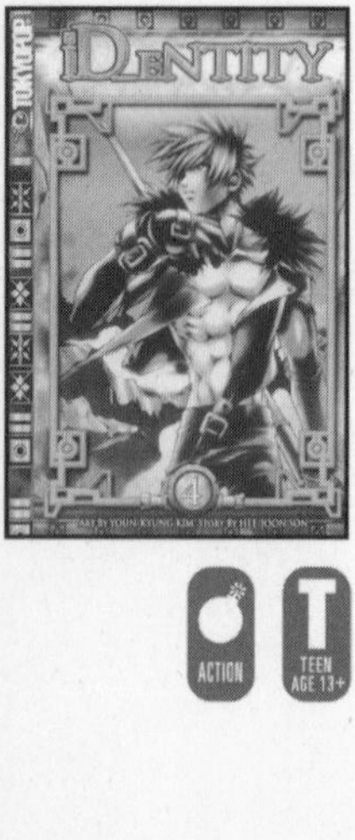
TOKYOPOP
iDeNTITY
4
ART BY YOUN-KYUNG KIM STORY BY HEE-JOON SON

ACTION

TEEN AGE 13+

ID_ENTITY

BY HEE-JOON SON AND YOUN-KYUNG KIM

As a fan of online gaming, I've really been enjoying *iD_eNTITY.* Packed with action, intrigue and loads of laughs, *iD_eNTITY* is a raucous romp through a virtual world that's obviously written and illustrated by fellow gamers. Hee-Joon Son and Youn-Kyung Kim utilize gaming's terms and conventions while keeping the story simple and entertaining enough for noobs (a glossary of gaming terms is included in the back). Anyone else out there who has already absorbed *.hack* and is looking for a new gaming adventure to go on would do well to start here.

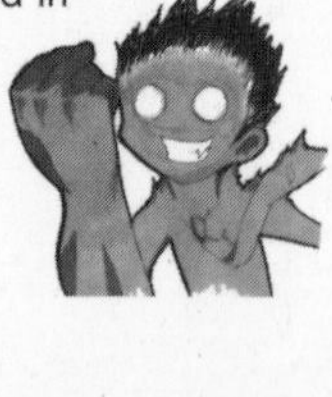

~Tim Beedle, Editor